A HISTORY
OF GAUL

Celtic, Roman and Frankish Rule

Fr. Funck-Brentano

Translated from the French by
E. F. Buckley

BARNES
&NOBLE
BOOKS
NEW YORK

Originally published as *The Earliest Times*

This edition published by Barnes & Noble, Inc.

1993 Barnes & Noble Books

ISBN 1-56619-392-3

Printed and bound in the United States of America

M 9 8 7 6 5 4 3 2

PREFACE

THIS volume contains the beginnings of French history from prehistoric times to the advent of the Capets. The works of our predecessors have been a great guide and help, above all the monumental work of Fustel de Coulanges on the institutions of Roman Gaul and the age of the Merovingians and the Carlovingians, a work which is unique in its precision and wealth of information, its clarity of thought and its accuracy of expression. Worthy of the master is the great work of his disciple, Camille Jullian. The magnificent picture he has drawn of Celtic and Roman Gaul is arresting by reason of its varied and abundant knowledge, and perhaps even more on account of its brilliance of style and its happy boldness of thought. *Gaule Mérovingienne* by Maurice Prou is a masterpiece. As for the marvellous *Prolegomènes* of Benjamin Guérard, praise is superfluous. And, as may well be imagined, the great works of Bayet, C. Pfister, A. Kleinclausz, and G. Bloch, the accurate studies of Louis Halphen, the stirring religious history of Georges Goyau and the clear, strong pages of Imbart de la Tour have not been neglected.

At the end of each chapter will be found, not the bibliography of the subject, which would have overflowed the limits of this book, but an indication of the sources and the works to which we have been more particularly indebted, as well as such works the perusal of which would, in our opinion most successfully complete the pages which follow.

To our predecessors we owe much; we have delved wholeheartedly into their works, and we cordially acknowledge our indebtedness to them.

FR. F.-B.

CONTENTS

CHAPTER I

PAGE

THE PREHISTORIC PERIOD 1

CHAPTER II

CELTIC GAUL 27

CHAPTER III

ROMAN GAUL 84

CHAPTER IV

THE MEROVINGIANS 210

CHAPTER V

THE CARLOVINGIANS 299

CHAPTER I

THE PREHISTORIC PERIOD

The territory of Gaul in the primary, secondary and tertiary era : the appearance of man. The divisions of the quaternary era. The quaternary era : the Chellean, Acheulean, Mousterian, Solutrean, Aurignacian, and Magdalenian epochs. The features of each of these epochs. The capital of the prehistoric period, the Eyzies in Dordogne. These six epochs make up the palæolithic, or the chipped stone age, succeeded after a long interval called the hiatus by the neolithic or the polished stone age. The palafittes or lake dwellings. The bronze age followed by the iron age which inaugurated the historic era.

THE territory to-day occupied by France, the boundaries of which have for centuries been unanimously considered to be the Rhine, the Alps, the Mediterranean, the Pyrenees and the Atlantic, has from the earliest times undergone certain transformations which geologists have made it their task to describe. This long period of formation has been divided by them into four epochs, each of which lasted several milleniums, and which they called the primary era, in which the continents first appeared and outside Europe a few chains of mountains were formed ; the secondary era, characterised by a great extension of the sea in southern Europe and the emergence of the northern regions out of the waters ; and the tertiary era when the waters once more covered the soil of Gaul, but when the central mountain mass stood out like an island, extending from the Morvan mountains in the north to the Montagne Noir and the Lacaune mountains in the south, and from west to east from the Limousin to the Cevennes. In the south, the Pyrenees reared their crests, and the Alps arose in the east. A second island then came to light—Brittany, to which were added the islands of Normandy, followed by a third, the Vosges. What we know

Prehistoric Gaul.

1

as the Basin of Paris was a gulf the waters of which washed the shores of Brittany, the central body and the Vosges. Lastly, in the quaternary era the continents assumed the shape in which we know them, and man appeared.

As regards organic life, the primary era is characterised by the reign of the nautilites—mysterious submarine creatures composed of a head and four members, all the species of which are to-day extinct—and by the appearance of the batrachians; the vertebrates being represented only by fish and above all by numerous reptiles.

In the secondary era appeared the first form of mammalia— the marsupials, whose young were born as embryos which remained attached to the mother's breasts before they could live independently of her. These primitive mammalia came to light during the tertiary era, and at the same time the great saurians developed their monstrous forms—the dinosaurs, an order of reptiles, with skins either bare or covered by bony scales. Reptilian birds disported themselves in the luxuriant vegetation.

The tertiary era was glorified by a magnificent flora. It was the age of the great lakes, and the reign of the mammalia —the pachyderms, the ruminants and the great mammalian fish, the cetaceans. The first monkeys swung in the branches of the trees, and the proboscideans, mammals with trunks like that of the elephant, trampled down the wild vegetation surrounding the marshes.

Some scientists place man as early as the tertiary era, but it was in the quaternary that he appeared as the master of nature and her products.

J.-H. Rosny the elder, a novelist who, like Balzac, made more than one incursion into the domain of history, and, like him, illumined it with flashes of genius, has given us a striking picture of the man of the quaternary era. Speaking of the man of over a hundred thousand years ago, he says :—

" Our ancestors of old used to light fires on the cold nights that were so full of terrors, when the fearsome machairodus **The Hunters.** (a meat-eating feline like the tiger) with its dagger-like canines was still hunting its prey in the same pastures as the mastodont, the tropical elephant, the tertiary rhinoceros, and the hipparion " (the ancestor of our

2

horse, with three toes, of which the middle one was the largest. Julius Cæsar's horse, to which he raised a statue in front of the temple of Venus Genetrix, was an animal of this description, and examples of it existed in the nineteenth century—an extraordinary phenomenon of atavism).

" Man," continues J.-H. Rosny, " doubtless already showed well-marked variations—sometimes endowed with the strength of the gorilla and of a powerful build, sometimes weaker and more dependent on guile—in fact, combining the characteristics from which the thousand and one varieties of the present day have been developed, a feeble animal compared with the wild beasts which could have annihilated our tigers with one blow of their claws, and the herbivores of which the mammoth and the elephant are but the dwarfed descendants. It is with a shudder of pity that we picture to ourselves a small band of men on our French soil, during the flint age at Thenay." Thenay is a *commune* of Loir-et-Cher, where the Abbé Bourgeois found in 1865 flint chippings which led certain archæologists to place the advent of man in the tertiary era.

" The band of men would be encamped on the confines of a forest, or by a river, bordering a plain intersected by swamps. Wild animals abounded in the woods, in the high grasses and waters. Terrifying creatures had increased and multiplied. Herds of herbivores wandered about under the leadership of ferocious males. As yet no metaphysic of Good and Evil existed. . . . The universal destruction of the weak by the strong, òf the stupid by the clever, of the solitary ones by the packs, went on without any reflection on the cruelty of natural laws. The beauty of the world was compounded of a colossal harmony of growth and murder, suffering and joy, love and hunting."

Man had not yet learnt the cultivation of cereals or of textile plants. He had not yet shut himself up in caves, or subterranean shelters; he lived in the open air, in the hollows of the valleys, in the depths of virgin forests, or else on the plateaux which stood out above the watersheds. On the heights from which may be seen the shining waters of the Somme, the Seine, and the Meuse, he made his first appearance in Gaul.

This was the period called by Camille Jullian " the age of

3

the hunters," the longest of the stages in human development. It continued for tens of thousands of years and only ended a few milleniums before our own age. Man required this long period of time to rid Gaul of the monsters which swarmed there —wild felines, cave bears and the giant hyæna. And it was only after this fierce fight of centuries that, feeling himself master of the soil, he was able to set to work to cultivate it, to sow seed, and enjoy the fruits of his harvests.

The four eras, which we have just enumerated—the primary, the secondary, the tertiary and the quaternary—were in their turn subdivided into several epochs, identified by geologists according to " strata." We are only concerned with the quaternary epoch, in which man made his first appearance.

But perhaps the reader may wish to interrupt us. These successive eras, he may object, existed thousands and thousands of years before historic times, they have left no written records, no inscriptions; how then can we form any idea, however vague, of what could possibly have taken place in them?

To this our master, Fustel de Coulanges, would reply:—

" In the absence of books and inscriptions, there remains the earth's crust . . . "; and he develops this idea with all the fine lucidity of his genius :

" In Denmark," he says, " there exist huge deposits of peat. Peat consists of a mass of vegetable substances collected for centuries. Every square yard of peat represents several centuries of forests.

" On digging, the various kinds of trees that made up this peat can be distinguished; the lowest layer is found to consist chiefly of pine; the layer above is oak, and the topmost layer is beech.

" Thus it becomes clear that in this territory the pine was for a series of centuries the chief feature of the forests, for another series of centuries it was the oak and for a third the beech.

" Now, with the succession of generations of trees and species of animals, generations of men and animals also succeeded each other in these ancient forests of which this peat is composed. The men who lived in them during the different epochs have left traces of their existence—instruments, weapons and utensils fashioned by hand. The men themselves have perished,

4

but their works remain. And, just as the various layers of peat differ from one another and are composed of the remains of various varieties of trees, so these objects of human manufacture show different characteristics at various depths.

" In the lowest layer, the pine layer, all the objects which have served a human purpose are of stone. In the next layer above, the oak layer, objects and instruments made of metal already appear; this metal, however, is never iron but bronze. Only in the topmost layer do we find objects of iron."

Now turning to Gaul, let us examine, not only the superimposed beds of peat, but also the crust of earth which forms the soil of the country. The rocks we find there are also arranged in various superimposed strata. The alluvials, that is to say, those layers which have been formed in the course of centuries by the mud of rivers, which, though similar in formation to the peat left by the forests, have taken much longer to come into existence, are also superimposed in parallel strata.

If we dig into them we find the same deposits of all kinds as in the peat, that is to say, remains of plants, shells, bones, and the same objects of human manufacture which are once again seen lying in the same order—in the lowest stratum only objects of stone, higher up instruments of bronze and still higher up weapons, utensils and instruments of iron.

It is these things which make up the whole history. If, in the lowest, which is the oldest stratum, only stone objects are found, it means that in the age corresponding to this deposit man did not yet know the use of metals. After that comes bronze, an alloy of copper and tin, and we need not be surprised that this alloy should have preceded the use of iron, which is a pure metal. It is more difficult to extract iron from its ore than it is to mix tin and copper in the manufacture of bronze. For iron is harder to work whether by fire or forge.

The quaternary era has therefore been divided into the Chellean epoch (from Chelles in Seine-et-Marne), the Acheulean (from Saint-Acheul in the Somme), the Mousterian (from Moustier, a *commune* in Pyzac-en-Dordogne), the Solutrean (from Solutré in Saône-et-Loire), the Aurignacian (from Aurignac in the Haute-Garonne), the Magdalenian (from La Madeleine, a *commune* of Tursac, Dordogne), and a final

5

epoch, which is the one preceding our own, called the Tourassian (from Tourasse in Haute-Garonne), to-day identified with the Azilian to be discussed later.

As no dates can be ascertained within thousands of years, and there are no historical landmarks, these epochs—or strata —have been named after the different localities, all situated in France, be it noted, where the various objects, consisting principally of weapons, have been discovered.

These six epochs, the Chellean, the Achulean, the Mousterian, the Solutrean, the Aurignacian and the Magdalenian, constitute the divisions of what is known as the palæolithic age— the early or chipped-stone age, in which the weapons used by man were made of flints roughly chipped into shape.

The Chellean epoch, which is the earliest of the chipped-stone age, and the first in which traces of man are indisputably found, is characterised by the primitive weapon, consisting of a sort of chipped stone axe in the shape of an almond, which also served the purpose of a tool, a scraper or a knife. Man was scantily clad, the climate was very mild, and our ancestors rejoiced in a vigorous constitution. Supple, agile, and with long and flexible arms and legs, the Chellean was able to climb the giant trees of the period. In addition to his axe-head of chipped flint, he was armed with a cudgel of wood and a spear. What was the quarry he hunted ?—It consisted of the antelope, the deer, the elk, the reindeer, the horse, and the auroch, a sort of wild bull like the bison. But he had to exercise the greatest caution in order to avoid the huge monsters which would have swallowed him whole—the mastodonts, the giant hippopotamus, the large felines, the cave bears and the woolly rhinoceros.

It is thought that Gaul was at this time joined to Great Britain by an isthmus, which was afterwards covered by the waters of the Channel. The climate was hot and damp, the vegetation tropical and the forests huge and dense.

Had the family yet come into existence ?—In an embryonic form it probably had. Men had to join together in groups in order to defend themselves. As J.-H. Rosny remarks : " We can imagine the little clans, in which the supremacy of the cleverest hunter, the luckiest slayer of wild beasts, was recog-

6

nised as a matter of course. The animal world was still too strong compared with man for the community not to bow before the necessity of acknowledging a strong and courageous chief."

The Chellean epoch was followed by the Acheulean and Mousterian epochs. The climate became colder and man found shelter in the caves and grottoes, among the most characteristic of which are the ones at Moustier, in the valley of the Vézère (Dordogne). This was the cave age *par excellence*, for the use of caves continued throughout the following epochs side by side with other kinds of habitation.

It has been pointed out that the troglodytes chose for their homes the caves in the proximity of running water. In Perigord, the classic territory of prehistoric man, the celebrated grottoes of Moustier, La Madeleine, Cro-Magnon, the Eyzies, the shelters at Murat, the grotto of Sainte-Eulalie, the Grotto of David, are to be found scattered along the Vézère, in Dordogne, the Drome and the Célé regions. The grotto of Chauffaut is on the Vienne, the Bruniquel caves on the Aveyron. On the lower reaches of the Vézère there may be seen, standing out along a stretch of twelve kilometres, a line of rocks hollowed out like a huge rabbit warren, which must have served as a shelter for a fairly large population. In other regions subterranean dwellings existed on the borders of the Loire and the Seine.

In the Mousterian grottoes weapons have been found which show a marked improvement on the clipped stone axe of the Chellean epoch—a lancehead, for instance, capable of inflicting a deep wound. Fastened to the end of a strong staff this must have been a most formidable weapon. The fashioning of flints had also improved. By a series of fine chippings a bevelled edge was cleverly produced on the axes.

In these caves the troglodytes must have lived a life more wretched perhaps than that of the free hunters of the Chellean epoch. We can only guess at the promiscuity of their sexual life. But their love of adornment is proved by the existence of shell necklaces, and earrings made of perforated teeth. Moreover, many of man's most formidable enemies had disappeared—the dinotherium, followed by the mastodont and the terrible machairodus. The lion still survived, together with

7

the giant hyæna and the great cave bear, all of which demanded a share of his shelter and often tracked him down in it.

Free entry into the caves had not yet been barred.

" The human family used to light a fire to act as a barricade. All around, the animal creation, either hunting or being hunted, roared, howled, belled, trumpeted or bellowed. Some huge wild beast would pass by with his mate; he would roar at the flame, then crouch down and wait. Behind him came the hyænas, the wolves and other beasts of prey which lived on whatever the monster left behind him. If the fire burnt full and clear, and wood was not lacking to keep it up, all these savage beasts became restless and grew tired of waiting; but if the flame died down, if, for lack of feeding, cinders gradually took the place of the light, then the time had come for the Beast to cross the boundary. He would leap the space in great bounds of ten yards and the struggle would begin. When men were there in numbers, it ended in their favour. But if there were only six or seven of them, it was an indecisive battle; if there were but two or three, the discarded pieces of the family which had been devoured remained for the prowlers and parasites " (J.-H. Rosny).

It is a remarkable fact that these caves of the primitive troglodytes were still inhabited down to quite recent times, in the Middle Ages and the seventeenth century. Several of them formed themselves into villages. In the glorious reign of the *Roi Soleil* (Louis XIV), Boileau, in his epistle to Lamoignon, described the subterranean village of Haute-Isle.

> Le village au-dessus forme un amphithéâtre :
> L'habitant ne connaît ni les chaux, ni le plâtre ;
> Et dans le roc, qui cède et se coupe aisément,
> Chacun sait de sa main creuser un logement.
> La maison du seigneur, seule un peu plus ornée,
> Se présente au dehors de murs environnée :
> Le soleil, en naissant, la regarde d'abord
> Et le mont la défend des outrages du nord. . . .[1]

---

[1] The village above forms an amphitheatre; the dweller therein knows neither lime nor mortar; and in the rock, which is yielding and easily cut, each man hollows out a dwelling with his hands. Only the house of the chief is a little more ornate, and is built outside and surrounded by walls: the rising sun looks first upon it, and the mountain shields it from the northern blasts.

Many of these grottoes were still inhabited fifty years ago. The troglodytes are indeed tenacious folk!

The Mousterian epoch was followed by the Aurignacian (Aurignac, Haute-Garonne). It is remarkable for the first appearance in human history of any attempt at art; and an interesting branch of art it was, consisting of work on ivory. The female head from Brassempouy (Landes) with long hair curling on to the neck and shoulders, is a most precious relic; and then there were the mural decorations, such as the rhinoceros painted in red on the walls of the cave at Font-de-Gaume (Dordogne).

The Solutrian epoch followed (Saône-et-Loire). The climate was particularly dry. The seasons were clearly marked showing all the varieties between a cold winter and a fairly hot summer. Horses and reindeer abounded. At the foot of the precipitous rocks of Solutré a terrible accumulation of horses' skeletons has been discovered, amounting possibly to 100,000. It is supposed that the men of the period in hunting them used to pursue them to the edge of the precipice where the animals threw themselves over and were killed. At this time man seems to have eaten horse as well as reindeer flesh. Some vague beginnings of poetry may perhaps have existed. At all events, the art which, as we have seen, first saw the light of day among the Aurignacians, was brought to an astonishing stage of perfection during the Magdalenian epoch. But we must not forget how slow was the course of evolution, seeing that the Magdalenians are separated from us by thousands and thousands of years, and that they in their turn were divided from the Mousterians by an even greater length of time.

The Magdalenian epoch—how charming is its name!—is above all interesting on account of its artistic character. It took its name from the celebrated grotto of La Madeleine in Périgord on the Vézère, where Edouard Lartet, one of the pioneers of prehistoric research, found in 1864 that marvellous engraving on ivory representing with extraordinary accuracy of drawing the figure of a reindeer—a veritable work of art of over twenty thousand years ago. The animal is shown in profile, grazing, and its proportions, the naturalness of the position and the fidelity and precision of the outline are perfect.

Engravings on ivory and reindeer bone are characteristic of the period, together with engravings on rocks, on schist, on stone and on pebbles. The first engraving on pebble was found in Lot, near Rocamadour, by the Abbé Lemozi. It represents a hind with her head turned licking herself. It is almost like a snap-shot, and even a photograph could not have reproduced the movement more accurately—a movement more complicated than in the case of the reindeer of La Madeleine which we have just been discussing.

Later still, in 1920, Abbé Lemozi discovered in the valley of the Célé—we are still in the department of Lot—a succession of grottoes divided into several large halls separated from one another by narrow corridors and galleries one of which is at least a hundred and fifty yards long. "The two last halls," writes Jean Labadié, who visited them, "compose a veritable landscape with architectural details, an elysian stage scene which would have delighted the soul of Hubert Robert. A stone cascade ends in a flight of convex steps carefully rounded, from which a river of rose-coloured marble flows between amber-coloured bushes with branches more diverse than coral."

The walls are decorated in black or red ochre, or else adorned with rock carvings, depicting all manner of prehistoric animals —mammoths, bisons, fish and equine creatures, the whole studded with hieroglyphic signs. The vault, eighteen or twenty feet above the ground, is covered with tracery and engravings. The arrangement of the place is reminiscent of a temple, and such it probably was.

These engravings carried out with flint chisels, these paintings in ochre or black—varied occasionally by sculptures like the astonishing bisons in the cave at Tuc d'Audibert, so vigorously and accurately modelled in clay—almost always represent animals. The ideas of man, in the prime of his vigour and physical strength, are still the ideas of a child. You have but to watch children drawing; they always begin by drawing animals.

In this wealth of artistic expression—and it may well be described thus—the reindeer occupies the place of honour. This may be due to gratitude, amounting almost to a cult, to the animal to which the Magdalenian owed so much. The women, taking up their position at the door of the grotto, roasted reindeer joints over wood fires; as clothes for themselves and their families they sewed reindeer skins with the help of tendons and needles, the latter made of reindeer bone; the reindeer provided everything. And man, with respectful attention, engraved the image of the invaluable animal upon which his own life so much depended.

To the reindeer in these works of art were afterwards added the rhinoceros, the mammoth, the horse and the bison.

These drawings are astonishing, not only on account of the period in which they were produced, but by their intrinsic merit. In depicting animals in full gallop, the movement is reproduced with an accuracy which in the course of centuries the eye of man has become incapable of seizing. It needed the help of photography for Aimé Morot, who was the first to attempt such a thing, thirty years ago, to give an accurate picture of horses in full gallop in his famous charge of the cuirassiers. Fifteen or twenty thousand years ago, the Magdalenians noted these elusive running movements and fixed them for ever on stone; over two thousand years passed by before modern art found a method of retracing them by mechanical means. This proves that primitive man was far superior to us in strength and vigour of constitution and keenness of vision. And doubtless the same was true with regard to his sense of smell and hearing.

It is round about the small area of the Eyzies in Dordogne that the most interesting palæolithic settlements are grouped— the grottoes of Cro-Magnon, Laugerie, La Madeleine, Font-de-Gaume, Combarelles and the Cap Blanc shelter.

Here was the bright hearth of art found in the earliest beginnings of our history, tens of thousands of years before the oldest artistic productions left us by the most ancient civilisations. France may well be proud of having possessed it in the region which two thousand years later she was to call Périgord.

At La Madeleine a complete painter's outfit was found—a palette, paint pots and stones for grinding the colours. Only the perishable articles were lacking—the brushes. The study of these rock frescoes revealed seven different shades of ochre, the complete range from yellow to red and from red to brown.

The Magdalenians produced their wonderful deep black from manganese salts.

So much has been found that a regular museum, the Louvre of prehistoric times, has been founded at the Eyzies, and this little place, which boasts of only a few hundred inhabitants, might be regarded as the capital of the troglodytes, the most ancient hearth of culture in the world. For, while it is true that other countries, such as Spain and Portugal, can produce prehistoric works similar to those of La Madeleine, nowhere else is such a large group of grottoes and decorated caves to be found, bearing witness to the activity of man's life in this district, to important reunions of hunters and nomads, and pilgrimages with possibly large assemblies of people meeting together at those seasons of the year consecrated to commemorative feasts.

Then one fine day our Magdalenians, who were hunters, artists and dreamers, saw appearing at the mouth of their valley unknown warriors armed with new weapons which dealt death from a distance. The reindeer became rarer, and migrated towards the north. Our artist-hunters followed it, preferring the rigours of life in arctic climes to bowing down before unknown masters. Whilst a few of them remained with the newcomers, to act as their slaves in the villages, the majority of them became Esquimos.

The Magdalenians, according to some archæologists, were followed by the Tourassians (La Tourasse, Haute-Garonne) and this epoch was characterised by the use of spears made of deer's antlers.

This quaternary, or palæolithic, or chipped-stone age, divided, as we have seen, into six epochs, was followed by the prehistoric period properly so-called, which preceded modern times but is still many thousands of years earlier than the earliest of ancient history—that of Egypt in the most distant days.

This prehistoric period, in its turn divided into the neolithic age, or the age of polished stone, the bronze age and the iron **The Hiatus.** age, was separated from the preceding era by an immense interval of time. Scientists, from an examination of the geological strata, have estimated that thousands of years must have elapsed before man replaced his

12

chipped flint weapons by polished flint weapons; and to this abyss of time they have given the characteristic appellation of " hiatus."

But other learned men, whose minds were shocked by the idea of the hiatus, as the ears of poets are shocked by a hiatus in poetry, fill up the space between palæolithic and neolithic times by a period of transition, which they divide into three periods—the Azilian (the grotto of Maz-d'Azil, Ariège), the Tardenoisian (Fère-en-Tardenois, Aisne)—how pretty are these two names—and the Campignian—this reminds one of a quadrille—a period called after the village of Campigny in Eure, marking the advent of the neolithic age. The Azilian, Tardenoisian and Campignian epochs were apparently the product of a race of negroid type, probably from Africa, who marked a return to barbarism as compared with the preceding epochs. There are no longer any signs of art, or at most only rough schematic or geometric decorations on pebbles or walls; there are no more needles made of reindeer bone, no more assegais, no more beautiful spear-heads. The instruments, writes Abbé Breuil, are reduced to " piercers of split bone, clumsy polishers, flat, perforated spears, fashioned without art." According to Jean Brunhes, African influence may be detected in these minor products of industry which filled up the hiatus between the palæolithic and the neolithic ages. However that may be, the invention of stone polishing coincides with the end of the quaternary era and marks the first centuries of modern geological periods.

And, indeed, the neolithic age was destined to see great progress in another domain. What an advance in the manufacture of weapons, for instance! Let us take the axe alone, the polished flint axe, set on to the end of a strong wooden handle. Wielded by a vigorous arm, it doubled the power of the blow or the shock. With its sharp edge, the axe could make deep cuts or notches; with its blunt edge it could crush and bruise. Man was now in possession of a weapon which made him master of his rivals. But though material progress was great, it is maintained that, compared with the chipped-stone age, it was one of moral and social decadence. Artistic gifts gradually disappeared, and a period of long depression

13

supervened which the following generations had great difficulty in overcoming.

The palæolithic, or ancient stone age (chipped stone), was **The Lake-dwellers.** therefore the cave age; the neolithic or new stone age (polished stone) was the age of the palafittes (lake dwellings).

During the winter of 1853 to 1854, the level of the Lake of Zurich having lowered considerably, the discovery was made in the mud of an accumulation of stones, mixed with bones and carbonised objects, and fragments of weapons, utensils and pottery. The lake was dragged, and soundings were taken in the other Swiss lakes and the lakes of Savoy, where lake dwellings were found built on piles rising above the water.

For hundreds, possibly thousands of years, a large proportion of mankind lived on the waters. The lake villages must have been very numerous. The Lake of Neuchâtel alone possessed thirty. Man had not only to defend himself against the wild animals, but also against man, a far more formidable animal, since, in the lake period, the most dangerous beasts, the mammoth, the lion and the rhinoceros, had disappeared from the territory of Gaul.

The population had increased. The human being had secured for himself a certain amount of ease, a few commodities, and the beginnings of luxury, which was nevertheless, for the period, true luxury. He harvested cereals and flax, he ground his grain, made blackberry and raspberry wine, and wove his garments, for spinning had not as yet been invented. The needles were made of small bones of animals or fish bones. The lake-dweller possessed flocks and stored provisions. He knew how to make earthenware pottery, soon to be followed by chinaware and bronze swords. And then it was pleasant to rob one's neighbour of his goods, not to mention his wives and daughters, so charming when they were young, and their men who could be reduced to servitude.

While these lake dwellings certainly afforded safety, the patience and skill of neolithic man in constructing his palafittes with the help of stone implements alone completely baffles us. " This struggle for a habitation on the bosom of the waters," says J.-H. Rosny, " is assuredly the most grandiose in our

14

evolution, and in contemplating it we are filled with feelings of poetic emotion."

Men were grouped together in tribes. The houses composing the lake cities were huddled close together, and joined to the bank by a gangway on piles.

In the peat deposits of the canton of Lucerne wooden floors have been found which were at least forty yards long and twenty broad. They supported huts either round or square in shape. The woodwork consisted of interlaced branches of trees, covered by a roof made of reeds and rushes. The walls were composed of clay tiles baked by fire.

Round about the lake stretched fields of crops—corn and barley for food, flax for clothes. The live-stock included the bull of the peat-bogs, the goat, the goat-horned sheep, the marsh pig and—oh, marvellous to relate !—the dog to guard them, the dog whose alliance with man secured the victory of the latter over the other animals and his mastery of the earth. The horse had been domesticated. The bones of domestic animals have been found in the lake cities in far greater numbers than the bones of wild beasts.

Finally, in the palafittes of a later date, that is to say the bronze age, pieces of yellow amber have been found. Now this fossilised resin called yellow amber could only have come from the Baltic. Consequently the lake-dwellers of the bronze age must already have been engaged in commercial enterprises.

As J.-H. Rosny observes : " With his shelter on the face of the waters, the owner of cultivated fields and pastures, provisioned for the winter, fed by the fruits of the earth, the flesh of his cattle, and of the urus, the aurochs, the wild deer and the fresh-water fish, neolithic man must have enjoyed some very pleasurable moments when circumstances were favourable."

For the lake-dwellers used to preserve the wild fruits, nuts, chestnuts and dried apples and pears. They baked unleavened bread. " Cakes of coarse flour," says Jean Brunhes, " have been found, at least two thousand years older than the famous loaves baked at Pompeii." According to Camille Jullian, the population inhabiting one of these great lakes must have numbered as many as 100,000; they probably stored their provisions and goods on the lake, and sought refuge there in time of emergency, their ordinary dwellings being on the surrounding banks.

They were places of refuge and shelter rather than regular dwellings.

Such at least they must have been in many districts up to the last centuries before our own era. Cæsar and Strabo both describe the Ardennes country where the tangled brushwood covered a far greater space than it does at present. This region was occupied by a population consisting of a mixture of Ligurians, Celts and Teutons. When threatened by an invasion of their enemies, these people barred the way into their country by interlacing the longer branches of the brushwood, mingled with brambles and thorns, strengthening the whole defence work with piles. They then retired with their families to the little islands in the middle of marshes, quite inaccessible to any army, says Cæsar, doubtless to the dwellings which had survived from the lake epoch and which they must have kept in repair.

Where no regular lakes existed, these houses on piles were erected in the middle of the marshes which were so numerous in those distant days. It is also possible that neolithic man hollowed out artificial lakes for the building of these edifices. The use of grottoes, moreover, had not been abandoned, and man made himself shelters of wood and leaves.

And it is now that we come across a proper name for the first time, the first proper name to be heard in the great silence of prehistoric ages—that of the Ligurians. It was first found in the writings of the Greek historians.

The Ligurians.

D'Arbois de Jubainville made a great historical discovery when he pointed out that the suffix *ascus, asca* is to be found neither in Latin nor in Umbrian, but that it must have belonged to the Ligurian language, a language which is also apparently of Indo-European origin. The Ligurians used the suffix *ascus, asca* when they wished to turn a word into the name of a place, just as we from the word *chêne* have made *chênaie* (La Chênaie), from *hêtre*, *hêtraie*, from *saule*, *saulaie*, etc. We find these terminations in *asco, asca, aschi, usco, usca, osco, osca*, not only in Upper Italy, in Liguria proper, but also in

16

Switzerland, in the valleys of the Rhine and the Danube and in northern Gaul. Now it is precisely in these regions that the lake dwellings are to be found and they belong to a period when the Ligurians were masters there. It is only in those districts, where the names of places bear these Ligurian suffixes, that the ancient lake cities have been discovered.

Whence it may be concluded that the lake civilisation was essentially a Ligurian civilisation.

It is true that these pleasing deductions are disputed to-day. Camille Jullian believes that the Ligurians and Celts spoke the same language, the Celts being a Ligurian tribe who founded a State on Ligurian territory.

In Gaul, the Ligurians occupied the entire basin of the Rhone. Some writers maintain that it was from here that they set out for the conquest of northern Italy, and later spread into the neighbouring regions of Gaul, the upper reaches of the basins of the Garonne and the Seine. Auguste Longnon even goes so far as to say that the name Thierache, the original form of which was Teorasca, proves that the territory of the Ligurians reached as far as the North Sea.

Thus we see that the lake dwellings coincide with the polished stone age and continued in use, after the comparatively short copper age, right into the bronze age. The latter began towards the middle of the third millennium (about 2500 B.C.) and ended towards the beginning of the ninth century B.C. But during this latter period a new style of habitation came into being which was destined to be characteristic of it—the underground dwelling. The ground was hollowed out more or less deeply in such a way as to form a shelter with vertical walls entered by means of a sloping path. The walls were then lined with wood in very much the same way as the trenches were in the Great War, or sometimes large stones were placed on the top of each other. A few stones composed the hearth, the smoke from which escaped through an opening in the roof. Inside were to be found seats and couches of stone, pieces of pottery, weapons and a few utensils in polished stone or bronze. Thus a regular system of cities grew up, uniting hundreds of these trench-like constructions which were built side by side, and in dimensions probably equalled the huts of the lake dwellings.

One can imagine what these conglomerations of subterranean dwellings looked like when seen from a neighbouring height—merely a juxtaposition of roofs hardly rising above the level of the ground.

Hard by the dwellings of the living were to be found those of the dead, the latter resembling grottoes, some of them natural, but most of them artificial. These have been found chiefly in the cretaceous subsoil of Champagne. The skeletons in them were arranged with their heads turned to the walls, and were divided from each other by flat stones. About them were placed the weapons, the utensils, the ornaments and other relics of the deceased. Beside the corpse dishes were placed filled with food for its sustenance, in keeping with the oldest beliefs of southern Europe, so well described by Fustel de Coulanges in his *Cité Antique*. The burial grotto was generally approached through a smaller grotto, forming a sort of vestibule or peristyle, entered by a corridor the ground of which had clearly been much trampled under foot by visitors—doubtless parents, friends and devotees coming to render pious homage to the departed and bring them offerings.

More numerous and more interesting than the monuments to the dead hollowed out in the grottoes were those which appeared above ground, often constructed in imposing dimensions—the dolmens, the menhirs and the cromlechs. These have often been regarded as Druidical monuments, but some of the most important of them have been found in districts which the Druids never inhabited. The megaliths are of far earlier date than the Celts and the Druids.

Like the polished stone age and contemporary with it, the period which witnessed their construction was called after these monuments of huge unhewn stone—it was known as the megalithic age (from the Greek words μέγας, large, and λίθος, stone).

Monuments similar to the dolmens and menhirs are to be found in Algeria and Syria, as well as in India and Japan, but they are most numerous on French soil. Dechelette estimates them at 4458.

The dolmens, made of huge stones placed side by side and on top of one another, were monuments to the dead. The

18

whole construction was covered with earth on which the grass grew. Viewed from a distance on a plain a dolmen looked like a kind of knoll or bank, in the shape of a great long tortoise with a turf-covered shell. From most of the dolmens the hand of time has removed the earth and sand, leaving behind only the granite skeleton.

Some of these blocks of stone, such as the great menhir of Men-er-Hroëck (The Fairy Stone), weigh at least 200 tons; l'Aiguille de Locmariaque weighs 347 tons. In order to place these granite columns where they stand, they had to be moved over twelve to eighteen miles.

Were the men who handled these cyclopean blocks giants then? we exclaim. Not a bit of it. They were small, puny men whose acquaintance we made in discussing the lake dwellings.

And ancient writers, as a matter of fact, tell us that the Ligurians were a dark-haired race of short stature, extraordinarily robust and endowed with great energy. Diodorus and Strabo describe them as small but possessing muscles of incredible elasticity. The Ligurian, who was an indefatigable runner, looked as though he were set on steel springs. His limbs seemed to obey the orders of his will without ever tiring. In running the light-footed Ligurian knew no rival. The Mediterranean people used to speak colloquially of the swift Ligurian, just as we speak of the light-footed gazelle or the agile squirrel. Æschylus praised his stamina.

The Ligurian was deeply attached to the soil, which he tilled with stubborn perseverance. Even the women worked on the land with unremitting diligence. In our own days we may still see the Arab women in Algeria going out to wash clothes in the neighbouring streams just before they are expecting the birth of a child, so that, sometimes, the little boy or girl arrives in the middle of the washing operations. And then, when the sun has gone down below the horizon, the mother returns to the hut, bearing on her head the palm fibre basket full of the clothes she has washed in the river and on the top of it the new-born baby. The Ligurian woman of ancient days resembled her. She would interrupt her hard work on the land to give birth to her child, which she washed in a neighbouring stream.

Then placing it in some safe place she would return to her digging and weeding as if nothing had happened, and in the evening go home with her baby in her arms.

This physical vigour was not accompanied by any sign of artistic gifts, however feeble. " The best drawings produced by megalithic man," says Camille Jullian, " were the geometric figures with which they adorned their pottery, which, however, were in no way different from or superior to what may be found among the least intelligent of savage races." They had no idea of literature. The women could tell no tales, and the old men no legends, unless it were to call to mind the stratagems which the Ligurians were so clever at devising, the ambuscades which no one knew how to arrange and carry out so well as they did. Nevertheless, even among the Ligurians, there existed some dim remembrance of that mysterious Kingdom of Ys, lost in the shadowy and distant past of the country of the menhirs, probably swallowed up by the waters, a legend common to the folk-lore of all races.

The religion of the Ligurians consisted, like that of many other primitive people, in a simple and straightforward worship of natural elements. Fire, Earth, the Sun, the Moon, the Evening Star, the Morning Star, were for them divinities who were sometimes evilly and sometimes well disposed towards them. Above all they worshipped the Earth in the form of a goddess, and on a lower and more limited scale local divinities, such as springs, lakes, trees and hills, which were haunted by their familiar spirits, fauns, sylvans, hamadryads, nymphs and naiads, elves and fairies. . . .

These were primitive, deep-rooted traditions. As late as the fourteenth century the girl friends of Joan of Arc used to seek for cures at the fountain of the currant bushes, over which a local divinity had cast its spell. Joan used to join the pretty processions which, on mysterious anniversaries, used to go and hang garlands on the fairies' tree; she would be one among the train of people who went to sing hymns under the tall trees on Ascension Eve. The priests and monks of Rouen were not far wrong when they accused the marvellous maid of worshipping the last survivors of their rival divinities, to whom, all unconsciously, like the true daughter of the soil of France that she

20

was, Joan had in her earliest childhood rendered this simple homage, not knowing it was the tradition of far distant ancestors.

The religion of the Ligurians, like that of the early Greeks, demanded human sacrifices. Until the beginning of the first century before our own era, the Ligurians of the Apennines sacrificed prisoners taken on the field of battle to their gods, until some new divinity, introduced into their Pantheon of nature-gods, taught them that it was more advantageous to sell their prisoners to the Greeks as slaves than to cut their throats on the altar-stones.

The erection of these megalithic monuments required the help of hundreds and hundreds of men all working together. Thus the dolmens and the menhirs presuppose the existence of an organised society divided into classes under the rule of a guiding aristocracy. Moreover, only the leaders of a strong aristocracy could have been honoured by funeral monuments of such dignified proportions.

Many bodies were buried in the same dolmen, which often resembled an ossuary, a magnificent family vault, in which generation succeeded generation.

In the districts were the dolmens where built were also to be found, dating from the same period, huge stones pointing skyward and fixed in the ground by their most pointed end. They were generally arranged in lines. These are the famous menhirs. If they were arranged in semi-circles they were called " cromlechs."

All kinds of wild hypotheses have been advanced to explain the meaning of the menhirs and the cromlechs, the most probable being that they were connected with the cult of the dead. The menhirs may have been funeral piles. Of the innumerable theories advanced on the subject of the rows of stones at Carnac in Brittany, " I prefer," says Camille Jullian, " that which explains it as a colossal funeral ground of primitive times, whence the dead after being burnt and stripped of their flesh, departed for their new abode."

The neolithic and megalithic age has been called by Jullian the epoch of the agriculturists. Social life had been established on a firm basis. The pursuit of comfort had developed human activity. Wheat was sown and harvested and bread was brought forth from the oven; for it is a remarkable fact that, of all cultivated grain, wheat was the first to crown the labours of man, and was followed by millet, barley, rye and oats. Fruit trees were picked out in the wild woods, selected and cultivated, particularly the pear and the apple tree; flax was gathered, to be followed later by hemp.

And the first efforts at industry had already yielded valuable results. In the lake villages weavers' combs, cords, thread and pieces of stuff have been found. Soon the wool was taken from the sheepskins and supplemented the rough furs of bygone ages with warm materials. Later on man learnt to dye them blue and red with woad and kermes. The art of pottery, with its utensils of various shapes, preceded the bronze age which ushered out the neolithic epoch. We have already discussed the bronze age in describing the last years of the lake period.

The bronze age coincides roughly with the period called by Camille Jullian the age of the migrations. The great migrations began no doubt before the end of the neolithic age, and the epoch of the warriors may have begun before the close of the bronze age.

The migrations proceeded from two main sources, one hailing from the Far East and the mysterious East Indies, the other from the north and snowclad Scandinavia. Now these migrations did not take the form of sudden huge overflows spreading over vast tracts like some impetuous flood. On the contrary, they were gradual advances, slow movements towards the west, or towards the south, on the part of races who, without any desire for war or plunder, were seeking less densely populated and more fertile districts, with a milder climate, but were often driven to acts of violence by the resistance they encountered or by despair of ever reaching the goal which seemed constantly to elude them. Tens, possibly hundreds of years, must have been spent by the Indo-Europeans and the Hyperboreans in their gradual conquest of Europe.

The bronze age is itself divided into the Morges period (from Morges in the canton of Vaud in Switzerland), when hatchets, daggers and swords made of bronze still showed very rough workmanship; and the Larnaud period (from Larnaud in Jura), which was also called " the fine age of bronze."

22

As a protection against these migrations walls and fortresses were built, some of them composed of the huge blocks of the megalithic period, like the formidable wall at Sainte-Odile made of giant stones, placed side by side, and joined by wooden bolts in the shape of a swallow tail—" dove-tailed " as we call it. In the course of time the wood rotted away, and only the cavity into which it had been fixed in the stone remained. When the difficulty of building a stone wall seemed too great, a substitute was found in the shape of ramparts of heaped earth.

Men succeeded in combining together for collective work. Marshes spreading over thousands of acres were drained, such, for instance, as those in Alimania, a colossal enterprise demanding all the more trouble and energy, and all the greater cooperation and organising power, seeing that man was still very poorly equipped with instruments for his task.

And this co-operaticn in enterprise, which meant that thousands and thousands of men had to work harmoniously together, bears witness to the high degree of social understanding and moral culture reached by man, not to mention some system of common legislation which inspired respect.

Moreover, as J.-H. Rosny has so clearly pointed out, the presence of civilising elements was due, not to the immigrants, but to the autochthonous races. The invaders found themselves in a small minority compared with the races which for centuries had been installed in the great oak or chestnut forests, on the cultivated plateaus or in the hollows of the verdant valleys.

They were no longer met by people who took refuge underground, but by a race who lived in dwellings built above ground and already possessed of many an object that tended to add to the amenities of life.

But is not this the invariable rule ? In ancient times invasion meant the overrunning of a conquered people by a race lower in the scale of culture : *Græcia capta ferum victorem cepit* was an oft repeated phenomenon. What the Goths were to the Romans, the Germans to the Gallo-Romans, the Indo-Europeans and the Hyperboreans were to the natives whom they found in Gaul.

The large number of fortifications which made their appearance towards the end of the bronze age proves how greatly man lived in fear of man. Surprise attacks, sudden sallies, and war-like expeditions became frequent. And lo! we enter into the iron age which Jullian calls the epoch of the warriors.

We are now on the confines of the historical period which we shall make it our task to describe. Already the name of one race has been mentioned—the Ligurians, to be followed now by the Iberians. It is true that, with regard to the latter, historians are not agreed. "Iberian" apparently was the name, not of a race, but of a State, the Empire of the Ebro, a name used by the Greeks for this district. At the beginning of the fifth century (500–475 B.C.) the Kingdom of the Iberians, stretching beyond the Pyrenees, may have extended into Languedoc as far as the Rhone. Bordeaux thus becomes Iberian. Euskarien, that is to say the Basque language, which, as we know, has survived with such wonderful tenacity in the mountain districts, must have been the language of the Iberians. Basque itself was probably composed of two elements, the one Iberian, possibly of Asiatic origin, the other Italo-Celtic. This much at least is certain, that the peninsula of Spain owes its name—Iberia— to the Iberians, a name of Greek origin, and that, in the first century before our era, a branch of these Iberians, called Aquitanians, occupied the region stretching between the Pyrenees and the Garonne, where Cæsar's soldiers came across them. But in the East civilisation had already adopted pulsating forms of life; Egypt bore witness to a magnificent culture; Greece was listening to the lays of Homer and was soon to produce works of art of the highest beauty, whilst the dawn of Roman greatness was already visible. In Gaul the iron age was inaugurated, which was also divided into two "stages." The first (from the eleventh to the fifth century B.C.) was called the Hallstatt period (from Hallstatt, a place in the Salzburg mountains in Austria)—a huge necropolis where, in hundreds of tombs, weapons, utensils and bronze and iron ornaments were found. The sword was still made of bronze. The iron sword made its first appearance in the iron age (the end of the second century B.C.) called the La Tène period

The Iberians.

24

(from La Tène, a place on the lake of Neuchatel, which became famous). With the La Tène period we enter into the domain of history. The skeletons found at Hallstatt and La Tène are supposed to be Celtic. Armed with the sword of La Tène the Celts, who were natives of the Danish isles and peninsula, and the lower plains of northern Germany, invaded Gaul in the fifth century before our era, conquered the Ligurians there, overran Europe as fiery victors, and founded an Empire in Asia Minor; with the iron sword of La Tène the Gauls of Vercingetorix were destined to be armed beneath the walls of Alesia.

To sum up, we have seen that a number of diverse races succeeded each other on the soil of France, beginning with palæolithic man, who was possibly not autochthonous, followed first by the Indo-Europeans and Scandinavians, and then by the Iberians, the Ligurians and the Celts. Next in succession came the Romans by right of conquest, the Goths and the Germans by invasion, the Syrians and the Semites by a process of infiltration, the Hungarians and the Saracens as robbers, and the Normans as robbers and afterwards as colonisers.

Like the soil on which it came into being, the French people too developed in race, in manners and in language, after the manner of alluvial deposits—the chief of these alone amount to a dozen—divers elements, each one of which contributed its share to all that is most striking, most original, brightest and strongest, in that magnificent whole, which centuries of social life, co-ordinated efforts, hopes and fears shared in common, and struggles endured side by side, have mingled into one incomparable alloy—the nation, the language and the civilisation of France.

BIBLIOGRAPHY.—Legrand d'Aussy. *Mém. sur les anciennes sépultures nationales*, from *Mém. de l'Institut, Sciences Morales.* Élie de Beaumont, *Recherches sur quelques unes des révolutions de la surface du globe*, 1829–30. John Lubbock, *Prehistoric Man*, 1889. Ém. Cartailhac, *La France préhistorique*, 1889. Alex. Bertrand, *La Gaule avant les Gaulois*, 1891, 2nd ed. D'Arbois de Jubainville, *Les Premiers Habitants de l'Europe*, 1894, 2nd ed. J. Flach, *Origine de l'habitation et des lieux habités en France*, 1899. Gabriel and Adrien de Mortillet, *Le Préhistorique*, 1900, 3rd ed. G. Bloch, *La Gaule indépendante . . .* from *Hist. de France*, published by E. Lavisse, 1901. Peyrony, *Les Eyzies et les environs*, 1903. Joseph Déchelette,

Manuel d'Archéologie préhistorique, 1908. Fustel de Coulanges, *Les Débuts de l'histoire de la Gaule*, from *Revue archéologique*, 1908. Camille Jullian, *Hist. de la Gaule*, Vol. I, 1908. [Maxime Petit] *Histoire de France illustrée*, s.d. [1909]. *Peintures et gravures murales des cavernes paléolithiques*, Cartailhac and Breuil, *La Caverne d'Altamira*, 1906. Capitan, Breuil and Peyrony, *La Caverne de Font-de-Gaume*, 1920. Jean Brunhes, *Géographie humaine de la France*, from *Hist. de la Nation française*, edited by Gabr. Hanotaux [1920]. Jean Labadié, *Une découverte archéologique dans les Causses du Lot*, from *Illustration*, 1923. Jean Fourgous, *La Capitale de la Préhistoire, ibid.* J.-H. Rosny *Les Origines, La Préhistoire* [1924].

CHAPTER II

CELTIC GAUL

The invasion of Gaul by the Celts towards the end of the 6th century B.C. The formation of the Gallic nation. The Druids. Physical Geography of Celtic Gaul. The divisions of society : the family, the clan, the tribe, the people. Primitive monarchy. The vergobrets. The movements of the Celts in the 4th century : their conquests. Ambigatus, king of the Bituriges. Character of the Gauls. Foundation of Marseilles. The States of Gaul in the 4th century B.C. The features of the principal ones. The civilisation of the Gauls : their houses, their industry, their clothes. Organisation of feudal Gaul. Picture of Gaul during the last century of her independence (second century B.C.). First invasions of the Romans. End of monarchy in Gaul. Conquest by the Romans of Transalpine Gaul (Provence). The three provinces of Gaul : *Gallia togata, Gallia braccata, Gallia comata.* Peculation of the Roman governors. Population of Gaul before the arrival of Cæsar.

THE Celts came from the north, from those nurseries of the nations—Jutland, Friesland and the coasts of the Baltic. They were the Normans of the sixth century before our era. They gave to themselves the name of Celts. They were also called *Galates.* The Romans called them **The Invasion.** " Galli." This word was used for the first time in Cato's *Origines* (the second quarter of the second century B.C.). From *Gallus, Galli*, was derived the name of Gaul and the Gauls.

To the ancients the three appellations, *Celtes, Galates*, and *Galli*, were synonymous; but Auguste Longnon is of opinion that originally they were applied to three different branches of the same race. A fourth branch must have been represented by the Volcæ, who, in the first century before our era, had settled down between the Danube and the Main. The name given to the Celtic tribes of the Gauls, after passing through an

27

intermediate Teutonic form *Walah*, came to be applied to the Wallachians, the Walloons, to the Gauls, and to those Gauls, whom the Germans were afterwards to call by a name which on their lips became a word of abuse, and was also derived from *Walah*—the Welsh.

Whilst the Ligurians had been a short, dark-haired, olive-skinned race, the Celts were tall and fair, with pink and white skins. The fair-haired Celts, writes Claudian, " proud of their tall stature, despised the shortness of the Romans " (Julius Cæsar). They must have resembled the Slavs more than they did the ancient Germans. It has been suggested that they should be called the Celto-Slavs.

It has often been asserted that the French nation was composed of a mixture of various peoples, among which the preponderating element was provided by the Celts. But, on the contrary, the latter, on invading Gaul, found themselves a small minority compared with the natives, just as the Germans were who succeeded them some centuries later.

If it were necessary to pick out from the various races which went to form the French nation one predominating type, this would certainly be found among the Ligurians and the autochthonous tribes, admitting that the Ligurians themselves were immigrants. To speak in general and none too precise terms, it would be safer to say that the French are not Celts but Ligurians.

The mixture might be very roughly apportioned as follows :—

In the formation of the French nation 50 per cent. were autochthonous Ligurians and Iberians, 20 per cent. Celts, 5 per cent. Latins, 16 per cent. Germans, including the Gothic element, 4 per cent. Normans and 5 per cent. various other elements—Greeks, Basques, Semites, Syrians, Africans, etc.

When, in the third century B.C. the Greek artists, who at this time had flourishing schools in Asia Minor, witnessed the arrival of the Celts—great big men, with steel blue eyes and quantities of fair hair which looked as though it were made of sunbeams—the Greek artists, filled with admiration for these warriors with their strong muscles, their virile proportions, firmly planted on their strong legs, abandoned their old models, decadent Greeks and Asiatics, and made statues and bas-reliefs of Celtic figures.

28

When the Celts arrived in Gaul towards the end of the sixth century B.C. they did not find the same race or the same culture everywhere.

Jean Brunhes points out that in the west, from the Pyrenees to the north of Brittany, the Ibero-Armoricans were to be found (Armorican meaning close to the sea); in the central regions, the north and the east, from the Alps to the Channel, were the Ligurians. The former constructed dolmens in which the dead were buried; the latter placed their dead, in a squatting position, in great jars or cists; the former were still a pastoral people, on the sea-coasts they were fishers; the latter were, as we have seen, agriculturists, reaping their harvests with bronze sickles.

The conquest of Gaul by the Celts seems to have occupied the whole of the fifth century B.C.

Between the Rhine and the Pyrenees the Celts found isolated tribes; and, as a matter of fact, the various groups of Ligurians never attempted to unite together. The only form of war they knew was brigandage. The fortresses they had built, their walls of giant stone and their ramparts of heaped earth, provided extremely efficacious defences against surprise attacks from some neighbouring tribe in search of booty; but they were not impregnable shelters against bands of warriors accustomed to mass manœuvres and battles on a large scale. The struggle could nevertheless be extremely bitter. Carthaginian and Phocian navigators, who used to sail within sight of land, very often witnessed a bloody battle, and had opportunities of seeing the ravages of war.

The Celts were triumphant, but the slow nature of their conquest bears witness to the smallness of their numbers. They came with their wives and children and their booty, which they bore in their train in long lines of chariots.

Their language, like the Ligurian, was intimately related to Umbro-Latin. Neo-Celtic dialects are still spoken, in parts of Brittany, in Ireland, in Wales, in the Highlands of Scotland and in the Isle of Man, but their idiom, changed in the course of centuries, shows but faint resemblance to the remains of ancient Celtic preserved for us by the science of epigraphy. This much at least is certain, that the Celtic language must be

29

placed in the great family of so-called Indo-European languages (Latin, Greek, Teutonic, Slav, Sanscrit and Iranian). Penetrating into Gaul, the Celts gave the name to the great stream of water which the Germans consider as *par excellence* the river of Germany; they called it the Rhine. In Celtic this word means " stream of water." This may possibly be the root of the German word *rennen*, to run, and of the French word *renne*, reindeer, which comes from the Teutonic *renn*, in Swedish *ren*.

Moreover, the whole Celtic nation did not invade Gaul. Part of it remained on the right bank of the Rhine, which thus became Celtic on both sides, just as both slopes of the Alps were Ligurian and both slopes of the Pyrenees Iberian.

The great body of Celts was divided into tribes, each of which was destined to conquer and settle down in a particular part of Gaul.

The conquerors and the conquered apparently intermingled very quickly. In primitive times, when social distinctions hardly existed and civilisation was still in an embryonic condition, the similarity between religious ideas and practices helped towards this fusion of races into one homogeneous whole.

The Celts, like the Ligurians, deified natural elements—the Earth, the Sky, the Sun, Fire and Thunder—and they honoured **The Druids.** local divinities, the gods and goddesses of the rivers, the springs, the deep forests and the wind-swept peaks, with an ardent worship. With a picturesque imagination they indulged in a belief in charming nymphs who kept watch at the sources of the great rivers, the Seine, the Saône and the Loire. The Celts, like the Ligurians, worshipped above all the Earth, which they pictured in the form of a woman, and doubtless, according to Camille Jullian, they went to pay her homage at the same altars and sanctuaries used by the Ligurians. The Celts, like the Ligurians, used to bow in reverence beneath the branches of the great trees surrounded by the mysterious murmurs of the woods. The Ligurians gave the place of honour to the beech, the Celts to the oak. This religious difference, which in a more advanced civilisation would certainly have led to copious bloodshed, was never emphasised either by the Ligurians or the Celts. They endowed both the beech and the oak with supernatural power in the shape of mysterious fairies which haunted them—the supernatural " dames " of ancient folklore.

" The Druids," says Pliny the Elder, " hold nothing more sacred than the mistletoe, that, at least, which is found on the English oak. The English oak is for them the divine tree *par excellence;* their sacred groves consist of this species, and the use of oak leaves is enjoined in all sacrifices. Also a tuft of mistletoe growing from an oak is a sign that it comes from heaven and that the tree has been chosen by some divinity. Mistletoe on an oak is, moreover, exceedingly rare. It is· cut in accordance with a strict and detailed ritual and takes place on the sixth day of the new moon, when she gives a fairly strong light but has not yet reached a full half. The priest, clad in a white robe and armed with a golden sickle, climbs the tree and cuts the mistletoe which must be placed at once in a white coverlet."

We all know how mistletoe is grown; the seeds are carried by birds from branch to branch, but the bark of the oak being particularly hard, the seed can only stick in it and germinate and take root with the greatest difficulty.

To the mistletoe gathered with this ritual of a golden sickle and white coverlet, the Celts attributed marvellous virtues; there was no malady it could not cure.

This cult of trees was destined to survive the passing of centuries, invasions and revolutions. The Catholic Church tried to fight it, but was quick to acknowledge its inability to deal with beliefs deeply rooted in the popular mind; so much so, that many a priest in the country, or even the town districts might have been found holding in deep respect the tree of magic properties; and this naturally led to the discovery of a remedy for the evil. About the supernatural power of the beech or the oak there could be no doubt; and, in order to render homage to it, a pious statue of the Virgin soon came to be fixed to the gnarled surface of the ancient trunks, purifying them and justifying the hymns, the garlands of flowers, the traditional rites and the rustic ceremonies.

Several of these fairy trees have survived to our own day. Others have preserved their pagan character, like the celebrated oak called Lapalud in the neighbourhood of Angers. The

Angevins honoured it with a curious attention as late as the nineteenth century. The custom was for every carpenter, joiner, wheelwright and mason who passed beneath the old oak to knock a nail into it. And thus the tree was covered with a coat of iron to a height of nine feet.

The same thing took place with the waters; and since many really did possess healing powers, the cures they effected prolonged the homage paid them. The town of Nîmes owed her protective diety, Nemausus, to the genius of the spring. Among these aquatic divinities there was one who enjoyed exceptional renown. This was the god who bore the name of Borvo or Bormo. Of how many thermal springs was he not the tutelary genius? And together with his name they also preserved the healing virtue with which he had endowed them—la Bourboule, Bourbonne-les-Bains, Bourbon-Lancy, Bourbon-l'Archambault, etc.

Unfortunately, like the Ligurians, the Celts also included in their religious observances the horrible practice of human sacrifice. It is impossible to think of this without a feeling of revolt, though it must be confessed that the early religious rites of all races included this cruel and detestable custom. The Greeks and the Romans who, at the time when they came into contact with the Gauls, had reached a more advanced stage of culture and had forgotten the sacrifices of Homeric days, or regarded them as legends and poetic fictions, speak of the sacrifices of the Druids with a horror which is indeed justifiable. They chose their victims as best they could, first of all from the ranks of those condemned to death; and in those rude ages capital punishment was of frequent occurrence.

Punishments varied in accordance with the variations in the Druidical Pantheon. All the gods demanded human sacrifices in their honour, but were not propitiated by the same kind of execution. Thus the powerful god Esus, the god of battles, preferred his victims to be hanged in the depths of the woods where he had his sanctuaries. The proximity of one of these was made evident to the traveller by the number of bodies swaying from the green branches. The good old poet Gringoire hymned " the fair orchard of the god Esus." An altar consecrated to this amiable personage—I mean the God Esus—was found fitted into a Roman wall on the site where Notre-Dame de Paris was afterwards built.

Taran, the god of thunder and lightning, whom the Gauls identified with the Roman Jupiter, demanded his victims to be burnt alive; whilst the great Teutates preferred them to be drowned in a tub of water.

Teutates was the great god of the Gauls. His name translated from the Celt means the " national god." He was the inventor of the arts. He protected commerce and was the patron god of merchants. Teutates possessed the most numerous and most crowded sanctuaries. These were as a rule not temples that had been built, but clearings made in the woods. Here the devotion of the pious heaped up treasures of gold and silver, coins and precious vases. After a battle a part of the booty was reserved for the gods who had given victory. This was prompted by the same feeling that makes mankind consecrate to God a part of the fruits of the earth. Later on this was done for the salvation of the soul, by the building of chapels and churches and the foundation of monasteries. By this means the great abbeys derived power which contributed to the progress of the country and it provided one of the sources whence the bishops secured the influence which also proved so beneficent in times of trouble.

The Celts, who were simple-minded in their primitive state of culture, heaped up their gifts to the gods in the spots devoted to their worship—the clearings in the woods or the depths of the sacred lakes, gifts consisting of ingots of gold and silver, sparkling jewels and precious vases. So great was the veneration—or fear—inspired by the god, that no greedy hand dared to touch the treasure. The consul Servilius Cæpio, sent to Gaul against the Cimbri (106 B.C.), sacked the Gallic temple at Toulouse and dragged the sacred lakes. By this means he amassed in ingots of gold and silver a treasure valued at 15,000 talents (£32,000,000 in English money). And, in the following century, the Romans, after having conquered the country, sold at a high price for the benefit of the Treasury the sacred lakes of the Gauls, from which the buyers possessed themselves of the treasure.

After the Gallic trinity, Teutates, Esus and Taran, come such

33

picturesque divinities as Belenus, the god of the thermal healing springs, and of the heights illumined by the rising sun. He taught those of the Druids, who undertook cures, old wives' remedies, and the uses of herbs and roots gathered at the solstices, and mysterious formulæ. He had as a companion Sirona, the luminary of the night and the dusky forests, the white Selene of the Greeks, Diana with her opal crescent. Sirona was originally a spring that gurgled beneath the moss of the woods. Then there was a rough and brutal god, the Vulcan of the Celts, the genius of fire and metals, who presided over the subterranean forces. Of none of these divinities have we any certain picture, with the possible exception of Epona, the goddess of the wild steeds and beautiful chargers. The Celts did not feel the necessity of imagining their gods in human or animal form and doubtless did not conceive them thus.

Besides the national gods, the worship of whom was common to all, there were the local and topical divinities, who dwelt in the branches of trees, in the beds of rivers, or on the sunny heights. But the topical divinities were generally vegetarians, satisfied with the wild or cultivated fruits, flowers and herbs presented to them by their worshippers. It was as a rule the great gods who were insatiable man and flesh eaters.

The great variety of the punishments invented by the Druids bears witness to their imagination. We have already mentioned the unfortunate victims who were hanged in honour of the gods, or burnt alive, or drowned; others were crucified, or killed by flogging or by being stoned. Some were shut up together with various animals in great hampers made of wood and osiers, and stuffed with hay and other inflammable material. The whole was burnt together amidst heartrending cries, howls and hoarse entreaties; the flesh crackled in the flames and gave forth a sickening stench—enough to rejoice the hearts of all the gods in the world.

These terrible customs survived for a long time in France, though they lost some of their ferocity, and, with the increasing refinement of life, occasionally adopted a certain picturesque charm. Burnt sacrifices to the gods usually took place in the height of the summer, in the months of June and July. The fires of St. John, which even in our own day are lighted in many

34

a country district, with their graceful rondos and joyous refrains, are but an old tradition, an echo which still resounds after two thousand four hundred years. It was for long the custom in France at the festival of St. John to throw various animals into the flames—cats and moles, foxes and wolves shut up in baskets. In Paris, the magistrates, in their robes of State, were present at the burning ceremony as a sign of its importance. This custom was still in existence in the reign of Louis XIV, when it died out. On the 3rd of July, a few days after St. John's day, they still used to burn in the *rue aux Ours*, a great wicker basket—the degenerate offspring, fortunately, of the hamper stuffed with men and animals that the Druids used to roast in order to propitiate their gods.

The Druids also made use of human sacrifice in their divinations. It was their custom, says Strabo, " to cut open a man's back with one stroke of the sword and to make their prophecies in accordance with the way the victim struggled."

As victims condemned to death were not sufficiently numerous for these frequent holocausts, which the Druids, be it said, made with the best intentions in the world, in order to get rain after a drought, or to heal some distinguished personage, or to secure the happy issue of some useful enterprise—innocent victims were sacrificed, unfortunate creatures who were bought as slaves to be killed, just as calves and pigs are bought in the market. Lastly an abundant source of supply was found in prisoners of war.

But the astonishing fact is that these same Druids who organised such atrocious sacrifices used to study the movements of the stars and the constitution of the elements, they talked of the grandeur of the universe, taught a lofty and refined morality, governed by the most noble belief in the immortality of the soul. They also combated idolatry.

" The Druids," says Ammianus Marcellinus, " joined together in societies, occupied their minds with profound and sublime questions, raised above human concerns." They possessed a fairly accurate knowledge of the past of Gaul, maintaining that their race was partly aboriginal and partly from beyond the Rhine, whence it had been ousted from its ancestral hearth by frequent wars and the encroachment of the sea—an extraordinarily accurate theory, proving that they studied and indulged in reflection.

The belief in the immortality of the soul was particularly ardent among the Gauls. So intense was it that the Greeks and Romans, who also shared it, were struck by it. To this belief they attributed the contempt for death which made the Gauls march with bared breasts against enemies armed with helmets and breastplates. The words applied by the Italians to the French noblemen of the time of Louis XIII might have been said of them : " They enter into battle as if they were to rise from the dead the next day." Diodorus Siculus says that the Gauls held death in such deep contempt that they fought duels and killed each other for the most trifling causes—just like the French noblemen of the time of Louis XIII.

In the traditions of the people of Armorica, with their clear-cut poetical conceptions, this belief in the immortality of the soul took a very picturesque form. The Armoricans believed that the kingdom of the Dead was situated across the sea beyond the setting sun. The crossing was made in a mysterious boat. This belief in the bark of the ferryman of the dead, the bark of Charon, was a popular belief in many lands. It is to be found in the most ancient hymns of the Serbians, in which the oars are held by St. Peter accompanied by the prophet Elijah. The Gauls believed that on the furthest coasts of Brittany a population of silent sailors undertook this imperative task. A long-drawn, low wail which made the air vibrate, like the wind kissing the waves, warned the ferrymen that the bark had arrived to all appearances empty, but really weighed down by the souls it was bearing. The bark swung out to the open sea, the oars beat the water, the crossing took an hour, and the bark neared its destination. A loud voice called out the names of the souls on board; as the recitation proceeded the boat emerged from the water; when the voice was silent the sailors returned with their empty bark.

The teaching of the Druids on matters of religion, morality and the mysteries of Nature was made orally in the form of poems which had to be learnt by heart and were handed down from mouth to mouth. This is a valuable hint which helps to explain the transmission of the Homeric poems, for the latter were composed at a period when writing had not been invented. And it is probable that the most important at least of these druidical poems resembled the poems of Homer, though they may not have possessed the precise literary and artistic form which the Iliad and the Odyssey owed to subsequent revision.

Thus the Druids had no knowledge of writing, or at all events did not wish to make use of it, in order that the sacred mysteries might not be divulged. They reserved their teaching for the children of the nobility, who were sent to live with them in the depths of the woods or in caves, in the dark shelters of legendary lore. Their teaching exalted the virtues of courage, strength and ambition. Women appear to have had no part in it. The Celts never had a Druidess like the Teutonic Velleda. The virgins of the island of Sein and the bacchantes of the Namnetes, mentioned by the Greeks, were figments of the imagination.

This hidden and mysterious religion from which the mob was excluded and which the priests kept jealously to themselves endured in a stereotyped form. It left its mark on the Roman religion, which was brought into Gaul after Cæsar's conquests; and this explains the popular welcome given to Christianity, which made its appearance under the Emperors. The religion of Christ was the religion of the humble, the weak and the poor. Woman was exalted in the form of the Mother of God. As soon as Christianity reached Gaul, the masses, the working masses of the country, bestowed upon it all their vigour and the irresistible power of their faith.

Nevertheless the Druids cannot be said to have formed a caste; they were an initiated priesthood grouped together under one leader, the chief Druid. The power exercised by the latter was very great, not only in the religious, but also in the social and political world. Religion, in the hands of the Druids, constituted the only national tie binding together the various peoples of Gaul. In the country of the Carnutes, the Druids held general assemblies attended by crowds of the faithful from every quarter. At Fleury, also called Saint-Benoît-sur-Loire, this religion had altars where sacrifices were offered by people from the remotest parts of the country.

The Druids, formed into tribunals, were the supreme judges of the people. Now in a nation possessed of no administrative machinery, the administration of justice constitutes all the government there is. The Druids used to judge all disputes, not only between private individuals, but also between tribes and even cities. They thus rendered a great service to the nation by maintaining relative peace between rival tribes and hostile clans. The Gauls described to Posidonius how their priests interposed as peacemakers and arbitrators between parties ready to tear each other to pieces.

In order to maintain their authority they made use of the most formidable means of constraint—excommunication. The thunder of the Catholic Church when it was at the height of its power, in the most troublous times of the Middle Ages, did not inspire greater respect and fear than the sentence of exclusion from the sacrifice pronounced by the Druids from the depths of a neolithic cave or the midst of a sun-dappled clearing in the woods.

Throughout the whole of Gaul an excommunicated man became a cursed being; he was refused all justice and was shunned by everybody, as he was no longer allowed to approach the altars of purification.

" If a private individual," writes Cæsar, " or even the chief of a tribe, refuses to submit to the edicts of the Druids, they cut him off from all religious ceremonies. This is the greatest punishment known in Gaul, and those upon whom it is inflicted are regarded as impious scoundrels. No one speaks to them or comes near them, as they would be sullied by contact with them; they can exercise no public function, and are not even allowed to demand justice before the tribunals."

And if it was a whole clan or tribe or city that had been excommunicated, religious death overtook the district thus penalised. No priest would officiate there, the stones of the altars were deserted, blackened by flames now extinguished, stained with the dark blood that had been shed over them. The bards no longer sang the glories of their ancestors, the magi no longer cured fevers, the sorcerers no longer dressed wounds.

Under the direction of the Druids the order of divine healers, called eubages, and the bards formed, as it were, a lower branch of the priesthood. The name of bard has been handed down to our own days together with that of the barz or village fiddlers of Brittany. They were jugglers who beneath the sonorous
38

whispering of the immemorial oaks, on the sunlit heights and by the side of the refreshing streams, used to sing their divine lays, hymning the mysteries of their religion, the beauty of the moral life, tales of the gods, the valour of their ancestors, and the courage of their warriors. " The bards," writes Ammianus, " sing in heroic verse, to the accompaniment of the lyre, the great deeds of the heroes "—which is an exact definition of epic poetry.

In poetry as in art all beauty is traditional. The poet or the artist of genius who produces a masterpiece owes it largely to his predecessors and his environment. At two different periods the French, who have the epic mind, produced national poems— in the primitive times of the Druids and during the age of chivalry, in the tenth, eleventh and twelfth centuries of our era. But both periods were followed by a break in tradition, in the first case by the Roman conquest, and later by the English invasion and the disturbances of the Hundred Years' War, which was followed by a " renaissance " inspired from abroad. The French, whose gifts would have enabled them to produce a hundred Iliads or Odysseys, renounced their birthright because they would not or could not remain faithful to themselves.

Under the rule of the Druids, the healing magi were much more numerous than the bards or jugglers. They are worthy of all respect. They worked, studied botany and practised chemistry. " The eubages," says Ammianus, " tried to explain the forces of nature." " They studied nature," writes Strabo, and from her learnt useful recipes, some of which have been handed down to us by Pliny and by Marcellus Empiricus. They sold unguents made of clarified fat and perfumed with the essences of herbs which they used to go out and gather on the magic nights by the light of the moon. Whether the magic of the nights and the rays of the moon possessed any great power we know not, but sterilised fat scented with herbs carefully distilled was certainly good for wounds. In the combating of disease the eubages also used amulets and cabalistic formulæ. These amulets and formulæ were infallible cures, unless the patient had a corrupt soul, which must first be purified according to the prescribed rites and by appeasing the wrath of the gods by sacrifices. There were occasions when this divine wrath was so great that neither amulets nor sacrifices prevented the sick man from dying.

Healers of this description still existed in Gaul under the Merovingians. Gregory of Tours relates how, in the year 587, the Bishop of Paris had one of them arrested, and on him was found a large pouch filled with divers herbs, the teeth of a mole, some bones of mice and some bear fat. The Bishop had the whole lot thrown into the river and banished the picturesque healer from his diocese.

Description of Gaul. We must not be surprised by the important part played by woods in the religious life of the early Celts. " Gaul with her huge forests," say the ancient writers.

Strabo has described in words that have become famous the harmonious aspect of Gaul, her mountains, her plains, her rivers and her valleys. " Such a felicitous arrangement of natural features, which seems to be the work of an intelligent being rather than the result of chance, would be enough to prove the existence of Providence." In this beautiful arrangement Strabo believed that the Pyrenees were parallel to the Rhine; but, harmonious though it may have been, the aspect of Gaul must nevertheless have been somewhat forbidding.

The district of Bedsia, with its fertile fields, was then but woods and marshes; it was famous, not for its cornlands, but for its iron mines. The districts of Orleans, Gâtin, Blois and Perche [1] were covered with tangled masses of prehistoric vegetation intersected by marshlands. The huge forest of the Ardennes, with its impenetrable undergrowth, was joined by the forests of Voivre and Argonne to the Vosges, which spread eastwards through the Hercynian forest of legendary lore, of which Cæsar says, " There are no Germans who after a sixty days' march can say where it ends, or know where it begins." The Vosges spread to the north through the impenetrable forests of Haardt and Hünsrück between the Rhine and the Moselle, and to the south through the thick woodlands of the Jura extending into the Alps. For centuries these forests formed between Gaul and

---

[1] There is no exact modern equivalent for these districts, which in Latin were Pagus Aurelianus, Vastinensis Pagus, Blesensis Pagus, and Pagus Pecticensis.—*Tr.*

Germany a barrier more difficult to cross than the flood of the Rhine. Smaller rivers, like the Sambre, the Meuse, the Saône and the Doubs, were swallowed up in them. Only the broad. Rhine, with the rocks and mountains along its banks, could make a clear space in their midst. Huge trunks drifted down the Rhine, and also down the Somme and the Meuse, brought down from immense distances by the rivers when they were in flood. In this way the great peat bogs of Belgium were formed.

Thus Gaul was covered with thick forests of trees centuries old joined by an impenetrable undergrowth. In the north were oak, beech and birch trees; in the east pines and firs.

The Ardennes, less imposing in aspect, were covered with a stunted, grey and forbidding vegetation.

Here and there were inhabited caves, sacred groves and marshes surrounding islands on which lake-dwellings were still to be found. Among the fauna various prehistoric monsters still survived.

The rivers, along the greater part of their course, were bordered by swamps and marshes which man would not or could not drain.

Such was the general aspect of the country. But if in the north of Gaul the forests followed each other in almost uninterrupted succession—north of the Seine the country was nothing but a vast tree-covered plain—the ground began to clear towards the south-east. The exploitation of the mines by the Bituriges (Berry) led to a clearing of the woods; the Auverni (Auvergne) and the Aedui (Burgundy) had destroyed many a forest for purposes of agriculture; the Carduci (Quercy) were famous for their flax fields. Cæsar on reaching Gaul found Provence covered with olive trees. It was the custom among the various tribes who were grouped together between the Rhine and the Pyrenees to leave the frontiers of their territory wild and uncultivated, and these districts were quickly covered with shrubs, which thus surrounded the territory of each tribe with a wide belt of green.

As physical conditions play a large part in the moral and material development of a nation, we must not be surprised at the slowness with which primitive man attained civilisation.

41

The Celts imposed their own social divisions upon the Ligurians, and they did so all the more easily in that they found the social structure of the latter very similar to their own. We are still very far, be it understood, from any legislative organisation. As regards law the Gauls knew nothing beyond certain patriarchal customs.

The Divisions of Society.

Let us turn to the period of the Tarquins in Rome, the Homeric age in Greece and the tenth and eleventh centuries in France. Camille Jullian in a few words gives us a precise picture of Gaul : " Gaul, in vaster proportions and more clumsy outline, presents us with the same political institutions as Greece and Latium; she remained a juxtaposition of City States."

In Greece several families (γένος) formed a phratry, several phratries a tribe, several tribes a city; in Rome several families (*gentes*) formed a curia, several curiæ a tribe, several tribes a city. In France in the eleventh century several families (gestes) formed a mesnie, several mesnies a fief, several fiefs a State (Île-de-France, Burgundy, Flanders, Champagne, Anjou). In Gaul we find several families forming a clan, several clans a tribe, several tribes a people or nation, or what the Romans called a city. By whatever name these various peoples were called—Celts, Ligurians or Iberians—there were no fundamental differences between them. " Among them all we find political forms and superstructures which are analogous " (Jullian).

We are in the presence of a family enlarged by the subordination of secondary branches to the principal branch ruled by the chief. And this grouping is preserved in the same shape in the larger divisions of the clan and the tribe. Historians were right to place the origin of the tribe in the family. The tribe was generally designated by a proper name, a family name, the name of the family or of the parent chief or the name of some ancestor.

" The tribe," says Jullian " was a collection of families and individuals rendering obedience to common chiefs, called by the same name, bound by one set of rules, leading a similar existence and living as neighbours on the same territory." Each tribe had its own traditions, its protective deity, and common interests; its members all derived from the same stock (*geste*)

42

lived together on common territory to which they gave their name, working together, fighting side by side and, in the larger districts, where several tribes were united, led by the same chiefs. The tribe, which grew out of the family, was the cell which was destined to develop and provide the various divisions of the State.

Each of the many tribes of Gaul derived its particular characteristics from the regions and country in which it lived; each tribe came to have its own traditions, owing to the development of the race and the unions between the young people of the same tribe, which were naturally frequent and possibly in the beginning even obligatory. Each tribe was moulded by the country in which it lived and which imposed on successive generations a particular form of labour, and also by its system of morality and the customs resulting therefrom. Thus as time went on each of these Gallic tribes developed clearly-marked characteristics. The toil of centuries was destined to give to the people of France, through the virtues of the soil, of the race and traditional occupations, their manifold type and variegated character. Could anything be more beautiful?

Here were the mountains, yonder the valleys. The wooded cantons were the home of the woodcutters, the Silvanectenses of the Senlis district; the waters which surrounded the island of Lutetia bred a race of boatmen, the Parisiaci ; the lands rich in minerals produced workers in metal, the Bituriges (Berry), the Petrecores (Périgord); the cantons which possessed silver mines gave birth to miners to work them, the Rutenes (Rouergue) and the Gabales (Gévaudan); on the delicate clay soil of Auvergne potters were trained. And this appropriation of man by the soil and of the soil by man was destined to increase and strengthen day by day. Even at the present time many districts of France still bear strong and healthy traces of the old Gallic tribes who, over two thousand years ago, took such firm root in them that many, like Médoc, Queyras, Condroz, the district of Buch, la Soule and so on, are still known by the names of those tribes.

The same process took place in Gaul before the Christian era as had already occurred on a small scale in Greece, and was to be repeated in France after the anarchy of the ninth and tenth centuries—the federation of neighbouring tribes owing to the development of social intercourse, economic necessity and industrial and commercial activity. Lutetia was the home of the boatmen, Bourges of the metal-workers, Gergovia of the potters, Bibracte of the workers in silver, enamel and bronze. By an exchange of services and of local products, the tribes came to form peoples or small nations on a larger scale, and navigation, iron-works and pottery, though still in their infancy, were more fully developed. Thus were formed the peoples, the " nations," who in their turn founded traditions, and had aspirations and interests in common and served under one chief.

It is estimated that Gaul was divided into four or five hundred tribes, grouped, according to Cæsar's calculations, into seventy-two peoples or nations, not counting the district of Narbonne. Thus a people consisted on an average of four or five to as many as ten tribes.

Though grouped into peoples, the tribes nevertheless preserved a certain independence; each one kept its distinctive character, its traditions and its communal life under its own chief. Such an one was Ambiorix, who, at the time of the wars of independence, was chief of one of the tribes belonging to the people of the Eburi.

These tribal chiefs exercised power in the larger divisions of the people or nation, acting as local magistrates with police jurisdiction. They formed a deliberative assembly within the union, a council, in which common interests were discussed and decisions reached for the benefit of the people or nation. This assembly the Romans afterwards called the senate of the city. The senates of the Gallic cities consisted of the chiefs of the clans or great families, the chiefs of the " gestes " who made up the tribe; the union of several tribes, generally five or six in number, constituted the city. In time of war each of these senators, these chiefs of clans or gestes, marched at the head of his people, like the feudal barons of the eleventh century. In the course of the struggle for independence six hundred senators of the Nervii died sword in hand in the midst of their followers; according to Cæsar only three survived. About the eleventh century the *Chanson de Guillaume d'Orange* told a similar tale.

Each tribe had its own sanctuary, its place of refuge, its

44

market-place, in which the heads of families met together, thus forming the headquarters or capital of the tribe. And the union of the tribes constituting the people or city also had its sanctuary, its place of refuge, in which the heads of families assembled, thus forming a capital in a spot fortified either by nature of by the art of man.

At the head of these peoples or nations, each consisting of the union of several tribes, themselves composed of several families, was placed, in the beginning, at all events, a common chief, a prince, or king, whose function was paternal or patriarchal and also religious, similar to the kings in early Greek and Roman civilisation and in France in the Middle Ages.

Monarchy had as a rule disappeared in Gaul towards the end of the second century B.C. As the families by means of the bonds created by " clients " gradually achieved class distinctions, the chiefs of the principal families came to constitute an aristocracy which freed itself from royalty.

This gradual grouping and co-ordination continued until the second century, when the Arverni succeeded in uniting Gaul into one great State under their authority. It was a premature unification, for as yet the interests, customs and traditions of the various nations had little in common; and it was impossible for it to survive.

Several of the Gallic nations, after abolishing their monarchical constitution, nevertheless put the reins of government in the hands of one supreme magistrate, who was, however, elected for a period of one or two years, and called the " vergobret." The vergobret exercised royal authority, but, in matters of foreign policy, important negotiations, or when it was a question of declaring war, he was powerless to act without the national council or senate.

The vergobret was the supreme magistrate, with powers of life and death. He was the chief of the armies, but in the same way as our own President of the Republic—he never went into battle with the troops, but left to the generals the task of leading them.

The vergobret was not allowed to leave the district he governed.

Young men of energy and resolution were frequently raised

to this position and through them a vigorous impulse was given to national affairs.

About the vergobret the chiefs of the tribes or principal families, and of the gestes, constituted the senate just mentioned, which acted as his guide, supervisor and support.

In concluding this sketch of the political institutions of Gaul, we must point out that the Gauls, after several centuries of evolution, experienced a similar struggle as the ancient Greeks of the popular parties against the chiefs of the great families, the aristocracy and the patriciate. In Gaul, as in Greece, the popular party, which did not possess the strong social constitution of its adversaries, I mean that organisation of families with sharp class distinctions under the leadership of their chiefs, placed its interests in the hands of a supreme chief, something like the tyrants of the Greek towns. And thus royal authority was revived in Gaul, but in a very different shape from that of the patriarchal and religious monarchy of the early times. It partook of the nature of a tyranny; either the people increased the authority of the vergobret, which amounted to the same thing, or in a still simpler way they chose a chief, with no particular title, whom they followed. As in Greece, aristocratic government meant liberty, popular government was the incarnation of tyranny; and it was this latter form of government which, as we shall see, formed the independent or national party.

Thus in Gaul of the so-called barbaric ages the essential elements of the various forms of government that the world has known were to be found in full activity, without having been borrowed from any outside source. Is it not one of the most natural and simple laws of human history that similar social and economic conditions necessarily produce similar institutions?

As soon as the Celts had made themselves masters of the greater part of Gaul, their need for activity and their warlike virtues drove them in search of fresh adventures. **The Conquerors.** We have already described the facility with which the Celts intermingled with the Ligurians; and their great expeditions were undertaken together.

From Gaul, the victorious Celts crossed the Pyrenees and spread over Iberia; they then turned to the south-east in the direction of Northern Italy, whence they descended into the plains of Latium and carried their warlike activities against the splendours of Greece and the seductive languors of the East. In 395 B.C. they entered Melpum, a flourishing town of Transpadane Etruria; in 390 B.C. they appeared before Clusium, where their altercation with the envoys of Rome took place. The legions, under the command of the consul Q. Fabius, were crushed in the terrible battle of the Allia, and the Gauls entered Rome. They seized the town and set fire to the greater portion of it, but failed before the strongly fortified Capitol. The incident of the geese is well known. The pick of the young men of Rome had shut themselves up in the sacred enclosure, whilst the women and children took refuge in the neighbouring cities. One night the Gauls were on the point of taking the Capitol by surprise, when the sacred geese raised the alarm. The Gauls only consented to retire on receiving a thousand pounds in gold. It was weighed out for them. The Romans complained of the weights the Gauls had brought. Whereupon Brennus threw his massive sword into the scales, crying " *Vae victis !* " and the Romans were obliged to balance the sword of the conqueror in addition to the weights complained of.

The recollection of the danger they had run, and the memory of their defeat were never effaced from the minds of the people of Rome. For many years afterwards, whenever there was a threat of attack by the Gauls, the *tumultus gallicus* was proclaimed. " Alarm ! To arms ! " and the shops were shut, business was suspended, and the citizens enrolled *en masse* for the defence of their country.

The fourth century B.C. marked the zenith of the Celtic Empire, which constituted the second iron age already mentioned. The Celts conquered Great Britain, they conquered the whole of Spain except its Mediterranean coast, and all France but for the basin of the Rhone, and the north of Italy. They ruled the whole of Germany except the northern districts, and Switzerland; their dominion was established on the Middle and Lower Danube and a part of Hungary; in Silesia itself it extended to Liegnitz, in Roumania to Isakscha, and in Russia as far as the Lower Dniester—the whole forming an Empire greater than that of Charlemagne or of Napoleon, an Empire reaching from the Straits of Gibraltar to the Black Sea, at the time when Alexander the Great was engaged in the conquest of Asia (334 B.C.).

In 283 B.C., the Gauls made their appearance in Greece, where they pillaged the treasures of Delphi (278 B.C.); they founded an Empire in Thrace, another in Phrygia, and, west of Phrygia, the district of Galatia is called after them to this day.

Thus the triumphant progress of the Gauls was one of the greatest the world has ever seen. Proper names connected with it, the names of the generals, the battles and precise details are unfortunately lacking. But if we may believe Livy, this colossal conquest was the work of one man, Ambigatus, King of the Bituriges, who won this vast Empire by means of two simultaneous expeditions, one under the command of his nephew Bellovesus, and the other of his nephew Sigovesus. Through the darkness of the ages and the mists of time, the name of Ambigatus, the old King of Bourges, stands surrounded by a halo of power and majesty which places that of Charlemagne in the shade.

The success of the Gauls was in a large measure due to the state of the world which they set out to conquer—here decaying nations fossilised in their outworn institutions, there peoples still in their infancy, and incapable of offering any effectual resistance. What, for example, could the Greeks, or the small kingdoms of Asia Minor avail against the impetuous onslaught of these howling masses, which swept down on them like a torrent, brandishing their weapons and despising death? The ingenious defences of the *strategi* and artists in military tactics were wiped out, just as diminutive dams made by a gardener are swept away by the avalanche which comes crashing down from the mountain heights.

The numbers of these conquering masses must not however be exaggerated. It can only have been 200,000 men and 20,000 horses that swept down like a hurricane upon the dainty little ornament of a State that Greece was at that time. But how could those savage, disorderly, improvident hordes have existed in the spots where they settled down? They had at their disposal no means of communication for supplies. It must be borne in mind that the numbers of the so-called barbarian invaders, where it has been possible to calculate them, were comparatively low. It is impossible to imagine 200,000 men and 20,000 horses being held in check by the geese of the Capitol.

We must beware of the emotion of the writers who, in subsequent ages, have described the disasters that overtook their country. The people of the time were impressed by the tall stature of the Gauls, by their masses of red hair, the dazzling whiteness of their skins, the thunder of their terrifying voices (Ammianus), by their swagger and their greed. They regarded them as half Titan. They reckoned up with amazement the quantity of meat and fermented liquor that one of these warriors was capable of consuming. A Gaul, writes Cicero, would have thought he was being poisoned if he mixed water with his wine. After these debauches the semi-Titans lapsed into a state of drunken stupor which made them even more exuberant, menacing, disorderly and tumultuous than they had been before.

And the Gallic women were no less formidable. Ammianus has drawn their portrait : " Several strangers together could not resist a Gaul with whom they happened to have quarrelled, especially if he summoned his wife to his help, for she outdid him in strength and savage looks. Look at her, inflating her throat and grinding her teeth; with her strong snow-white arms she made use of her fists and delivered blows as vigorous as the blows from a catapult."

Polybius depicts the Gauls as fire-eaters, bawlers, scoffers and grandiloquent braggarts. " They are entirely guided by passion ; reason has no hold over them, and they know not how to obey." " The common characteristics of the Gallic race," writes Posidonius, the successor of Polybius, " are irritability, mad love of war and promptitude in coming to blows; otherwise they are simple folk devoid of malignity." " Anyone provoking the Gauls," says Strabo, " is sure to find them ready for a fight without possessing any better defence than their own strength and valour."

If we may believe Aristotle, the Gauls, like great wilful children in a rage, would have shot arrows against the lightning to frighten it; they would have hurled themselves armed into the waves of the stormy sea in the hope of beating back its hostile waves. Nicholas of Damascus says that the Gauls regarded it as cowardice to leave a falling or a burning house. Aelian says the same thing. These are legends, no doubt, but they reflect the opinion of antiquity. " They made straight for their enemy," says Strabo, " attacking him from the front, without any precaution. They were easily routed by craft."

The Romans also bore witness to the bravery of the Gauls, which they carried to the pitch of temerity, their spirit, their love of talking and their fickleness. " The Gauls," says Cato, " have two ruling passions—fighting and talking." Cæsar and Hirtius describe them as " frank, open and candid people, waging war by their valour alone without artifice." " They were ready for war at any age; the old men went into battle with just as much courage as the young. They scorned danger, and no man among them ever cut off his thumb, as Italians have done, in order to escape the toll demanded by Mars " (Ammianus).

Add to this a generous spirit, enthusiastically following the first impulse—for good, quick to defend the oppressed. They were chivalrous, and punished the murder of a stranger more severely than that of one of their own citizens; they were so honest that they left the doors of their houses open; but they were also very thrifty, says Strabo. Diodorus calls them " extremely miserly."

The Gauls were very changeable, they would not carry out any complicated enterprise, and grew tired of any sustained or painful effort.

With such faults and qualities, the Gauls could easily achieve brilliant victories over decadent or very primitive nations, or over disunited or newly-founded States. It was much more difficult for them to organise and govern their conquests or to found a lasting Empire.

The bluster and uproar with which the Gauls opened battle soon ceased to terrify their enemies. At the beginning of the battle of Telamon (225 B.C.) the Latins were for a moment terrified by the same spectacle as had filled their ancestors with fear on the banks of the Allia (390 B.C.). In the ranks of the barbarians there was a terrific rattle of arms and armour borne by giants. To the blare of trumpets and war horns the Gauls added shouts and yells; the Latins answered by a cloud of javelins which proved more efficacious in spreading disorder in the ranks of the enemy than were ferocious howls and the clash of brazen instruments. In the hand-to-hand fighting, the Roman sword, which was easily wielded and could cut and thrust, soon got the better of the heavy and cumbrous blade of their adversaries.

During the third century B.C. the Celts lost their great Empire. The Carthaginians took from them the possession of Spain, the Romans subjugated Cisalpine Gaul. The Celts only remained a sovereign people in Gaul itself, and even so, from that time onwards German tribes from across the Rhine were constantly coming to settle in the northern regions, thus forming to the north of the forests of the Marne that nation consisting of a mixture of Germans, Celts and Ligurians of which the Romans were to make their province of Belgic Gaul.

Several centuries before this time the Greeks had established themselves on the Mediterranean coasts of France. They were, **Marseilles.** moreover, not the first Eastern nation to land on these shores. As early as the tenth century before our era the Phœnicians had held sway in the western Mediterranean, but only vague traces of their sojourn are to be found in certain names of places.

The foundation of Marseilles by Phocian emigrants took place about the year 600 B.C.—in 598 B.C. say those historians who are not afraid of giving a precise date.

The Greeks came in search of tin for the making of bronze, and also for amber and coral. Yellow amber was only to be found on the shores of the Baltic, for the ancients did not know of its existence in Sicily; but grey amber, with its sweet scent, formed from the internal concretions of cachalots, was fairly common along the coast of Gascony.

To the foundation of Marseilles is attached a pretty legend which historians have discarded somewhat over-hastily. It is told by Aristotle, who lived two hundred years later; but Aristotle had a critical mind and had given some attention to a study of the past. According to him, a young Phocian merchant called Euxenus—others say his name was Protis—landed about the year 600 B.C. on the coast of the Mediterranean just where the Rhone, with its waters the colour of powdered glass, joined the blue waves of the sea. The Phocian made himself welcome to the natives, the Ligurians. Now it chanced

51

that Nann, the king of the country, with his capital at Vego-briga, wanted to find a husband for his daughter Gyptis. Painters depict Gyptis as a beautiful lithe girl, with long hair the colour of ripe corn. But as Gyptis was a Ligurian from the south of France, she must certainly have been dark. Nann called her suitors together. Euxenus was one of the guests. It was a custom of the country that a young girl should hold out a cup of clear water to the man she loved best. To the astonishment of everybody, Gyptis offered the cup to the stranger. Where-upon Nann gave his daughter to the Phocian together with sufficient land for the foundation of a small empire.

The anecdote is so pretty and our artists have drawn such charming pictures to illustrate it that it would be a pity if it were not true.

If it is not true we may console ourselves with the reflection that nobody will ever know. Perhaps the truth lies in Camille Jullian's ingenious theory of the king of a primitive tribe wel-coming a stranger, who brings him charming gifts from distant cities, and giving him one of his daughters and lands to settle down upon. At all events from this pleasant page of poetry we may gather the welcome given by the Ligurians to strangers who landed with those invaluable treasures—the olive, writing and money.

And this explains why the first alphabet used by the Gauls was the Greek alphabet.

The band of immigrants from Asia Minor was considerably reinforced fifty years later. Driven out by the Persians, the Phocians took to their ships, which formed quite a formidable fleet, but the Carthaginians, together with the Etruscans, inflicted a grave defeat on them just off the island of Corsica (537 B.C.) and the ships were scattered. The majority of them reached Marseilles. The town prospered and became the headquarters of the trade in tin, which was sent there from Great Britain by land and water routes. From the shores of the Channel to the delta of the Rhone the journey took thirty days. Marseilles was crowded. The people of Marseilles founded Agde (from ἀγαθή, the good), Nice (from Νικαῖα, the Victorious) Antibes (from 'Αντίπολις, the Citadel) and 'Ολβία, the fortunate, close to the present town of Hyères. . . . Right into Spain did they carry the seeds of colonies destined to grow and flourish.

The friendship between the Phocians of Marseilles and their neighbours the Ligurians did not last very long. After the death of King Nann the town was attacked, but succeeded in holding out. Warned by this alarm, she strengthened her ramparts. It was owing to this hostility and their marked differences in custom and culture that the Greeks of Marseilles tried to isolate themselves from the surrounding people, thus preserving intact the traditions and the civilisation of their own country. But this did not prevent the inhabitants of Marseilles from carrying their trade into the heart of Gaul, travelling up the valley of the Rhone, descending the Garonne and the Loire as far as the Atlantic coast and the Seine as far as Rouen. In the Atlantic ports they again met Greeks embarking for Great Britain in search of tin.

The decadence of the Phocians, who were obliged to give way before the attacks of the Persians, the Etruscans and the Carthaginians, prevented the people of Marseilles from receiving any new elements of strength or prosperity; but, through its own energy the town developed its industries and its military virtues in such a way as to secure hundreds of years of active and glorious life. The coins of Marseilles, and especially the silver pieces, were eagerly sought for throughout the west and as far as the banks of the Danube.

In the fourth century B.C. Marseilles was the headquarters of Greek culture on the Mediterranean, from the shores of Sicily to the Straits of Gibraltar. Her temples were the most highly venerated sanctuaries of the worshippers of the Homeric gods. Her culture, it is true, was not of a very high order. The remains of ancient art handed down to us through Marseilles do not bear the imprint of the classic age of Greece; but after Tarentum had been violated by the soldiers of Pyrrhus and Syracuse by Hannibal, after Mummius had sacked Corinth and Sulla had entered Athens, the civilisation of Pallas Athene was only preserved in all its purity in this Phocian colony.

The people of Marseilles maintained their vessels of war with jealous care, and transformed them in keeping with the progress of poliorcetics. Strabo says that they were particularly clever in the construction of machines of war.   Decadence, it is true, set in during the course of the third century B.C.   The Carthaginians, Hamilcar and Hasdrubal, wrested her Spanish colonies from Marseilles (236–220), whose people thereupon threw themselves into an alliance with Rome.   G. Bloch is of opinion that Hannibal chose the route of southern Gaul and the Alps because he was afraid of the fleet of Marseilles in alliance with Rome.

The defeat of Carthage (146 B.C.) gave Marseilles the monopoly of trade with the East, but the alliance with Rome had become a protectorate.   The fleet of Marseilles was used to carry the Roman legions into Spain.   The Roman allies were transformed into masters, against whom, it is true, the brilliant colony rose in a sudden outburst of energy, so that Cæsar at one time was afraid that the engineers, the sailors and the citizens of Marseilles might shatter his destiny.

At the beginning of the fifth century B.C., when they crossed the Rhine in order to occupy Gaul, the Celts were apparently **The States of Gaul.** already divided into various peoples, each of whom set out for the conquest of a particular part of the territory they invaded and settled down as rulers of it.   Cæsar found them in their original cantons.   Each people gave its name to the occupied region, and these regions in their turn were responsible for the name of the town which was destined to become the capital—if this word may be used at such an early date—a capital which served the tribe scattered over the district as a fortress, a place of refuge and a centre for supplies.

In the heart of Gaul the Bituriges settled down in the district of Bourges, the Senones in Sens, the Aedui in Autun, the Tricassi round about Troyes, the Carnutes in the region of Chartres and Orleans, the Arverni in Auvergne, the Allobroges in Dauphiny, the Lingones in the neighbourhood of Langres, the Nervii on the Sambre, the Treveri on the Moselle, and the great people of the Aulerci in the district of Le Mans and Evreux.

At the time of the Celtic invasion the Bituriges seem to have been the dominant people, and they did not take long to make Bourges the strongest fortress and the richest town of Gaul. Cæsar praised its beauty.   Its ramparts, the defensive power of which was increased by a belt of marshland, were thirty-nine

54

feet high, and the country surrounding it was bounded by moors and marshes. The territory of which Bourges was the capital was the proud possessor of iron mines, and the Bituriges worked them with a skill and energy which made them famous. The celebrated Ambigatus was king of the Bituriges in the third century B.C.; he was a patriarchal monarch whose rule partook of an epic and religious character. He has been called the Charlemagne of the Celts.

Ambigatus had at his disposal the most formidable military power of the time, due, no doubt, in large measure to the skill of his people in forging weapons of war out of the iron extracted from their soil. To the Bituriges was due the invention of tinning.

But two hundred years afterwards, in the first century B.C., Cæsar found the Bituriges among the clients of the Aedui. For the Celtic tribes of Gaul obtained the suzerainty over one another in different ways; some were protective tribes, other tribes were clients subjected to the former in " faith " and " friendship." There were tributary peoples and sovereign peoples. We read that the Arverni held the Vellavii (the people of Velay) " under their rule." And there were allied peoples, federations in which one of the allies held command.

The power of the Aedui had increased as that of the Bituriges declined. Bibracte, their stronghold was, owing to its position, probably the most impregnable in Gaul. It is known to-day as Beuvray in the district of Nièvre. In Bibracte we find the Celtic root " bebros "; Bibracte seems to have signified " the town of the beaver springs."

With its pointed peak dominating the countryside, and commanding the valleys of the Loire, the Saône and the Seine, the haughty fortress of Mount Beuvray reared its head above the plain below. This capital of the Aedui disappeared, and was only found again in 1867, when it was excavated. One wide thoroughfare ran through it, cutting it in half like an apple, from one gate of the town to the other. The houses, which in front were level with the street, at the back were five or six feet underground. Their foundations were made of masonry, their walls, made of partitioned clay, were framed with huge supporting rafters. They had neither windows nor chimneys. The Aedui made their capital not only a stronghold, but also an industrial town, with sounding smithies, buzzing workshops filled with bronze-workers, metal gravers, and enamellers, trades each of which occupied a different quarter of the town.

The art of enamelling was at that time the glory of the Celts. The Greeks and Romans marvelled at it. They would not believe the tales of the first travellers who told them that over there, in the land of the setting sun, the barbarians poured liquid purple on to partitioned metal and made it stick on as hard stone. Philostratus mentions it with the greatest admiration. The excavations at Bibracte brought to light instruments and articles made by the enamellers. The Celtic enamels were generally red, in close imitation, it would seem, of the coral which the Gauls were so fond of setting in glittering gold.

Thus in the third century B.C. Bibracte was the most important industrial centre in Gaul. In these smithies and workshops half hidden underground, the subjected workman spent his days in dark and unremitting toil, like some slave chained to his task. Workmen's tombs have been found under the vices and anvils from which they were not separated even in death.

The Aedui maintain that they were akin to the Romans.

Gradually they extended their power over the neighbouring peoples, some of whom became their clients, and others their allies, but allies subordinate to them. Their patronage extended from the Loire to the Saône, and in the north to the Seine, and they might have succeeded in uniting the whole of Gaul under their authority, just as the Parisii in the centuries that followed realised the unification of France, if they had not fallen foul of the power of the Arverni, who also aimed at the hegemony, which indeed they apparently attained towards the end of the third century, at the time when Hannibal crossed Gaul.

A strong race, with great energy and strength of character, having made the rough territory which in all its bleakness had formed the central core of Gaul their own, the Arverni consisted of stubborn workers on the land, amongst whom a class of skilled artisans had also come into being. The Bituriges were smiths, the Arverni were potters. At Lezoux (Puy-de-Dôme) the ovens

56

were " baking " night and day, and hardening the clay. Even in the most rustic-looking villages muffles were to be found in full activity. The Arverni supplied domestic utensils for the greater part of Gaul.

Like the Bituriges, the Arverni were ruled by an elected monarch assisted by a senate—an office held for life with sovereign authority, an elective kingship which, as a matter of fact, frequently became hereditary. Two kings of the Arverni, Luernus and his son Bituitus, who became king on the death of his father, provided a short but brilliant page of history. They lived in the second century, and their authority extended over almost the whole of Gaul. They even held sway over the Belgæ.

Greek and Italian travellers saw Luernus advancing along the road at the head of a picturesque train of followers including howling dogs of war. A collar and bracelets of gold gleamed against the purple and gold of his dress. He rode erect on a chariot studded with silver. Behind him soldiers bore the Gallic standards, with their device of the wild boar, and at his side a bard sang his valour to the accompaniment of the lyre. With a grand gesture, which the poet compares to that of a husbandman sowing seed, Luernus threw handfuls of gold and silver coins to the subjects who followed his chariot.

On a certain day in the year, in order to " feed " his subjects, Luernus had a space enclosed measuring over two miles in circumference. Here all manner of food was collected, vessels full of wine or ale were crowded side by side. In this gargantuan enclosure, every man could drink and stuff to his heart's content.

Later on we shall read about the battles of Bituitus against the Romans, which covered the Arverni with glory; but their greatest triumph was the production of Vercingetorix.

The Sequani established themselves between the Saône and the Jura, and spread northwards as far as the valley of the Ill between the Vosges and the Rhine. They occupied the cantons which afterwards formed the Franche-Comté, Burgundy and Upper Alsace. They were agriculturists who devoted themselves more particularly to breeding cattle—sheep and pigs. From them the Romans obtained the salt pork of which they were as fond as the English are to-day of Danish bacon. They exercised

57

great power owing to their energy, their unremitting toil and their robust valour. But their territory was, as it were, cut in two by huge forests which made communication difficult between the northern part of their Empire and the southern cantons.

The Sequani were particularly hostile to the Romans, and sometimes joined the Germans in their incursions into Italy. " The Germans," writes Strabo, " became formidable when the Sequani joined them, and ceased to inspire fear when they did not."

The Sequani were always in the opposite camp to the Aedui. The two nations were separated by the Saône, but they each claimed both banks of the river, for the sake of the towns standing on it and the tolls collected in them.

Thus the four most powerful people of Gaul at different periods were the Bituriges, the Aedui, the Arverni and the Sequani. But all the peoples of Gaul deserve mention, for each of them had a character and an individuality of their own.

The Allobroges, in the mountains of Dauphiny, showed from this time onwards that love of independence which was to characterise them for centuries. Their descendants are proud to-day of having had as ancestors during the period of the great Celtic wars the most ferocious champions of liberty—progenitors of those who two thousand years later became the promoters of the Revolution.

The Remi, in Champagne, seem of all the Gauls to have been the richest and most advanced in culture, with aristocratic tastes and a love of comfort, which led them to accept with less hostility than the rest of Gaul a civilisation which paved the way to Roman domination. From the beginning they were the allies of Rome and remained faithful to her. Their country was rich in pasturage and renowned for its horses.

The Parisii, who at one time formed one nation with the Senones, had separated from them. The island of Lutetia was their capital. They were remarkable neither for their numbers nor for the extent of their territory. Some scholars maintain that the root " Par " means " boat." Thus the Parisii were called boatmen. Lutetia, and the island of that name, was their stronghold, protected by a double line of defence, the first consisting of the river, and the second of the marshes, at least in the south, for in the north there were hills covered with woods. In the territory of the Parisii the population became very dense owing to the favourable position of their lands and their exceedingly remunerative calling on the waters.

In the north of Gaul, the territory which is to-day Flanders and Brabant was covered with forests and marshes, and was inhabited by very rough people—the Nervii and the Menapii. In the country of the Atrebates the sheep produced the wool which supplied the cloth industry of Tournai and Arras. The cloth made by the Morini (western Flanders and French Flanders) was eagerly sought for as far south as Italy.

We must end this rapid survey of the chief peoples of Gaul by a description of the Veneti, who were established on the south coast of Brittany, a valiant race of sailors. They used their mighty oaks for the construction of their ships, which were huge and massive vessels, propelled by means of heavy sails made of skins with thongs of knotted hide, and chains for ropes. The Veneti carried on trade with Great Britain, and, as a matter of fact, felt they were nearer England than the mainland of Gaul. From England they were separated, or rather joined, by the sea; whilst from the continent they were divided by impenetrable forests, those forests of English oak with their tangled undergrowth.

These States of Celtic Gaul, amongst which various peoples were distributed, numbered about seventy-five. They left such an indelible mark on the soil of France that centuries have not been able to efface it. They gave to the country those internal divisions adapted to the configuration or the nature of the soil; they presented her with her checkboard of towns and boroughs, her character of over two thousand years' standing, and her territorial arrangement. Until the period just preceding our own, until the Revolution of 1789, when the ridiculous division of the provinces of France into departments took place, the old Gallic States still preserved their names, their boundaries, and, in the words of Fustel de Coulanges, " a sort of existence in the memories and the affections of the people." Until 1789, and even in our own day, this proud memory of their ancient lineage may still be found in the various *countries* of France.

The Civilisation of Gaul. In building their houses, the Gauls made little use of stone; until the arrival of the Romans they were but clumsy masons and mediocre quarrymen. Even their gods possessed but few temples built by man.

Strabo describes the houses of the Gauls in the following words : " Built of planks and wattles of reeds, they were spacious and round in shape, covered with heavy arched roofs " —roofs of thatch. But these were more or less important buildings.

In the first century before our era Vitruvius describes the homes of the Gauls as follows : " Some are caves hollowed in the mountain side, others shelters resembling swallows' nests, made of clay and branches of trees."

The floors were made of beaten earth, and the only chimney was a hole in the roof by which the smoke escaped. There were small square windows, without glass, of course, closed by outside shutters. The door was made of wattles of reeds.

There is a picture of a Gallic house on an antique bas-relief in the Louvre depicting a Gaul defending his house against a Roman. It looks like a bee-hive.

Moreover, a fighting Gaul was proud of cutting off the head of his vanquished foe and bringing it home at his saddle-bow in order to hang it up on the wall of his house. A Gaul of any standing always had a small stock of these trophies preserved in cedar resin with which to renew this decoration, a stock which he was never tired of showing with pride to his visitors. Among the favourite subjects of the coiners of the Bituriges and the Aedui was the head of a warrior with a triumphant halo of severed heads around it ; another was the figure of a warrior brandishing a trumpet in one hand and the head of his vanquished foe in the other.

They had little furniture, nothing but some low tables and coffers that also served as seats. Meals were taken sitting on the skins of wolves or dogs (Diodorus Siculus), or on bundles of straw and dead leaves (Strabo). At night these skins and straw heaps served as beds. The more well-to-do Gauls had carpets and mattresses of wool.

60

As luxury developed, the rich decorated the outsides of their doors with slabs of silver or some other shining metal.

The Gauls loved isolated dwellings in rustic surroundings, on the bank of some river full of fish, or on the confines of a forest abounding in game.

They lived on milk and venison, and also on fresh or salt pork. " Their pigs," says Strabo, " larger, stronger and swifter than those of other countries, wandered loose in the fields. They were as formidable as wolves."

The Gauls loved beautiful dogs and fine horses, and they paid a very high price for the mastiffs they imported from Great Britain.

It is not to be wondered at that hunting was their greatest passion, for it was not only a great pleasure to them, but also of practical use, since the fruits of it constituted a large proportion of their food. The most abundant form of game, if not the most sought after, consisted of the wild pigs from which the Gauls bred their domestic pigs. They crossed their hunting dogs with wolves. On leaving the woods, the huntsman would emerge into some clearing consecrated to a druidic god—a propitious spot for cutting up the game and sacrificing part of it to the protecting divinities.

The towns of the Gauls served as places where people met together, provisions were stored, and fairs and markets held, even more than as centres of habitation. In them Cæsar depicts Gauls eager for news, questioning travellers, surrounding merchants and pressing them to tell all they had learnt.

" The capitals," says Fustel de Coulanges, " were merely small towns in which the senate met on the days it assembled." They were strongholds and centres of worship. In ordinary times few people visited them. Strabo describes the town of Vienne, the capital of the Allobroges, as a simple village.

The capital was by preference chosen in some spot protected by natural defences. To quote Strabo once more, " It is considered good for a town to occupy as strong a position as possible," a rugged rock, the sides of a mountain, like Gregovia, Alisia and Bibracte, or to be surrounded by water, like Lutetia and Melun, or, like Bourges, to be encircled by a belt of muddy marshland.

The area included within the confines of a town was often

very large, the houses occupying only a small portion of it. Camille Jullian compares these Gallic towns to the great cities of central Africa " where, inside the dykes or palisades forming the enclosure, empty spaces and nondescript domains alternate with groups of huts, in the midst of which are found open market-places, cemeteries, alleys lined by workshops, warehouses for arms, barns and granaries and the palaces of the chiefs." The Greeks, accustomed to their marble cities, their pediments decorated with the most wonderful works of art, were appalled by this mixture. " Nothing," they said, " is more hideous than a Gallic town."

It is important to note that all the towns of Celtic Gaul were situated in the centre, the west or the south. The cantons of the north-east, into which the Germans gradually percolated, possessed none.

Serving as places of refuge and market centres, the Gallic towns resembled the acropoli of ancient Greece and the castles and fortified towns of the Middle Ages. The days devoted to business, to the exchange of agricultural and industrial products, were also the days of religious observance. The priests profited by the " assembly of people " as much as the merchants.

We have already mentioned the industry of Gaul in connection with Bibracte, where the inhabitants knew how to get iron from the ground and forge it. We have shown how they invented tinning and the art of enamelling. They extracted silver from sulphur of lead and discovered the art of plating copper with it; they found gold in the sands of the rivers, and even knew how to extract it from the soil, or by smelting; they invented the best kind of dyes—vegetable dyes—and were the first people to make soap. " Soap," says Pliny, "invented by the shining-haired Gauls."

These marvellous and fruitful discoveries alone shed an unexpected light on the " barbarism " of the Celts.

Meanwhile what were the Germans doing? Nothing. What were the Germans doing at the time they invaded Gaul? Nothing. Thus one sees the difference between a nation carrying within it the seeds of an original civilisation and a barren race incapable of civilisation except under the aegis of its neighbour.

In glasswork the Gauls succeeded in producing colours of

incomparable depth and clearness, which our own age has been unable to reproduce. It would not be unreasonable to expect this art of making stained glass to have been preserved by tradition in the centres where it was first produced. At all events it is certain that it was in France that religious edifices first had windows by which the light poured in through glass of the brightest colours, and that it was in France of the twelfth century that the art of making stained glass windows reached a magnificence and a perfection which no other nation and no other period have ever been able to equal. The Gauls also applied their technique for stained glass to the production of jewels in imitation of coral and amber—the yellow amber, and the pink coral, so much sought after.

To come down to the more practical appliances of industry, the Gauls invented the coultered plough, the mechanical reaper, and the great scythe. " The Gauls," says Pliny, " use for the reaping of corn an apparatus composed of a trough with dented edges, mounted on two wheels and drawn by a team of horses, arranged in such a way that the ears of corn, cut off by the teeth, fall into the trough." They also gave to the world the bulging casks in which the juice of the grape grows mellow in its sleep.

Even the most superficial study of the facts just mentioned must lead to the conclusion reached by Camille Jullian that mankind to-day owes hardly less to the Celto-Ligurians, that is to say, the ancestors of the French people, the Gauls, than it does to the Greeks and the Romans of classical antiquity.

The transport of goods was never made on the backs of men. It redounds to the credit of the Gauls that they never regarded their fellow creatures as beasts of burden. Goods were conveyed on two-wheeled or four-wheeled carts, which have hardly altered to this day. It might even be said that the cart with two large wheels was used in the same districts of France as it is in our own time—the centre, the west and the south; and the cart with four smaller wheels in the north and east, where they are still to be seen. So tenacious, in the depths of a nation's heart, are the customs of its traditional existence.

The coach-building of the Gauls was so famous that the Romans even went so far as to borrow from them the principal terms of the trade.

It is true that the high roads were widened, strengthened and improved by the Romans, but they only followed the course of the long roads of the Gauls, which crossed the country and united their capitals in a way so well suited to their communal existence. These Gallic roads have never been appreciated at their true worth. They were wide and strong enough to allow Cæsar to march his armies with all their *impedimenta* over them. The rivers and streams were crossed by means of wooden bridges and the marshes on causeways made of piles of wood and trunks of trees.

The rivers were the scenes of busy traffic. Regular flotillas went up and down the Seine, the Saône, the Loire and the Rhone; the celebrated confraternity of Parisian boatmen dated from before the Roman conquest. Transports were organised to carry the merchandise from the Rhine and Saône on to the Loire and Seine ships, and *vice versâ.*

It is easy, from the produce of the soil and from what has just been said about their industries, to imagine the kind of goods the Gauls exchanged with each other. Trade with foreign nations was also developed. From the shores of the Baltic came yellow amber, from Great Britain tin and the great war dogs; the Gauls, on their side, and more particularly the Veneti, loaded up their ships for England with linen and woollen goods, the grey amber from the shores of Gascony, the products of their metal industries, bronze and silver-plated copper, their glasswork, their pastel from Languedoc, which the inhabitants of Great Britain used for tattooing themselves, and wine carried no doubt in their own rounded casks.

From Marseilles Gaul exported to Italy agricultural implements and carriages and cloth. Strabo says that the Gauls supplied the whole of Italy with the *sagum*, a kind of heavy cloak made of thick, hairy wool. They sold to the Romans the soap of which they were the inventors, and in the way of food, oil and figs and pork, and more particularly the smoked hams of the Sequani and of the Menapii extolled by Martial. The fat geese of the Morini were also regarded as a great delicacy on the banks of the Tiber. They were delivered within sight of the Capitol, which had once been saved by their illustrious sisters, in large flocks driven by gay peasant boys ; for, with necks outstretched,

64

they made this long journey on foot, owing to the curious belief that the flesh of geese is more delicate when the birds are tired.

The use of money as a means of exchange was widespread. The Greeks and Carthaginians had taught its use, and from the third century B.C. onwards the Gauls struck their own local coins, an art never achieved by the other so-called barbarian peoples, more particularly the Ligurians of Italy, in spite of their contact with the Romans and with the Massaliotes along the coast of Provence, nor yet by the Germans, who, it seems, were summoned to regenerate Gaul, but as regards money never handled any coin that had not been stolen from their neighbours.

The Gallic coins did not, it is true, possess the delicacy and finish of the Greek and Roman coins, but many of their devices, with their worn inscriptions, are full of life and virile imagination to which the engraver, within the limited means at his disposal, succeeded in giving a happy turn. The profile and name of any given individual, a war chieftain, or the king of a city, appear but rarely before the last days of independent Gaul, the days of Dumnorix and Vercingetorix; but the inspired treatment of these little figures both, on the obverse and reverse, shows originality and an occasionally disconcerting but always pleasing fancy.

We have just mentioned the esteem in which the Latins held the industry of the Gauls; but they admired their agriculture no less, and the way in which they bred cattle, more particularly their cows, sheep and pigs, and the good account to which they turned them. The corn of Gaul was famous, as was also their beautiful white bread, and the ancestors of the French people had already the reputation of being the largest bread eaters in the world.

From barley the Gauls brewed their ale, a light-coloured beer, in honour of which the Emperor Julian wrote some charming verses :

" On Wine made from Barley.

" Who art thou, whence dost thou come ? A new Bacchus ? I know thee not. I swear it by Bacchus, the true Bacchus. I know by this name only the son of Jupiter. His scent is the scent of nectar. As for thee, thy smell is that of the he-goat.

For want of grapes, the Gauls have made thee from corn. Well mightest thou be called ' the wine of Ceres.' "

The Gauls knew the value of manures. They fertilised their land with lime and marl, that marl for which they sometimes dug deep down into the soil, to the bewilderment of the Romans, who were astonished to see people " manuring earth with earth."

The study of the clothing of the Gauls is full of interest. The dress of the peasant in the fields, both male and female, has hardly changed since the third century before our era to the present day. This may be seen from Roman bas-reliefs. It consisted of breeches, that is to say trousers, and the Celtic smock held in at the waist by a belt. Many of the peasants used fur, more particularly goat skins, instead of material.

Thus the three principal articles of the Gallic dress were the breeches (trousers), sometimes with wide legs, sometimes with fairly narrow legs drawn in at the ankles. In the rural class the breeches very often ended above the knee. The body was covered by the tunic or smock, slit down the front, sometimes only down to the waist, sometimes all the way, drawn in by a belt and having long sleeves; and lastly the *sagum* or cloak, hooked sometimes on the right shoulder, sometimes on the breast, and often provided with a hood. The Romans, after making fun of this style of dress, ended by adopting it, so much more practical was it than their own togas and tunics; and in our own day the dress of the old Gauls has become the costume of three-quarters of the world.

These are facts of great ultimate importance. It is customary to talk of the Latin civilisation of France, but is this not one of the most grievous errors of official history? To their ancestors, the Celts and the Ligurians, the French owe much more than to the Romans, even leaving out of account their blood and race. We have already mentioned the agricultural implements, the coach-building, the art of working in metals and stained glass. But the bed with a mattress was also a Gallic invention, and it was from the Gauls that the Romans borrowed it. We have seen that the Roman roads merely followed the tracks of the Gallic roads. And when Christianity arrived, which contained nothing, or very little, that was Roman, Gaul breathed her own

66

spirit into it. And, as we shall see, it was the same with regard to language.

Writing and the use of money came to Gaul, not through the Romans, but through the Greeks.

The Gauls had a greater influence over the Latins than the Latins had over them. They gave the Romans many of the essential elements of life—dress, agricultural implements, bedding and coach-building. The truth is—and it cannot be too often or too loudly and emphatically repeated—the truth is that French civilisation, modern civilisation, is essentially a Gallic civilisation, born from the fusion of the two elements of Celt and Ligurian, of which the latter, as Camille Jullian has already observed, was responsible for the greater part.

The rich Gauls loved luxury on their persons much more than in their houses. They covered themselves with jewels, rings, bracelets, necklaces and golden fibulæ set with coral. They were particularly fond of this combination of gold and coral, which harmonised with their long fair hair, and the brilliancy of their child-like pink and white complexions. They used to wash their fair hair in lime water in order to make it fairer still. When they did not let it flow loose in the breeze, they knotted it up in a bunch on their heads, which, according to Diodorus Siculus, made them look like the god Pan.

The Gauls, said Ammianus, were very clean in their persons, tending their long hair, their drooping moustaches, and their fresh complexions. And he adds : " You will never find among them, as you find elsewhere, a man or woman, however poor, in dirty or ragged clothes."

They loved bright and variegated colours in their clothes, and the materials of the rich were worked with gold thread, Their *sagum*, or hooded cloak, described by Diodorus Siculus, was generally made of material with coloured stripes or checks, a bright contrast to the monotonous white of the Roman togas, and the monotonous black of Spanish clothes. They did not wear the same cloaks in summer as in winter. In winter the wool of which they were made was thick, coarse and as it were hairy; in the summer, on the other hand, it was very fine. Strabo says that in order to make some of their sheep grow finer wool the Gauls used to cover them with skins.

Not only their cloaks, but their other garments were also usually made of wool, home-grown wool strongly woven; only the poor continued to wear the linen of neolithic times. The poor labourer, says an old song, " is clothed in canvas like a windmill."

The war dress of the rich and noble Gauls was even more magnificent. Their helmets and shields were encrusted with gold and coral. Their helmets were pointed; in very early times they finished up in one very long point.

Virgil gives a beautiful description of a Gallic chieftain climbing the Capitol. His thick red hair seemed made of sunlight, over his brilliant tunic he wore a cloak with bright coloured stripes and a collar of gold sparkled on his milk-white neck.

On State occasions the warrior would dress himself up in terrifying horns, the head of an animal, or some other curious fetich; the fantastic tourney helmets of the mediæval jousters were of this description.

The Gaul of noble birth never went out without his sword, which he wore on the right side, whilst the Roman only carried this weapon into battle; and this is a custom which the Gauls handed down to the knights and nobles descended from them.

Feudalism in Gaul. By the third and second centuries before our era the progress of agriculture and industry had borne fruit and wealth had become concentrated in the hands of the strongest.

The Celtic race had founded its social organisation on the family. The power of the father was absolute, as it was in Rome. Until he was old enough to bear arms, a son was not allowed to accost his father in public. The subordination of women was complete and polygamy was allowed.

About the principal branch of a family were grouped the minor branches in such a way as to form, under the authority of the chieftain, a society composed of clans. The clan in Gaul became the living and active cell of society, similar to the *gens* in Rome.

There has been much discussion regarding the tenure of property among the Gauls. It was their custom to appropriate not only articles, but also land. We know from Cæsar that

68

litigation in connection with the inheritance of estates frequently occurred in the time of the Druids.

Like the Romans, the Celts extended the family by means of clients.

Thus their social system was one of clientage, if we call it after the subordinates, one of patronage, if we call it after the protectors. But this is feudalism.

Feudalism, which we must beware of regarding as exclusively military, is a form of society through which all great peoples have passed in the early days of their history. It existed in Egypt, Greece, Rome and Gaul; it will be found again at the beginning of French civilisation. It also existed in an identical form during the corresponding period of Japanese history. The picture drawn by Maurice Croiset of the social organisation of Greece in Homeric times, and by Benjamin Guérard of France in the tenth century, are exactly similar, whilst the patronate in Rome and in Gaul was identical. And it is impossible to maintain that either of these people borrowed from the other, for at this epoch in their history they were unknown to one another. In each case similar social and political conditions produced similar institutions.

Thus, in the third and second centuries B.C. in Gaul the patronate, that is to say feudalism, was, as in early Rome, a very living and vigorous institution. Cæsar observed that it formed the essential element in Gallic society. He called the chieftains of the great families " knights," the subordinates " clients " or " ambacti," attached to the patron by ties of faith and devotion in return for the protection he afforded them, just like the vassals in feudal France. Vassals! Fustel de Coulanges actually called them by this name. Beneath the clients came the slaves, corresponding to the serfs of the Middle Ages.

The tie binding the client to his patron, the " ambactus " to his " knight " and later the vassal to his lord, was a very close one. " It is a crime," says Cæsar, " it is sacrilege among the Gauls for a man to abandon his patron if the latter is in danger." The patron on his side owed his client similar devotion. " No man," says Cæsar, " allows his clients to be oppressed."

Some have regarded the ambacti as forming a superior class

among the clients, and consisting of those who lived in the society of the chieftain, following him and helping him every day—the *comites* and *familiares* of the Romans. It seems certain that this class of clients existed, consisting, no doubt, of those among them devoted more particularly to the profession of arms, like the mail-clad vassals of the ninth century; but is it correct to attribute to them alone the title of ambacti? As a matter of fact this quibble, which is purely verbal, is of little importance.

The number of clients might be very large and add considerably to the authority of the patron. Cæsar says that the prestige and power of a man were measured by the number of his clients. Aduaticus, King of the Aquitani, had 600 men under his patronage; Vercingetorix was able to raise an army from among his clients, whilst the clients of Orgetorix of the Helvetii could have peopled a whole canton. There were nobles in Gaul who as patrons or suzerains governed a whole city, whilst a few among them had an entire district under their authority.

The feudal lord of the Gauls was the judge of his people, just as later the feudal lord in France was the judge of his vassals. We have already mentioned the tribunal of the Druids, which was common to the whole of Gaul; a similar institution in later days was the royal parliament. It adjudicated differences between cities, tribes and overlords, as well as private cases, just as the royal tribunals and the Church tribunals afterwards did in France. But over the clients whose suzerain he was, the Gallic patron was supreme judge.

This personal power was strengthened by the possession of wealth, for the seignioral mansions of the Gauls were no longer in the second century B.C. the old round thatched huts decorated with gaunt skulls. They were filled with all kinds of furniture, jewels of gold, coral and amber, weapons encrusted with gold and silver and coffers holding shining piles of chinking coins.

These heads of noble families had their mansions in the fields, on the confines of the woods which they cleft with their noisy hunting parties, or on the banks of streams. They went to the capital for the assemblies at which the nobles discussed their common interests.

70

Round about the mansion of the overlord and a few houses reserved for clients of distinction lay scattered the village of primitive hives which sheltered the servants—the slaves. A noble Gaul, such as Ambiorix, king of the Eburones, lived in a veritable castle, one of those castles which is almost a town, like the castle-towns of the twelfth century. Uxellodunum was built on a height, and protected by a belt of ramparts which sheltered the working and fighting masses, the clients of the master.

Might it not have belonged to some lord of the manor like Coucy or Guillaume d'Orange?

What were the elements composing this feudal aristocracy? A tempting theory is to regard it as a nobility of warriors, consisting of the victorious Celts who had imposed their authority on the Ligurians and reduced them to the condition of a people deprived of its rights. This is the opinion adopted by Auguste Longnon. But we must hesitate before agreeing with him, seeing that a similar theory applied to the German conquerors of Gaul has been entirely discredited for the last forty years.

On the contrary, it is most probable that feudalism in Gaul was of Ligurian origin. The Celts, on entering the country, adapted themselves to it with all the greater readiness since they themselves had already put it into practice.

The causes which brought this system of feudalism into being, by means of clients, were the same as those which organised it among every people at a corresponding stage of their social development. It is impossible, both for material and moral reasons, for a people suddenly to develop a common organisation, a feeling of nationality, a centralised power and a general system of administration. For this centuries of struggle and effort are required, a steady, patient work of co-ordination and understanding. And, in this long process of formation feudalism is the first step, the first " stratum," to use a prehistoric term, but an inevitable and fruitful one.

This Gallic feudalism has been dubbed organised anarchy; but it was quite the contrary of this; it was essentially an organic organisation, if such an expression can be used—and one full of the most vital energy.

It is easy to imagine the little incidents that occurred under the system, those distressing little incidents of everyday life. In the absence of a national authority, a sovereign judge and administrator, wielding a power respected by all, the weak begged protection from the strong—the small enclosure against the neighbouring domain, the merchant against the brigand, the agricultural labourer against the marauder, the families of lesser importance against their more numerous rivals who were in a position to reduce them to servitude.

" The poor and weak," says Fustel de Coulanges, " sought the protection of the powerful and rich, in order to be able to live in peace and protected from violence. They rendered him obeisance in return for his protection."

The overlord had among his supporters all sorts and conditions of men—warriors, labourers, artisans, coiners who struck coins, in the later days with his own image engraved on them; around him were bards, like the troubadours and jugglers of the twelfth century, who sang his glory and the great deeds of his ancestors, the bards of the " *chansons de gestes* " who extolled his lineage. The story is well known of the Roman general who saw approaching him a Gallic chieftain surrounded by his vassals in arms and his war dogs, preceded by the bard who, to the strains of the lyre, celebrated his exploits. First of all the bard sang, hymning the illustrious birth and valour of his master, and the Romans laughed as men laugh who imagine they are clever.

Such were the divisions of society in Gaul in the third and second centuries before our era, though there are still a few elements we have not mentioned. As in France in the twelfth century there was a good deal that escaped the power of the patron—adventurers, bandits in the strictest sense of the word, isolated, fierce creatures, embittered and wretched, living a hard life of daily toil in lonely districts; there were also tramps and pedlars, braziers, tinkers and menders of agricultural implements, who went about from farm to farm and village to village; in the towns the independent elements were fairly numerous, including a proportion of the working classes.

These independent elements gradually increased in importance; to Vercingetorix' call to arms they were the first to respond, and after the fall of the young hero, Correus, King of the Bellovaci, in his turn, formed them into groups, with the result that the senate of the Bellovaci, says Hirtius, " had less authority than the ignorant populace."

Below the overlord and his clients came the subject people, and below them again was the mass of slaves, who were either men taken in war or bought in the market. The traffic in slaves between Gaul and Italy was very active from the second century B.C. onwards. It was the custom, on the death of an overlord, to burn his chief slaves, together with his favourite animals, at his funeral. The belief of the period in material survival after death is well known. Food was placed near the tomb, and slaves and domestic animals were sacrificed in order that the departed might still make use of their services. Cæsar says that this custom only died out shortly before his arrival in Gaul.

It is astonishing to find Fustel de Coulanges arriving at the following conclusion : " There was a great difference between the old institutions [the system of overlords and clients in Gaul] and those of the Middle Ages. A sort of vassalage already existed, but outside the State. This vassalage among the Gauls did not give birth to State feudalism."

It is difficult to understand the meaning of the illustrious historian. Vassalage among the Gauls played the identical part it afterwards did in the Middle Ages—without, however, supposing that the latter institution was a development of the former. It constituted a feudal State, and although in Gaul it may not have existed on the grand scale of its counterpart in the Île-de-France, this was because, as we shall see, its development was brutally arrested by a foreign Power.

On emerging from their earliest period, the Gauls entered upon the most glorious epoch of their civilisation, which, after having been imposed, in all its essential elements, upon the Romans themselves, extended over the Rhine into Germany. Under the strong protection of their feudal system, they were advancing towards a brilliant destiny, when an invasion more terrible than that of any savage tribes suddenly burst upon them—the invasion by a nation which, in spite of all its wicked cruelty, was regarded as civilised. Julius Cæsar, a man of genius, of a selfish, hard and narrow genius, enslaved Gaul at the time of her early development and the Roman Power stifled the national aspirations of a race full of youthful promise in the toils of a wretched utilitarian administration. The roads were improved, aqueducts built, great monuments in stone raised, sophists gave dissertations in the schools, rhetoricians held forth in the pretoriums, the idle rich mouthed fried sow dugs, washed down with Falernian, on tables of sardonyx, in marble halls. Poets devoid of originality fitted together their verbal mosaics in spondees and dactyls; howling mobs went mad over the bloody games in the arenas ; a detailed and wise legislation was put into force—but the early sap of a great people, about to flower into an original civilisation, was thrust back to the lowest roots; it required ten centuries—and of all the fair spectacles afforded by the history of France this is perhaps the fairest—it required a whole millennium for this sap to rise up again slowly, with difficulty and determination, into the open air, the sun, the wind and the rain which give life, and thus to unfold its blooms.

There once lived in Germany a celebrated historian, Professor Th. Mommsen, who in eight volumes of a History of Rome wrote a great deal about the Gauls. In it he said :

" To all appearance Gaul, at the time when Cæsar entered it, had reached the pinnacle of any culture of which she was capable; she was already descending the downward slope."

So far was the " culture " of the Gauls from having reached the end of its tether when the Romans arrived, that it was destined to continue its development in spite of the most serious obstacles and to fertilise the whole of modern civilisation with its genius.

The centuries of Roman rule were for Gaul a period of lethargy. She was beaten down to the ground, but the germs of life were still in her, sleeping like seeds in the fields under winter snows. And after centuries of disfigurement, the old Celtic and Ligurian stocks appeared once more. They had been exploited by Romans and Germans, but nothing could destroy either their traditions or their customs. Closely bound to the land, the Gallic nation preserved its life and habits intact, and from the day it was able to move freely it produced, with all the magnificence with which we are familiar, the incomparable history of France.

74

The country was occupied by the Ligurian race, with whom the Celts had intermingled. To the south of the Garonne there was a different stock, the Iberians, whom the Romans called the Aquitani, and who spread over into Spain. The Ligurians of northern Italy spread, through the Alpine passes, into the neighbouring cantons of Gaul.

The Last Century of Independence.

The Celtic invasions stopped in the third century B.C. On the north-east frontiers the Germans were making their power felt. They had already thrust back into Gaul the Celts who had established themselves on the right bank of the Rhine, after which they themselves crossed the river and increased their settlements in the valleys of the Somme, the Oise, the Aisne and the Moselle, mixing with the natives, and thus forming north of the Seine and the Marne that people, quite different from the Celto-Ligurians, known as the Belgæ.

The Belgæ, formed from a mixture of Ligurians, Celts and Germans, adopted the language of the latter. In a passage of great interest Strabo says that the Belgæ did not speak the same language as the Gauls, but that they were very like them, whilst the Aquitani, who lived between the Garonne and the Pyrenees, resembled in their looks and ways, not the Gauls, but the Iberians of Spain.

Thus we find, in the second century before our era, the following races in Gaul :

North of the Seine and the Marne, the Belgæ, a mixture of German immigrants, Ligurians and Celts.

In the centre, between the Seine and the Garonne, the Gauls properly so-called, being a mixture of Celts and Ligurians.

South of the Garonne, the Aquitani, an Iberian people mixed, no doubt, with Ligurians.

On the west coast, in the peninsulas of Brittany and Normandy, were a people called the Armorici, apparently a mixture of Ligurians, Celts and Belgæ, for the Breton language, which is spoken in the Armorican peninsula to-day, must have been imported from Great Britain by Britons, who, at a later date (the fifth to the seventh centuries A.D.), had sought refuge there from the Saxons.

The Phocians were established along the coast of the Mediterranean.

And, on the eastern frontier, beyond the Rhine, were the savage Germans; beyond the Alps, the Ligurians, properly so-called; and beyond the Ligurians, the Romans.

In 155 B.C. the Massaliots invoked the help of Rome against the Ligurians, who were harassing them, and Flaminius, sent to give the Ligurians a lesson, was met by a shower of stones. The consul Opimius defeated the Ligurians (154 B.C.) and took from them part of their territory which he gave to the Massaliots.

Thirty years later there was a fresh intervention on the part of the Romans on behalf of the latter, against a Celto-Ligurian tribe whom the Greeks called the Sallyes (people of Provence). The Sallyes were defeated first in 125 B.C. by the consul Flavius, and a year later by the consul Caius Sextius, who sold most of the population by auction, and on their territory founded a colony, " the waters of Sextius," *Aquæ-Sextiæ*, Aix.

The Allobroges (Dauphiny), a rough and free-spirited race, tried to drive out this colony of foreign soldiers, who were of no use to them. They were allied with the Arverni, who aspired to the hegemony of Gaul; whereupon the Aedui, in order to get the better of the Arverni, made advances to Rome.

The Aedui, like the Romans, had under the name of a republic an aristocratic form of government; whilst among the Arverni under the rule of their king, the celebrated Bituitus, the popular element predominated, the " commons," as it was called in the Middle Ages.

The Allobroges welcomed the fugitive Sallyes with all honour. As the Aedui had declared themselves in favour of Rome, Bituitus, the ally of the Allobroges, ravaged their territory. In 122 B.C. the consul Gnæus Domitius Ahenobarbus set out with a strong army, including elephants, with which he hoped to terrify the Gauls, who had never seen any before. The meeting between the ambassador of Bituitus and Ahenobarbus has become famous. The Arvernian arrived accompanied by his bards, his war dogs and his ensigns with the device of the boar. The bard began by singing to the accompaniment of the lyre the glory of Bituitus and his messenger, which the Romans thought extremely funny. Bituitus sent them offerings to conciliate them, but Ahenobarbus would not listen, and a battle took place at the confluence of the Isère and the Rhone.

The tactics of the Romans, the superiority of their equipment and their huge elephants won them the victory (121 B.C.). According to Latin historians 120,000 Gauls perished as compared with 15 (*sic*) Romans.

After his defeat Bituitus begged an audience of the conqueror. But when once the Roman had his adversary in his grasp he preferred to keep him. The noble chief of the Arverni was dragged to Rome and displayed like a fatted ox in the triumphal procession. The Roman populace shouted enthusiastically at the sight of the Gallic prince in his shining armour. But were they ever told to what blackguardism they owed this fine spectacle? Probably not; and if they had been told, they would no doubt have thought it all the funnier.

In order to make sure that the efforts of Bituitus would not be repeated, the Roman Senate had his son, Congentiatus, delivered up to them by the aristocracy of the Arverni, and felt they were thenceforward safe in that quarter.

The fall of Bituitus ended the monarchic system among the Arverni, and, out of sympathy, in all the other states of Gaul in which it had revived. The heads of clans, representing the aristocracy and what the Romans called the cause of liberty, everywhere obtained the upper hand—a sorry change for the friends of independence.

After despoiling the Sallyes of their territory (123 B.C.) the consul Sextius laid hands on that of the Vocontii, and the cantons to the east and south of the Cevennes were obliged to submit to the yoke of the Roman wolf. Not only the Sallyes, but also the Volcæ and the Allobroges found themselves obliged to exchange the alliance with the Arverni for the rule of Rome. The octopus was spreading its tentacles. West of the Alps, the Romans organised the territory they had conquered, and called it " the Province," *Provincia*, the Provence of to-day, otherwise known as Transalpine Gaul, and soon, on account of the town of Narbonne which became its capital, designated the Narbonnaise district.

From this time forward the three provinces of Gaul are found mentioned in Latin literature—*Gallia braccata*, that is to say the part of Gaul in which the people wore breeches or trousers—Provence; *Gallia comata*, where they wore their hair long, that is to say the whole of Gaul beyond Provence, and, lastly, *Gallia togata*, where the Roman toga was worn, otherwise known as Cisalpine Gaul, on the Italian side of the Alps, in touch with Rome, and subjected and organised by her much earlier.

And now that part of Gaul from the Cevennes to the Alps, from the town of Vienne to the delta of the Rhone, was admitted to the benefits of Roman administration. The Roman senate, and the host of meddlers and merchants, business agents, hangers-on and tax-farmers, publicans, land developers and slave merchants, who clung round their white togas, got full measure without delay. There was the farming of taxes, public works, transport facilities, tributes, customs and dues, the salt monopoly, etc.—a cloud of flies buzzing round the beautiful golden honey.

To the exploitation of the public coffers the gold-ringed knights, speculators and money-lenders added that of private property, mines and quarries, forests and pastures. The unfortunate Transalpines, impoverished by the conquest and despoiled of part of their possessions, were now subjected to every kind of levy and taxation. They were forced to pay; in order to pay they had to borrow, to pawn what remained of their patrimony, to produce the interest, to repay the capital, and as, when the time came, they had no more than on the day they started borrowing, it ended in complete expropriation under the menace of the severe legislation passed against insolvent debtors, which was particularly cruel in the case of a conquered race who seemed to exist only in order to be exploited.

It is true, appeal could be made to the Governor of the province, but the latter was in the hands of the financial magnates of Rome; or complaint could be lodged at Rome, with the Senate—with what result, it is easy to guess.

The Roman Governor was all-powerful in his province where his word was law. Taxes and statute labour, payment in kind and requisitions were all levied at his pleasure. He it was who decided what contributions should be demanded from the vanquished. As supreme judge, he passed capital sentences, and his decisions were final. It is easy to imagine the whims of such a despot in connection with a conquered race, whom he regarded as inferiors, sheep to be fleeced. The case of Fonteius, pleaded by Cicero, gives us some idea of it.

78

This noble personage was Governor of Gaul from 79 to 76 B.C. In 69 B.C. he was accused of peculation by the Gauls, whom he had indeed exploited a little bit too flagrantly. What with levies on the upkeep of roads, casks of wine in return for contracts for public works and the auditing of accounts, taxes and arbitrary impositions, the whole gamut of accusations against him can easily be imagined.

Cicero, who had prosecuted Verres, pleaded in defence of Fonteius. What a wonderful counsel! In the first place, who were these witnesses who came to give evidence against him, demanded the advocate? Allobroges, barbarians! They might be seen walking in the Forum in their breeches and cloaks. And, what was even worse, they seemed to be confident of their cause. These witnesses spoke with assurance. But, for that matter, what confidence could be inspired by people who made sacrifices of blood to their gods? [It is true that the Druids were guilty of a great wrong in sacrificing human beings on their altars, but that had nothing to do with the extortions of Fonteius.] My client, added Cicero, is a valiant soldier. The town of Marseilles [which had nothing to do with the matter] and the colony of Narbonne [consisting of Romans] gave evidence in his favour. Lastly, pleaded Cicero in conclusion, could one tear Fonteius from the arms of a loving mother, and from the affections of his sister, Fonteia, who was a Vestal Virgin? They would both weep at the very thought, and Fonteius too would weep. . . .

From all this the innocence of Fonteius was clearly established.

Moreover, we must not forget the passage of the Roman armies, who maintained that in pillaging these people clad in cloaks and breeches they were conferring a great honour upon them; nor the billeting of troops, the requisitions, the arbitrary imposition of fines, the exploitation of confiscated territory—in short, the whole system of usury.

Prohibited in Rome, in the provinces usury was tolerated; moreover, the gold-ringed knights knew of no better transaction than to borrow in Rome in order to lend to Transalpine Gaul. In the worst years this yielded thirty per cent. And if the debtor did not pay up, there remained the fine alternative of selling him into slavery. In addition to this, since it was necessary to secure a market for Italian wine and oil, Rome forbad Transalpine Gaul to cultivate what best suited her soil and climate—the vine and the olive.

Indeed Transalpine Gaul paid a somewhat heavy price for the honour of being admitted into the civilisation of Rome.

Gaul was divided into peoples, or city States, as the Romans called them, which did not agree together, were jealous and quarrelsome, and plundered one another. We have seen that the only common bond between them was the organisation of the Druids with their general councils; but the power of the Druids had gradually declined with the development of feudalism. These divisions resulted in regular wars, with offensive and defensive alliances, strategic campaigns, the capture of strongholds, pillage, murder and robbery, which left bitter hatred in their train. It was rare, said Cæsar, for a year to pass by without a city taking up arms in order to attack a neighbouring city or to resist an attack.

These divisions between the States prevented any national understanding in face of foreign aggression; and this has been brought up against the Gauls. Why did they not form a national federation? They would then have been able to resist the Roman invasion and the incursions of the Germans.

The Gauls would have been able to resist these invasions just as well had they possessed grenades and machine guns. Moral and social discoveries have not been less difficult to make than scientific inventions, and their diffusion has been no less arduous. The growth of modern political ideas has of necessity been slow and gradual, and has been achieved only after many a struggle and effort, and much suffering. Camille Jullian has pointed out that the idea of national unity never occurred to any race of antiquity. Even in France, how many wars, bloody battles and terrible conflicts took place before the south allowed itself to be assimilated by the north. Even on the eve of the Renaissance, Burgundy, as we know, was in alliance with England against the King of France.

In addition to this France was, in reality, practically eighty or a hundred times larger than she is to-day. The extent of a country must be measured by the time taken to establish communications. A distance of forty miles is a short one for a motor car going a hundred miles an hour, it is a very long way for the pedestrian who would require a whole day's march to cover it and in the end would arrive tired out. In those days there were no railways, motor cars, telegraphs, telephones or newspapers to spread ideas, writing was known only to a very small minority, whilst the difficulty of communication and the great distances were increased by huge forests, which very often had to be skirted, by marshes, and by the rarity of bridges over the rivers. The Romans became menacing on the Alpine frontier; but under such conditions how could men's minds be awakened to sentiments of a common nationality of which they had no conception, how could they be aroused to a general call to arms, when the Veneti were in Armorica, the Morini along the northern seaboard, the Treveri beyond the Ardennes and the Carnutes in the district of Chartres?

The union of the various peoples of Gaul could only have been achieved as it was in Italy by the dominion of one of them over the rest.

Outside the feudal families—the patrician families as the Romans would have called them—there was a fairly numerous crowd of people who were not connected with any clan, the populace of the rural districts, artisans, adventurers, and independent individuals—" the commons," in short. Men of wealth and energy, who had at their disposal those two great levers birth and riches, after having formed the " commons " into groups for their support, succeeded in establishing what the Greeks called tyranny. As " tyrants " they ruled the State. We have already seen how Bituitus was seized by the Romans and how they compelled the surrender of his son. Fifty years later Celtillus, among these same Arverni, again made the attempt, and for a time re-established the supremacy of his people over the neighbouring tribes. The lasting success of his enterprise might have brought about the unification of Gaul, and, through this unification, her independence. But Celtillus was overthrown by a rival faction, by the heads of the patrician families who combined together in horror of tyranny. He perished at the stake; but in the traces of his father's footsteps was to march one of the greatest of men—his son Vercingetorix.

The divisions which separated the Gauls occurred, not only

between the various peoples, but also between the different factions in the bosom of a single State. The noble families were, like the Montagues and the Capulets, in a constant state of rivalry and conflict. The head of a clan, in his desire to rule the State, would turn to the populace, the " commons," the mass of rural workers and artisans, who enjoyed the protection of no patron, the malcontents, in fact, and thus roused against him the families organised under the feudal system. A similar conflict occurred again and again in similar circumstances. And thus we find the patricians, when their immemorial power was threatened, soliciting alliance with Rome in order to secure the defeat of a rival, actually becoming her allies, and endeavouring to maintain their existence with the help of the very people who had invaded their territory.

On the foot of the statue raised to Vercingetorix on the heights of Alise-Sainte-Reine, these words of Cæsar have been engraved : " United, Gaul would have defied the world."

This union, alas ! at the time when Cæsar appeared, was impossible.

As it was, the union of Gaul in the war against the Romans was more complete than the circumstances might have led one to expect. Strabo makes an unexpected but nevertheless an apparently very true remark when he says that the Gauls were quickly subjected because they resisted the Romans in great masses. " The slightest check meant a general defeat." The result of a single campaign, or even of a battle, decided their fate. If the struggle had been broken up and spread over many localities and divided into various episodes, as it was in Spain, where the Iberians " cut up their wars into small and scattered battles, after the fashion of brigands," says Strabo, into guerilla warfare, in which the Romans spent two hundred years before establishing their rule, the Gallic war might have lasted for ever and might even have ended in a very different way.

One last subject to be discussed is that of the population of Gaul on the eve of the Roman conquest. It is generally estimated at five or six million inhabitants ; but some historians have placed the figure at ten millions, and others as high as twenty or thirty millions. The most densely populated districts were valleys fertilised by rivers, such as the Seine and the Oise, the Saône and the Loire. It would be as well perhaps not to rely too implicitly on the description given by Cæsar. His wonderful *Commentaries*, written in the simplest possible language, in order to be accessible to all, were destined for political propaganda.

It was to the interest of Cæsar to exaggerate the numbers of his vanquished foes.

We must bear in mind the huge spaces that were covered with woods or marshes; more than half of northern Gaul was waste land. Flanders was one vast forest, in which the only clear spaces were quagmires, and wild beasts were the sole inhabitants—"the pitiless forest," as it was still called by the chroniclers of the Middle Ages. It is true that a number of these forests were inhabited. An import trade existed, but it could only contribute in a very small degree to the subsistence of the people. The territory of Gaul, which to-day supports a population of forty-seven or forty-eight million people, could, it would seem, hardly have contained more than twelve or fifteen millions at the time Julius Cæsar was making ready to subjugate it, a figure which is very near to that suggested by Camille Jullian.

BIBLIOGRAPHY.—Cæsar, *Commentaries*. Cicero, *Pro Fonteio*. The Works of Strabo, Ammianus Marcellinus, Diodorus Siculus, Vitruvius, Pliny, Plutarch, in various editions. The Emperor Julian, *Complete Works. Letters*, edited by J. Bidez, 1924. Alf. Maury, *Les Forêts de la Gaule*, 1857. Fustel de Coulanges, *Hist. des institutions politiques de l'ancienne France*, 1875. Bulliot et H. de Fontenay, *L'Art de l'émaillerie chez les Éduens*, 1875. D'Arbois de Jubainville, *Introduction à l'étude de la littérature celtique*, 1883. D'Arbois de Jubainville, *La Civilisation des Celtes et celle de l'époque homérique*, 1899. D'Arbois de Jubainville, *Les Celtes depuis les temps les plus anciens*, 1904. Meitzen, *Siedelung und Agrarwesen der Westgermanen und Ostgermanen, der Kelten* . . . 1895. Bertrand, *La Religion des Gaulois*, 1897. Jacq. Flach, *L'Origine historique de l'habitation et des lieux habités en France*, 1899. G. Bloch, *Les Origines, la Gaule indépendante* . . . from *Hist. de France*, edited by Lavisse, 1901. J. Dechelette, *Recherches sur la religion gauloise*, 1904. Blanchet, *Traité des monnaies gauloises*, 1905. G. Dottin, *Manuel* . . . *de l'Antiquité celtique*, 1906. Cam. Jullian, *Hist. de la Gaule, II, la Gaule indépendante*, 1908. [Maxime Petit], *Histoire de France illustrée* [1909]. Aug. Longnon, *Origine et formation de la nationalité française* [1912]. Loisy, *Essai hist. sur les sacrifices*, 1920. Jean Brunhes, *Géographie humaine de la France*, from *Hist. de la nation française*, edited by Gabr. Hanotaux [1920]. Imbart de la Tour, *Histoire politique des origines à 1515, ibid.* [1921].

CHAPTER III

ROMAN GAUL

Cæsar's conquest. The pretexts given—the invasion of Gaul by the Germans of Ariovistus and by the Helvetii. First victories of Cæsar (58 B.C.). The divisions of Gaul—the patriciate and the popular party. The first period of the Gallic Wars (58–55 B.C.). The Gauls not yet aware that their independence is at stake. Second period (54–53 B.C.). Vercingetorix. Defeat of Cæsar before Gergovia. Alise-Sainte-Reine. Conquered Gaul. The task of the conquerors. Gaul subjected to Roman civilisation. The administrative work of the Romans. Reasons of the romanisation of Gaul. Latin Gaul (second century B.C.). The Gallo-Roman towns. Paris under the Roman Emperors. The culture of Latin literature—Ausonius. Organisation of the land—the large estate, the villa. Spread of Christianity—its beginnings in Gaul, its development. Persecution. The martyrs of Lyons, Sainte Blandine. Saint Denis and the Martyrs' Mount. The basilicas. The German menace on the Rhine. Invasion of the Cimbri and the Teutons (second century B.C.). Defence of Gaul organised by the Emperors. First appearance of the Alemanni and the Franks. The terrible avalanche of the years 275–276. The Germanic peoples protected and entrusted with the defence of the Empire. Germans established in Gaul by the Romans. Gaul in the fourth century. Saint Martin. Arianism. Its spread. Its importance. The great estates of the fourth century. The colonies.

A BOUT the year 62 B.C. the pressure of the Germans on the Rhine became more and more menacing.

The most important of their nations, the Suevi, occupied Suabia and Franconia. They rendered obeisance to a certain Ariovistus, a sort of barbarian genius, who lived always **Cæsar.** under canvas, was greedy for battle, and was carving out a great Empire for himself by the sword. Ariovistus hastened to respond to the appeal of the Sequani, who were established in the present district of Franche-
84

Comté, and were impatient of the yoke of the Aedui, the most powerful nation in Gaul since the fall of the Arvernian hegemony.

Ariovistus marched to the help of the Sequani with about 15,000 men, most of them mounted. The Aedui were beaten. They abandoned their territory on the banks of the Saône, which was seized by the Sequani, gave hostages and surrendered to their rivals most of the peoples who had been their clients.

Thanks to a handful of German knights, the hegemony of Gaul had passed into the hands of the Sequani (Besançon).

But Ariovistus aimed at deriving some advantage from his victory. He began by laying claim to Upper Alsace and added it to his empire, which now extended from the Vosges to the Oder. To his summons the most divers peoples from across the Rhine hastened to respond—Harudes, Marcomanni, Triboc and Vangiones. It has been maintained, mistakenly no doubt, that the Teutonic idiom spoken in Alsace to-day dates from this period.

Amongst his allies Ariovistus played the part of a potentate, levying contributions, taking hostages, and dividing among his own followers land confiscated from its owners. The Sequani rebelled; they took up arms, summoned their clients, and a battle took place; they were beaten.

Many years previously the Aedui had concluded a pact of amity with the Romans. Ariovistus and the Sequani had forced them to take an oath not to have recourse to this alliance; but one of their chiefs, a Druid named Diviciacus, a rich man, of influential family, had refused to take it. He went to Rome, where he continued his intrigues. He showed himself everywhere, anointing Cicero with the unction of his flattery, and hanging on to the white togas of the senators in order to pour into their ears the woes of his fellow citizens.

On their side, a party of the Helvetii, a Gallic nation of Switzerland, in view of the menace from Germany, made up their minds at the instigation of one of their chiefs, a certain Orgetorix, to leave their country, and, following the traditional route of the emigrations, to enter Gaul, and march towards the Atlantic, in order to seize lands. They crossed the Jura, went through the land of the Sequani and arrived among the Aedui, pillaging all the way. The Aedui redoubled their complaints to Rome and the Allobroges joined them.

A young man, belonging to a patrician family so illustrious that it claimed it had sprung from the loins, if not of Jupiter, at least of Venus, a young man who until that time was hardly known in Rome except for a life of gallantry, extravagant elegance, tasteful luxury and wild prodigality, the young Julius Cæsar, was at that time, as a red-cloaked proconsul, Governor, not only of Illyria, but also of both Gauls, Cisalpine and Transalpine. He was immensely clever, probably the cleverest man that has ever lived, and equally ambitious, vaguely aspiring to the highest destiny. Cæsar saw in the conflict that would be the result of the double invasion of Gaul by the Suevi and the Helvetii the opportunity for a success which would at once raise him head and shoulders above his rivals, mediocre politicians who were tiring Rome by their squabbles and intrigues. The enterprise which Cæsar had planned would secure for him, not only the fabulous halo of some far distant triumph, but also a devoted army and immense resources in money and goods of all kinds.

The Senate hesitated. Cæsar succeeded in convincing it. He assembled the troops placed at his disposal as proconsul in both provinces and set forth in order, as he said, to intervene in favour of the Aedui, the allies of Rome, and protect the Gauls against the Germans. The beginning of the Gallic Wars has been fixed as the 28th of March, 58 B.C.

The Helvetii, to the number of about 400,000, including women and children, had invaded the country of the Aedui, when Cæsar, crossing with his army over the Saint-Bernard pass, engaged in their pursuit, overtook them at Montmort, near Bibracte and not far from Mount Beuvray, and inflicted upon them a total defeat, forcing those who survived to return to their own country.

After this it was necessary for Cæsar to turn against the Suevi, who, under the leadership of Ariovistus, were descending the valley of the Saône, and threatening the Roman province of Cisalpine Gaul. Here, once more, the victory of Cæsar was complete. Ariovistus and his Suevi fled to the Rhine, which the Romans reached at the same time. In the neighbourhood
86

of Bâle a terrible massacre took place—soldiers, women, children and old men, Cæsar had them all put to the sword. Numbers of Germans were drowned in trying to cross the river. The Teutonic peoples who were waiting on the right bank for an opportunity of crossing in their turn retreated in disorder and were massacred in small parties at a time by the inhabitants of the districts they traversed. Soon afterwards Ariovistus died of wounds. These events took place in the year 58 B.C.

The Gallic War had been inaugurated, and Cæsar made up his mind not to end it until it had provided his ambition with the pedestal it required. " I waged this war," he said, " as much in the interests of Gaul as of Rome." And, indeed, the Gauls did not at first recognise the Romans as enemies, but regarded them rather as allies against the invaders. And even when they did understand that the campaign undertaken by the red-cloaked proconsul would turn to anything but their advantage and that, under pretext of doing them a service, the Romans were only aiming at extending their own Empire, in the majority of the aristocratic cities the rich still declared themselves in favour of Cæsar. Government by an aristocracy represented public liberty in the eyes of the Roman senators, and thus Cæsar, in conquering the Gauls, could pose at Rome as the defender of liberty. The cause of independence in Gaul remained in the hands of the masses, the populace, the " commons," who followed the voice of any capable man who, moved by the noblest motives or, on the contrary, like Cæsar, following the path of personal ambition, was willing to lead them against the conquerors.

Thus the proud patrician Julius Cæsar treated with disdain the disorderly hordes whom he had to fight—wanderers, outlaws, vagabonds, adventurers, brigands and thieves, as he often called them, adding that these wanderers, adventurers, brigands and thieves had left the cultivation of their fields and their daily toil in order to defend their country, which made them adventurers and brigands of a peculiar type.

The wicked cruelty with which Cæsar stained his glory is in part explained by his fury roused at the resistance offered by this rabble and the checks it inflicted on him.

Thus some peoples, among whom the rule of the aristocracy

was undisputed, like the Remi (Rheims) and the Lingones (Langres), remained obstinately attached to Cæsar. Others had a wavering policy, now in favour of alliance with Rome, now on the side of national resistance, according as to whether the patriciate or the " commons " were more powerful in the city. The Aedui occupied a place apart, inasmuch as they succeeded in protecting their own prosperity and power from the storm. They may be compared to the Burgundians in the Middle Ages whose territory they occupied. In the first century B.C. they followed a policy similar to that which was so successful in the case of the subjects of Philip the Bold and Philip the Good during the struggles of the Hundred Years' War.

Thus Gaul was very far from offering united resistance to Rome.

We must bear in mind also the great difference between the Gauls and the Romans in the field of tactics, in military organisation and armament.

For two hundred years the Gauls had scarcely altered their method of fighting, which they still carried on like the primitive warriors of the time of Ambigatus and Sigovesus. To march straight at the enemy without any precaution, without sending scouts ahead or protecting their flanks, without dissimulating their forces, or finding out the strong and weak points of their adversary—such was still their entire tactical method.

They went out to war in large crowds, accompanied by their women and children, and carrying an incredible collection of personal property, plate and utensils of all kinds on interminable files of wagons : and, in spite of all this *impedimenta* they never succeeded in having enough provisions for a campaign of any duration. How often was not the success of one of their armies ruined from lack of victuals ! Peoples and tribes on the march remained in their separate groups, divided from each other by long intervals. How could military operations be carried out in such conditions ?

The generalissimo, elected at the beginning of the march in a tumultuous assembly, remained virtually dependent on those who had appointed him. Ambiorix told the Romans " the mob has as much power over me as I have over them."

A chieftain, such as Vercingetorix, even if he had thought out

88

a better conceived and wiser plan of campaign, adapted to the means and resources of the enemy, would have had the greatest difficulty in preventing his soldiers from rushing upon their foes blindly, and hurling themselves in serried ranks into the attack, running forward so as to arrive breathless and exhausted to grips with the enemy without precaution of any kind, like a swarm of ants hurling themselves against a wall.

The Gauls never thought of surrounding their encampments with trenches and ramparts. A huge entanglement of carts, chariots, wagons and *impedimenta* of all descriptions was piled up at the back of the camp—their sole protection for a last desperate stand should the army flinch. All they knew of military works was reduced to these clumsy infantile devices.

As regards armament they had made no progress whatsoever; they were still armed with the long, heavy and massive sword which had only a cutting edge. They also had lances and pikes. A few used bows and slings. They had no breastplates. The Gaul believed he was in honour bound to present his bare breast to the foe. He was armed, it is true, with a shield, which he took the precaution to fasten to his left arm by means of straps. This shield was very large, the height of a man, but it was made of wood or of wickerwork which the Roman javelins pierced at the first attempt. Bristling with javelins, like a pincushion full of pins, the shield remained fastened to the left arm of the warrior, who was obliged to unstrap it and remain without protection of any kind. The Gauls very often ranged themselves for battle in serried ranks one behind the other, those at the back raising their shields above their heads so as to form a huge tortoise, the scales of which consisted of the overlapping shields. Cæsar describes how his soldiers, with one thrust of the javelin, would pierce several of these shields, and as the iron bent, they would remain nailed together.

The helmet was worn only by chiefs. To the hero who carried this ornamental headdress it imparted an aspect of refulgent splendour, with its crest in the form of some fantastic bird, or the head of an antediluvian beast with a huge trunk and fearsome horns, or more simply adopting geometric shapes with effulgent superstructures, or else displaying the bolts of Taran, the god of thunder and lightning. But beneath this impressive adornment the face remained uncovered and one thrust of the javelin would demolish the whole concern.

At first, it is true, the Gallic army filled the enemy with terror, with its packs of howling dogs, the braying of the brazen trumpets, and the wild and frantic cries and hoarse shouts of the whole army—a regular din of hell enough to drown the voice of the thunder. But the legions soon grew accustomed to this method of intimidation.

The armies of Cæsar, however, were well disciplined. They were never very large, but they consisted of the best soldiers in the world. In the Gallic wars Cæsar never employed more than eleven legions, each of which consisted, on an average, of 5,000 men.

Whilst the Gauls had no knowledge of machines of war, Cæsar possessed a formidable equipment. The Romans not only had javelins, but also *balistas*, which shot shafts weighing almost two hundredweight a distance of 160 yards; for siege purposes they had *onagers*, consisting chiefly of a strong beam which a spring suddenly released turned into a powerful projector; they had catapults, and large iron hooks to undermine the ramparts. In siege assaults they were protected by tortoises, or mantelets (*musculi*) on wheels, machines made of wood and wattles covered with earth and skins.

To the Gaul, who met him with bared breast, the Roman soldier appeared clad in iron and leather. In the fight he had only to think of attack, his accoutrements provided the defence. The Roman sword, easy to manipulate, was a very superior weapon to the heavy and cumbersome Gallic blade.

While the Gallic army encamped carelessly, wherever it halted, without even troubling to choose a spot protected by nature, a height, shelter afforded by the waters of a river, or by marshes, every Roman camp was safeguarded like a town by a triple line of defence, a ditch, a rampart and a palisade. The four gates were guarded by sentinels. The Gauls never succeeded in capturing a Roman camp.

Thus Camille Jullian might well say that Cæsar possessed in his legions " the most solid body of infantry that any nation has ever produced." Their power was increased by the resources placed at the disposal of the proconsul by the various peoples
90

that Rome had subjected to her Empire, and whose warlike gifts he knew how to use in accordance with their respective military habits and traditions—there were Balearic slingers, Cretan archers, Numidian horsemen, not to mention Celtic knights, who were at that time considered the best in the world and whom Cæsar recruited, not only from Cisalpine and Transalpine Gaul, but only too often from the ranks of the long-haired Gauls themselves, and particularly from the Aedui.

In addition to all these advantages the Romans were under the command of a leader who was doubtless the greatest soldier in history, not endowed, perhaps, with the genial impetuosity of a Hannibal, or the magnificent grasp of generalities and prodigious yet precise judgment of a Napoleon, but, with his varied gifts, possessing everything required for a leader in war—clarity of thought, rapidity of decision, precision of execution, an astonishing power of calculating the means to an end and a wonderful talent for organisation which left nothing to chance, an astonishing lack of scruple, the cunning to pose always as the defender of virtue and right, the art of making all means appear just that attained his end ; and finally the gift of inspiring the love and enthusiasm of his men.

Cæsar demanded the roughest and sometimes the most repulsive duties of them, harassing marches, the most stubborn and dangerous engagements; but his men always found him in their midst in any trouble or danger. He exposed himself to the blows of the enemy like the meanest of his followers, after which he would heap honours and rewards upon his legionaries as much as on himself. His officers, whom he chose with discernment, knew that fighting under his command meant coffers full of sesterces. Cæsar crammed and stuffed them with gold pillaged from the towns and sanctuaries; the most insignificant soldier knew that after a victory he would be given at least a slave as his share of the booty.

Moreover, he had spies, secret agents, whom he knew how to maintain among the enemy and chosen from their own ranks. Duratius among the Pictones, Vertisco among the Nervii, Cingetorix among the Treveri, and many another helped Cæsar to gain the information he required, or propagated among their fellow-countrymen the true or false reports and news which the Romans desired to have spread.

Cæsar in his *Commentaries* gives us to understand that it was well-nigh impossible for the cause of independence to triumph.

After the defeat of Ariovistus, the Aedui imagined they were masters of Gaul, as the Sequani had been before them. But Cæsar was on the watch. He did not divulge his plans, and more than one Gaul allowed himself to be deceived by his assurances. The Aedui and the Remi regarded him as an ally, an ally who began by making sure of the support of the patricians among the Aedui and even of the vergobret himself, as well as of the chiefs of the Sequani. He even did the cavalry of the Aedui the honour of incorporating them with his own legions, and few indeed among the Gauls suspected the hidden designs of the proconsul.

Cæsar decided to begin the conquest of Gaul in the territory of the Belgæ, who, with the Arverni, were everywhere renowned for their martial prowess. Cæsar and Strabo both agree that Belgic Gaul reached as far as the Marne, and point out that of all the Belgæ, the most courageous were the Bellovaci (Beauvais) and the Suessiones (Soissons). When once the Belgæ were subjected, caught between their own territory and Transalpine Gaul, Gaul proper would be at his mercy. The Belgæ seem to have realised the danger. The sacred spirit of independence seems to have breathed within them. Nevertheless one of their peoples, the Remi (Rheims), remained faithful to the alliance made with Rome.

The campaign was a hard one, conducted by Titus Labienus, Cæsar's best lieutenant. It ended, under the command of Cæsar himself, in the bloody defeat of the Nervii (Hainault) on the banks of the Sambre. The victory was so hotly disputed that at one moment Cæsar found himself obliged to fight in the front rank like a common soldier. After this he seized the *oppidum* (a place of refuge and a fortified centre of supplies) of the Aduatuci, in the valley of the Meuse, and 52,000 Aduatuci were sold by auction, standing with a wooden yoke on their necks and their hands bound behind their backs. Let it not be forgotten that in this war the Romans represented civilisation and the Gauls barbarism. Cæsar crowned his victory by pushing a salient across the Rhine, in order that the Germans might catch a glimpse of the Roman eagles.

The Gallic Wars have been divided into three periods—the first, from 58 to 55 B.C., consisted, on the part of the Gauls, of unorganised efforts, that is to say, devoid of any common plan, some rushing to arms whilst others gave way. The Gauls did not understand, it was as yet impossible for them to understand, that their independence was at stake. Unfortunately, this period was turned to terrible account by the conquerors. The second period, including the years 54 and 53 B.C., was characterised by increasingly important movements in favour of independence and by attempts to realise it on the part of an ever larger number of united peoples. The repeated crimes of the Romans had ended in awaking the national sentiment.

The campaign of the year 56 B.C. consisted of the war in Armorica and Aquitainia. The peoples of the west had risen up under the active and energetic leadership of the Veneti (Vannes). The Veneti were masters of the sea. We have already described their trade with England, and their great ships driven before the wind by means of leather sails.

Cæsar and his lieutenant Brutus accomplished an astounding feat in improvising a fleet to fight the Veneti on their own element. Cæsar sent for oarsmen from Provence, and found auxiliaries among the Aquitanian Celts of Saintonge and La Vendée, whom an ancient feud made the envious rivals of the Veneti. Brutus invented great hooked knives modelled on the mural hooks, with which the Romans undermined the base of the ramparts they were besieging. By means of these hooks, he succeeded in cutting the ropes which fastened the sails to the masts of the enemy's ships, and made them fall flat on deck. The heavy vessels, with their high prows, found they could not move, whilst the oarsmen from Provence could manœuvre the Roman boats at will. Cæsar's triumph was complete. There was a great massacre, and the survivors were taken prisoner. The Veneti had fought a noble fight for the greatest of causes. They never submitted to Rome, but Cæsar called their attempt to safeguard the freedom of their country " rebellion," and,

93

as everyone knows, rebels must be punished. All the senators of the country had their throats cut, and the rest of the population were put up for sale like cattle. " The strong and industrious nation of the Veneti," says Camille Jullian in conclusion, " whose race and power reached back to the time of the dolmens, the oldest and most original people in all Gaul, perished in slavery and death," and the life characteristic of Armorica was extinguished until the Middle Ages. It must not be forgotten that in this war the Romans represented civilisation and the Gauls barbarism.

Whilst Brutus covered himself with glory against the Veneti, the young Crassus was distinguishing himself against the Aquitani. Crassus was one of Cæsar's best lieutenants, the cleverest and most determined after Labienus. The Aquitani showed more forethought in their military operations than the Gauls. They sent to Spain for soldiers who had trained in the school of Sertorius, able men who knew how to construct a camp and realised the importance of a well-chosen position. Nevertheless the Roman legions carried the day.

But these great deeds were surpassed by Cæsar himself in his expedition against the peoples of the Rhine (fourth campaign, 55 B.C.). The proconsul marched against the Usipetes and the Tencteri, whom he found collected together in a great mass, including women and children in large numbers. The chiefs of the nation addressed him in moving terms. Cæsar replied by summoning them and the leaders of the people to his camp. The Usipetes and Tencteri, thus invited, went to the appointed place. "I was delighted by the opportunity," writes Cæsar. He had not forgotten the glorious tradition bequeathed him by Ahenobarbus, who seized Bituitus when he had entered his tent in full confidence. Cæsar made his soldiers surround the chiefs and nobles of the Usipetes and Tencteri who had entrusted themselves to him, and deaf to their prayers and entreaties, had them bound hand and foot, whilst the bulk of his army attacked the mass of their fellow-countrymen deprived of their leaders and for the most part disarmed. A few were able to make some show of defence behind the barricade formed by their chariots. Women and children were put to the sword. Those who took flight found themselves caught in the angle formed by the junc-

94

tion of the Meuse and the Rhine, where the Roman cavalry, sent in pursuit, put them to death at their ease. Cæsar had won the most glorious of his victories. He writes about it with pride : " The Romans, delivered from a terrible war, in which they were opposed by 430,000 of the enemy—[really!]—returned to their camp without loss."

In Rome this event caused a great stir. Plutarch says that in the Senate Cato Uticensis made a vehement speech, denouncing the infamous deed and proposing that Cæsar should be delivered up to the enemy in order to appease the gods. But the senators laughed in his face and decreed feasts and sacrifices in honour of this fresh triumph so worthy of the annals of Rome.

Cæsar wanted to complete his attack on the Germans by invading Great Britain, the hearth of the religion of the Druids, the fires of which animated the spirit of Gaul. He made his pretext the help the Armoricans had received from the Britains. The expedition required two campaigns. The first landing was only marked by an ephemeral victory. Was it a victory at all? The British chariots, the tanks of the period, which advanced to the accompaniment of a shower of missiles, spread havoc among the legionaries, who were put to flight by these machines which they had never encountered before. It was necessary to return with all speed to the boats.

But Cæsar renewed the attack. He took ship as far north as Boulogne, drove back the Britons, under the command of Cassivellaunus, beyond the region of London; but his heart was not in the game in this country where there was nothing to pillage. Plutarch is careful to point this out.

Cæsar derived no great profit from it, he says, " for he could not take or win anything of value from poor and necessitous men, so that the war had not the result for which Cæsar had hoped." Thus he set sail once more for Gaul, after extracting from the Britons " a scrap of paper," their solemn act of submission and fidelity sworn on oath.

The Romans had expected marvellous results from this expedition to Great Britain. The isle of tin and fine war dogs shone in their imagination like a seductive mirage; pearls were to be found there as large as the fist. The French under the

Regency had similar dreams about the Mississippi. The conquerors set forth not only in ships of war carrying arms, balistas, onagers and stones, but also in trading vessels which they were doubtless to bring back filled with the most marvellous treasures. The lieutenants, the stewards, the inspectors and the minions of Cæsar, anxious to dazzle Rome by their luxury, and to enlarge and embellish their villas in the Campagna, had surrounded themselves with merchants of every description, in anticipation of the pearls, the metals, the slaves, the great hunting dogs and other even more precious and magnificent treasures of which they had but a vague idea.

This was the period when Rome amassed untold treasures. Her armies were covering themselves with glory in the East as well as in Gaul. It was a time of unbridled luxury for which Cæsar set the example; precious furniture, statues by the greatest artists, celebrated pictures, brilliant mosaics, strange and rare ornaments, gold and silver plate, Cæsar bought everything from every quarter. Suetonius says that in Gaul Cæsar " more often destroyed towns for the sake of pillage (*ob praedam*) than as punishment for some crime." He filled the temples of Rome with votive offerings stolen from the sanctuaries of the Gauls in order to magnify himself in the eyes of the Romans; in Italy and the provinces he sold gold by weight, at the rate of 300 sesterces to the pound. At his own expense, that is to say at the expense of the Gauls, he undertook the construction in Rome of a new forum, in which he hoped to see his own fortunes flourish, and the cost of which was estimated at 60 million sesterces. He lent money to anybody—the agents and servile heralds of his glory. "He subjugated the Gauls by the Roman armies," says Plutarch, " and the Romans by Gallic gold." He lent money to Cicero, the prating orator; he took Cicero's brother Quintus with him as his legate on the expedition to pillage Great Britain. Whereupon Cicero, who for the time being was very much concerned with the spoils that might be won in those islands, set to work with unparalleled conviction to sing the glory of the conqueror of Gaul and of Great Britain, and as his prose, flowing though it was, seemed to him inadequate, he added verse. Catullus too wrote verses, also about Cæsar, and they were better than Cicero's :

" Debauchee, spendthrift and robber ! who lettest thy favourite devour the treasures of the long-haired Gauls and far away Britain ! Cæsar ! the vilest of the Romans ! Debauchee, spendthrift and robber ! Thy favourites strut about and wallow in wealth. Cæsar, the greatest debauchee of Rome ! Thou free liver, spendthrift and robber ! Oh general most rare ! thou didst go to the most distant isles of the·west, with thine infamous minions, only to devour hundreds of millions ! "

With Cæsar's fifth campaign, marked by the second Belgic War (54 B.C.), we enter upon the second period of the Gallic Wars, in which the Gauls, who had been outraged for four years, deceived, robbed, put to the sword or sold into slavery, during one of the most hateful periods in the history of the human race, began to unite, as far as it was possible at this epoch, for the deliverance of their country.

Before his second expedition to Great Britain, Cæsar had had some warning as to this possibility in the conduct of Dumnorix, an Aeduan noble, the younger brother of that Diviciacus, whom we have already mentioned as importuning the Senate, and son-in-law of Orgetorix, the Helvetian, whom he had expelled during the exodus of 58 B.C. Dumnorix had in him the makings of a leader of the people and of a war-chieftain. Immensely rich, he was followed by a large band of cavalry, whom he supported at his own expense. His attitude, moreover, had been vague, like that of the nation to which he belonged. Declaring allegiance to Rome, he served Cæsar, but only to betray him ; then he returned to him again for some low service. Dumnorix was one of those men who possess clearness of vision and noble aspirations, but whose characters are not as lofty as their designs, which are little more than intangible dreams— characters so vividly portrayed by Shakespeare in Hamlet and by Musset in Lorenzaccio. He made moving speeches about the fair independence of Gaul, but without having the necessary force of character to gather any large body of revolutionaries around him. Cæsar, put on his guard, attached him to his suite, and in order not to leave him behind in Gaul, wanted to take him to Great Britain. Dumnorix pretended that he suffered from sea-sickness and that his religious convictions forbade him from taking part in any hostilities against the country of the Druids. Meanwhile he left no stone unturned to spread among the Gallic chiefs who were to accompany Cæsar all manner of ideas calculated to win them over to the cause of independence. As the proconsul was on the point of embarking, Dumnorix suddenly left the camp with his followers. Pursued by Cæsar's cavalry, the noble Gaul died bravely. " I die a free man, the citizen of a free nation," were his last words.

Cæsar's rapid conquests resulted, and could not fail to result, in a merely superficial settlement. A few districts, such as that of the Veneti, where everything had been devastated and the population put to the sword or sold into slavery, might have been described as pacified; but in the others hatred and rebellion simmered. M. G. Bloch points out in a very interesting way how the Roman rule, by placing all the nations of Gaul under the same yoke, had destroyed the struggle for hegemony which had armed the various peoples one against the other, so that the road was now opened for union in the sacred cause of independence.

On his return from Great Britain to the continent, Cæsar found the great countries of Gaul, which, in his own famous words, he thought he had reduced to silence, in a state of fermentation. The disaster inflicted by Ambiorix, the chief of the Eburones (valley of the Meuse), on the legions of Sabinus fell like a thunderbolt.

Ambiorix was one of the most interesting figures of his time; despising the refinement and luxury of a civilisation in which he took no interest, he lived on his farm on the edge of the woods, supervising the work on it, hunting in the forest, and loving the open air, the woods and freedom. He was endowed with rare qualities as a soldier, being full of guile and with a genius for planning ambuscades. In his sullen and bitter hatred of the Romans, he pretended to be their friend in order the better to be able to cut their throats. Sabinus, Cæsar's lieutenant in the north-eastern cantons, fell into the trap. He was routed by the Eburones, and massacred together with all his legion. Quintus Cicero, who happened to be in the neighbourhood with his troops, succeeded in saving the remains of the vanquished army. He rallied it together and shut himself up in a huge camp fortified in the usual Roman way. In vain did the Eburones, who had been reinforced by the Menapii and the Nervii, endeavour to take the entrenchments by assault. Cæsar came up with his customary speed, and succeeded in raising the siege. But the repercussion of this event was felt throughout Gaul. The Carnutes (Chartres and Orleans) and the Senones (Sens) massacred or drove out the chiefs who had been placed over them by the Roman faction. Cæsar took a high hand; he gave up his visit to Italy and increased his army to ten legions. The Aedui (Autun) and the Remi (Rheims) remained subject to Rome and by means of garrisons cleverly dispersed throughout the various States the general upheaval was averted. The Belgæ took up arms. Ambiorix, of the Eburones, and Indutiomarus, of the Treviri, were their brave and determined leaders; but against the organisation of the Roman army, under the direction of the genius of Cæsar, any local effort in one of these regions of Gaul was doomed to failure. The ravaging of several Belgic cantons by the Romans was terrible. As Ambiorix and his Eburones had beaten the Romans, Cæsar describes them in his book as " scoundrels," and these " scoundrels " had to be punished in an exemplary manner. The Romans cut down the standing corn, delivered up the villages to the flames, and put women and children to the sword, whilst the old men perished under the most terrible tortures. Terrified, the Carnutes and the Senones begged for mercy from the conqueror. Indutiomarus had fallen in battle against the legionaries of Labienus, but it was Ambiorix whom Cæsar had set his heart on capturing. Cæsar would tolerate no resistance on the part of his adversaries; victory above all was not allowed. With the help of his supporters, his spies and the agents whom he kept in the country, he organised a savage, minute and clever manhunt. Sometimes Ambiorix was seen fleeing in the distance; Cæsar or his lieutenants would send their cavalry in pursuit; but Ambiorix knew all the features of the country better than they did. In order to lay hands on his hated foe, Cæsar lowered himself so far as to turn for help to the Germans. Ambiorix was supported by four faithful companions, energetic, ardent and swift

99

as himself. In a few weeks he and his heroic little escort became, as it were, the heroes of legend. They were seen everywhere at once and the Romans were maddened by their endless efforts to catch them without success. These comings and goings, marches and countermarches, criss-crossing each other in every direction, were not, of course, undertaken without the inevitable slaughter, pillage, burning and devastation. The faithful Hirtius writes in this connection : " Despairing of getting his fugitive and trembling [sic] foe (Ambiorix) into his power, Cæsar thought his dignity [sic] demanded the destruction in the States belonging to Ambiorix of men, cattle and buildings, so that, an object of horror to those whom chance had spared, Ambiorix might never return to a country upon which he had drawn down such disasters." " Everything," adds Hirtius, " was destroyed by murder, fire and rapine." The whole proceeding was base and cruel beyond description. Finally it became necessary for the Romans to evacuate territory which they had so thoroughly ravaged that they could not live in it themselves, and Cæsar brought back his soldiers to Rheims and the Remi, his faithful friends (Sept. 54 B.C.).

Here another picture was unveiled.

At Rheims, before the representatives of Gaul, Cæsar discoursed on the rebellion of the Senones and the Carnutes. He condemned Acco to death, one of the leaders of the Senones, who was regarded as the soul of the movement of independence. Cæsar insisted upon death by flogging, as though he were some low deserter from his legions. For was not a noble Gaul, who desired the freedom of his country, a deserter from the cause of Rome ? Others of the accused, who had escaped this dread penalty by taking flight, were ordered by the proconsul to be forbidden " water and fire." By this treatment at the hands of the stranger the Gauls tasted the lowest depths of slavery. As for the conqueror, he was once more able to announce to the Roman Senate " that Gaul had been reduced to silence."

This proud proclamation was made at a moment when Gaul was about to make her voice heard, and this time with a magnificence and splendour which would put the glory of the victor for ever in the shade.

A rapid glance at the five years that had just passed showed the Gauls what the help brought to them by Cæsar had cost. The aristocracy of the country had summoned him and welcomed him, and Cæsar had not hesitated, in the interests of his own policy, to put tyrants over them—tyrants whom they abhorred. Whole senates had been massacred or reduced to servitude; the " chiefs " of the country had been dragged by Cæsar in his train, as pitiful hostages, treated as slaves who were too untrustworthy not to be bound hand and foot.

What had become of the fine cavalry which was the pride of Gaul? Cæsar had sent it to Great Britain or to the Rhine. The auxiliaries which the proconsul raised in Gaul were systematically placed in the most dangerous positions in battle, wherever the slaughter was greatest, for he was always anxious to spare his legions. His procurators and foragers stripped the country bare in order to meet the needs of the army; Latin merchants and speculators swooped down upon the towns and estates like a cloud of hungry sparrows on to fields sown with corn, and Cæsar's lieutenants, not to mention Cæsar himself, set them the example of how to make a clean sweep of everything. At the assizes held in Rheims shortly before, an assembly of Gauls was forced to pass sentence at the dictates of the master. The mockery of freedom which remained to Gaul was laid bare in this lurid light.

Vercingetorix ! At this great and sonorous name the soul of a Frenchman still leaps after two thousand years. " Vercingetorix " was a proper name, well suited to the hero; it meant in the Celtic language " grear king of warriors," and this name, which has re-echoed, and will ever re-echo, down the ages, was already as resplendent as a standard, as a call to arms. " It seemed made to inspire terror," says the historian Florus.

Vercingetorix was the son of Celtillus, King of the Arverni, whom the patrician faction had burnt at the stake. His son had grown up with the desire of vengeance in his heart, and when he saw his country enslaved by the enemy, his hatred burnt even more fiercely against the foreign oppressor than against those who, as unconscious instruments of the latter, had been the aiders and abettors of his father's death.

Vercingetorix was young, ardent, rich, handsome, tall and

101

strong. He had a numerous following. He is usually represented with long drooping moustaches; but the coins struck in his image show him with long hair and the face entirely clean shaven. He was one of those men whom it is an honour to meet, in whom Nature seems to have achieved a masterpiece, not so rare as might be supposed, but who rise to eminence but rarely, since neither men nor circumstances conspire to make their value felt. Their strength of character, firm and lofty convictions, fine generosity and nobility of spirit shine out all the more resplendent because those connected with their history, beginning with their illustrious foe, display a mediocre, shrivelled spirit, with a selfish outlook. Nevertheless Cæsar, so little able to understand him, was bound in his *Commentaries* to bow before him. "Vercingetorix," he writes, "never took up arms for his own personal interests, but for the liberty of all."

Vercingetorix not only possessed the gift of command, he was also eloquent, persuasively, irresistibly eloquent. He had the power of pleasing the masses, though it was by means of manly virtues, with which was mingled that curious charm peculiar to leaders of men.

Under his guidance the resistance of Gaul took on a different character. It no longer consisted of unskilled marches, and simple-minded and primitive forms of attack. Vercingetorix had studied Cæsar and his soldiers, he had also studied his own countrymen. With wonderful versatility of intellect, an abundance of moral resource and incomparable scope of imagination, he was destined to make the Roman leader tremble.

Cæsar was master of his army; a single word from him—less than a word, a gesture, a nod of the head—and as one man the legions would get into motion, manœuvre, fight or halt with all the precision of clockwork. "The legions," said Cæsar, "show what the discipline of the Roman State can accomplish." But Vercingetorix had to reckon with his followers, to discuss with them, submit his plans to them and have them approved, not only by the council, but by the mass of the soldiers in arms; he had to struggle to secure the support of his allies, who, at the slightest reverse, threatened to abandon him. Throughout the whole of the war in which he commanded he had beside him supporters who thought of nothing else than how to give him a blow in the back.

"Vercingetorix," writes Fustel de Coulanges, "did not have at his disposal the one prerequisite for all great wars—he was not in command of a united nation. The divisions which exist in society are also to be found in armies, and their counterpart in the heart of the soldier is indecision, lack of discipline, doubt and distrust. In vain did Vercingetorix collect a large army, for however great his own energy, genius and personal valour may have been, he seems never to have succeeded in endowing that army with the organisation and cohesion necessary to face the Roman legions."

In the accomplishment of the great task for which he had opened his heart, he had in his own country, in his own city, his own family, enemies who would not lay down their arms, who hampered his efforts, thwarted his plans and betrayed him to the foe. His uncle Gobannitio and the chiefs of the Arverni, infeoffed to the aristocratic party, and devoted to Rome, the masters of Gergovia kept watch over him, and would fain have put him in chains.

The exact strength of Vercingetorix's forces was always known to Cæsar by means of deserters, his very words were reported by traitors; very often, sometimes every day, the proconsul was told what his smallest movements would be.

Before coming to active measures, Vercingetorix had allowed his plans to mature for a long time; he had made them with care, and had surrounded himself with auxiliaries and allies judiciously chosen; the conspiracy remained secret. Cæsar was in Italy watching over his own interests and his political career when the insurrectionary movement broke out, as had been arranged, in the district of the Carnutes.

On a fine January morning (52 B.C.) Gutratus and Conconnetodumnus, two of the bravest and most resolute confederates of the Arvernian chieftain, penetrated into Orleans at the head of a well-armed band of men. From the beginning of the rebellion, Gutratus was the terror of the Romans; from the very first days he assumed superhuman proportions in their imagination, and they regarded him as a sort of exterminating monster spreading fear and death wherever he went. The Roman

103

merchants established in the town, who were even more hated than the soldiers on account of their nefarious dealings and their eagerness to found fortunes on the misery and sufferings of the conquered, had their throats cut in a trice. Amongst them perished Cita, the real head of Cæsar's commissariat. The Carnutes and the Arverni had learnt to unite; the first promoters of the movement, they remained its heart and soul.

The news of the morning's events in Orleans spread like wildfire. Heralds had been posted in relays at various points, and by means of this organisation which was surprisingly swift, Vercingetorix was informed of the result that same evening at Gergovia in Auvergne. He called his clients to arms, but from the first moment the obstacles which were to bar his road rose up before him. His uncle Gobannitio and the patricians would not support the cause of liberty, but drove the hero out of the town. He became a fugitive. Who was the leader of this great people fighting for their freedom? A fugitive, an exile!

It would be as well to ennumerate the peoples who took part in the war of independence which we may call the war of Vercingetorix. They were the Arverni (Auvergne) and the Carnutes (the district of Chartres and Orleans) who were the originators, and were joined without delay by the Parisii, the Senones (Sens), the Aulerci (Maine), the Lemovices (Limoges), the Turoni (Tours), the Andecavi (Angers), and the peoples belonging to the confederation of the Armorici, in both peninsulas and along the coast, between the mouths of the Seine and the Loire. The Pictones (Poitou) also joined the movement, but only partially, their capital Limonum (Poitiers) remaining true to the Roman cause.

South of Auvergne, the Nitiobriges (Agenais), the Gabali (Gévaudan), and those of the Ruteni (Rouergue) who had not been swallowed up in the *Provincia Romana* gave their help, drawn in by the Cadurci (Quercy), who were the resolute agents of national independence in these cantons. The other peoples of this district were forced to be prudent on account of the vicinity of the *Provincia Romana*.

Belgic Gaul had been decimated and ravaged by the last war and, in a state of constant fear of German pressure from across the Rhine, could only come to a tardy and partial decision.

The Bellovaci (Beauvaisis) pronounced against Rome but would not follow Vercingetorix. The Remi (Rheims) and the Lingones (Langres) declared in favour of the Romans. " Among these two peoples," writes Jullian, " hatred of independence had been raised to a virtue." The Aedui (Burgundy) continued to waver between one side and the other. The Santones (Saintonge) declared for the Romans. The Aquitani (Gascony) remained neutral. Lastly the Narbonnaise was for Cæsar and the Allobroges (Dauphiny) seemed to have resigned themselves to the suzerainty of Rome.

Thus Vercingetorix was very far from having the whole of Gaul on his side; he had barely a third of it—generally speaking the part corresponding to the north-east and the centre of France, Celtic Gaul properly so-called.

Even in that part of Gaul which supported the cause of independence the aristocratic faction continued to show indifference, not to say hostility, towards the young patrician who had been saluted as king by the popular elements of Auvergne; they were always ready to betray him and did indeed often do so.

Excluding the Belgæ, the Armorici and the Aquitani, and not taking the Narbonnaise into account, Gaul was divided into two great confederations, the one following the Arverni (Auvergne) and the other the Aedui (Burgundy); a division, as Jullian points out, similar to that which had divided Greece between Athens and Sparta, and France in the fourteenth and fifteenth centuries between the Armagnacs and the Burgundians. And in each State this division was reproduced again. The city States which followed the lead of the Arverni also provided followers for the Aedui, and *vice versâ*.

The Aedui represented the patrician party, the *meliores*, equivalent to the Armagnacs of the end of the fourteenth century; the Arverni, the popular party, the *minores*, like the Burgundians of later days, the popular party with its " tyrants " and its impetuous mobs. But, unlike the struggle against England, it was the democrats who represented the national party in the fight against Rome.

In the war he had undertaken, Vercingetorix no doubt disposed of superior numbers to Cæsar, but the difference was not nearly so great as the author of the *Commentaries* made out, and this difference was more than compensated by the discipline of the legions, their armament and their siege equipment; in short, by the organisation of his command.

It would have been interesting to see these two adversaries coming to grips with forces numerically equal, but equal also as regards quality, armament and war material, each of the two leaders enjoying full authority over his troops. In such circumstances it is not at all certain, very far from it, that Cæsar would have won the day. For if Cæsar perhaps had on his side a superior intelligence and a greater knowledge of the technique and tactics of war, Vercingetorix surpassed him through the power bestowed by his devotion to a sacred cause, by his disinterestedness, by the enthusiasm which doubled his strength and his faculties, as compared with the futile ambition, the harsh pride of the baldheaded Cæsar, the wan proconsul, whose wrinkled features bore the traces of nights of sensuality, whose heart was withered up with debauchery and excited by the ghastly pre-Neronian dilettantism which made him rejoice in the hideous task of bloodshed and rapine, and in the morbid pleasure of blasting and trampling under foot human destinies, just as the Roman plebs, his beloved fellow citizens whom he flattered and whose suffrages he craved, delighted in seeing the red blood flow on the white sand of the arena.

Cæsar was in Italy. The plan of Vercingetorix was to let loose upon the Narbonnaise his best lieutenant, Lucterus the Cadurcian, " a man full of audacity," says Cæsar, to make trouble there, and perhaps awaken a desire for independence, whilst he himself remained in the heart of the country among the Bituriges, whom he would rally to his cause, and thus bring his weight to bear against the Aedui. In this way the Roman legions which had been left in Gaul would be separated from their leader, and threatened at their base of supplies.

In Lucterus the Cadurcian Vercingetorix possessed the most faithful of his companions, who from the beginning of the war to the end was his most courageous and trusted lieutenant. He deserves a place by the side of his glorious leader in the forefront of the field of honour. And after having served as his indefatigable helper, Lucterus enjoyed the supreme honour
106

of being his companion in captivity and of dying by his side in the talons of the Roman eagle.

But the jealousy of the Aedui had already been aroused. The echoes revived by the young King of the Arverni when with such a noble gesture he assumed the leadership of the movement for liberty made them suspicious. With Cæsar all powerful in Gaul, their own pre-eminence was assured; but lo, it was passing into the hands of the hated Arverni !

Nevertheless they decided to follow the movement; but they did so reluctantly, glancing back the while, and praying for the success of the enterprise, since they were engaged in it, whilst at the same time trying to safeguard their own interests, in case the struggle did not have a favourable issue. From the very first day, Eporedorix and Viridomarus, who were in command of the Aedui, did not regard Vercingetorix as a chief to whom they owed devoted obedience, but as a master whose orders they executed because it had become difficult not to do do.

Cæsar was in Italy when the news of the insurrection in Gaul reached him. He was surprised. The secret of the conspiracy had been well kept; but he knew the Gauls. In the depots of Italy he raised all the legionaries that could be spared, crossed the Alps and traversed the Cevennes in the snow and the mud. Thanks to the inertia of the Aedui and the complicity of the Lingones, Cæsar arrived in Auvergne, the territory of Vercingetorix himself, where he appeared like a thunderbolt.

What was the young Arvernian to do ? Stick to his plan and maintain and reinforce if possible the human barrier in Gaul which would separate the Romans from their base—the Narbonnaise and Italy, and thus cut off their reinforcements in men and materials, and in other directions prevent Cæsar from communicating with his legions in the north; or else remain in Auvergne, the heart of the rebellion? Among the Arverni the powerful party, which had driven out Vercingetorix, joined the enemy, and Cæsar found in it, among the most influential personages in the land, his wholehearted partisans. To allow them to act meant the loss of Auvergne, and what sort of a figure would Vercingetorix cut in trying to command other cities if his own fellow-countrymen submitted to the foe? To the appeal of his own folk he could not turn a deaf ear.

Thus a road was opened between Cæsar and his legions in the north. With his customary clearness of vision and rapidity of decision and movement, Cæsar took it. Through the territory of the wavering Aedui and the friendly Lingones, he rejoined the main body of his troops in the north, and quickly appeared in the neighbourhood of Sens with his ten legions, his whole army being now reunited under his own expert guidance. The plan so finely conceived by Vercingetorix, and which from the very beginning would have secured his final success, had been destroyed. The mistake the young Arvernian had made was forced upon him by the lack of unity in his own country.

And now the two generals had come to grips, each at the head of his army. Vercingetorix failed in his attack on the fortified strongholds. He had neither the knowledge nor the equipment for siege warfare. " The Gauls," said Cæsar, " surround a place with all their forces, hurl stones at the ramparts to put the defenders to flight, and then, covering themselves with their shields, make for the gates and sap the walls." A very primitive proceeding ! In the capturing of towns, by means of poliorcetics and ingenious appliances, Cæsar, on the other hand, succeeded almost without striking a blow.

In a pitched battle, the exact site of which has never been determined, the Gallic army suffered a serious check, and Vercingetorix learnt to understand that in a war of sieges and pitched battles he would never be able to get the better of his enemy. Against his sounder instincts, which were always in favour of courage and open attack, he conceived a new plan, and by his energy and conviction succeeded in imposing it upon his council and his army.

Cæsar himself copied the designs of the young Arvernian chief, going so far as to use the very terms the latter would have employed to make his allies in the war adopt them. " Let us change our tactics," he said; " no more battles in open country. Let us aim at depriving the enemy of food and supplies. Our large force of cavalry can easily accomplish this task. Crops must be destroyed, farms stripped bare, villages set on fire. Thus day by day we shall gradually destroy a famished army, seeking for its daily bread, in isolated detachments which we shall take by surprise and put out of action separately. We must ruin the towns in which the enemy might find shelter, with the exception of fortresses built on a height and considered impregnable."

This terrible programme was adopted, and it was immediately put into execution with a savage, almost sublime ferocity. In the very centre of Berry twenty villages and towns were burnt to the ground in a single day.

Alas! Vercingetorix allowed himself to be moved by the Bituriges, who implored him at least to spare their capital, Bourges, *Avaricum*, the most beautiful city in Gaul, says Cæsar. The Bituriges had only joined the cause of independence with some hesitation, and Vercingetorix was afraid they might desert it, if too great a sacrifice were demanded of them. It was always the same fear of disunion and defection which made the young chieftain flinch in the execution of his best laid plans. The Bituriges, moreover, promised to defend their city resolutely, and they kept their word when Cæsar had surrounded them with his army.

The siege began, harsh and inexorable. The Romans constructed their siege towers with their leather revettings; the besieged set fire to them. Clever at mining and forging, the Bituriges multiplied their means of defence. They caught the siege hooks with which the Romans tried to undermine the ramparts in nets; they countermined their mines; they met the attacking towers with defence towers of equal height. They passed along red hot balls of pitch in metal containers from hand to hand; the last man in the chain, standing erect on the ramparts, would throw the burning shell on to the wooden buildings of the besiegers. But no sooner had he appeared and hurled the burning pitch, than he fell, striken down by the Romans. It meant certain death, and yet not for one instant was the post allowed to remain empty. The siege lasted twenty-seven days, and the town was taken in a heavy thunderstorm which spoilt the defence. The massacre which followed was terrible, truly Roman and truly Cæsarian, the whole garrison being annihilated. It was an outrageous murder of 40,000 human beings. Women shrieked and hugged their babies to their breasts, and like lightning one of the legionaries would kill both mother and child.

In Avaricum Cæsar found food and a comfortable shelter for his troops, who now had abundant supplies.

This was in April of the year 52 B.C., and constituted the second grave defeat suffered by the Gauls. Vercingetorix did not lay down his arms.

After this success, Cæsar sent Labienus, his most skilful lieutenant, to the north, in order to suppress the rebellion there, an enterprise in which he obtained much assistance from the Germans; not that the latter consented to support him by means of open alliance, but the constant menace from them, directed chiefly against the brave tribes of the Treviri, obliged both these and the neighbouring peoples to remain inactive behind the protection of their own frontiers. The barrier of the Rhine was once more thrown open to the invaders, but this time the Romans winked their eye at it. The menace allowed Cæsar to complete his conquest of Gaul.

When all was quiet on his northern front, Cæsar thought he might strike a decisive blow by carrying the war into the very heart of the insurrection, into Auvergne. He proposed to take Gergovia, the stronghold and capital of the Arverni, situated on the plateau to the south of Clermont, which has kept its name to this day. Vercingetorix hurried up to the defence of the place, but took care not to shut himself up inside it. He, together with the pick of his men, took up their station on a neighbouring height, keeping in direct touch with the besieged. Cæsar, afraid lest his army should be caught in a vice and only able to obtain supplies with the greatest difficulty, owing to the attacks of the enemy's cavalry, made up his mind to tempt fortune. He ordered an attack. But he was repulsed with much bloodshed. In order to avoid a complete rout, he was obliged to hurl himself into the *mêlée*, in which he lost his sword and was almost taken prisoner. A swift retreat was his only alternative, and he resigned himself to it with a heavy heart. Could anyone have foretold that one day Cæsar would be forced to flee before " barbarians " ?

Vercingetorix made a triumphal entry into the city of his ancestors, from which he had been driven some years before.

110

The masses acclaimed him with enthusiastic shouts, bestowing upon him the title of king, of which his father had been deprived at the stake. It was a glorious day for the young soldier and for the whole of Gaul. How wonderful it must have been to see his large blue eyes light up for a moment with the ray of beneficent joy and holy pride which must have illumined them that day! And indeed his allies themselves solemnly placed in his hands the supreme command over the confederate forces, which until now he had wielded only through the magic of his personal valour and prestige.

The defeat of Cæsar at Gergovia had yet another result—the Aedui deserted the Romans and joined the cause of freedom. They brought the Sequani in their train. Vercingetorix marched to Bibracte, the stronghold of the Aedui, and there convoked an assembly of all the Gallic peoples. All the Celtic cities were represented, with the exception of the Remi and the Lingones, who remained stubbornly faithful to Rome. The star of the young Arvernian was now burning brightly in the ascendant. He was able to hope for victory; but the seeds of weakness still remained. It is true that Vercingetorix now had full authority over the whole of the Gallic forces, but this was in no way comparable to the authority enjoyed by the Roman general over his legions. Every decision of the Gallic prince was subjected to interminable discussions. In the gravest crisis he was obliged to summon a council of the various tribal chiefs, explain his plans, and have them approved. This council was full of rivalry, jealousy, and hatred. How often did not the clear-sighted leader have to give way in despair on points he knew it would be disastrous to cede. He was even accused of treachery, and before his own soldiers the brilliant general was reduced to pleading in his own defence. And in the end he was obliged to take pledges and hostages to ensure the fidelity of his allies. Surrounded by untrustworthy men, feeling himself frequently betrayed, he was driven to have recourse to the most rigorous, sometimes the most cruel, measures against perjurers, turncoats and deserters. He knew that he was playing for great stakes. Was Gaul to live on free, glorious and independent, following her national destiny along the open road, or was she to vegetate beneath the yoke

111

of the despot, the destroyer of fruitful initiative, at the mercy of corrupt foreigners?

In the northern districts, the skilful Labienus, who had been separated from Cæsar since the defeat of Gergovia, was marching against Lutetia, the capital of the Parisii, which seemed to be the key to the basin of the Seine. The Parisii were ready for the fight. They had chosen as their chief a veteran of previous wars, Camulogenus of the Aulerci. Camulogenus no longer possessed the spirit, the strength or the youthful endurance which the Gauls loved, but his experience of military matters inspired confidence. Labienus, with four legions, had posted himself on the right bank of the Seine, on the spot where the eastern wing of the Louvre and Saint-Germain-l'Auxerrois now stand. Camulogenus had taken up a position on Mt. Sainte-Geneviève. The engagement took place on the plain of Grenelle. The left wing of the Gauls was driven back at the first encounter, but the centre and right wing, under the command of Camulogenus himself, resisted without yielding a foot. The Parisii engaged were killed to the last man and their old and valiant leader, Camulogenus of the Aulerci, fell in their midst.

Nevertheless the situation of Cæsar remained critical. Vercingetorix had returned with pitiless severity to the strategy of the campaign of Avaricum—the burning of farms, the destruction of forage depots, avoiding pitched battles and preventing the enemy from receiving supplies by lying in ambush for his convoys and destroying them—in short, by starving the foe and putting his bases out of action.

And now, quitting the jungles of the Ardennes, Ambiorix once more appeared, savage and redoubtable.

The tribes of the north joined the movement, the Morini (Flanders), the Nervii (Hainault), the Ambienes (Picardie) and the Atrebates (Artois) in answer to the call of one of the most extraordinary personages of the time—Commius of the Atrebates.

Until the year 53 B.C., the war having then lasted five years, Commius was acting in Belgic Gaul as the agent of Cæsar, to whom he was apparently devoted. Was he one of those men who in the depths of their heart bear an indomitable love for the freedom of their country and wish to begin by studying the enemy in every nook and corner in order the better to fight him later on? At all events he was suddenly found showing himself in a hundred different places, rousing the sluggards, exhorting the wavering, and the insurrection let loose by him was animated by his devouring activity, his rare energy and indomitable courage. Thanks to him, even the Bellovaci ended by sending a few men to the league. But, even more serious for Cæsar than the rising of the tribes in the north was the victorious thrust of the patriots in the south, in their attack on the peoples of the Roman province of Transalpine Gaul; the Arverni and the Gabali had hurled themselves against the Helvii (Vivarais), and the Ruteni and the Cadurci had attacked the Volcae Arecomici. The Allobroges, aroused by the emissaries of Vercingetorix, seemed to be wavering. Cæsar, fearing to find his communications with Italy cut off, decided to retreat.

He crossed the country of the faithful Lingones and that of the Sequani (Franche-Comté), who had given but fainthearted support to the national movement, and reached the cantons of the Allobroges, who were hesitating but had not yet openly declared themselves. On gaining the Narbonnaise, he reorganised his forces and awaited a favourable opportunity for renewing the attack.

What could have passed through the mind of Vercingetorix at this juncture when the situation must have seemed so favourable to him? What arguments could have led him to abandon the plan he was following and the success of which seemed certain? Did he yield to his Gallic temperament, always eager for action and battle? Did he think that victory without a victory was unworthy of him and of the name he bore, unworthy of the people who had placed him at their head and of the sacred cause of which he was the responsible champion? Did he imagine he was certain of victory if he fell upon Cæsar in his retreat, where he was hampered by impedimenta and baggage of all kinds?

Or was the reason for his decision to be found rather in the perfidious conduct of the Aeduan chiefs, embittered by the humiliation they had suffered at the hands of the assembly of Bibracte which had placed them under the command of the young Arvernian, the king of their detested rivals? Did Vercingetorix, feeling his authority dwindling, aim at re-establishing it by means of a brilliant stroke which would also bring the campaign to a triumphant conclusion? He relied on the superiority of his cavalry. But was he ignorant of the fact that Cæsar had sent for a corps of picked cavalry from Germany? The fact remains that he attacked Cæsar. The exact spot is not known, for the *Commentaries* are deplorably vague as regards topography. But it was on the bank of a river—the Armançon perhaps or the Vingeane. Vercingetorix was defeated.

It was a serious defeat. The young general rallied his soldiers in their flight, and reached Alesia, the fortress of the Mandubii, on the summit of Mt. Auxois, above the present village of Alise-Sainte-Reine (Côte-d'Or).

We are entering upon the last act of this great and stirring drama.

Alesia was not only a stronghold fortified by nature and the hand of man, it was also, for the Gauls, one of their legendary sanctuaries, a sort of holy city. From the military point of view, the position of the town was not equal to that of Gergovia. The hills around Alesia, which were as high as the one on which it was built, provided Cæsar with a site for his encampments.

It has been calculated that Cæsar had 70,000 men at his disposal before Alesia, all admirably armed, picked soldiers. The number of Gauls confined in the place with Vercingetorix amounted perhaps to an equal number; but, were it only from the point of view of equipment, the two forces were in no way comparable. It must also be borne in mind that in an army such as that under the command of the young Arvernian, recruited from the masses, there were many men of little use.

The town was closely invested. Cæsar had surrounded it with a double line of entrenchments with high ramparts. Those nearest the town were as high as a wall, and along them wooden towers were built at intervals. In these trenches his legionaries could take shelter. From the top of the towers they rained down missiles spreading fire and slaughter. This double line of trenches was in its turn protected, on the side furthest from the town, by a palisade of pointed stakes, set obliquely, with
114

the pointed end towards the outside in order to stop the attack of a relieving army. The stakes were entwined with boughs and brushwood. Finally a fourth line of defence, over a fairly wide extent of territory, was composed of deep pits, in the bottom of which upright stakes were planted, which made any surprise from the outside, and indeed an attack of any kind, so difficult that it might almost be called impossible.

The plan of Vercingetorix, shut up in Alesia, was to hold his own against Cæsar's army, to fix it to the spot, to inflict as much damage on it as possible and to organise a formidable attack upon it by the whole of the forces of Gaul summoned from every quarter of the land. It was a plan of simple grandeur and magnificence. It was no longer a question of strategy, or of a well-ordered and disciplined fight; it was a matter of overwhelming the Romans scattered around his stronghold beneath a human avalanche so formidable that the superiority of their tactics, their equipment and their scientific manœuvring would be of no avail. This plan, in all its rare beauty of conception, was under the circumstances in which it was conceived the one which had the greatest chance of success, for it must always be remembered that the divided state of Gaul, with its various factions and rival peoples, would not allow of any hope of a long and patient resistance such as could be expected in a united and well-organised country.

The appeal of Vercingetorix was heard, but the response was not what it should have been. The young general had expected an onrush of a million men, of the whole of Gaul rising up *en masse*. In this alone lay salvation. The very thought of it filled Cæsar with fear. But the *levée en masse* did not take place. Only 250,000 men, it is said, marched upon Alise-Sainte-Reine. This figure is possibly correct; but in all this huge crowd—though it was insufficient for the object proposed—in this rabble, what a number were badly armed, badly equipped and without any experience of war! More-over, in the absence of the supreme chief, who was shut up in Alesia, the direction of operations was confided, not to one active, energetic and resolute leader, like Lucterius or Ambiorix, but to a council of four, only two of whom were well chosen—Vercassivellaunus the Arvernian, a cousin of Vercingetorix, and the wonderful Commius of the Atrebati, one of the heroes of the war. The others were Eporedorix and Viridomarus, two Aedui, political intriguers and men who could manœuvre, not on the field of battle, but in the back corridors of popular assemblies. Hence the delays, the hesitation and changes of plan may easily be imagined. In Alesia the besieged were dying of hunger. The non-combatants of the city were expelled. They presented themselves before Cæsar's lines and offered themselves up as prisoners and slaves. Cæsar refused. He was determined that they should die of hunger under the very eyes of their fellow citizens who had driven them out, holding up their hands in supplication, howling in their anguish, the agony of death mingling with their words of reproach and with their rage, and so harrow the hearts of the defenders that their will would be broken.

At last the Gauls appeared in sight of the besieged city. It was a solemn moment, the gravest in the history of France. Was Vercingetorix right, had his plans been faithfully carried out, had his appeal been heard, had it met with unanimous response? The destinies of France hung in the balance; with the Gauls, France was following the course of her own civilisation, begun by the Ligurians and carried on by the Celts; she would not have had to submit to that branding by Rome which it required over six hundred years of untold misery, fearful catastrophes, terrible anarchy and sublime effort to obliterate.

But the fate appointed had to be fulfilled. The attack, weakened by discussions in the high command, carried out with studied indifference by many of the leaders, in successive waves, in which the Gauls performed miracles of heroism and valour, and Vercassivellaunus and Commius wore themselves out with superhuman efforts, but Eporedorix and Viridomanus displayed criminal negligence, failed grievously; the Gallic army, exhausted by its own efforts, broke up into little groups, each of which returned separately to its native village (September, 52 B.C.).

Vercingetorix, clad in his finest armour, jumped on his charger, which he had adorned in its most sumptuous trappings, and delivered himself up, proud and free, before the tribunal of the pale proconsul in his scarlet robes. Still sitting on his steed, he rode round Cæsar, then dismounting, he took off the ornaments set with gold, silver and coral, with which his charger was harnessed, threw them, together with his own armour, at the feet of the Roman, and sat down beside the trophies he offered without saying a word. Such is the description given by Plutarch.

Vercingetorix gave himself up as an expiatory offering, hoping to save his fellow-countrymen by this voluntary sacrifice, for he knew the hardness of his enemy's heart.

It was a final act of sublime and incomparable beauty, worthy of the hero who acted it with such wonderful simplicity. Vercingetorix was taken to Rome, where, after having been kept in prison for six years, Cæsar had the baseness to have him put to death on the day of his triumph. We have seen how Cæsar behaved during the war in Gaul. The way in which he conducted it and the way in which he brought it to an end alike cover him with dishonour. He was no doubt endowed with a rare intelligence, as bright, nay brighter, than the sun; but a man devoid of honour cannot be a great man. Nobody can refuse this title to Vercingetorix; the verdict of history is bound to refuse it to Julius Cæsar.

Shortly afterwards Cæsar succeeded in laying hands on Gutratus. With his legions he crossed the country of the Carnutes, which he had already ravaged, burnt, pillaged and covered with ruins and bloodshed several times. The unfortunate inhabitants came and implored him on their bended knees to spare them at least this once. Cæsar replied that he would be satisfied with a single victim—Gutratus. The wretched Carnutes, mad with despair, set to work to find him; and they succeeded. It is probable that, like Vercingetorix, Gutratus came and delivered himself up, like a sacrificial victim to the sinister proconsul. I will quote Camille Jullian :

" Cæsar ordered the execution of Gutratus, an execution carried out in the Roman fashion, with rods and axe, and allowed all the soldiers to have a blow, so that each one might taste the blood of the man who had given the signal for the war. They fell with such fury on the body of the Gaul that it was but a corpse when the lictor's axe completed the execution."

Ah, proud civilisation of Rome, thou foster-mother of Gaul regenerated, what hymn could be sweet enough to sing in thy honour?

The name of Gutratus, which, together with those of Vercingetorix, Ambiorix, Lucterius the Carducian and Commius of the Atrebates, was one of the five most glorious in the war of independence, was doubtless but a surname. " Gutratus " is the Celtic for " priest in the service of the god." Like the famous Archbishop of the Hundred Years' War, he may possibly have held some religious office, or he might even have been a Druid who offered sacrifice to the gods.

The capture of Vercingetorix did not put an end to the struggle for independence. Cæsar distributed his legates over the various provinces and inaugurated a new system, one of clemency, nay even of favour and consideration towards those who decided to submit, and of extreme severity towards the " rebels." This severity generally consisted in cutting off the right hand of any Gaul criminal enough to love the liberty of his country, and sending him forth carrying his right hand in his left, to show it to the various peoples who were still unsubjugated, and thus teach them what it meant not to love Rome and allow themselves to be pillaged by her glorious representatives. Bands of these unfortunate creatures might be seen wandering about, dying of gangrene and exhaustion along the roads or on the edge of the woods. Terrorisation and clemency combined had their effect, but the image of Vercingetorix continued to shine in men's minds. The Aedui submitted, but many others continued to resist. The Bellovaci had hesitated to take part in the struggle. The patricians were for Rome, but the people rose up at the voice of an ardent leader, Correus of the Bellovaci, and the Senate was obliged to yield. The brave peoples of the Treviri, who had been forced to inaction hitherto by the menace from Germany, also joined in the war against Rome. From the virgin forests of the Ardennes, Ambiorix once more emerged, and his indomitable energy and prodigious activity were displayed now among the Bellovaci, now among the Treviri, spreading the sacred fire. At the voice of Commius of the Atrebates, the Aulerci (Evreux and Maine) also rose up. Dumnacus, Drappes the Senonian

118

and Lucterius the Carducian burnt with an ardour that nothing could quench. The Romans held Poitiers, but in Uxellodunum (Le Puy d'Issolu), a stronghold comparable to Gergovia, Lucterius held out against them, surrounded by the bravest of the Pictones. What glorious names—Ambiorix, Gutratus, Correus, Commius, Dumnacus and Drappes the Senonian, which with that of Lucterius the Carducian should never be blotted from the annals of France! They revived the policy of Vercingetorix of making a desert round the Roman armies, harassing them, making the supply of provisions difficult, and engaging them in detail without offering battle; but this fine effort came too late. The majority of the Gallic peoples were exhausted, tired and weakened, and, moreover, the attempts of the various tribes were not co-ordinated. They were no longer led by a Vercingetorix, who imposed his will by his genius, his race and his dazzling popularity.

This last final stand of Gaul was a grand example of courage and virtue, but it was doomed to failure.

" The wars in Gaul had lasted ten years. Cæsar had taken by assault eight hundred fortresses and subjugated three hundred tribes, he had fought against three millions of the enemy, leaving a million dead and taking a million prisoners." What a terrible picture! That was how Cæsar went to the " help " of Gaul!

The whole country was devastated. Cæsar only spared the corn and forage in the regions where he needed them for his own troops and where, moreover, he did not fail to seize them.

Some districts were plundered root and branch, two or three times, or even four times, as in the case of Beauce, the territory of the Carnutes. The numberless towns taken by assault were sacked, pillaged and burnt, whilst their inhabitants were put to the sword or reduced to slavery, sold like cattle—the just punishment for " rebels," that is to say people who were criminal enough to defend themselves when they were attacked. The looting of temples and private houses was carried out methodically with all the regularity worthy of the great administration of Rome. And there was plenty to be done.

The proconsul of the Gauls was indeed a warrior of genius.

119

"But robbers have no niche in the Panthéon . . ." says Paul Déroulède in his verses. Certainly there could be no niche there for Julius Cæsar.

"Independence had meant perpetual war; the Roman Empire brought peace "; with these words Fustel de Coulanges **The Work of** comes to the conclusion that the Roman conquest **the Conquerors** was a blessing.

100 B.C. Independence meant war; true, but it was creative war, in which a free people gradually formed their institutions, their customs, their traditions, their religion, their art and their literature. Was not the warlike eleventh century the making of France, at the same time enriching the whole world by the highest art, the most virile literature, the loftiest beliefs, the most fruitful customs and creations of eternal beauty, when the soul of France found self-expression by means of the sublimest originality?

Camille Jullian sums the whole matter up perfectly when he says : " France would have been born earlier if Rome had left Gaul her kings and her liberty; and because she prevented her from remaining strong and united, from ruling and educating herself in her own way, it is impossible to hold the Roman Empire in too great detestation. It arrested the task at which so many centuries had toiled, and it retarded by hundreds of years the moment when a French nation would come into existence within the boundaries ordained for her on earth."

The *Pax Romana* meant for France five hundred years of spiritless, mediocre and powerless insignificance, of drab and narrow sentiment, and of sterile egoism, five hundred years of puerile or senile imitation, which you will, from which nothing came or was ever likely to come.

Moreover, what had the balance-sheet of this " *Pax Romana* " to show? On the debit side was the terrible slaughter of the "pacifier." All the wars that might have been the result of the continuance and development of Celtic feudalism would not have demanded such a huge number of victims. And what about the unprecedented massacres of the third century, of which we shall hear later on? And what of the German invasions and the terrible wastage and destruction resulting from them, due to the debasing influence of the *Pax Romana* ?

On this point again we cannot agree with our loved and admired master, Auguste Longnon, who in his lucid pages on the early beginnings of France maintains that if Gaul had not become Roman she would have become German. In the course of its struggles the race was gaining strength, the fiefs were becoming larger, and unification was being gradually achieved in a virile fashion. The military virtues would have been kept alive by independence and the Germans, during their terrible invasions of the third century, would have found a strong nation capable of driving them back, instead of a subject race, lowered in vitality by a nebulous peace in which the robust virtues which produce warriors can no longer either be reared or preserved. From the reign of Tiberius, the successor of Augustus, Gaul lost the practice of arms. The Roman patron had taken upon himself the task of defence, and when the patron sank into shameful decrepitude, he forsook his client, without leaving him either the social conditions or the institutions and equipment which would have enabled him to defend himself against the barbarian.

" It has been constantly asserted that Rome saved Gaul from German invasions," says Camille Jullian. " This is not true. As long as the proconsuls appointed by the Senate did not cross the Alps in order to weaken and divide the peoples, the Gaul of Ambigatus and Bituitus had nothing to fear from the Barbarians across the Rhine. It was Rome, in short, who delivered France over to them, through the criminal stupidity of her squabbles, by the puerility of her dreams of peace and by the incompetency of her organisation at the frontiers." Bravo Jullian !

In the two centuries, which were to be followed by the dreadful and tragic times we are about to examine, the only sign of life, of vigour, of health and activity was to be found in Christianity, that religion which, in spite of the language which it was to introduce into France, had nothing of Rome in it. Rome, in her usual way, persecuted it cruelly. And, let us make no mistake about it, the elements which founded Christianity in Gaul were the same as those which had animated with their faith the masses who fought for independence, that is to say, the popular elements. Whilst the upper classes became Romanised in their urban centres, their villas, and in their courts of rhetoric, with regard for nothing but foreign traditions, the people remained the people, cut off from all touch with civilisation, but remaining true to itself, keeping its strength and energy intact. In this Christianity which addressed itself to the soul of the masses with a fulness, a freshness and a simplicity which from the very beginning made it welcomed and understood—ah! the lovely breath of pure fresh air!—in this guise so different and unexpected that it was unrecognised, there was nevertheless born again in all its greatness and generosity the popular soul of Vercingetorix inspiring the heart of France to beat once more.

It has been regarded as surprising that Gaul should so easily have accepted the rule of conquerors who had made her suffer so terribly. It seemed a sudden change. Cæsar, with his activity, his subtlety and charm, as well as by the prestige his victories had given him, was the first to contribute to it. He had planned a civil war in order to make himself all powerful, and it was important for him to have both the Gauls on his side.

Labienus, who had been Cæsar's favourite lieutenant, his right hand in Gaul, joined the side of Pompey; the Gauls supported Cæsar. After having " pacified " them by violence, Cæsar scoured Gaul, heaping favours on his adherents. In the Narbonnaise he formed his famous legion of Larks, called after the bird so common in the fields of Gaul; an occasion which was marked by the promise of Roman citizenship to several thousands of Gauls; and this process of naturalisation continued to increase. Cæsar even went so far as to give certain Gauls seats in the Senate. His fellow citizens made fun of them when in Rome the newcomers with heavy tread and outlandish accent asked the way to the Curia.

The Romans were even driven to the conclusion that in his anxiety to win the good graces of his late adversaries Cæsar went a little too far. Was he not Gallicising Rome rather than Romanising Gaul? " From the Alpine peaks, the friend of the Gauls (Cæsar) has let loose the fury of the Celts." Cicero was no longer pleased. Gaul had sent orators to Rome who could make longer speeches than he could. " Adieu to Latin

urbanity," he groaned, " adieu to our fine and polished wit !
The breeches of the Gauls—once more—invade our tribunals ! "

Cæsar and his legions once satiated, Rome took care not to
hinder the assimilation of the conquered. To make a vanquished
nation resemble the victor is a modern idea. The boundaries
of the Gallic " cities," as fixed by the Romans, coincided with
those of the territories of the various peoples whom Cæsar had
found already established in the country. The Romans left
them their ancient names, and later on Christianity adopted
the same divisions for its bishoprics, which survived with but
insignificant differences almost as late as 1789, and more than
one of the departments of France possesses the same boundaries
to this day.

Gaul was annexed to the Empire. She gave up her religion,
her language and her customs, at all events among the upper
classes. For the unwritten law, under which the tribes had
lived, Roman law was substituted. For Gallic feudalism, like
mediæval feudalism, knew only the law of custom under which
the suzerain was the judge of his vassals, the father-master of
his family. The clan system was to all appearance abolished
in favour of a magistrate sitting in his tribunal. Women and
children won a measure of freedom and the ties of the clients
were relaxed; but Roman law in Gaul was harsher to the lower
classes. Nevertheless it must not be imagined that the country
was fundamentally Romanised. Fustel de Coulanges goes much
too far in the conclusions he draws. We are more in agreement
with Kurth, who maintains that Celtic customs survived among
the populace. This is a very important fact, for the seed of
French history lies hidden within it. " Nowhere," says Kurth,
" even in the best-governed districts, was the assimilation complete at the time when the final crisis broke out."

Among the people the Celtic language survived, and the
great mass of the nation still spoke it when the German kingdoms
were founded. Some historians are even of opinion that the
Bagaudæ, those thousands and thousands of rustic rebels, who
were free men and Roman citizens, still spoke Celtic at the end
of the third century. In Bordeaux, where the culture of Latin
letters was then at the height of its glory, the family of Ausonius,
the greatest Latin poet of the period, still spoke Celtic at home

123

(fourth century). The Treviri were considered one of the most completely Romanised of all the Gallic peoples, Treves having become a sort of second Latin capital; and yet the people of that city still spoke Celtic, according to St. Jerome, at the end of the fourth century and the Arverni still spoke it in the fifth century under the Visigoths. As with their language, the people remained faithful to their old beliefs, they continued to venerate their sanctuaries and their local divinities, and to preserve their ancient customs. And their habits retained the roughness, rudeness, if you will, of the good old days of independence.

But the Gauls abandoned at least their warlike practices. Thirty years after the conquest Strabo observes that all their energies were concentrated on works of peace. A few rebellions, it is true, broke out, like the revolt of the Bellovaci in 46 B.C. But they were insignificant. And from that time onwards a single cohort of 1200 men was sufficient to guard a huge territory. About the middle of the first century A.D. the Emperor Claudius was able to say to his senators :

" Never, since she was conquered by the divine Julius, has Gaul wavered in her allegiance; never, even in the most critical circumstances, has her attachment been broken."

" I can never understand," says Camille Jullian, " how Gaul consented to remain a Roman province."

But let us consider the state of Gaul. We have seen how important peoples, like the Remi and the Lingones, and towns like Poitiers, were from the first devoted to the cause of Rome. The Aedui, the most powerful people in Gaul, were on her side. Moreover, we must not regard this as the chief reason for the Romanisation of Gaul, for it is abundantly clear that the differences between Celto-Ligurian civilisation and Roman civilisation were not as great as might be supposed. Camille Jullian makes this quite clear. The great historian reminds us that a thousand years previously the Celts and Italians had spoken the same language, that this ancient bond not only with Italy, but with Greece, had left strong traces in the constitution of the family, in the structure of society and in religion. The Romans of the first century represented a civilisation more advanced in many particulars than the civilisation of Gaul, but

124

they fitted into each other. There is, however, an even more important consideration. We have seen how in all the States, even among the Arverni, the patricians were on the side of Rome. Now the triumph of Rome made the patriciate all powerful. Not only did it once more resume the direction of affairs, but from the very fact that it was the patriciate, the cultivated class, it exercised a preponderating influence over the manners and customs and everything which constituted the life of the nation. Even before the conquest, the sympathies of the patrician Gauls were directed towards Rome; and they willingly became Roman. Cæsar heaped favours upon them and flattered their vanity.

Religion, in spite of the similarities we have just mentioned, might have proved an obstacle to the Romanisation of Gaul; but, as we have seen, the religion of the Druids was a religion of caste, of the patrician caste, in fact, and the patricians became Romans.

There remains the language. The love which all modern nations have for their own tongue did not exist in ancient times, at all events among peoples who had no literary past. Writing had only been known in Gaul for a short time, the Greek alphabet was used, and then only by a very small minority. To-day we cling to our own language as we cling to life itself, because it represents a magnificent mass of masterpieces created by the spirit of our nation, created by our own spirit, and is for us almost like the air we breathe. Nothing of the kind existed for the Gauls in the time of Cæsar, when Vercingetorix had the inscriptions round his image on coins inscribed in Latin.

Language was only a means of communication between men, and of all the various forms it had taken, the simplest, the most widespread and most useful appeared the best.

.   .   .   .

Augustus, the successor of Cæsar, divided Gaul into four provinces—the Narbonnaise, Aquitainia, and Celtic and Belgic Gaul.

The Narbonnaise included the old Roman province, Transalpine Gaul, to which some neighbouring districts, such as those of the Allobroges, the Volcæ and the Helvii, had been added. It was roughly bounded by the Mediterranean, the Pyrenees, Haute Garonne and the Cevennes, by that part of the Rhone

125

which runs east and west and, lastly, by the Alps. In the first century A.D. Pliny the Elder describes the Narbonnaise as follows : " In its flourishing civilisation, its abundance of wealth, the nature of its customs and inhabitants, the Narbonnaise is second to no other province, it is, in fact, not a province at all, it is Italy."

Aquitainia extended from the Pyrenees to the Loire and included the Pictones (Poitou) and the Bituriges (Berry). It was the most Latin of the provinces after the Narbonnaise, and enjoyed the happiest fate, as it was furthest removed from the seat of the German invasions. In the fifth century, Salvienus described it as " covered with vineyards, studded with flowery meadows, rich in abundant harvests, happy in its fruitful orchards, its woods with their shady groves, its rivers breathing freshness—a veritable paradise."

Celtic Gaul or the Lyonnaise extended between the Loire and the Atlantic and was separated from Belgic Gaul by the Marne. It included the old Armorican federation, the Carnutes, the Senones and the Empire of the Aedui. Lastly, Belgic Gaul, between the Marne, the Somme, the Channel and the Rhine, was inhabited by the great, rough and warlike nation of the Belgæ.

The three provinces of the long-haired Gauls, the Belgic and Celtic territory and Aquitainia, were as a rule grouped under the administration of the same Governor, a great personage, some-times even a member of the Imperial family, Agrippa, Drusus, Tiberius or Germanicus.

The old leagues and federations disappeared, there were no longer suzeraine nations and client nations. Gaul became a union of peoples independent of one another, which the Romans called " cities."

The word " city " was applied, not only to the most important town in the district, but also to the whole of the territory which formed a living whole, with its capital as the gathering place for the various manifestations of the life of the community; and in this respect the constitution of the old Gauls maintained its original character and gained the upper hand over the Græco-Latin type of city. The town, the " chief place," made its power felt throughout the whole city, in the towns, boroughs,

126

villages, backwaters, and country estates, which were governed by it, though they on their side carried on the administration of the town.

Autun, for instance, was the capital of the Aedui, and had as its satelites Nevers, Châlon, Mâcon, Beaune and Bourbon and a number of villages and villas. The country folk at their work, the foresters in their shady woods, were active members of the " city," enjoying equal rights with the artisans of Autun at their stalls and the shopkeepers in their shops. In fact, the rural population had most influence in the State; in order to be a member of the curia, which had jurisdiction over public affairs, a man had to possess at least twenty-five acres. The " city " burghers consisted of landed proprietors.

Imagine one of the departments of France inhabited by a Gallic people, one of the old peoples of independent Gaul, with a capital, some towns of secondary importance, several *pagi*, territorial groups from which the *pays* of France were developed, a certain number of villages, the *vici* and numberless country estates, each one ruled by its master, who lived in his *villa*, and constituting a separate social cell. Such, after the Roman conquest, and for eight or nine hundred years afterwards, were the essential elements of social life in Gaul until the time of the Carlovingians.

As to the name which was given to the " city," the *processus* varied. Sometimes the people gave their own name to the town —the Parisii, for instance, christened Lutetia. This was most frequently the case. Sometimes, on the other hand, the town gave its name to the people. From their capital, Vienne, the Allobroges were called *Viennenses*, the Viennois.

And just as each " city " had its capital, so Gaul as a whole was to have hers, which hitherto she had never possessed. In 43 B.C. Lucius Munatius Plancus, one of Cæsar's lieutenants, traced at the confluence of the Rhone and the Saône, on the hill of Fourvières, the boundaries of a town, in which he settled some of his veterans, who were joined by colonists from the Narbonnaise. The position was happily chosen at this point where the two rivers met. And Lyons became not only the economic and political capital of Gaul, but, with the deification of the Emperors, her religious capital also.

Augustus carried on the policy inaugurated by his predecessor, Cæsar. He appointed as Governor of all the Gauls a prince from his own family, his son-in-law Claudius Drusus, one of the finest figures of his age.

Drusus was young and willing, endowed with a clarity of vision and activity which were reminiscent of Cæsar, but with the additional gift of nobility. He succeeded in inspiring veritable enthusiasm in the breasts of the Gauls. He understood the danger of German pressure on the Rhine, and after the massacre of some Italian merchants by the Usipites and the Tencteres, he made his first expedition against them (12 B.C.). The following year he undertook a further campaign, during which he penetrated as far as the Lippe district and reached the Weser. In the year 9 B.C. a third expedition brought him to the banks of the Elbe. He had crossed the Hercynian forest of ancient legend. The young hero died on his way back, in the heart of Germany.

The policy of Drusus was continued by Germanicus and Tiberius, but it had received a definite set-back. The young prince had at least marked his sojourn in Germany by a splendid undertaking carried to a successful issue—that canal of Drusus (*fossa Drusiana*) which diverts some of the waters of the Rhine and the marshes in its delta into the Yssel, and through the Yssel into the sea.

In the year 12 B.C. on the eve of his departure for the war in Germany, Drusus had built at the confluence of the Rhone and the Saône, at the " confluence," as it was more briefly called, an altar to the two great divinities of the day, Rome and Augustus, the high altar of that cult which was to take the place of the religion of the Druids—the worship of the deified Emperors.

It is difficult in our days to understand how anyone could adore a living person, even if he were Emperor, and render him the religious homage due to a god.

The very name of " Augustus " was a proof of the worship given. It was not the name of a man. It formed part of the Roman ritual and signified " sacred, divine." The Roman Senate bestowed it on Octavian, the heir of Cæsar, and from Octavian it was handed down to his successors.

The altar at the confluence dedicated to Rome and Augustus

128

was unveiled by Drusus in the presence of the delegates from sixty of the old Gallic peoples and was surrounded by devices representing these sixty peoples. This took place on the 1st August, 12 B.C. A regular cult was established, the high priest of which, the Primate of the Gallic Church, was called " the priest of Rome and of Augustus." From that day forward, on the same date every year, in the presence of pilgrims from every quarter of Gaul, the ceremonies of the cult were solemnly repeated.

The cult spread to all the " cities," in the capitals of which its altar was erected, with a high priest elected by the " city " and a band of clergy ordained for its ceremonies. The inscription at Narbonne ran as follows :

" The people of Narbonne have dedicated this altar to the divine Augustus and have vowed him an annual feast for ever. May this be to the honour and glory of the Emperor Cæsar, son of the divine Julius, Augustus, father of our country, sovereign pontiff, and to the honour and glory of his wife and his children, and of the Senate, the Roman people and the town of Narbonne, which dedicates itself and devotes itself for ever to the worship of his divinity."

Thus was the worship of Augustus celebrated, and was followed by the worship of Drusus, Vespasian, Marcus Aurelius and the other Emperors. The dignitaries connected with it were persons of exalted rank, members of the noblest families; their chief took precedence of the highest magistrates, and the cult was enriched by annual festivals. It was to be found, in a humbler guise, in the villages and dwellings of the poor.

This homage rendered to living men must not be regarded as sycophancy. To the ancients it seemed quite natural. Similar worship existed among the Egyptians and the Greeks. To the Iberians Sertorius and to the Lusitanians Viriathus were demi-gods.

The very nature of religion in those days led to such deification. The family *manes* were worshipped, that is to say libations were poured to dead relatives, and offerings placed on the altars consecrated to them. Every family had their *lares*, the founders of their " house." And if men became deified after their death, why not during their lifetime? It was

129

but a short step from one to the other, and if there were reason to take it, surely it would be in the case of the master of the world.

Moreover, the meaning which we apply to-day to the word " god," as representing the creator and sole ruler of the universe, was not that used by the ancients. They honoured thousands of gods, each of whom enjoyed limited power and possessed the virtues and vices of human nature. Ajax, under the walls of Troy, wounded the god Mars and made him howl in agony. A spring, a tree, a hill, each had its god; why should not Rome, the mistress of the world, have hers? " The queen of towns," said Ausonius, the poet of Bordeaux, " is Rome, the golden town, the abode of the gods." Let us also remember what to the French of the old *régime* was the person of the king, reigning by the grace of God, anointed with oil sent straight from Heaven by a dove which was the Holy Spirit, the King clad in the Church's raiment, working miraculous cures to the beat of the drum. Strangers used to say " The French worship their King." Was this very far removed from the deification of Augustus as the ancients understood it?

And do not we too place men on pedestals—the saints, to whom we render an obeisance differing but little from that paid by the ancients to their *lares* and their demi-gods, as well as to their gods. Saint Michael is an angel, but Saint Joan of Arc was a woman. They stand side by side in our churches.

Thus, if we reflect a moment, and remember above all what deification meant in the beliefs of the ancient world, we shall be the less surprised by the worship of Rome and of Augustus.

We have already mentioned the decay of the religion of the Druids at the time of the Roman conquest. Rome did not even think it necessary to fight Druidism, but merely contented herself with forbidding human sacrifice. So far were the Druids from being proscribed that their name is still to be found in the fourth century. And in their fall they even seem to have survived the priests of the Roman religion, and to have disappeared only with the rise of Christianity.

Truth to tell, the upper classes, the educated people whom, until the arrival of the Romans, the Druids had almost entirely ruled, recognised them no more, and humbling themselves,

130

they became the counsellors and priests of the common people. Fustel de Coulanges calls what survived of their teaching mere superstition. But it should perhaps be described with greater respect. This persistence of the Druids until the Frankish conquest proves the survival, with their customs, their beliefs and their familiar energy, of the old Celto-Ligurian race; it seemed to have lost its vitality, or rather pre-Christian writers no longer mentioned it. But it still lived on with all its forces intact. Pass on, Romans and Franks, you who despise it as that whereof slaves and serfs of the soil are made; pass on and salute; it will outlive you all !

We find similar testimony provided by their language. The Celtic tongue disappeared from Gaul very much more slowly than is generally supposed. The upper classes, it is true, quickly adopted the language of the conquerors, it was the language of the officials, the legislature, the tribunals, of edicts and imperial proclamations; the civil administration would allow no other. But this did not apply to the lower classes.

A proof of the importance of the Celtic language and of its persistence for many a long year is to be found in the manner in which it penetrated even into Latin itself, at all events in Gaul, and that even in the case of the most common words; from the Celtic Latin borrowed *bladum* (*blé*, corn), *alauda* (*alouette*, lark), *braccœ* (*braies*, breeches), *leuga* (*lieue*, league), *arepennis* (*arpent*, acre), *cervisia* (*cervoise*, ale), etc.

Now the French language, which, taken as a whole, is nothing but a slightly modified form of Latin, is derived, not from the language of Cicero and Virgil, the language of the imperial proclamations and edicts, of the Roman administrative bodies and deliberative assemblies, it does not even owe its origin to the influence of the native aristocrats who spoke the literary language of Roman society—the French language was derived from popular Latin, which was very different from classical Latin both in structure and vocabulary. And this popular Latin was propagated in Gaul by Christianity which, from the second century onwards, gradually established it wherever Christianity itself had triumphed.

It was by means of popular Latin that Christianity spread in Gaul and it was by the missionaries of this religion that it was taught to the masses, so that, from the very beginning, Christianity attacked the local divinities and the rustic myths, veneration for which was still taught by the descendants of the Druids, or, at all events, was handed down from generation to generation of the humble. Christianity, in combating these enemy gods, these beliefs and practices, which found a very different existence in the heart of the nation from that of the cult of Rome and of Augustus, also at the same time combated the native tongue. And with the triumph of Christianity came also the triumph of popular Latin.

As the diffusion of popular Latin in Gaul, that is to say of the French and Provençal languages, cannot be attributed to the influence of the aristocracy or of the officials, or of the laws and decrees, or of the teaching in the schools, which would certainly have been very great, an explanation has been sought in the influence of the military garrisons and the Roman colonies. A poor explanation indeed!

" The Latin people," writes Fustel de Coulanges, " never settled in Gaul. The few Romans who went there were negligible. The legions themselves were not composed of Italians." There were armies on the Rhine; the other provinces had no garrisons. There was no Latin colony in Aquitania, only one in Celtic Gaul—the city of Lyons. The new towns founded after the conquest, Autun, Clermont, etc., remained Celtic towns (C. Jullian). If these Latin garrisons and colonies were estimated at three or four per cent. of the total population of Gaul, it would be an exaggeration of the real proportion. This three or four per cent. might have exercised some influence upon the language if it had included the governors and the officials, the magistrates, the members of the aristocracy, and the schoolmasters, and not merely the common soldiers and colonials. Far from giving their language to the Gauls, the colonies and the garrisons must have been submerged by the Celtic language.

As for the merchants, their number was far too insignificant to produce such a result; moreover, the Roman merchants, like all merchants in all countries under the sun, were forced to speak the language of those with whom they had to deal—the Latin of Cicero with the upper classes, Celtic with the people.

132

It was Christianity, the religion of the people, addressed to the people, practised and spread by the people and covering everything with the flood of popular power it had created, it was Christianity which gave to France the language she speaks to-day, though it may be admitted that the garrisons and colonies may to a certain extent have paved the way.

" Gaul was a part of the Roman Empire for five hundred years," writes Fustel de Coulanges, " and, throughout that long period of time history cannot find that she made a single effort to separate herself from that Empire."

The Gauls tried to make the best of their situation. They anxiously solicited the title of Roman citizen, which secured them the protection of Roman law and guaranteed their prosperity. Augustus and Tiberius gave it sparingly, but with the Emperor Claudius it became common.

It must be remembered that until the advent of Christianity, when we speak of the " Gauls " we mean what we would now call the ruling classes, who allowed themselves to be moulded by Roman culture.

The rest of Gaul, and that the most important part, the part which constituted the nation, remained silent until the arrival of the Christian creed; it made no sign, it wrote no inscriptions, it raised no monuments, it shone neither in rhetoric nor poetry, nevertheless it was this part that counted, it alone which was of any importance ; and yet from the time of Vercingetorix to the advent of Christianity, of it alone no mention is made.

Claudius, who was born at Lyons, was the son of the popular Drusus. He was an original thinker who wrote a history of the Carthaginians and Etruscans and insisted that the master who killed his slave was guilty of murder.

He came to Gaul and granted the right of Roman citizenship to whole towns *en bloc*, and especially to Lyons, and insisted that this title bestowed upon the Gauls should not be merely honorary, but that it should confer upon them civil and political rights, the right to receive honours, *jus honorum*, and inclusion in the ranks of knighthood.

Referring to this event, Tacitus made the general, Petilius Cerialis, tell the Gauls, " You share the Empire with us, you often command the legions, you administer the provinces; between us and you there is no longer any division or barrier."

About the middle of the first century a few insurrectionary movements were fomented by certain nobles. But they came to nothing. The unfortunate insurgents possessed neither military organisation nor weapons. In 68 the rebellion of Vindex broke out. This was something of a very different nature. Nero was on the throne of Rome, and at the moment was at Naples. Caius Julius Vindex, a Roman senator and Governor of Celtic Gaul, was a Gaul by birth, a member of an illustrious race and of royal descent. He did not aim at severing Gaul from the bonds of Rome, but declared that he was outraged by the crimes of the Emperor. He wished to depose Nero in favour of Galba, the Governor of the district of Tarragon (a Roman province of Spain). Galba was well known in Gaul, and held in high esteem; he had once been Governor of Aquitania and Upper Germany. The Celts responded to the appeal of Vindex. Verginius Rufus, who was in command on the Rhine, arrived in haste with his legionaries, and Vindex was defeated in the neighbourhood of Besançon and committed suicide (April–May, 68). But the rebellion was none the less important, even more so for the history of the Roman Empire than for that of Gaul; for the Gauls had proved the power of the provinces to elect an Emperor. Moreover, in spite of the victory of the Rhine legions before Besançon, the cause of Galba triumphed; the army in Spain proclaimed him " Augustus." Nero committed suicide and Galba marched across the Narbonnaise to Rome to assume the purple. During his reign, short though it was, for he was murdered by the Prætorian Guards on the 28th of January, 69, he was able to show his gratitude to Celtic Gaul by lowering the tribute it paid to the Empire and increasing its right to Roman citizenship.

Galba was succeeded by Vespasian, Titus Flavius Vespasianus, who inaugurated the era of the Flavian Emperors—Vespasian, Titus and Domitian (69–96 A.D.). It was a period of peace, work and order. The Roman legions drove back the Germans and the Rhine cities were organised. The Gauls were able to turn their industrial gifts and love of agriculture to account; it was an epoch of material prosperity. They were only troubled for a short period under Vespasian by the revolt of Civilis, a German from Batavia, whose appeal for independence nevertheless found an echo in Gaul. Veleda, the German prophetess, inflamed the hearts of the insurgents, who seized Cologne, which had quite recently been founded by the Romans. The Druids in Gaul were aroused and harangued the people. The enthusiasm was sufficiently great for delegates from the various cities to hold an assembly at Rheims. Tacitus has described their deliberations; the conclusion reached was that it would be better not to continue the movement; and, in the circumstances, this was perhaps best. For a whole century too many vital, vigorous and well-organised elements had been weakened and stifled, or else had atrophied in inactivity. Gaul felt the German menace weighing her down. She could not longer hope to struggle against it single-handed with the diminished forces at her command. Safety and self-interest both prompted her to remain faithful to Rome. Moreover, the delegates who met at Rheims were drawn exclusively from the patrician class.

It was on .this occasion that Cerialis, the Governor of Lower Germany, made the speech to the Treviri reported by Tacitus.

His words to the Gauls were :

" The Germans are poor, you are rich. If we Romans demand military service from you, if we impose tribute, it is in order to secure you peace. . . . We have had bad Emperors and we have suffered at their hands more than you; we have had good ones and it is you who have reaped the benefit. . . . You must learn to submit to inevitable evils as you submit to the scourges of nature. Shoulder your burdens for the sake of the reward they bring you. Our city is not closed against you. We place at the service of all the benefits she confers. How often have you not been in command of our legions, governors of our provinces ? Therefore love Rome and respect her ! For what would happen, ye gods ! if she were to fall ? "

After Domitian the Imperial throne was occupied by Nerva (96–98), who was succeeded by Trajan and after him by Hadrian (117–138). It was a flourishing period for the Empire. If Gaul did not fulfil the vigorous, fertile and original destiny promised her by such leaders as Ambigatus, Bituitus and Celtillus, and for which Vercingetorix had laid down his life, at least she enjoyed peace and tranquillity. " The whole of Gaul," says the historian Josephus, " Gaul, which was neither effeminate nor degenerate, rendered willing obedience to twelve hundred Roman soldiers." Even on the Rhine the Germans ceased, for a time, to be menacing—the great *Pax Romana* mentioned by Pliny the Elder had been inaugurated, *immensa Romanæ pacis majestas* (" Natural History," XXVII. 1, 3).

The towns increased in beauty and prosperity. The geographer Pausanias describes Gaul as one of the richest, best populated and most civilised provinces of the Empire. The Emperor Hadrian himself was astonished at the zeal displayed by the Gauls in trying to transform themselves into Romans. " When the Gauls might behave in their cities in accordance with their own laws and customs, is it not astonishing to see them transforming them into Roman colonies? " were his words.

In 138 there ascended to the throne of the Empire the monarch who gave his name to the dynasty and to this golden age of Roman history—Antoninus Pius. Nîmes was the birthplace of his paternal grandfather, and the Gauls were able to salute a fellow-countryman in him. In 161 he was succeeded by his adopted son, Marcus Aurelius (161–180). A noble spirit, worthy of his predecessor, he brought all the virtues with him to the throne; and yet his reign was a period of decadence. The frontiers were menaced, the undertaking of public works slackened, the roads were neglected and the industry of Gaul decayed. Her famous red-figured pottery in which she excelled died out, and Christianity, which had taken vigorous root in Gaul, suffered the most terrible persecution. Under Marcus Aurelius, the most virtuous and wisest of the Emperors, the year 177 was marked by the horrible torture of the martyrs of Lyons.

In 178, a German tribe, the Chauci, broke through the barrier of the Rhine. By way of Cologne and Bavay they reached Tongres, pillaging, burning and massacring as they went. Didius Julianus at last succeeded in driving them back. From 180 to 193, that human monster, the Emperor Commodus, presided over the first catastrophes suffered by the Empire. After him, Septimus Severus, a provincial, an African, born in the district of Tripoli, nevertheless made an effort to renew

136

its stability and cohesion. Rough, decided and energetic, he aimed at restoring order in the vast establishment, but it was too great a task for the activities of one man. His Punic origin and his Carthaginian accent were mocked at. To deprive the senatorial oligarchy of the authority it still enjoyed, to complete the assimilation of all the imperial provinces to Italy, by depriving Rome and the Senate of their supremacy, were his main objects. It meant the destruction of the old Cæsarian conception, organised by Augustus, and the latter found a defender in the person of Clodius Albinus, who was in command of the legions in Great Britain. Albinus came and installed himself at Lyons. Severus, with the troops which had been encamped in the region of the Danube, hastened to the spot. Gaul became the theatre of the struggle.

A furious battle, in which 150,000 men were engaged, was fought at the gates of Lyons; in a hand-to-hand fight the combatants entered *pêle-mêle* into the town, which was set alight in the confusion. The beautiful city at the confluent had to be rebuilt. Severus won the victory and Albinus committed suicide. The policy of decentralisation had definitely triumphed.

Aurelius Antoninus, surnamed Caracalla, the son and successor of Severus (211–217) accentuated the policy of his father by the famous edict, the exact date of which is not known, bestowing upon all the free-born subjects of the vast Empire the title and rights of Roman citizens.

There is no need, however, to pay homage to his greatness of soul; he was merely concerned with increasing the revenues of the imperial exchequer, by making a large number of people pay the tax of five per cent. on all estates.

Caracalla, a rough and brutal soldier, who succeeded in making the barbarians respect the Rhine frontier, inherited his father's tastes and had but little sympathy for Latin civilisation. He was born at Lyons, and wore the costume of the Gauls, whence his name " Caracalla," which meant the Gallic tunic with a hood, a dress which the Emperor not only wore himself, but imposed upon his followers.

The reign of Alexander Severus (225–235) is like an oasis in the history of the period. He succeeded Heliogabalus. The Prætorians proclaimed him Emperor in his fourteenth year, and in the freshness of youth he possessed a charming nature. He was a Syrian, his mother probably being a Christian. He is credited with the idea of wishing to transfer the seat of Empire to the East. He hastened to the defence of Gaul against the Alemanni. His was a sentimental and mystic nature; he was a sort of Marcus Aurelius endowed with the charm and inexperience of youth, with a philosophy based on idealistic aspirations. The soldiers murdered this young dreamer at Mayence in 235. With him came to a close the sunny era of the Antonines, in which, nevertheless, many a cloud had obscured the horizon since the end of the second century.

Roman Gaul was formed in the first century; the second century saw the completed picture; with the third decadence had already set in.

Latin Gaul in the Second Century. In the second century Gaul was divided into nine provinces—the two Germanies (Upper and Lower), the three Alpine provinces (The Maritime Alps, the Cottian Alps and the Graian and Pennine Alps), the Narbonnaise and finally the three provinces of the long-haired Gauls (Aquitania and Celtic and Belgic Gaul). The latter, which were the most important, owing to the extent of their territory and their population, were generally called " The Three Gauls." From Lyons northwards the Latin atmosphere grew ever more rarefied; only a few towns basked in its rays amidst the surrounding deserts. Not only the Narbonnaise, but even Aquitania enjoyed a more advanced state of Latin culture. An exception must be made of the borderland of the Rhine; the charm of the country and the navigability of the beautiful river together with the necessity of keeping active watch against the German menace, making it a centre of Roman civilisation.

Even the districts in its neighbourhood had been converted to the culture of the Emperors.

The three Gauls had a common capital in Lyons, where, amid a vast concourse of people, the cult of Rome and of Augustus was celebrated. The festivals began in the month of August —the month of Augustus.

A vast space had been consecrated to the Roman divinity, a whole town round about the altar dedicated to Rome and Cæsar, though minor deities were also worshipped there. It was a veritable sacred city with temples, altars, tripods bearing the sacred fire, the various images of a hundred different gods belonging to that manifold and hospitable mythology, stones for offerings and sacrifices, houses for the priests, porticoes where the people thronged, and also, for the needs and pleasures of the masses, amphitheatres reserved for games, arenas in which gladiatorial combats took place, merchants' stalls and hot baths—huge establishments open to the people who went there to pass their leisure hours.

Here the Concilium of the three Gauls met, solemn sessions at which Gaul could make her voice heard.

The Concilium of the three Gauls sat in the temple of Augustus, and included delegates from the whole country. Sixty cities were represented in it, and it consisted of about two hundred members. Though they were primarily religious delegates, they also played a political part, sending addresses to the Emperor expressing their satisfaction with or airing their grievances against the Governors of the various provinces and their procurators, demanding the reduction of taxes, and drawing up plans of reforms to be carried out. These assemblies, instead of being subject to the Governors appointed by the Emperor, sometimes even laid down the law to them. "Behold our proconsuls," said a certain Roman senator in the days of Nero, "they are like candidates soliciting the votes of their subjects; they stand in fear of their accusations and beg for their commendation."

The head of the Concilium, the prince of the *Sacerdotes*, was a great personage, who took precedence of all others in Gaul.

Thus in addition to the religious ceremonies there were also secular attractions of all kinds—dramatic representations, fights and bloody games. As at the Olympic Games in Greece, a place was reserved for literature. A rhetorical competition in the language of Cicero, or even in that of Demosthenes, did not seem out of place between the sacrifices to the deified Emperor and the bloody gladiatorial shows. At the annual meeting of the Concilium there already existed, though in a more solemn guise, those familiar features described by the mediævalists who studied the pilgrimages, the fairs and assemblies of the twelfth century, but with this difference, that the latter never provided

139

spectacles in which unfortunate human beings were devoured by wild beasts, and that for the declamations, not always very entertaining, of the orators of Bordeaux and Autun, were substituted the " light " lays of the merry jugglers.

As a mark of his position, the Governor of a province wore the purple cloak, the imperial mantle. He had a bodyguard of lictors. He enjoyed extensive authority, including the power of life and death. To fill these offices personages of high rank were chosen, senators, and by preference the richest among them, in order that their wealth might save them from the temptation of peculation and enable them to maintain in the provinces a train worthy of the Emperor they represented.

The town in which the Governor resided was regarded as the capital of the province. And it soon assumed the aspect of it on account of the traffic, the luxury, the officials and the clients which it attracted.

The financial administration was in the hands of the commissaries or procurators of the prince (*procuratores*). A head procurator commanded them, "the procurator of the province," who was himself under the authority of the Governor. It sometimes happened that in the case of provinces of minor importance, like the three Alpine provinces, the offices of Governor and procurator were vested in the same person.

The office of procurator was exceedingly lucrative. He had in his hands the management of the public moneys, which in those days, as in many others, left a fairly large deposit behind in the coffers that had once held them. As the head of the financial administration, the procurator was cognisant of the disputes, litigation and delinquencies arising therefrom. Judge in all such matters, he tried to extend his jurisdiction in other directions, which brought him into conflict with the Governor.

Such were the most important wheels in the administration of a province, but in Roman Gaul the most essential element of it was the city.

The city was governed by a Senate, like Rome herself.

We have already seen that the Gallic cities were ruled by an assembly of the heads of clans, a feudal aristocracy; and in Roman Gaul this was left unchanged. The local aristocracy

140

continued to direct affairs. In order to have a seat in the Senate the payment of a high rate of taxation was a prerequisite.

Members of these local Senates were called " decurions."

Thus the composition of the Senate in the Gallo-Roman cities remained the same as it had been in the days of independence, but its functions were quite different, being more extensive, detailed and complicated—a regular administration, in fact. And this is one of the most important and interesting points in connection with this transformation. It is not sufficient to change the name, or even the dress of the members of an assembly in order to endow them with a new character, fresh gifts and a different understanding of the requirements of social life and the means of meeting them. What did these gatherings of " senators " in the heart of a people mean in the time of Vercingetorix?—a reunion of feudal lords, each one of whom governed his own territory in accordance with the manners and customs peculiar to it, but met with the rest in order to discuss the common interests of the whole people. The Romans intervened and destroyed this feudal organisation, these customary rights and these local authorities, and thereupon invited these same feudal lords, or their sons and grandsons, henceforward called " decurions," to administer the same people henceforward called a " city." Society had been levelled. It was no longer the patron who ruled, but money. The feudal lords were transformed into financiers and administrators. But the poor were no longer dependent on anybody. In their inexperience they ran the cities into debt and soon it was necessary to appoint curators over them.

The office of decurion was unpaid as had been that of the Celtic senators, though the latter were compensated by the feudal organisation of which they were the heads and by the legitimate profits they derived from their position.

And here it would be well to repeat the very true observation made by that great historian Jacques Flach, that under the letter of the laws, which are not always in accordance with the life of the people to whom they are supposed to apply, we should try to discover the real life and customs of the community. There is legislative history, which is abstract and theoretic,

141

and there is the history which brings to light facts as they actually existed.

It was easy for the Romans, by one sovereign edict, to suppress the organisation they had found in Gaul, to decree the destruction of the various social classes, to establish an equal division of property which gave the death blow to the feudal form of society, and to suppress the various rights enjoyed by the aristocracy; but it was only very slowly that these reforms could become active realities in face of existing manners and customs. Just imagine the state of Gaul with its deeply-rooted social institutions as opposed to the administrative machinery, so rudimentary on the whole, at the disposal of Rome. The administration of the cities was in the hands of the old aristocracy, who did all in their power to continue a state of affairs upholding traditions which were of benefit to themselves; nevertheless, in the long run, the reforms decreed by Rome were put into practice. How was this brought about? The responsibilities of the senators, which in the early system were compensated by the very conditions under which feudal patronage was exercised, were little by little deprived of their privileges, so much so that from the second century onwards the office of decurion became a burden to those who were honoured with the title. Laws had to be made to compel those concerned to accept the offices thrust upon them. It was even found necessary to prosecute and hunt down the fugitives. Camille Jullian very rightly says that the Roman organisation in Gaul confused the terms " political senate " and " social class." It was a continuation of the old state of affairs, but the useful privileges appertaining to this class of society before the conquest and which made this confusion legitimate having disappeared, uneasiness became more and more acutely felt.

The responsibilities of the *curia* in the Gallic cities weighed heavily upon those who composed it. The decurions were responsible for the collection of taxes; they had to see to the victualling of the town, provide festivals for the people out of their own pockets, and undertake public works, also frequently at their own expense; and so heavy were these burdens that those of them who had been ruined in the service of the city had to be granted alimony by law. In return the decurions were

142

covered with honours—mere hot air; and they took precedence at the spectacles and public banquets.

The Gallic *curiæ*, that is to say, the assemblies of the decurions in the various cities, were thus recruited from one social class, like the old Gallic Senates, and were of the same status. The office was conferred for life and was hereditary. In theory, the Senate of the city was renewed every five years, but the operation was limited to the addition of new members to fill the gaps.

One of the results of the innovations was the strengthening of the landed aristocracy. Another was the formation of a middle class, a moneyed class, and by this is meant not only bankers, but agents for agricultural or industrial products, transport contractors and slave merchants. The power of money began to rival that of land and was destined to increase. The bourgeoisie made their appearance and the liberal professions, at least in some of the large towns, writers, artists, doctors and engineers, exalted it with their brilliance.

Thus the Gallic *curiæ* were assemblies similar to the Senate at Rome. Like the latter they had at their command the organs of the executive—the two duumvirs, the successors of the old vergobrets. The duumvirs were to the Gallic cities what the consuls were to Rome.

To the office of the duumvirs, also unpaid, though the appointment was for one year only, the same remarks apply as to the curial office; it gradually became more and more onerous and for the same reasons. The Antonines issued a decree which ran :

" If any man appointed to a magistracy take to flight he shall be pursued, and if he be not found, he shall be deprived of his fortune, which shall be given to him who is appointed duumvir in his stead; if he be found, his punishment shall be to bear the burden of the duumvirate for two whole years."

And thus an organisation of society was reached which seemed extravagant. But at the beginning it was not so. Nevertheless a clear example is here to be found of that fatal distortion of sometimes exceedingly wise institutions, when the letter of the law remains immutable in the midst of social and economic conditions which are in process of transformation, resulting at

143

last in the most grievous though occasionally most comic discord.

The duumvirs were elected by the assembly of decurions. They were, like the consuls, magistrates with judicial powers, though not extending to the High Court, which was in the hands of the representatives of the Emperor. Like the consuls, the duumvirs sat on curule chairs, clad in embroidered togas and a red-bordered tunic. They were accompanied by lictors with fasces, but without the axe denoting supreme power. In order to increase the prestige of the duumvirate, the Emperors sometimes accepted the office, exercising it by means of a representative.

Under the command of the duumvirs were placed the ædiles and the quæstors. The latter were financial agents.

To the ædiles was entrusted the upkeep of the roads, the public monuments, the baths and the markets. They had to arrange the distribution of corn and presided over the organisation of the games and public festivals. The ædiles were more important personages than the quæstors, and were associated with the duumvirs in the administration of the city in such a way as to form with the latter a college of four magistrates.

The financial resources of the Gallic cities consisted in the revenues belonging to them, the common property of the old peoples which the Romans had left untouched. In addition there were donations, legacies left by rich citizens and the forced largesse of the decurions, the duumvirs and the ædiles.

The proceeds from taxation went into the coffers of the procurators; they belonged to the State. These taxes were of various kinds—the capitation tax, a personal tax, similar to the poll-tax of later days; the *chrysargyrum*, which may be compared with the modern tax on turnover; the legacy duty; a tax on sales and markets; market tolls, the salt monopoly, payment in kind for the army, and the obligation to billet soldiers and officials on their journeys, and finally all the impositions by means of which the taxpayer was made to pay for the upkeep of the roads and bridges. These taxes were still in existence in the Middle Ages.

The weight of these various taxes does not seem to have been crushing. They were not even increased under those

Emperors who spent incalculable sums in ostentation and display. The heads of the Empire found it more expedient from time to time to cut the throats of a few rich persons and confiscate their goods.

Like a fascinating mirage of the past the picture of the Gallo-Roman towns charms our imagination. The fine ruins they have left, the *Maison Carrée* at Nîmes, the arenas at Arles, the temple at Vienne, the arch called after Tiberius at Orange, the Porte-noire at Treves, and the baths at Lutetia bring to our minds the shining image of a civilisation stamped with the beauty of Greece, but grander and more powerful. In addition there were the magnificent roads, so indestructible that to this day they still form an essential part of the French system of communication.

The Towns.

The Gallo-Roman towns had a forum. Those which were built on a navigable river or by the sea placed it on the quay, the others in the centre of the city, a vast and noisy square out of which the principal roads radiated. It was adorned with statues, including, as a rule, an image of the Emperor, such as that which stood in the forum of Paris. The forum was surrounded by buildings and porticoes. The basilica was built in its neighbourhood, as well as the public prison and *horreum,* as the municipal granary was called in which the reserves of corn were stored.

The basilica (from the Greek βασιλεύς, king) was the most important and for us the most interesting of all the buildings.

The Gallo-Roman basilica was a large building, rectangular in shape, supported by colonnades and entered by a portico. Inside was a huge well-lighted and airy hall, which occupied almost the entire edifice. At the sides there were occasionally small semi-circular apses, somewhat resembling the side-chapels in Romanesque churches. All round the hall on the first floor, or at all events on either side, ran a gallery, from which a full view could be obtained of the whole building.

The basilica was the place in which business was transacted, where public questions were discussed, and votes canvassed, as in the forum itself. At the end of the basilica was the court in which sat the duumvirs, the prætor or, in the capitals, the Governor himself. The merchants had their counters in the

145

apses at the side, and, at appointed hours the nave was used as a stock exchange. It was in the basilica that the decurions met in their curia. A *tabularium,* a building in which the archives were kept, frequently adjoined it.

The Gallo-Roman basilicas are of peculiar interest to us because they were afterwards used by the Christians for their meetings and the celebration of the divine sacrifice. It is easy to understand that the early Christians preferred them to the temples consecrated to idols. Thus at first churches were also used by the Christians as meeting places. Out of the basilicas the Romanesque churches were developed, and from the latter the Gothic churches. And this explains why no Gallo-Roman basilica has survived. The Christians transformed them as their religion developed, and in accordance with the demands of a new style of architecture.

The temples consecrated to the gods were copies of Greek architecture, but mere Roman imitations, the work of clever and attentive pupils, who had good examples to go by, but lacking the delicate mastery of their model, and the fire and life of original work.

From the second half of the second century there was a marked tendency to erect buildings of vast dimensions. The walls were enormously thick, some even measuring thirty feet in width. From the reign of Hadrian especially buildings reached grandiose proportions constructed according to plan, and were decorated in a style very far removed from classic simplicity. Thermæ and amphitheatres assumed formidable dimensions. In the Middle Ages a vast concourse of people could assemble in the arenas at Nîmes, which contained a belfried monastery and chapel—a small town within the town, living an independent existence, with peculiar privileges. The inhabitants of it were called " the knights of the Arenas."

In the thermæ, or public baths, people went to bathe in large parties, spending many hours in them talking and hearing the news of the day. They consisted of a succession of sweating-rooms, basins and chambers of varying temperature—the *tepidarium* in which a gentle heat prevailed modified by a *piscina* of tepid water; the *caldarium,* which was so hot that if the limbs were moved at all rapidly they felt as though they

146

were being burnt; and in addition rooms for games and gymnastics, porticoes, courts, terraces and gardens. The halls were decorated with paintings or mosaics; and in the porticoes there were statues. In these haunts of pleasure part of the town found the most agreeable amusements. Many a pleasant hour was spent there of which an echo is found even in epitaphs of the dead. And in watering-places these thermæ, in all their varied luxury, enjoyed an even greater importance; for the Romans were familiar with the great French watering-places— Mont-Doré, Vichy, Luchon, Aix-en-Savoie, Neris, Luxeuil, Royat, Chaudesaigues, Dax, Bagnères and the three Bourbons, Bourbon-l'Archambaut, Bourbon-Lancy and Bourbon-les-Bains. Moreover, following the example of the Gauls, the Romans learnt to appreciate their curative properties, which they continued to attribute to the protective deity of the spring. The thermæ, which possessed healing waters, also assumed a religious character. Baths and a temple would be found side by side, and the votive offerings discoveied there bore witness to the ardour of the cult.

Entry to the thermæ was open to the public and on certain days it was free.

Together with the thermæ, the most important buildings in the town were the arenas and theatres, huge edifices arranged to hold large crowds of people; for the spectacles were free. Everybody was granted admittance, even the slaves.

The cities devoted large sums to them, and rich private citizens made them the object of their munificence. The theatres must not be confused with the arenas—the Paris theatre occupied the site of the present Lycée Saint-Louis, and the foundations of it have been discovered. The building consisted chiefly of a large semi-circle, open to the sky, with graduated tiers of seats. An open semi-circular space between the lowest row of seats and the stage was called the orchestra. The stage, shut in at the back by a high wall calculated to arrest and reverberate the voice of the actors, naturally faced the seats. Adjoining the amphitheatre and the stage were porticoes where the spectators could walk about and chat before the opening of the spectacle and between the acts, or where they could take refuge in case of rain. On each side of the stage, like a sort

147

of proscenium, boxes were built above the vaulted corridors leading to the orchestra. It was in these that important personages were seated, just as they are in our own day. The exterior of these buildings was very simple, almost bare. The only ornament consisted of pilasters or colonnades; but inside were countless statues and altars forming a most animated scheme of decoration.

The Paris arenas, so happily reconstructed in the Rue Monge, were even vaster. They were nevertheless only of modest dimensions, like those of Lillebonne, Lisieux and Valognes, compared with the great arenas of the south. They were oval enclosures, and the arenas were protected, for a very good reason, by strong barriers. The tiers of seats were built up the side of Mount Sainte-Geneviève. The semicircle facing them had no seats, and was reserved for various shows, triumphal ceremonies, pantomimes and processions.

The site was happily chosen. From the tiers of seats the view must have stretched over the town, which as yet knew nothing of sky-scrapers, towards the verdant plain; it is true that the great awning, with which the arenas were probably covered, must have hidden the landscape.

In these imposing edifices all manner of spectacles, for the most part repugnant enough, used to be given—gladiatorial shows, in which the defeated combatant was put to death, unless the mob chose to give him his life. The victors received crowns and large sums of money, like our own boxers, who console themselves for not being rewarded with crowns by receiving even larger sums of money. As the gladiators, whose bodies were too well protected by armour, did not shed enough blood, criminals condemned to death were also kept for these exhibitions, and, under the eyes of the besotted crowd, delivered over to the beasts. In the brilliant second century, Christians were even dragged to the arenas. The panting mob watched the red blood flow, and the limbs of the victims writhe in an agony of terror, pain and death. What a charming amusement !

" They make a game of watching men torn to pieces," writes Salvienus, " whilst the circus re-echoes the shouts of joy given by the assembled populace, applauding the ferocity of the bears and lions.

" In order to procure these beasts, no forest is left unsearched; the Alps raise their peaks to the clouds, the valleys are buried in snow; but nothing can stop our hunters. There is no country in the world too remote for the search for wild beasts, for the citizens must be provided with festivals at which they may taste at their ease the pleasure of seeing these animals make a quarry of men and devour their entrails."

And this was all that the imagination of several centuries of Latin civilisation was able to devise for the raising of the masses, for their amusement and recreation from their daily toil. The rich were given the phrases of the orators, the nonsense of the sophists, the laborious compositions of the versifiers. Truly Latin civilisation in Gaul was a fine thing! And to think that it has been asserted, as is even still asserted, that French culture grew out of this!

The streets of the towns were narrow, the monuments crowded together. The principal artery was a continuation of the road, which joined district to district in the countryside—the high streets of the modern French towns, with which we have already met in the Celtic towns. Except for the forum, which was the centre of public life, there were no pleasure grounds or walks. Nothing was done to embellish the Gallo-Roman towns by means of open spaces, symmetrical buildings, vistas or parks. All such ideas—and this has not been sufficiently noticed—came into being only with the Bourbons—the Place Royale (Place des Vosges) in Paris marks an era; it was built at the instigation of Henry IV, and was framed by palaces and houses of harmonious outline and colour, so that the whole presented a pleasing aspect. Then, too, for the first time, a space was set aside in the town for the health, pleasure and recreation of the citizens. Monuments, it is true, were not lacking in the Gallo-Roman towns, and of the most ornate description, decorated with statues, pilasters, cornices, friezes and pediments; but they were never grouped into a decorative whole. Each edifice was built on its own account, for the utilitarian or moral purpose which had inspired it—the altars of the neighbourhood, fountains adorned with syrens, Tritons and other divinities with flowing beards ending in fishes' tails, statues of Emperors or of tutelary deities, altars consecrated to the local genii, some under pent-

149

houses, others under porticoes or the arches of a colonnade, some in niches, others fastened to the walls of the houses, protected against pollution by the figures of two serpents, which kept guard over them just as police notices do in modern towns.

The shops and the various trades all had their respective quarters, just as they had in the Middle Ages; here were the sandal-makers, yonder the tinsmiths and the metal-workers, further on again the butchers and potters. In Paris the potters were congregated together on the slope of Mount Sainte-Geneviève, which they had riddled with numberless holes. It looked like a giant rabbit warren. These were the pits from which they dug the clay necessary for their work, grey clay or red clay. Both kinds were to be found there. The Parisian potters had succeeded in entering into competition with their fellow workers in Auvergne, and used to send their " vessels," often decorated with figures, as far as Rome. Their table-ware in glazed and figured pottery had no rival; but here again originality was lacking—the models came from Italy.

The shops were numerous and occupied the ground floor of the houses looking on to the street. Wine merchants tried to secure shops at the corner of two streets, or in the squares or the forum; the Gallo-Romans were already acquainted with the " pub " at the corner. They not only retailed wine and ale, but also olives, oil, pickles and dried vegetables stored in large terracotta jars fitted on to the counters. Small covered stoves kept their alcoholic and spiced drinks hot.

The houses of the rich proved the luxury and wealth of the day, with their roofs of glazed tiles or gilt metal, their porticoes so designed that one side was in the sun whilst the other was in the shade, their marble or porphyry colonnades, their airy vestibules, cooled by a basin of water or a fountain, their central heating, the hot air being distributed by means of cleverly arranged stoves and pipes. The halls were decorated with pictures, mosaics and statues, and contained sardonyx tables, rare pieces of furniture beautifully carved, fashionable ornaments, bronzes, china and glass.

These works of art were not original productions any more than were those which decorated the temples and public buildings in Gaul. The beautiful marbles which have been found in France came from Italy. With the example of America before us to prove how difficult if not impossible it is for a great people to produce an art of their own, when they are not natives of the soil but colonials, it will the more readily be understood how it was even more difficult for the Gauls of the second century to produce anything bearing the mark of their own genius.

Nevertheless in their sumptuous abodes the richest of the Gauls led a magnificent existence; some of them even had companies of comedians and ballet dancers in their service, for whom a stage was built at the end of the vestibule.

But all this luxury was at the expense of a slave population, which included the majority of the people, a fact which should not be forgotten by the apologists of that life of antiquity which in Gaul no longer even bore its old fruit—the terrible basis of that incomparable art and literature of Greece (that miracle of Greece extolled by Renan) and in Rome of a military and administrative grandeur such as has never been seen again.

In the middle class which was gradually being formed—as yet a comparatively small class—a pleasant family life did indeed exist, a centre of gentle radiance and of the culture of those mediocre but solid virtues which thrive on the common round of everyday life; but it would be vain to expect to find in it any idealism or enthusiasm, any exaltation of high enterprise or aspiration towards the beauty which elevates and which alone, in the blind alley of civilisation into which he has wandered, can enable man still to live a life worth living.

Private possessors of large fortunes spent them in the construction of arenas for gladiatorial shows and the slaughter of Christians, or temples dedicated to an uninspired worship of Cæsar; or more usefully to the provision of public baths for the health and pleasure of the people and the building of splendid aqueducts by means of which drinking water was conveyed to the towns.

According to Camille Jullian, it was not until the best period of the Middle Ages in France, the twelfth and thirteenth centuries, that such a fever for building broke out as that which devoured the Gallo-Romans of the second and third centuries; but in the latter the spirit of charity was lacking. There were none

151

of those wonderful works of the Middle Ages in which the soul of a generous nation palpitated, and the fervour of faith merged into devoted activity. But there were banquets worthy of Luernus and Bituitus, free baths for the refreshment of the citizens in their lesiure hours—the distribution of corn, against which, however, Jullian places a mark of interrogation—and above all the blood-stained sand of the arenas, *panem et circenses!*

As may well be supposed, luxurious dwellings were the exception and not the rule. Most places could not boast of any, and even in the most beautiful towns there were numberless hovels, legacies from the past, the old beehives with their thatched roofs and floors of beaten earth. The shops were of wood or pisé, and there were also strange and outlandish erections inspired by visitors from the East. And it must not be supposed that these various dwellings were built in separate quarters for the upper and lower classes, like the eighth and twelfth arrondissements in Paris, the Grenelle and the Ménilmontant quarters. Primitive huts stood side by side with the most sumptuous buildings.

The towns were, as a rule, well kept, and the cleanliness of the Gauls was proverbial.

Though free from the perpetual bustle and uproar which constitutes the charm of modern towns, the Gallo-Roman towns were never quiet. There were the various cries of the street-vendors with their baskets to which the rattle of the scrap-iron carts and the hoots of the motors have alone put a stop in our own day—divers loud and strident cries, some of them already set to music. There was the din of the flaming forges, with the hammers falling in cadence on to the sounding anvil, and of the carpenters' benches, the town criers mingling with the lowing of the oxen and cows standing in rows on the market-place or going along the streets, which they filled with greenish dung. And in the bird-fanciers' shops the birds sang in their cages.

The women were free to come and go, and kept shops. The sale of perfumes was their speciality. The shrill nasal voices of these costermongers were everywhere to be heard. More generous than Louis XIV, the Roman Governors allowed them

152

to carry on the trade of barbers, barbers for men, of course. There were no women lawyers as yet, though there were women doctors.

The Gallo-Romans of the towns gave up wearing their brilliantly coloured clothes, their cloaks with bright stripes of red and light blue, which imparted such life and gaiety, the gaiety of youth, to their national dress in the days of independence. The colours they now wore were all in one scale, ranging from white to brown, through the various shades of grey, yellow ochre and burnt sienna. They kept their breeches or trousers, their woollen tunics or coats and the hooded cloak, the caracalla, which was adopted by one of the Emperors and provided him with his surname, just as later on Hugh Capet was called after the cape. The colours of the caracalla, of a dark russet shade, was simply that of wool in its natural state.

The Governors and their lieutenants, carried about in their litters, wore their deep red togas in public; the decurions were clad in white togas with red borders. A few of the Gauls wore the tunic, and a struggle arose between Gallic and Latin fashions, in which the former won the day even in Italy.

The adoption of Gallic fashions by the Romans gave a great impetus to the cloth trade in France, which, together with pottery, became the trade *par excellence* of Gaul. " It is Gaul that clothes me," exclaimed Martial. The cloth of Artois and Hainault, of Champagne and Normandy, of Rheims and Elbeuf, was already famous; but Flanders, which was destined to become the leading cloth-making industry of the world, still lived outside the pale of civilisation, sombre and wild in the depths of her forests.

With the help of the details just given the aspect of Paris in the second century before our era can easily be reconstructed. The banks of the Seine were bordered by forests and marshes, the latter more especially the left bank. In the plain dominated by Montmartre the water stood stagnant, as the stream of Ménilmontant drained it too slowly. The Bois de Boulogne was a real forest. There was a villa at Passy, another at Neuilly. The Bièvre ran clear and bubbling through a forest of reeds.

The town of Paris was still chiefly concentrated in the island of the City, where numerous houses and a few fine buildings, especially the temple of Jupiter on the actual site of the present cathedral close, had replaced the old Gallic huts. The island was joined to the left bank by the Petit Pont and traversed by a broad street, which reached the right bank by means of the Grand Pont, and was an integral part of the great high road joining the northern to the southern districts of Gaul. The Island of the City was already a sacred spot in which the gods of Gaul and the gods of Rome hob-nobbed together; Esus and his cranes, Cernunos and his horns, did not frighten away Castor and Pollux in their temple smiling down upon them from their starry height.

On the left bank, ascending the slope of the Mont de Lutèce (Colline Sainte Geneviève) was a conglomeration of buildings of all kinds, public buildings, rather than an inhabited quarter; with the exception of the houses and workshops of the potters, who had made the ground of the hill look like a sieve. (These are the conclusions of the Comte de Caylus which have recently been attacked by Monsieur de Pachtere.)

On this left bank was also the forum of Paris, which occupied the space between the Boulevard du Palais and the Rue de la Cité of the present day; the theatre was on the site of the Lycée Saint Louis, and the arenas in their present position. The Emperor Julian inhabited the *Palais de Justice* which in a changed shape afterwards formed the residence of the old kings of France. A market stood on the site of the Rue Soufflot; and finally a large building with strong arches, the remains of which may still be found in the Rue Cluny, seems to have been a gathering place where the members of the watermen's guild, or patrician boatmen of Paris, used to discuss their interests and organise the festivals of their corporation. The watermen, who provided the town of Paris with its coat-of-arms, can apparently be traced to the days of independence.

The dimensions of the arenas and the theatre bear witness to the importance of the town at that early date, and the residence there of the Emperor Julian, who describes it so charmingly, together with the industry of its sailors and potters, combined to give it a brilliant reputation.

" I had taken up my winter quarters in my beloved Lutetia,"

writes the Emperor Julian, " for that is what the Celts call the little town of the Parisii. You reach it from either side by a wooden bridge. The volume of the river varies but little and is nearly always the same at every season."

This uniformity in the low-water mark of the Seine was due to the large number of forests covering the valley. Since then the deforestation has been responsible for frequent and disquieting floods.

" The water of the river," continues Julian, " is agreeable to look upon and excellent to drink." Alas, poor waters of the Seine ! Julian observes that " shut up on an island, the inhabitants could get no other water but that of the river."

" The winter is mild, which the Parisii attribute to the vicinity of the Atlantic and the warm effluvia borne by the breeze, for it seems," says Julian, " that the water of the sea is hotter than fresh-water."

" The country is covered with good vines, and also fig-trees, which they take care to wrap round with straw or some other covering to protect them against bad weather."

" This year (358)," he continues, " the winter was exceptionally hard and the river was covered with ice. You know," he said, addressing the inhabitants of Antioch, " you know the blocks of marble which come from the quarries of Phrygia. I cannot give you a better description of the enormous blocks of ice which float on the water, one after the other without ceasing, almost forming a bridge from one bank to the other. The inhabitants protect themselves against the cold in their houses by means of stoves."

Thus in the second and third centuries everything within the walls of the Gallic towns was Romanised in appearance at least. The decorations of the cities drew their inspiration from mythology, poetry and Greek and Roman history. The statues, the friezes, the bas-reliefs, the mosaics, the paintings— the subject matter of them all were Greek legends, Roman gods or Roman emperors. The forum of Besançon was decorated with statues of Scipio and Pompey; the Arverni claimed descent from Priam, the Remi from Remus, placing at the entrance gate to their town the figure of the she-wolf suckling the twins of the god Mars and the vestal virgin Sylvia. From the medley of Homer and Virgil the materials were drawn supplying most of the iconography of the towns.

And this was not surprising. For we have only to remember Louis XIV, who was thoroughly French in taste and sentiment, and to look at the decorations of Versailles. Are there any signs there of the past of France of which the great king was the magnificent representative? Where is there a picture of Bertrand du Guesclin or of Joan of Arc or the Chevalier Bayard; where is there an echo of the old French epic legends, of Rolando, Guillaume d'Orange, the Round Table and the four sons of Aymon? . . . Nowhere. But Apollo smiles at Venus, Pluto carries off Persephone, Polyphemus hurls his great stones and wanton Naiads are chased by Tritons. When Le Brun wanted to paint Louis XIV he made the absurd suggestion that he should depict him in the guise of Hercules, but the king had enough good sense to put a veto on this ridiculous notion. But after this can we be surprised that the Gallo-Romans should have forgotten Luernus and Bituitus, and old Ambigatus and his nephews crossing Europe with their terrifying train in order, like fantastic precursors of the Crusaders, to found a kingdom in the East? To this oblivion of everything glorious in the past of Gaul the teaching in the schools and the diffusion of Latin letters contributed in no small measure.

The glory shed by Roman civilisation upon the towns of Gaul aroused feelings of admiration which led them to **Belles Lettres.** the culture of letters and the opening of schools held in high honour.

And indeed the Gallic aristocracy were successful in their zeal to assimilate the civilisation of the conquerors, and from the second century onwards produced famous writers who wrote in the Latin tongue.

The great schools of Marseilles and Autun were the first to set a shining example, those of Marseilles being renowned for their Greek learning. Autun became the university town *par excellence*, whilst second in importance was Toulouse, called by Martial " the town of Minerva." The three brothers of the Emperor Constantine were educated there. Rheims also had a brilliant reputation for the culture of letters. The rhetorician Fronto saluted it as the Athens of Gaul. The schools of Treves

156

produced celebrated masters—Harmonius, who was admired as far as the East as a commentator on Homer. Saint Jerome went there to study.

The authors who were most studied were Homer and Virgil. On the verses of Homer children took their first steps in Greek. Among the educated classes Horace stood second in favour to Virgil, and was followed by Menander and Terence. But Lucan soon equalled them and surpassed them all, except Virgil, in popularity. The prose writers were not appreciated so much.

The cult of Aristotle had not yet been inaugurated. Plato was hailed as the god of philosophy, though neither his work, nor, indeed, that of any other philosopher, was very much studied. Historians took Sallust as their model, without copying him, and orators of necessity imitated Cicero. That was their main object—phraseology, the cult of the right word for its own sake. What they said had to be well said. And what was meant by " well said "?   It meant to be said as others had said it before.

M. Bloch has written an admirable passage on this subject :

" There was but little study of either science, philosophy or even law; but rhetoric remained.   A text to be commented upon and a theme to be developed, this was all the end of education.   Oratory, once the virile art of ancient society, had become an empty and frivolous toy.   It had played such a grand rôle that it seemed impossible to oust it.   But it was reduced to entirely conventional exercises, in which the main object was, under elegance of phraseology, to hide an entire absence of ideas.   This discipline, which we have not yet altogether abandoned, had its uses.   It made the mind supple and refined; but, practised for its own sake, as an end not as a means, and isolated from all serious study, it was barren and dangerous. It accustomed young men to put words before subjects and to hold the essence of less account than the form; it impoverished and stultified the mind, and if we study its effects in the most admired productions of the time, in the speeches of Himerius, the panegyrics of Eumenes, and most of the poetry of Ausonius, we realise the extent to which they were all devoid of substance and poetry and we shall not be far wrong in attributing

157

to this teaching a large proportion of the general decadence and ruin of Europe."

It was two Gauls, Plotius and Griphon, who in the first century opened in Rome the earliest schools of rhetoric, where they taught the art of apt phraseology; they had been preceded by the actor Roscius, also a Gaul, who had instructed the contemporaries of Cicero, and Cicero himself, how to use words with proper effect.

Indeed Gaul became so distinguished in the realm of oratory that she eventually furnished the Romans with their best speakers—Domitius Afer, the master of Quintilian, who placed his gift of eloquence above that of any other orator, was a native of Nîmes; Montanus came from Narbonne, Julius Africanus was born at Saintes.

Julius Africanus seems to have cultivated a singular species of eloquence. He pretended he had come in the name of his countrymen to congratulate Nero on having murdered his mother, and framed the following compliment in his honour :

" Thy Gauls, O Cæsar ! conjure thee to have the courage to bear thy good fortune."

The Gauls, moreover, seem to have furnished the Romans with " debaters " who were more vigorous, more alive and more effectual than the descendants of the Ciceronian school, if we may judge from the words which Tacitus puts into the mouth of the representative of their eloquence in his dialogue of *The Orators* :

" You seek perfection and you imagine it is a sign of health. . . . Come, come ! " exclaims the Gaul of Tacitus. " The true orator is judged by his strength, gaiety, vivacity, his wealth of words and variety of movements. Only to be in good literary health is already a sign of weakness; the advocate is not ' a man of letters,' he is a combatant."

The schools of Bordeaux, though the latest to be founded, were not the least brilliant. The town did not owe its prosperity to a Roman colony, as did Lyons, Arles or Treves. It grew spontaneously, thanks to its favoured position on the river and to the industry of its inhabitants, and its schools ended by eclipsing their rivals, for through its geographic situation it suffered less from the invasions.

Greek, at least in the second century, still occupied an important place in education. The only masters who were not Gauls were Greeks, and education even started with the study of the Greek language. Marseilles, at the beginning of the second century, possessed a university in which, of all the universities then in existence, Greek was best taught, so much so indeed that many wealthy Italians used to send their sons to study there.

And just as they produced orators, the Gallo-Roman schools also succeeded in rearing poets; but the latter did not reach their full brilliance until the fourth century in the person of Ausonius, and in the following century, in Apollonius Sidonius. It was indeed a paradox full of irony that the land which had been martyred by the divine Julius in the name of Rome should give to Rome the last Latin songs to celebrate her glory.

But here again the incurable vice, which makes this factitious literature so bloodless, was the lack of originality. It is impossible for writers to express sentiments and emotions that will arouse interest unless they draw them from the depths of their being; and they cannot experience emotions worthy of arresting attention except by striking their roots down into the deepest traditions of their race and native soil. The most celebrated of the Gallo-Roman poets was Ausonius. He was born at Bordeaux, and it was there that he wrote and taught. His masterpiece is a poem on the Moselle, and by this alone it suffices to judge Ausonius himself and the whole of the pseudo-literature of his day. They were exercises by skilful writers of Latin verse. And here we have the inevitable process of all decadence—though the word is inaccurate since there was never any ascent—literary snobbery, the worship of form for form's sake, and, in the end, what the troubadours were to call the *trobar clus*, esoteric poetry, from which the profane were excluded and of which they understood nothing, and also be it said the initiated who did not understand very much. Little verses, unworthy of Molière's Oronte, were hawked about and recited right and left, and by means of good comradeship and *savoir faire* a reputation was won by an epigram. The whole of Latin literature, which existed for hundreds of years without ever during all that period having shone with any very great

159

lustre, ended in that vapid poet, with his head lost in mist and clouds, who has been surnamed the Virgil of Toulouse.

This lamentable decay of Gallo-Roman literature, in spite of all the efforts, the intellectual gymnastics, wasted time and constant encouragement from a Government and a society enamoured of fine language, wrests from Camille Jullian a cry of beautiful and poignant regret :—

" How much better would it have been for the Gauls to have used the teaching of their own masters to convey the ideas and descriptions of their own country; their history was fair enough for this, their nature rich enough. . . . But the idea never occurred to them to preserve or to imitate the poems of the Druids and the lays of their bards, and these works died a double death, a death that knew not decadence "—killed by the Gauls themselves " traitors to their past." The phrase is Jullian's.

On a tomb in the Gallo-Roman cemetery of Lectoure the following epitaph was found :

" In the beginning I was naught and then I became somewhat, and, if I remember, it is to know that I am no longer and that for me there is naught."

These lines full of bitter scepticism, if they are not applicable to life as it should be, at least furnish a fitting conclusion to this rapid sketch of Gallo-Roman literature.

Outside the life of the towns there was the life of the country, which was the most important, and by a very long way. For Country Estates and Villas. between the furrows on the brown earth, in the valleys, on the slopes of the hills, on the confines of the deep forests, on the banks of the clear rivers and along the coasts of the restless sea, the French nation came into being.

As we have already seen, the " city " included a wide stretch of country in which the large landed proprietors formed the Senate. The villages were comparatively few; and instead of villages there were huge tracts of cultivated land developed from the great domains of the old days. Scholars have estimated that for sixty villages there were a thousand country estates. As in our own days, the majority of these villages were conglomerations of small peasant proprietors; and the rest, situated

160

along the high roads to serve the needs of travellers, consisted of groups of shops, cottages, posting-houses, inns and workmen's booths.

Nine out of ten of the villages of to-day were developed, not from the Gallo-Roman villages, but from the large estates. These seignorial properties were divided into two parts— the *villa urbana*, reserved for the master, his family, his guests and personal servants, and the *villa rustica*, where all the working machinery of the estate was to be found, together with the slaves and their overseers and the cattle.

Thus, at some distance from the master's house there were the farmsteads with their various buildings, the latter surrounded by the huts in which the slaves lived. In the middle of these huts was the *Ergastulum*, a sort of underground dungeon destined for the confinement of such of these miserable creatures against whom the master or his underlings imagined they had grounds of complaint. A glance is sufficient to realise the difference between the serfdom of later days and Gallo-Roman slavery. The serf lived in a separate dwelling in the bosom of his family, on the patch of ground to which he belonged and which he cultivated; the slaves wandered about the estate in bands, or rather in flocks, under the command of the keeper of the convict gang, who incited them to work.

The principal building of the farm was constructed round a rectangular courtyard enclosed by galleries supported by wooden columns. On the ground floor was the kitchen, the dining hall, the wash-house, the horses' stables, the cowshed and the pig-sty; on the first floor were the bedrooms above the stables, for the smell of manure was already considered exceedingly healthy; then there were the granaries and lumber-rooms.

In farms of any importance there was double stable accommodation, one set for the summer, the other for winter. They were flanked by small rooms filled with rustic odours, and inhabited by the shepherds and herdsmen. There were barns for the corn and hay, cellars for the oil, wine and winter fruits, besides the mill for grinding the corn into flour, the presses for the grapes and olives, the wheelwright's shed, and the dovecot, all of which buildings were grouped round a huge court (*cortis*), a name which was soon applied to the farm itself, and later, in

161

the fifth century, to the whole estate. As the farm continued to develop through a series of transformations, the old word, so modest in its origin, ended, after passing through all the links of the chain, by being applied to the royal Court and the Courts of Law.

The master's house was built on a pleasant site, and one from which the administration of the estate could easily be carried on. The banks of a lake or pond were often chosen, with a view over the smiling valley, and on the horizon wooded hills blue in the distance. The wooden buildings of the noble Gauls had been replaced by edifices of stone and brick, often with certain parts in marble. It was no longer the country house described by Cato the Elder and Varro. The *atrium*, with its *impluvium*, the basin built to catch the rain, was replaced by spacious galleries, numerous colonnades, some open to the air, others shut in by means of glazed partitions, and some of them supporting terraces of flowers. The portico, adorned with statues, led to the peristyle, which was paved with beautiful mosaics, many of which have been preserved to our own day. Out of the peristyle opened the reception rooms, the dining-rooms, the *diversorium* or drawing-room, arranged for all kinds of games, and sometimes a room for theatricals. The rooms reserved for intimacy were also grouped around, and everything was duplicated, so that there were winter quarters and summer quarters. And in both of them there were all the comforts which the Romans knew how to provide for their homes. The bath-rooms were heated by underground furnaces (*hypocaustes*) and there was a scent room.

The façade and the porticoes were adorned with sculpture, under the arcades there were statues, and on the walls medallions framing busts in high relief. Paintings decorated the inside walls, and among them portraits of the family were already to be found, and the badges of the high offices with which its members had been honoured.

The kitchens, which were lofty and large enough to serve as gathering places for the domestic staff, were placed outside the master's house, in a special building, an arrangement which was later also found in the seignorial mansions of the Middle Ages; whence arose the custom of carrying covered dishes to table and the expression " *mettre le couvert* " which is still used in France.

Lastly, not far from his house, the owner had built for himself the marble or granite monument, which was destined to serve as a mausoleum under the shade of beautiful trees.

The Gallo-Roman villa, like the great estate of the days of independence, formed a complete economic and political unity. Though the master had lost the feudal rights of the olden times, he still ruled a large number of people. He bore the title of senator, and exercised the functions of the office in the town. The combination of the two titles, senator and great landowner, was so frequent that the words came to be regarded as synonymous.

It is not difficult to imagine the life of these great Gallo-Roman nobles, busy in town with their public functions, and in the country directing important operations on the land, assisted by their stewards, indulging in the pleasures of the chase, receiving their guests, and according to the taste of the age, cultivating literature, the whole standing out against a background of the besotted mass of slaves, sweating, panting and crying out beneath the lash of the whip.

Some idea of the grandeur and magnificence of these Gallo-Roman domains may be gathered from the fact that the ruins of some of them, like the one at Chiragan on the Garonne (Martres-Tolosane) covered over twenty thousand square yards and that excavations have brought to light over a hundred busts and statues, admirable bas-reliefs, such as the rape of Proserpina and the labours of Hercules; and that even these represent but a small proportion of the treasures of art the place contained.

In addition to his slaves, the " senator " maintained a host of free servitors, mercenaries, parasites and retainers, the remains of the old Gallic clients. Slavery, which gave the master absolute power over his subordinates, was an easier institution for the landed proprietor to manage, and his fortune enabled him to acquire possession of large numbers of slaves.

And this brings us to another important consideration—the disappearance, or at all events the weakening, of the freeborn persons surrounding the patron. The old Gallic system of

163

clients and vassals was still a system of liberty; but under pressure of law it gave place to slavery. This was a change of the greatest importance, for it included the majority of the people. And we should like to ask the admirers of the " progress " achieved in Gaul under Roman domination whether this horrible retrogression into slavery, due to Roman law and administration, was not in itself sufficient to counterbalance the material advantages which the conquerors introduced into Gaul—better roads, stone buildings, thermæ, aqueducts, halls for shows and amusements of all kinds. The Romans may have increased the happiness of the upper classes, but to the nation as a whole they brought moral and physical degeneration, and an undermining of character and energy, the consequences of which made themselves felt all to soon.

The great landed proprietor on his estate directed the work, not only of the agricultural labourers, but also of the artisans. Hard by the groups of " cells " open to the air, the sun and the warm light of day, inhabited by the slaves who worked on the land, might be heard the buzz as from a busy hive coming from the " cells " of the artisans, also, alas ! occupied by slaves. Thus the great work of cultivating the soil had its counterpart in the production of manufactured goods. All kinds of things were made which were not all destined for the use of the patron and his family. The master used to sell the produce of his mills, his smithies, his mines, his workshops, his carpenters' benches, his brickworks, his potteries, his glass-works, his iron-works, his looms, and also his agricultural implements, just as he sold the produce from his farms and vineyards, his wine, his corn, his oil, his cattle, his smoked hams, his preserved game, his milk, his butter, his cheese and eggs.

Thus if we can conjure up in our imaginations one of these vast concerns, possessed and administered by a " senator," some of which covered an area of ten thousand acres, and supported an agricultural and artisan population of a thousand souls, we shall understand what, from the social, economic and political point of view, the " villas " which covered the whole of Gaul meant in the life of the nation.

Nevertheless, it must not be supposed that Gaul in the second century was composed entirely of large estates. There were never any of those colossal domains occupying an entire province which were to be found in Italy. Roman law, from the very fact that it put a check on the feudal sytem of clients, hindered the process of centralisation, which drove small proprietors, the weaker elements who could not protect themselves, to cling to the stronger. The development of the liberal professions, of the " commonalty " and of urban industries created small- and medium-sized estates belonging to those who could earn money. Until the end of the second century, and as long as the Roman Empire was flourishing, estates in Gaul, far from becoming amalgamated, continued to grow in numbers.

All that precedes has already enabled us to foresee the influence that Christianity was destined to exercise in Gaul and the im-

Christianity. portance it would secure. From the religion of the Druids the masses had been excluded. It is true that they were allowed to indulge in the worship of the minor local divinities, the springs, the trees, the neighbouring hills haunted by their familiar spirits; and a whole host of reciters of mythical lore, inspired healers and malevolent or benevolent witches kept alive these traditional beliefs, to which was added a vague worship of the deified dead; for it was believed that their souls could not have perished—a simple-minded religion strongly rooted in primitive thought, which survived the conquest. Whilst the upper classes burnt incense to Rome and Augustus, whilst the Druids, under the ban of the Romans, gave way before the *flamens*, the Gallic people clung to their old and deep-rooted primitive mythology, reinforced by its old wives' remedies and by the miraculous cures at the gurgling springs, at the clear fountains and the great gnarled trees, which tradition had endowed with supernatural powers.

But what could be the development, in the course of time, of this decapitated religion, bereft of priests and all superior guidance, teaching or doctrine?

We have already seen the state to which the lower classes of the nation were reduced—a state of slavery, of toil on the land, and labour in industrially exploited workshops. In isolated districts, in unknown spots, in lake-dwellings among the marshes, in the depths of the woods and along the sea coast, a by no means despicable fraction of the people still lived outside the

pale of the spurious and superficial civilising process organised by the Romans. Strabo, fifty years after Cæsar, declares that Gaul was not entirely subjected to Rome, and points out that the woods and marshes were inhabited by a population which had no industries; whilst Hirtius says that after Cæsar's victories the towns were denuded of those who fled into the depths of the country in order to escape the rule of the conqueror. As late as the fourth century Ammianus speaks of regions of Gaul which had remained inaccessible to Roman culture. And it was here that the most interesting remnants of the people were to be found, those who still preserved their strongest social instincts. And lo, Christianity appeared ! It is easy to imagine the echo it found in the hearts of the disinherited, and the support it received from them—Christianity which was born of the people, created by the people, which deified the son of a carpenter and was propagated by the apostles Peter and Andrew, James and John, who were the sons of fishermen, Christianity with its doctrine so full of humility and beauty, so stirring and generous, " Blessed are they that suffer for they are the elect of God."

By the irony of circumstances, the first evangelists had to preach the gospel to the towns; and behold, the great religion of the people swept down upon Roman society, which was leading such a pleasant existence in its luxurious palaces, learning wisdom in the schools of the rhetoricians and finding its amusement in the games in the arenas; never was a more formidable boulder flung into a pool of minnows.

Nevertheless the rise of Christianity in Gaul is shrouded in obscurity precisely on account of its popular origin. The poor did not write, they did not know how to write. And even if they had known how to write books, they would have had neither the means nor the leisure. And if they had written them, nobody would have preserved them.

It is believed that it was in the reign of Nero, about the year 63, that the first evangelists made their voice heard in Marseilles. They came from the East and spoke Greek, and the people of Marseilles were able to understand them.

It took a century or more before the doctrine spread up the Rhone and gained a footing in Vienne, and afterwards in Lyons.

166

Moreover, at first it was everywhere received with suspicion. The first missionaries had to begin by addressing themselves to the educated classes, for they understood Greek and through them the evangelists hoped to secure a more rapid spread of their gospel. One may well imagine the astonishment with which these wealthy Romanised patricians, who frequented the temples and were disciples of the sophists, received a religion so different from anything they had ever seen or heard before. The religion of the Greeks fitted into that of the Romans like a woman's hand fits into a glove of the right size, as did also the religion of the Romans into that of the Gauls. Zeus, Jupiter, Taran—Hermes, Mercury, Teutates—Ares, Mars, Esus—it was all so easy. Cæsar spoke of Mercury, Apollo, Mars, Jupiter and Minerva, and observed, " The Gauls have very much the same conception of these deities as other nations " : but the Olympus of the Christians was like nothing else in the world. What idea could be formed of a God who had no body, no passions, no human shape, a God who was one God, though he was three Persons, a God infinite and invisible although He was everywhere? It was unheard of! And then the morality which taught contempt for the good things of this world which the rich Gallo-Romans, no less than the sophists in their schools of wisdom and the rhetoricians in their schools of eloquence, were very far indeed from despising. It was the contradiction of everything they had ever believed.

Nevertheless the followers of Christ began to form themselves into humble societies which made converts round about. The first little church was founded at Marseilles, followed by the churches of Vienne and Lyons. They were organised in local and very secret conventicles, where the rites peculiar to the religion were observed and were imagined by those who did not participate in them to be something outrageous and monstrous.

The churches of Lyons and Vienne were in time joined by churches founded at Toulouse, Autun, Besançon and Treves. In the third century the churches at Rouen, Bordeaux, Paris, Bourges, Cologne and Sens came into being.

As Camille Jullian has so wisely observed, Christianity did not win the masses—the people who, as we have just seen, were so restive under the rule of Rome—or become a popular faith,

167

until she produced her martyrs whose bodies were laid to rest in tombs placed preferably along the side of the road, unless they were reverently dismembered and divided among numberless reliquaries which were venerated in every district and became " sanctuaries for the healing of disease and the protection of harvests." Thus the hundreds of local divinities worshipped by the old Celts, at last supplanted, were able to die in peace, leaving their crowds of worshippers to the new Deity in all the glory of a radiant sky blushing with the blood of the martyrs.

Christianity had no need to make any very great effort in Gaul against the worship of Rome and Augustus. The marble statues were not very firmly fixed upon their gilded altars, and the halting dithyrambs in spondees and dactyls sung by sycophantic poets were but little calculated to steady them. To make the mysterious fairies, the protecting deities and the laughing gnomes fall out of the great oaks and desert the crystal springs and the sunny slopes was, however, a very different matter.

The very true explanation given by Camille Jullian must be supplemented by another based upon language. The first evangelists, who came from the East, spoke Greek. With the advent of missionaries who spoke Latin, popular Latin, a sort of dialect, which was easily understood and to which in many places, at all events in the towns, the ears of the people were accustomed, their message raised a different response.

The persecution of the Christians began under the wisest of the Emperors, Marcus Aurelius. It is astounding that this true moralist, the author of that wonderful book, *The Meditations*, who in his outlook upon life was so nearly akin to Christianity, could possibly have unloosed such a terrible persecution. It is enough to confound the imagination, though on reflection it will appear less surprising. For Christianity not only taught new religious ideas, but its doctrines were subversive of the whole social and economic organisation of the Roman Empire, of which the Emperor was the keystone of the arch. Later on the Church modified her teaching, she connived at slavery and even practised it; but the first neophytes insisted upon an absolute and radical application of the doctrine. Thus to persons of established wealth and dignity they appeared like some sort of Socialists—and indeed they actually were Socialists, truer Socialists than those of our own day, who are not Socialists at all. They appeared in the light of anarchists with their furious anathemas against the rich, and their belief in the partition of goods and the equality of men.

The sublime story of the martyrs of Lyons has been handed down to us in an epistle which the Christian churches of Lyons and Vienne addressed to their " brethren in Asia and Phrygia," and which has been preserved for us by Eusebius. It is a unique document on account of its date, A.D. 181, and its authenticity. It describes for us the Christian community of Lyons towards the end of the second century.

It was an extraordinary mixture—a lawyer, a rich merchant from Pergamos, a doctor from Phrygia, a lady who seems to have belonged to the best Roman society, but above all members of the populace, numbers of slaves, young men and young girls of fifteen or sixteen, and the little " flock " grouped about the crook of a nonagenarian Bishop, Saint Pothinus. It is easy to imagine the impression such a hotch-potch created in the minds of a hierarchy such as was the Roman society we have described. They were convinced that in the Christian conventicles terrible things were done, and that children were sacrificed. Under torture some of the slaves confessed what they were expected to confess. Christians were arrested at Lyons and Vienne. At the command of Marcus Aurelius, those of them who were Roman citizens were beheaded. The rest were reserved for the games in the circus. Their Bishop, St. Pothinus, died before paying the extreme penalty, under the torture they inflicted upon him. Their common martyrdom was synthesised in that of a young slave who answered to the charming name of Blandine, better fitted, it would seem, for one of Perrault's fairy tales than for the martyrs' calendar. Her mistress, who was also a Christian, was afraid that she might show weakness under torture, deny her faith and bring accusations against her co-religionists. But Blandine did not falter. In the agony of torture, she constantly repeated to her executioners in a clear, calm voice : " I am a Christian, and nothing wrong is done amongst us."

She had sustained her younger companions when they were

on the point of death, as well as her little brother of sixteen. Then her own turn came. She was flogged with rods, in the Roman fashion, and then thrown to the wild beasts amid the ferocious howls of the yelling mob. The beasts mauled her severely, stained the white arena with her red blood, and then slunk away leaving her still alive. Whereupon they burnt her poor little body with red hot irons on a stove and, putting her in a net, threw her once again to the beasts—the poor little bleeding, palpitating bundle, hurled to the unchained brutes. A bull picked her up on his horns and tossed her in the air; the body fell back again. The bull snorted, bellowed and turned aside. Blandine was still alive, and kept repeating to her executioners in a voice waxing ever feebler, " I am a Christian, and nothing wrong is done amongst us."

The crowd stamped in spasms of hysteria, intoxicated by this human suffering. If any philosophers, like those in Couture's picture, chanced to have been among them, they must indeed have thought that Roman civilisation was a wonderful thing. The executioners decided to have done with this slave " rebel " by cutting off her head—a great honour for a slave; for this death was a privilege reserved for Roman citizens.

The Christians of Lyons and Vienne, in their epistle to the Phrygians, pointed the moral of the tragedy, by saying that the martyrdom of the sweet little slave girl inspired by Christ was " to show to men that what in their eyes was vile, misshapen and despicable was held in high honour in the kingdom of God ! "

Hush, hush, ye wretches ! Know ye not that ye are destroying the foundations of society !

Renan, in his sympathetic phraseology, draws the conclusion of history : " The servant Blandine proved that a revolution had been carried out. The true emancipation of the slave, emancipation through heroism, was largely her doing."

St. Blandine, pure sweet martyr, is worthy of giving her hand at the same altar to that other popular heroine who was martyred at the same age, Joan, the good Lorainian peasant girl of Domremy.

St. Irenæus succeeded St. Pothinus as Bishop of Lyons (178), appointed to the office by St. Polycarp, Bishop of Smyrna, the direct disciple of St. John the Evangelist. Irenæus was a man in the prime of life, of great intelligence and learning and of prodigious energy—a true fighter. The infant Church of Gaul found in him a leader. His evangelical activities happily coincided with the reign of Commodus, the son of Marcus Aurelius. Marcus Aurelius had been a sage; Commodus was a brute, but a brute to whom all the religions in the world, whatever their doctrines, were of one account. His reign was a mere sequence of murders and spoliation. If the death of Christians had been profitable to him, he would have had them killed; but since they were generally poor or else had given away their possessions before embracing the faith, Commodus regarded their martyrdom as devoid of interest and allowed them to preach, catechise and evangelise to their hearts' content throughout the Empire. Under his rule the Gallic Church made rapid progress.

Irenæus writes : " I was still a child, but I remember the things that happened then better than those which took place later on. I could tell the spot where the blessed Polycarp sat to speak; I remember his bearing, his way of life and his features. I could repeat the sermons he addressed to the people, how he told them of his friendship with St. John and with others who had seen the Saviour, and recalled their words; how he gave details about the Saviour, about his miracles and doctrine, which he had learnt from those who had seen the Word of Life; how he recalled it all, and how it confirmed the Scriptures ! "

Commodus died in 192 strangled by Narcissus the athlete. Septimus Severus renewed the edicts persecuting the Christians, whose progress was becoming decidedly menacing to society. Irenæus in his turn suffered martyrdom in 202. But the triumphant propaganda of the new doctrine could not be arrested. It had on its side the force of faith, the glow of youth, and the beauty of idealism, that power of idealism which is the only truly great power in the world and of which Roman society had been deprived.

Fustel de Coulanges is bound to admit that in the society of the day Christianity alone was filled with life and energy. St. Cyprian, Bishop of Carthage (249–258), was its leader. He was a native of the East, or rather of Africa. But a few years later

171

the motive force was supplied by Gaul, by the mass of the people, who had at last emerged into the light of day. At last, thou ancient stock of Celts and Ligurians, the hour had come, awaited with infinite patience, to show the world the wonderful seed thou hadst hidden in thy bosom !

The Church of Paris had her martyrs about the middle of the third century under the reign of the Emperor Decius (249–251) in the persons of St. Denis and his companions Rusticus and Eleuthereus. Truth to tell, their history is shadowed in obscurity. All that is known about them is to be found in a few lines by Gregory of Tours, who lived three hundred years after their martyrdom.

Gregory relates how, in the reign of Decius, seven men were consecrated bishops and sent to preach the Gospel throughout Gaul—" to the people of Tours, Bishop Gatianus; to the people of Arles, Bishop Trophimus; to Narbonne, Bishop Paul; to Toulouse, Bishop Saturninus; to the Arverni, Bishop Austremoine; to the people of Limoges, Bishop Martial; to the Parisii, Bishop Denis."

" The blessed Denis, Bishop of Paris, having suffered divers tortures for the name of Christ, ended his earthly life beneath the sword."

That is all we know and it comes from an authority who lived three hundred years later. Tradition has it that St. Denis and his two companions were beheaded on the hill in Paris which was called the Mons Martyrum, the Martyrs' Mount, Montmartre. But it seems more probable that the Bishop of Paris was beheaded at Saint-Denis. It was at Saint-Denis that his tomb was built, at the side of the Roman road where St. Geneviève was to raise her basilica. The Mons Martyrum was founded on a fable invented in the ninth century by Hilduin, the Abbot of St. Denis. According to Fredegar, who lived in the seventh century, Montmartre was at that time called Mons Mercore, that is to say, Mons Mercurii, the Mount of Mercury, from which the word Montmartre was derived. But is not the text of Fredegar corrupt? The tonic accent of Mercurii is on the second syllable, and the word which gave birth to Montmartre must have had it on the first. In the time of the Romans there stood on this legendary hillock, not only a temple of

172

Mercury, but also a temple to the god Mars. Now the word Mars would produce Mons Martis, of which the correct development would be Montmartre, as the inhabitants of the hill and the whole of Paris still call it, thus once more giving spectacled pedants a lesson in etymology and in the proper pronunciation of the French language.

When by their energy, their lively faith and the blood they had shed, but above all because their doctrine responded to the requirements of a new type of society, the Christians had increased in numbers throughout Gaul, they used to meet together for the celebration of their religion in the Roman basilicas, which were better suited to their taste than the temples sullied by the worship of false gods. Moreover, it was not long before they built churches specially designed for their meetings and ceremonies, moulding them on the plan of the basilicas to which their form of worship had become adapted and calling them by the same name.

The entrance to the basilica, or Christian church, was through a front portico leading to the *atrium,* that is to say a court open to the sky and surrounded by galleries like cloisters; this led to a vestibule, the *narthex,* through which entry was made into the church proper—a vast rectangular hall covered by a roof with naked rafters. A double row of columns with antique capitals divided the hall into three naves, in which the crowd was not allowed to circulate as it pleased, the right being reserved for men, the left for women, and the centre for the clergy. At the end of the central nave was the altar, a very simple, plain erection, without statues, illumined by a few lights, in remembrance of the first masses celebrated in the darkness of the catacombs. It consisted mainly of a large rectangular stone, slightly raised above the ground, behind which the priest said Mass facing the congregation. There were two lecterns for the reading of the gospel for the day and the epistle. At the end of the apse was the " cathedral " desk reserved for the celebrant. The outside roof had a double slope, like ordinary roofs in our own days. With the growth of Christianity in Gaul, many of these basilicas attained to fine proportions and were lavishly decorated—the ceiling was gilded, and the columns were made of different coloured marbles.

173

Those of the basilica of Our Lady Mary in Paris, found in 1847 in the sub-soil of the close, were in the Corinthian style and made of white marble. The poet Fortunatus gives a valuable description of this primitive Parisian basilica in the sixth century :

" The pile of this church rests upon marble columns, and the care with which it is kept enhances its beauty. It was the first to be lighted with windows filled with transparent glass which let in the light. It would seem that the hand of some skilful craftsman had imprisoned the light of day in the sanctuary. The trembling fires of the early dawn seemed to sport even in the dizzy vaults above, and the temple was lighted as by the light of day, even when the sun was not shining."

Two great upheavals shook the Roman Empire during the third century—the spread of Christianity and the German invasions. It remains to discuss the latter.

The Germans. As early as the first century B.C. the Romans had realised that the Rhine constituted a deep gulf separating them from the barbarians, and by means of military works and numerous garrisons they did their best to increase its value.

The populations who inhabited the right bank of the river and the unexplored districts beyond it were not different in their origin from the Celts and Belgæ who were spread over Gaul. They worshipped the same natural forces, though still in a crude and primitive way. They enjoyed a similar social organisation, that of the clan, but also in its most primitive form, including lands held in common. These populations were, like the Gauls, divided into peoples, each one of which, in the first century B.C., was still under the rule of a monarchical chief, whether king, priest or judge—a primitive form of monarchy.

The Celts and Belgæ, descended from the same stock as the Germans, had, on establishing themselves in Gaul, intermingled with the native populations, the Ligurians and the Iberians, and had mixed their stock, their language, their customs and their gods to an extent which it is difficult to trace. The Germans, on the other hand, regarded themselves as a pure race, and if they had mixed at all with foreign peoples, it could only have been with the savage hordes who ranged the eastern steppes of Europe. The name German did not represent any ethnic

174

group, but appears to have been applied to these peoples by the Romans, on account of their similarity to the Gauls (*germanus*, fraternal, consanguineous); but the modern Germans trace the word to Teutonic roots—*wehr*, war, *man*, man, the warriors. However this may be, each of the great peoples into which the race was divided bore a name peculiar to itself and they had no designation common to them all.

They were a rough, warlike race, endowed with great physical strength, tall of stature and ever ready to draw the sword.

It might be said that at the time when they first appeared in history, the Germans possessed no civilisation. The Gauls, it is true, on the arrival of Cæsar, were still in the early stages of their culture, but at least they had built towns and possessed industries, which in many ways were not only flourishing but more advanced than others of the same period; they struck coins, and made use of writing. Nothing of the kind existed among the Germans.

They built no towns and knew nothing of money, except what they had taken from their neighbours, and they lived a primitive life of hunting and pasturage. This is a fact of the greatest importance, an essential fact upon which their history during the first centuries of the Christian era was founded. For peoples who live only by means of hunting and pasturage, and deprived of the wealth derived from the practice of agriculture with its multiplication of the fruits of the earth, require vast territories in order to live, territories so vast indeed that the Germans soon had insufficient. And thus began the famous thrust towards the West—*Drang nach Westen*, as the modern Germans call it—that thrust towards the West which after three thousand years has not yet been arrested—that movement towards those happy districts where land made fertile by the toil of man is to be found. " The Germans," says Tacitus, " crossed over into Gaul in order to exchange their forests and marshes for a fertile soil."

Each of these numerous invasions, or, to use the characteristic expression, each of these numerous German thrusts into the territory of Gaul or other parts of the Roman Empire, was provoked by a similar thrust by another German people into the territory of those who were forced to emigrate. It was like a swarm of bees coming to occupy the hive of a feebler swarm, which was thus obliged, under pain of extinction, to seek a new home elsewhere. The people who had been driven out thrust themselves upon their neighbours, who in their turn thrust themselves upon a third party, who thrust themselves upon Gaul.

Another reason for these continual migrations was to be found in internal dissensions. A people would be divided into two parties, and the side that won the day would drive out its feebler adversary and seize its lands, so that the oppressed were obliged to go in search of land to live on beneath other skies. It is clear that these dissensions resulting in the expulsion of a portion of the people were also due to the impossibility for the whole people to find a livelihood in the district it occupied. The primary cause, the motive force for the movement we have described, was, as we have already said, the impossibility for the Germans to feed a relatively large population within the limits of a given territory through their ignorance of systematic agriculture.

The invasion of the Cimbri and the Teutons at the end of the second century before our era had covered the soil of Gaul with blood and ruins. The magnificent way in which Marius dammed the barbarian avalanche at Aix-en-Provence (110 B.C.) is well known, and the grateful remembrance of his feat still survives throughout the whole region as far as Marseilles, where to this day there is hardly a boy who is not called Marius.

In the following century (first century B.C.) some German peoples established themselves in a few of the cantons on the left bank of the Rhine, under very varying conditions. Cæsar was of opinion that the Aduatuci, in the territory of the Belgæ, in the district of Tonges, were descended from a detachment of Germans left behind after the invasion of the Cimbri and Teutons. The Eburones were also regarded as Germans, as well as various other peoples in the valley of the Meuse. Agrippa, in 38 B.C., and Drusus in 16 B.C., conceived the plan of protecting Gaul against the Germans by means of a *limes*, or military zone, on the right bank of the river, plans which were never carried out owing to the disaster of Varus (A.D. 9). Germanicus, the son of Drusus, a young hero worthy of his father, defeated

Arminius and regained the Roman eagles which had been lost in the Teutoburgerwald (A.D. 15–16); but Tiberius, in his jealousy, had Germanicus poisoned and refused to discuss his plans. There was no longer any question of forming on the right bank of the Rhine the protective and protected zone of which Drusus had dreamt and which was only realised eight hundred years later by Charlemagne. But at least the strong garrisons stationed along the river and the creation of two provinces called German provinces, the government of which was entrusted to military legates, secured the safety of Gaul for a time. It was an imperative necessity. For in disarming Gaul, in stripping her of her strong armour, and in depriving her, under their administration, of her warlike valour, the Romans had incurred the obligation of defending her.

Accordingly the Roman legions were stationed all along the Rhine—a population of 200,000 souls perpetually on the *qui vive !* living in redouts, in camps and cantonments such as the Romans alone knew how to construct. It is true that the quarrels of the Germans among themselves helped to keep them at bay for some time. Tacitus records the fact with satisfaction. Arminius himself, the hero of the Teutoburgerwald, was put to death by his own followers, and in A.D. 47 his own people, the Cherusii, sent a delegation to Rome to demand a king from the hands of the Emperor. Nevertheless these same dissensions thrust the defeated fugitives towards the frontiers, where they ravaged the country on both sides of the Rhine, which they frequently succeeded in crossing.

The Romans enlisted Germans for their armies. The example had already been set by Cæsar. In A.D. 69, when Vitellius entered Rome with his army, the Germans in it aroused the ridicule of the Roman people on account of the skins of wild beasts in which they were dressed. And sometimes the Romans even settled in their Empire and gave land to certain of these emigrant bands who presented themselves at the frontiers as suppliants, when they were not numerous enough to make their appearance there as warriors.

Throughout the second century, the great century of imperial Rome, the barrier of the Rhine was efficiently guarded. For twenty years Marcus Aurelius successfully repulsed all attempts at invasion; but they were renewed and threatened not only the line of the Rhine, but also that of the Danube. The Goths appeared in the Balkans; very soon they penetrated into Macedonia (A.D. 251).

These migrations, as we have already pointed out, were a necessity for the Germans. Beaten by the Romans, who sent punitive expeditions into their territory, they saw their lands ravaged, and were obliged to pay tribute and conclude humiliating treaties. But, shortly afterwards, a fresh invasion was let loose—the Franks were thrust out by the Saxons, the Alemanni by the Burgondes. It became necessary to advance.

The Roman army was the only rampart of Gaul and indeed of the whole Empire; for a similar abandonment of the warlike virtues which Rome had forced upon Gaul had also taken place among the Romans themselves. Their armies were composed of mercenaries, and even of the very barbarians which it was their mission to repulse; hence the growing importance of the legions in the constitution of the Empire. What meaning could the senate and people of Rome, S.P.Q.R., any longer possess?

The armies alone now had the power of making an eloquent appeal, for they alone had the power of making themselves heard. They created and destroyed Emperors, raising the good and the bad at random to power and then massacring them, killing the best of them, like Alexander Severus (A.D. 235).

And, at the beginning of the third century, with the accession of the Sassanides to the throne of Persia and the awakening of a fanatical lust of conquest, the Empire was confronted by the Eastern peril as well as by the German peril.

At this period there appeared for the first time two German nations who were destined to play a great part in history—the Franks and the Alemanni. These peoples, like all the invading hordes, came from the north, from the coasts of the Baltic, and the basins of the Elbe, the Oder and the Vistula. Their names, Franks and Alemanni, do not seem to have been ethnic in origin, any more than the names of the Belgæ and the Germans themselves. They were war names applied to themselves by peoples of divers origin united under one chief or one family for the purpose of war. Frank no doubt

178

meant " Brave "; Alemanni, " people of all kinds " (*alle*, all; *man*, man).

The Alemanni appeared in 213 in the reign of Caracalla, who inflicted a defeat upon them from which he derived his second surname " Germanicus "; the Franks first began to be mentioned in 241, under Gordianus, also in connection with a defeat inflicted upon them by the Roman army commanded by Lucius Domitius Aurelianus, the future Emperor Aurelian, at that time a military tribune.

The Franks occupied, on the right bank of the Rhine, the region lying between the North Sea and the Main; the Alemanni extended further south, from the Main to the Alps.

To these two nations was added a third, whose name was destined to resound through the ages—the Burgondes or Burgundians. In the first century they were to be found on the shores of the Baltic, as neighbours of the Goths. The Gepidæ, a Gothic people, attacked them and seized their lands. The Burgondes pushed southwards, and reaching the district of the Black Forest, they halted in the neighbourhood of the Alemanni. It was not long before the Burgondes formed connections with the Roman garrisons which acted as advanced guards on the right bank of the Rhine, and the families of the two nations became closely joined by marriage. Thus the manners and customs of the Burgondes were modified; they built properly arranged villages instead of the scattered dwellings characteristic of the Germans, and in the third century we find them established on the right bank of the Rhine with a culture similar to that of the Gauls.

About 257 bands of Alemanni forced the barrier of the Rhine, crossed the Alps and appeared before the walls of Ravenna; but they were utterly routed on the plain of Milan by the Emperor Gallienus; meanwhile other bands traversed Gaul diagonally and crossing the Pyrenees, seized Tarragona, and by way of Spain went and lost themselves in Africa.

It is easy to imagine the ruin they left everywhere in their train and the sorry spectacle afforded by Gaul and Spain who, when once their frontiers were violated, found themselves abandoned by their masters, the Romans, who had conquered

179

and disarmed them, and defenceless before a danger which had already threatened them for hundreds of years.

In 268 the Alemanni were again defeated in Italy by the Emperor Claudius II.

In connection with these various victories of the Roman troops over the Germans, Fustel de Coulanges emphasises the facility with which the Empire got the better of its enemies. " We are apt," he writes, " to exaggerate the strength of these barbarians. But they were conquered by Roman armies exceedingly small in numbers, often amounting to fewer than 30,000 men. These barbarians, who were badly led, only took towns that were undefended, and advanced into a country only as long as they did not meet the Roman army; they avoided battles, fought without either order or tactics and at the first check begged for peace."

The Romans continued to attribute these easy victories to the fine organisation and discipline which the leaders had established among the troops, and the contrast between the Germans and the legionaries was well illustrated on the occasion of a visit paid by two kings of the Alemanni to the Roman camp :

" They found themselves among equals—the Alemanni robust and bigger, the Romans disciplined by the practice of arms, the Germans savage and tumultuous, the Romans calm and prudent, confident in their strength of character, whilst their adversaries were proud of their bodily splendour."

It is a striking picture.

And thus we reach the terrible years 275–276, which let loose upon Gaul the most terrible cataclysm. The Germans broke through the barrier of the Rhine at many points and spread themselves right and left in devastating hordes. The country was at their mercy. There were no garrisons, no fortresses, no arsenals. The invaders could sack, kill, burn, pillage, rob and violate at will. Far from encountering the armies of the enemy, these savage bands found crowds of the invaded population hurrying to swell their ranks—slaves escaped from the *ergastula,* workers who had been exploited by the Gallo-Roman autocracy and divers elements who had never been subjugated to the yoke of Rome. There followed a series of wild orgies, unbridled gluttony, unbridled lust, destruction and incendiarism. Sixty

180

towns were destroyed, innumerable villas were pillaged and delivered up to the flames, whilst works of art patiently and tastefully collected for two centuries were reduced to fragments; crops were destroyed, women disembowelled, old men beaten to death, and babies' brains dashed out against the walls. Amid intoxicated yells torrents of crystal wine flowed from the beautiful Gallic casks. Of how many basilicas, thermæ, theatres, temples and other sanctuaries, granaries, cellars, wine stores, warehouses, shops, haylofts and barns, farms and dwellings of all kinds did not the walls blackened by fire alone remain to tell the tale ! The ruins of numbers of these villas may still be found beneath the burnt rubbish together with the bare bones of the inhabitants—hundreds of miniature Pompeiis buried beneath the German flood more destructive than the lava flow of Vesuvius. And, proving how true was Fustel de Coulanges's assertion, the few fortified towns, such as Treves, Autun, Lyons and Narbonne, were spared. Paris was destroyed. Alas what a wonderful thing was the great majesty of the *Pax Romana—immensa romanæ pacis majestas* (Pliny the Naturalist) —hymned by poets and historians !

" This invasion," writes Camille Jullian, " destroyed almost all the towns in the three Gauls "; the Narbonnaise alone was spared.

It is true that under Probus there was a reaction. He was an intelligent Pannonian, rough and energetic, and seems to have been the best of all the Roman Emperors. Probus crossed the Rhine (277) and drove back the Germanic peoples to the Neckar, promising his soldiers a gold piece for every head of a German they brought him. He was able to write to the Senate that after having won back seventy cities, he had delivered Gaul. He brought back into Gaul a large number of Germans in chains in order to make them put the devastated fields into cultivation again. This forced exodus has been described by a contemporary writer, who watched these German immigrants in their chains during one of their halts lying *pêle-mêle* under the porticoes of a town. The men with their ruddy locks no longer had the savage gait which had terrified those who had seen them fifteen years previously spreading terror, torch in hand. Beneath the fetters that bound them, the young men and young girls maintained an air of freshness and good cheer and, in spite of their distressful situation, continued to exchange words and smiles of love.

Julian gained another victory over the Alemanni in the neighbourhood of Strasburg in 357, but after he left Gaul in order to wield the imperial sceptre in Constantinople, the invasions from across the Rhine began afresh. Julian died in 363, and Valentinian (364–375), in order to keep the barbarians more easily in check, took up his residence at Treves. Between Constantinople and Treves the defence of the Empire fluctuated over a vast sector. Valentinian spent most of his reign at Treves, and it was the same object—the struggle against the barbarians—which made Charlemagne choose Aix-la-Chapelle as the capital of his Empire. For half a century Treves once more became the capital of the Western Empire (from Diocletian onwards the Roman State was divided into two).

And now the struggle against the Germans was entrusted, partially at least, to the Germans themselves, which led, not only to their settlement in Gaul, but also to the formation of their kingdoms. And indeed the Romans adopted a better policy than that of incorporating the Teutons in more or less large numbers in the armies of the Empire, by handing over to Germanic peoples, organised in their own way, certain regions of Gaul to protect and defend.

This policy had been outlined as early as the first century B.C. by Julius Cæsar himself. The great proconsul had established the Germanic people, the Ubii, who were no less faithful allies of Rome than the Remi and the Lingones, in the region of Cologne, where they became Romanised to at least the same extent as their neighbours the Treveri. Hard by the Ubii, though further north and still on the Rhine, the Romans established the Sicambri about the end of the first century B.C. Remnants of the army of Ariovistus had been left at Cæsar's pleasure in certain districts, the Triboci round about Strasbourg, the Vangiones at Worms and the Veneti at Spiers. Thus the Romans aimed at forming all along the valley of the Rhine, from Bâle to the sea, a line of defence consisting, not only of their own garrisons, but also of Germanic peoples under their protection.

In order to realise the consequences of this policy, which was put into practice as far as the interior of Gaul, let us consider for a moment how these colonies of Roman soldiers were organised. The legionaries were stationed in the districts they were expected to defend, and each man settled down with his wife, his children, his elders and his slaves; for under the Roman Empire the career of a soldier was a profession which lasted a considerable time. In the end soldiers even came to be branded with an indelible mark on their bodies to make it impossible for them to escape from their profession. In return for the protection afforded by the legionaries each district had to house and feed them. The region in which a band of troops was settled became, not its property, but its domain. The soldiers themselves together with their dependants had the right of being housed in it; this was called *hospitalitas*, and as a consequence they were allowed to requisition food, forage, beasts of burden and clothes.

In the course of time regular customs were established, and a landed proprietor was expected to devote to this " hospitality " a third of his dwellings and buildings of all kinds and produce in proportion to the revenue from his domains.

The consequences of this were as follows. When the Romans agreed that Germanic peoples should fulfil the same rôle as the legions, these peoples were treated in the same way. They were settled in regions the inhabitants of which were obliged to house, clothe and feed them. And these peoples established themselves there, like the legionaries, with their wives and their children. Thus the Romans, after having triumphed over the Burgondes, gave them Sabaudia, meaning that they installed them in that region in the manner just described. Gascony, Poitou, Perigord, Angoumois and Languedoc were " given " in the same way to the Visigoths. Consequently there soon arose in Gaul a kingdom of the Burgondes and a kingdom of the Visigoths, though in the beginning their chiefs were only called upon to exercise an authority in these parts similar to that which the Roman *duces*, that is to say, the Generals of the Roman armies garrisoned along the frontiers, exercised over the districts assigned to their command.

This lucid explanation is due to the brilliant genius of Fustel de Coulanges.

And the Empire did not only give the Germans lands to guard, they also gave them lands to cultivate. Whole districts had been turned into deserts as a result of the invasions, the effect of Roman law, and of the taxes which weighed heavily on the landed proprietors, and the ever-increasing difficulty experienced by the small proprietors to eke out an existence after the beginning of the third century.

It was not merely a question of bands of prisoners in chains that the legionaries conducted to the waste lands in order to force them to work there, but of solid masses of these immigrants from beyond the Rhine who were settled, not only in the frontier regions, but in the very heart of the country. A contemporary, filled with admiration, addressed a dithyramb on the subject to Maximianus Herculius, the Emperor with the title of Augustus, and to Constantine Chlorus, his colleague (end of the third century) :

" Thanks to thee, Maximianus Augustus, the Frank, subjected to our laws, has cultivated the fields abandoned by the Nervii and the Treveri; thanks to thee, Constantine Cæsar, all that remained uncultivated in the districts of Amiens, Beauvais, Troyes and Langres blossomed again under the care of barbarian tillers of the soil."

Towards the end of the third century another event took place in Gaul to which the attention of historians has not been adequately directed—the popular movement of the Bagaudæ. The word is derived from the Celtic *bagad* or *badad*, meaning " assembly." The Bagaudæ, Celtic by name, were peasants and labourers, free men for the most part. They joined together under arms, and their forces increased rapidly. Their weapons consisted of agricultural implements. About 285 Diocletian instructed Cæsar Maximianus to fight them. Once more great massacres took place. Tradition has located the most important of these in the neighbourhood of Paris, at the confluence of the Marne and the Seine, in the plain of Saint Maur des Fossés. But the Bagaudæ were not exterminated. They reappeared fifty years later in the same guise as before, and it was the task of the great Aetius to march against them at the head of his troops.

These events are among the most important of the period, but writers have not deigned to discuss them. With what disdain

184

the Romans must have regarded these poor wretches armed with scythes and ploughshares ! But Salvienus adopts a different tone with regard to them :

" If they were turned into Bagaudæ, it was owing to the corruption of the judges, the proscriptions and the peculation of those who, charged with raising the public dues, converted them to their own private use."

It is important to remember the following facts—that the Bagaudæ were numerous, that they were rustics and determined in their efforts; some scholars add that they spoke Celtic and that they were Christians.

After the terrible avalanche of the years 275–276, reconstruction could be the only possible aim; the towns had to be **Gaul in the** rebuilt, the fields cultivated, and the bases of **Fourth** society re-established. This was the task of the **Century.** fourth century, approximately from the accession of Diocletian (284) to the death of Theodosius.

It was necessary to establish security. A terrible experience had taught men how fragile was the barrier of the Rhine and that each town and each domain must in future secure its own safety. This meant farewell to the smiling towns with their sumptuous edifices, their charming thermæ and gigantic arenas. What was required for the future were strong fortifications and high walls. The space over which the town spread was reduced and confined to the central quarter. The remains of the funeral monuments which lined the approaches to the towns, forming beautiful avenues which had been sacked by the barbarians, were fitted into the foundations of the ramparts, to strengthen them, not only by means of their hard material but on account of their sacred character as funeral marbles and sculptured sarcophagi. The towns became fortresses, as well as numbers of villages and hamlets and the principal villas. The inhabitants from that time forward called them *castra*, fortified camps; strongholds and garrisons were stationed in them. They no longer relied upon a general system of defence depending on the good will of the Emperor, the valour of a general or the discipline of a legion. The historian would perhaps go too far in saying that the Middle Ages began in the fourth century, although it witnessed the same preoccupation with the problems of local defence which arose again during the centuries of anarchy after Charlemagne. Moreover, there was a great difference in the aims of the two periods, the men of the fourth century desiring to protect themselves against a common danger and the flood of invasions, those of the tenth always on the *qui vive* against private menace on the part of their neighbours.

Camille Jullian has described the walls of Bordeaux, built of huge layers of enormous stones held together by their own weight alone. These blocks had been taken from the buildings of the town which had been ruined by the barbarians, forming quarries of architectural and artistic *débris* of all kinds—friezes, cornices, capitals, shafts of columns, fragments of statues, plinths and architraves. The lower parts of the walls were held together by the strong cement of the Romans. Lines of red brick broke up the monotony of the whole. The walls were from eighteen to twenty-four feet thick and thirty to thirty-six feet high and shut out the bright view over the smiling countryside and the neighbouring hills. The corners, which battering-rams would quickly have demolished, were fortified by means of towers. " The square enclosure raises its proud towers so high that their tops cleave the clouds," writes the poet Ausonius. The gates were small, with straight lintels, mere holes in the walls.

The villas were also protected in the same way as the towns, as they had suffered even more than the latter beneath the flood of invasion. They were no longer pleasure resorts, as they had been in the second century, but fortified places, *castra*, camps after the Roman style, or at all events *castella*, whence the word " château." Villages became more rare, and the more important among them also protected themselves like the *oppida* which Cæsar had found in Gaul. And lo and behold ! under the fair *Pax Romana*, Gaul bristling with fortified strongholds !

But it was not sufficient to have ramparts strengthened with towers; it was necessary also to have soldiers.

The Emperors of the first century, Vespasian and Domitian, thought they could secure the safety of Gaul by the construction of that barrier, known as the *limes*, which stretched the whole

186

length of the frontier facing the barbarian world. This was not a wall, as has often been imagined, but a strategic road, a huge patrol road, with fortified gates, *castella* in which more or less important garrisons could find shelter. This road was protected on its further side by an embankment twelve to fifteen feet wide, bordered by a trench and palisade, followed by an open zone of about half a mile to a mile broad, devoid of buildings and trees. Along vast stretches of the *limes* sufficient defence was afforded by a river, like the Rhine, wherever there happened to be one. A fleet of boats keep constant watch up and down. It has been observed that the little forts with which the *limes* was protected—some fifty in number, most of which dated from the time of Drusus—that these *castella* were built in places which were more pleasant and convenient than strategically desirable.

The *limes* had been formed to prevent bands of marauders from making surprise sallies into the Empire rather than with the object of stopping attacks by armed forces. But above all it served as a Customs frontier to prevent the export of forbidden goods, more particularly arms, and of certain food commodities, and the passage of persons whose movements were subject to restriction.

But walls and ramparts required soldiers to guard them.

In the fourth century the profession of arms had fallen into disrepute. It was no longer held in respect. The reasons for this were various. With the growing menace of barbarian invasions it had become more dangerous, and at the same time military courage had weakened. Armies were beginning to be recruited from the ranks of adventurers of all kinds. From the time of Caracalla (beginning of the third century) all the subjects of the Empire were Roman citizens, a fact which robbed the military profession of its chief advantage. The Emperors tried to remedy this by making the profession hereditary, and, moreover, compulsorily hereditary, in the same way as the workmen's corporations and the senatorial curiæ were hereditary bodies. Valentinian (365) decreed that the sons of soldiers were to be soldiers; but compulsion had results which might easily have been foreseen—those who did not wish to obey had recourse to all manner of means for escaping military service.

187

The recruits deserted. They had to be pursued and traced to their hiding places, and those who gave them shelter had to be found out and punished. Young men cut off their right thumbs in order to make it impossible for them to hold a sword. The dearth of soldiers became so great that the Empire was forced to forbid the centurions to give their men any leave.

The land was tapped to provide its quota for military service. Every estate was called upon to furnish a number of men in proportion to its size, the small estates being grouped together to form a unit. And soon the State—and the landlord himself —preferred to replace the " ordinary " man by the " mercenary." The rich kept their servants, and the State, by means of the money thus derived, procured recruits of better quality; and as such recruits, even in Gaul, became more and more rare, they were obtained from the barbarians. And thus it came about that the defence of the Empire against the Germans was entrusted to the Germans themselves.

This system filled Fustel de Coulanges with the deepest admiration. " By means of a slight increase in taxation," he says, " military service was reduced to a minimum, and through this system of standing armies it might be said that the civil population enjoyed perfect peace to go about their business."

We have just seen what was the price paid for this peace and security in 275 to 276, and before long we shall find them paying a far more terrible price.

Within the ramparts which surrounded the towns the life of the citizens was also modified. Camille Jullian writes :

" Behold the state of the country after three hundred years of Roman rule—the towns destroyed by the soldiers or by the Germans, the fields lying fallow, the population reduced by more than half, and misery and anarchy everywhere. Never was the soil of France more terribly devastated or more miserable than under the Roman Emperors."

The inhabitants of Paris came down from Sainte Geneviève in order to shut themselves up in the Island of the City as they had done in the time of Camulogenus.

From the top of their narrow ramparts the citizens were able to contemplate in what had once more become a rural setting the ruins of their beautiful monuments. The artisans' colleges crumbled into decay. The industrial arts, the making of pottery, iron, bronze and enamel work, fell into a state of decadence from which it seemed that nothing could rescue them. And the countryside afforded an even more desolate spectacle. The barbarians had ravaged everything, and destroyed the harvests, and the stores of corn as well as the grain for sowing, and ruined the vines and orchards; the strong men and youths had all been killed or reduced to slavery. And in the midst of this desperate misery bands of men out of work were formed. From the hiding-places in which they had taken refuge during the terror, from the depths of prehistoric grottoes, from the midst of the woods and from the picturesque huts which had still survived from the time of the lake-dwellings on the islands surrounded by the green waters of the marshes, emerged emaciated, half-starved creatures without any means of subsistence.

They were killed in thousands—a facile solution for social problems; but the result of thus dealing with the scourge was merely to deprive the countryside of the hands required for the grape and corn harvests.

In the midst of this anarchy the State endeavoured to confine society within rigid limits. From the top to the bottom of the social scale in this vast Empire men were forbidden to leave the position in which they were born. The slave was not only chained to slavery, but also to the house and to the estate on which he lived. If the property was sold he was not allowed to be separated from it. The cultivator who tilled his own land, which had often been given to him by the State as a reward for his services, was also forbidden to leave it. Those who worked on the domain of a landed proprietor were bound to it for ever, and the bonds which tied them to their master were made ever more rigid; the labourer could no longer part with his own property or even go to law without the consent of the master for whom he worked.

Not only in the country districts, but also in the camps and towns a deep desire for stability tended to make the whole of society static. Artisans found their colleges transformed into gaols in which they were kept captive by law. A beginning had been made with those bodies whose activities seemed to serve

189

some public end; and the movement spread. Artisans were forbidden to leave the towns in order to take refuge " in unknown localities," and they were, moreover, forbidden to aspire to the functions of the nobility, the senatorial order.

Rome could see salvation for the society she had deliberately organised only in the creation of castes. Even the nobility, on account of the burdens they were obliged to shoulder, found themselves forcibly attached to the posts of honour which they too would fain have escaped.

Matters reached such a pitch that those who occupied a certain rank in the city, the owners, for instance, of over twenty-five acres, were forced to shoulder the municipal burdens and, willy nilly, to take their seats in the curiæ and never resign them. " The legislation of the fourth century," writes Imbart de la Tour, " consisted of a prolonged struggle against widespread desertion of duty." Under the inexorable slavery of these social bonds the vast Roman Empire might be compared to the giant trees that are sometimes found in pleasure gardens— trees which have grown old and whose trunks and branches are no longer fed with the life-giving sap drawn from the fertile ground. Nevertheless an attempt is made to save the tree with its picturesque branches and its great gnarled trunk covered with thick moss. But as it withers the tree begins to fall apart and the gardener tries to hold it together by means of iron bands, rough rings fastened by rivets. The blacksmith is summoned with his hammers and anvil. The tree raises its head once more in all its impressive grandeur, but its existence is only artificial, the life ebbs from it, and the sap dries up. Such was Gallo-Roman society in the fourth century.

Everywhere there were signs of exhaustion, and means were even sought to force people to have children.

Nevertheless, if we examine the Roman Empire as a whole, we find that in this general decay of an exhausted society it was Gaul that preserved the most life and vigour.

The old Gallic people, the Celto-Ligurians, had not disappeared; they still lived on, patient and humble, dogged and persevering. And this was sufficient to animate Gaul, beneath her carapace of foreigners, with a vigour that the other provinces of the Empire no longer possessed. Gaul had her own Emperors.

190

And from this fertile soil Constantine was destined to go forth to proclaim the triumph of Christianity.

Alas! poor Gaul, mutilated by Cæsar, yet bestowing the last remnants of her strength upon the Roman world, and becoming the final stronghold of Latin culture. Italy and Spain were dumb, Gaul alone still chanted her lays in the language of Virgil and Horace. The celebrated words applied to Rome and Greece—*Græcia capta ferum victorem cepit*—might be modified into " Gaul subdued and crushed became the support of her conquerors."

Julian, a member of the Flavian house, Flavius Claudius Julianus, arrived in 355, entrusted by the Emperor Constantius with the government of Gaul. The general anarchy of the country had been aggravated by internal dissensions, and Magnentius had appealed to the Germans, whose devouring hordes had penetrated as far as Autun. Julian, born at Constantinople, and educated at Athens among men of letters, rhetoricians and philosophers, seemed a young dilettante, an eccentric dreamer. But he proved himself to be a great soldier and a strong administrator. The taxes, which weighed down the Gauls, were burdensome chiefly on account of the extortions of the tax-gatherers. Under the administration of Julian they were reduced by seventy-five per cent. without the Treasury suffering. The Alemanni found in him a triumphant adversary. In the rapidity of his movements, he resembled Cæsar. He recaptured Treves and Cologne from the Germans and inflicted a crushing defeat upon them in the neighbourhood of Strasbourg (357), and crossing the Rhine he recovered 20,000 Gallic prisoners. His government marked an epoch in the history of France on account of the importance he gave to his beloved Lutetia, which from that time forward assumed the position of capital of the country. It was at Paris that Julian was proclaimed Emperor Augustus (May 360). In later days, when he had assumed the Imperial purple in the East, his thoughts reverted with a shade of regret to the delightful hours he had spent on the banks of the Seine.

The Christians were angry with the Emperor Julian for having returned to the worship of the old divinities, after embracing the Catholic religion; but he did not persecute them. His

191

return to the mythology of Olympus was accomplished without friction in remembrance of the poetic grace with which the finest literature in the world had filled his soul during the years when as a young man he had lived in Athens, the seat of that charming renaissance of Hellenism in the fourth century, listening to the light debates of the sophists, the lively disputes of the scholars, and the glowing verses of the greatest poets of the world gathered together in his honour. To this garden of brilliant flowers Julian returned with a free and easy gait which we of to-day can but greet with an indulgent smile.

In addition to the brilliant charm shed by Julian the Apostate over Gaul in the fourth century we must also bear in mind the contribution made by Ausonius of Bordeaux. The celebrated poet was born in that town about 310, in the reign of Constantine. It was possible to dream of a new era. The cult of letters held a high place, and Ausonius was destined to enjoy a brilliant career thanks to his talent and the favour it secured him. At the age of twenty-five he was a professor in the school at Bordeaux. Aquitania had suffered relatively less than the other provinces. Its lands were rich, and the district recovered very quickly.

The schools of Bordeaux enjoyed a great reputation. Their rhetoricians were spread over Italy and the East, and even became teachers in the Imperial household. The public bodies lavished favours on these schools, and they are well known to us from the poetry of Ausonius. He was a duumvir of the city, perhaps a " defender," according to the term already in use.

The University of Bordeaux, moreover, existed for a considerable time; we find it still flourishing in the fifth century, in spite of the arrival in the district of the Visigoths, who attended its courses and held its professors in high esteem. It only disappeared with the advent of the Franks.

To return to Ausonius—after having won the highest honours in his native city, he was appointed tutor to Gratian, the son of the Emperor Valentinian, in 369, and received the title of Count in honour of the occasion. He afterwards became Commander of the Prætorian Guard and, in 378, Prefect of Gaul. And thus we find the poet holding important public offices, and placed

192

at the head of the civil administration of the country. His authority extended from Mt. Atlas to the Moselle; for the Commander of the Prætorians in Gaul held command in Great Britain, Spain and Morocco. On the 1st of January, 379, Ausonius was at last honoured with the title of consul, and he almost died of joy. The consular attributes had become little more than honorary, but, next to the glory of the Imperial purple, this honour was the greatest to which a man could aspire.

Ausonius was the greatest poet of his day, and yet his work leaves us cold. It is artificial. It is true that we find in it an echo of society at that time, when the poet speaks, so superficially, alas! of his dear villa, his family life, and his colleagues at the University; but it fails to arouse our emotions. In order to judge his verses at a glance it is only necessary to compare him with Gregory of Tours. The latter is incorrect and heavy in his writing, he indulges in the crassest tomfoolery in order to tell us tales which do not actually bore us because it is impossible not to be amused by them, but which bear witness to his vulgar simplicity of mind. Ausonius is refined, intelligent and fluent, he knew all sides of society and had taken part in the most important events of his day, and had sometimes presided over them. And yet what remains to us after all this versification?—ashes and verbiage, sometimes harmonious but more often limping; and in spite of all its honours, brilliance and variety, depicting an empty life, full of vanity, though endowed, it is true, with a certain familiar grace of language and rhetoric. Whilst with Gregory of Tours—what floods, by Jove, overflowing into swirling eddies, carrying everything including ourselves along, and in which we love to plunge again and again up to our necks! For Gregory followed a very different current from that in which the bard of Bordeaux so skilfully guided his bark. For whilst Ausonius and his contemporaries among the aristocracy of Gaul delighted in the play of wit, and towards the end of the fourth century lived in the villas they had rebuilt an agreeable life enriched by a light literature and frivolous arts, surrounded by every comfort it was possible to desire, the honest life so well described by the grandson of Ausonius " in a convenient dwelling, with large rooms arranged for the various seasons of the year, a clean and well-spread board, young slaves and plenty of them, abundant furniture, precious silver, artists of all kinds, stables full of horses with shining coats, safe and elegant carriages "—the Christian populace of Bordeaux were already stoning a heretic, and St. Hilary was preaching at Poitiers. Hilary was inspiring with the enthusiasm of his faith his disciple Martin, the soldier who had come from far distant Hungary, the rough apostle who was to rouse the restless mobs, the military tribune who, to the consternation of the rich cooped up in their barren egoism, shared his woollen cloak on the Amiens road with a poor wretch shrivelled up with cold and hunger.

The populace came and tore Martin away from his ascetic life in order to place him, all pale as he was, covered with rags, with unkempt locks and looking like a Bohemian vagabond, with emaciated features and ecstatic gaze, upon the episcopal throne of Tours, and that in spite of the Bishops who were taking part in the election and who considered that even for a popular Bishop, this personage was really a bit too much of a guy.

In the market-place of the town a sick man remarked to Brice who was destined in his turn to become Bishop of Tours :

" I am waiting for the sainted man, but I don't know where he is."

—" You are looking for that lunatic ? . . . See over there, that creature who as usual is gazing at the sky like a man deprived of his senses. . . ."

The policy and influence of this mitred son of the people became tremendously powerful. The energy of his will, the passion of his convictions, his biting and brutal eloquence in which, nevertheless, his infinite goodness shone forth, his sublime disinterestedness, his unaffected voluntary poverty, triumphed over every obstacle. Only compare Saint Martin with Julius Cæsar and you will at once realise the pettiness, the mediocrity of a vulgar and ambitious mind and the empty vanity of the old *imperator* who hid his premature baldness beneath a laurel wreath of gold. . . .

Saint Martin bestowed upon Gaul those two great main-springs of the new life—the monasteries and the rural parishes. Miracles abounded wherever he trod, and after his death signs and wonders were continually repeated at his tomb when his

194

relics were touched. Pilgrims came from every quarter of Christendom chanting their hymns. The *atrium* of the basilica was filled night and day with swarms of invalids, the blind and those suffering from fever and hysteria. There were paralytics stretched out on their long litters, awaiting a cure, and remaining in the sacred enclosure for days, weeks and even months. Nearly all the churches in central and south-western Gaul were dedicated in the name of the venerated saint.

The aristocracy fled from the towns, which were full of a populace vibrating with Christian ideas, and took refuge in the country, in their gilded villas, and their pleasant amusements, and, to the distant thunder of the new religion, sadly contemplated their Roman gods on their marble altars, calling to mind the delightful spicy tales of these divinities with their various attributes, in whom they no longer believed, though it is true they had never believed in them before. There they led a life of hunting, and riding, with packs of dogs whose genealogies were recorded, playing tennis and wrestling, varied with games of dice and hot and cold baths. They listened to light lectures stretched out on couches covered with wolf skins, and attended endless banquets at which sows' udders were washed down with Falernian wine to the sound of the zither and the flute.

Meanwhile neither the senators, the prætors nor the duumvirs, nor even the " defender " who had replaced the duumvirs, any longer governed the cities, which were now ruled by the Bishops elected by the people and speaking the language and preaching the religion of the people. The people of France had burst its bonds. It had come out into the light. Let us listen to its voice. It had been dumb ever since the days of Vercingetorix, of Commius the Atrebatian and of Corres the Bellovacan, except for certain paltry revolts which had been smothered in blood. For a moment its voice was heard again; listen carefully, for all too soon this beautiful voice will be drowned beneath the tumult of the barbarians, until the day when, towards the end of the tenth century, it will appear once again the master of its own destiny, at last unfolding freely, until our own times, the fairest of all the histories of the world.

In pointing to this renaissance of the Western world in the midst of the ruins of the Gallo-Roman society, whose decadence we have described, it is seldom realised that this society did not really enter upon a stage of decadence, for the very good reason that it had never risen any higher than it was at the end of the fourth century. It had always been factitious and artificial when once it had been uprooted from its native soil and grafted upon a foreign culture. The world, it is maintained, was regenerated by the Germans. But the Germans, as we shall see, regenerated nothing at all, because they would have had to begin by re-generating themselves. On this point the proof brought forward by Fustel de Coulanges admits of no reply. Then if society was not regenerated by the Germans, it must have been regenerated by Christianity? This contention is truer; but the value of a doctrine depends on the men who champion it, on those who are its incarnation and of whom it is the expression. Now what was Christianity at the end of the fourth century? It was the people of France who pushed it forward with all the life and power that had remained within them. With a wave of the hand they cast down the Roman edifice which had lasted all too long. All that remained of it were certain insignificant shapes, words and formulæ. Gaul was regenerated by the Gauls.

Of the work of Rome all that was left was that which Christianity wished to keep—in the first place the administrative framework. The bishoprics were founded on the old cities, the Roman *civitates*, the archbishoprics on the provinces; but we have already seen that the Roman cities were merely the continuation of the old districts inhabited by the Gallic peoples. There were also the basilicas in which the Christians were to celebrate their religion and which, moreover, were quickly transformed.

A few ceremonial details were also kept, such as those connected with marriage—the ring, the nuptial veil, the crowns on the heads of the bridal pair; as well as certain details in ecclesiastical dress—the priest's alb being derived from the Roman tunic, the chasuble from the *pœnula*. But these were insignificant items. In its schools and monasteries Christianity saved the remnants of Roman culture, the classic language of the writers—the only salvage from a vast wreck.

If to this we add the roads, which were themselves built on the tracks of the old Gallic roads, we shall have included everything. And it amounts to nothing ! The argument of language is being continually brought up; French, it is maintained, is simply Latin. But in the first place it is not the Latin of Roman civilisation; the Latin from which French is supposed to be derived has nothing in common with Virgil and Cicero, nor even with the code, the pandects and the digests. And what did the Gauls do with it? They inspired it with their own genius, spirit and temperament, only preserving its empty shell. " France," says Jullian, " only kept the Latin language on condition of transforming it into its proper shape." By this we mean, of course, the beautiful pure French of the lays and fables and of the first chroniclers, the French of Villehardouin and Joinville, and not the language that began to be corrupted by the Burgundian and Flemish writers of the fourteenth and fifteenth centuries, Froissard, Chastellain, Jacques de Guyse and Olivier de la Marche, and was later on even more terribly mutilated by the humanists of the Renaissance. What fine writers Ronsard and Rabelais would have been had they not spoilt their language with such a large admixture of antiquity ! In its essence and construction and its innate character Latin is allied to German, with its declensions, its three genders, the position of the complements in a sentence, and the part played by the tonic accent, much more than to French. To maintain that the French of the *Chanson de Roland* was derived from Latin amounts to saying that Rheims Cathedral or the dungeon of Coucy were inspired by the Capitol and the forum. Moreover, we have seen that popular Latin had been imported into Gaul, not by the Romans, but by Christianity. " Let us say no more about the Latin genius," exclaims Jullian, " or about France being the pupil of that genius. She is worth more than that."

Let us make no mistake about it; Christianity in Gaul of the fourth century was a revolutionary movement, much more nearly akin than one might believe to the Revolution of '89 and founded upon the same principles of Liberty, Equality and Fraternity. The element of violence was excluded from it, because it was not led by ambitious politicians, greedy of power and gain; it was compounded entirely of faith, enthusiasm and love. Far from reaching its goal through ambition, it triumphed

197

by means of devotion, renunciation and sacrifice—Saint Martin.

"It was a strange spectacle," writes Camille Jullian, "that was presented by Gaul at the end of the fourth century. On one side the barbarians, who formed the armies of the Empire, on the other Roman society, entirely civilian, one might almost say intellectual, which gave to men of letters most of its wealth and authority";—but this authority passed into the hands of the Bishops. Between the barbarian armies on the one hand, and on the other the intellectual but uninfluential society of the Roman Empire, was the mass of the people who, as Jullian tells us, lived outside the pale of Latin culture; the plebeians and the peasants, the Gallic people, had once more found themselves beneath the ægis of Christianity.

And again, as Camille Jullian most aptly remarks, "Rome, after having deprived Gaul of her national existence, destroyed even her works and the very memory of her own history. It laid her low in the present, obliterated her past, and postponed her natural destiny.

"But Nature in the end imposes her will upon men, and the dead force themselves upon the minds of the living. Rome had not been able to destroy the native forces of Gaul nor those to which the unremitting toil of bygone generations had once given birth. These forces were destined to reappear and become active once more when the Roman Empire in its turn began to crumble to decay."

The agents of the Revolution of 1789 were elected by the people composing the National Assemblies—the Constituent and the Legislative Assemblies and the Convention; the agents of the Christian revolution of the fourth century were also elected by the people—the Bishop in each city. The Bishop was the sovereign head of the municipality. The " defenders " elected by the curia, the " Counts " nominated by the State, sank into insignificance beside him. Moreover, the defenders, who filled the first and most important office in the city, were in reality the nominees of the Bishop, on account of the influence the latter had in the assembly that elected them and of which he was the president. The same applies to the nomination of curators. In the fourth century it was the Bishop who exercised the only really strong authority in Gaul, because his was the only authority which rested upon popular foundations. He directed the administration of the city, acted as judge and arranged for the feeding of the people.

Nevertheless Christianity triumphant had yet to deal with further adversaries. According to Salvienus, "Minerva continued to be held in honour in the schools, Venus in the theatre, Neptune in the circuses, Mars in the amphitheatres, and Mercury in the palæstras." But they were merely gods on paper. Much more serious was the opposition of the old Gallic divinities, with their sanctuaries hidden away beneath the tall trees and served by priests who lived by means of the forbidden cult. The emblems of the rustic gods were still carried across the fields for the blessing of the harvests beneath great white palls; the lakes still received their offerings; and if the sacrifices did not call for the spilling of human blood in honour of the legendary deities, they were at all events still very numerous. And it will be readily understood that the Christians resolutely tracked down these obstinate survivals, not only by proscribing the old Druidical practices, but by trying to make the followers of the condemned religion forget the very language they used.

The Bishops of the cities met with adversaries of another kind in the monks of the great monasteries which developed on a prodigious scale in Gaul in the fourth century.

Saint Martin was a monk as well as a Bishop, but the other Bishops encountered great rivalry in the work of the monasteries. They tried to extend their authority over them; but the monks resisted. Cassian advised the monks to avoid women and Bishops. This conflict between the seculars and the regulars continued to develop with various vicissitudes; but the Bishops and the monks nevertheless fulfilled a common task; there were the episcopal schools and the literary activities of the monasteries, the great works undertaken by the Bishops for the defence, the extension and the sanitation of the towns and the magnificent task of clearing the land carried out by the monks; whilst moral teaching was inculcated by both branches with equal ardour and success.

Moreover, both the Bishops and the monks were united in the

fight against Arianism, which was one of the most important phenomena of the period and entailed most serious consequences.

Arianism first came into being in Alexandria about 318. It was a question of explaining the mystery of the Trinity composed of three Persons, each one of whom was God, but who together were but one God. Tertullian had taught that Christ was an emanation from the Father, "proceeding from the Father before the creation of the world, but not from all eternity."— " God existed before everything he created, therefore he was not always Father. For he could not be Father before the birth of the Son. There was a time when the Son did not exist." It is not our intention to enter upon a theological discussion. Suffice it to say that the doctrine of Tertullian was taken up by Arius in opposition to Origen, who maintained that the Word, that is to say Christ, had existed from all eternity like the Father. Moreover, Origen denied that the Son was of the same essence as the Father.

After having adopted the doctrine of Tertullian, Arius also adopted the second half of the doctrine of Origen. Alexander, Bishop of Alexandria, set to work to attack him, and the conflict opened. Was Christ in His beginning eternal like the Father and of the same substance as the Father, or was He merely an emanation from the Father?

This was the theological problem which was to play such a prodigious part in the destiny of the world and more particularly in the fate of France.

Even in our own day, the brigands of Abyssinia who, in the interval between two plundering expeditions and several murders, contrive to rob the caravans, when they sit round their bivouac fire at night still have hot discussions on the problem of consubstantiality.

The birth of Arius is shrouded in obscurity. He seems to have been born in Lybia or in Cyrenaica in the second half of the third century (between 256 and 270). He was ordained priest and just failed to be elected Bishop of Alexandria about 312, Alexander being his successful rival.

It was from an explanation of the Trinity given in 318 by the Bishop of Alexandria in an assembly of the clergy that the doctrine of Arius sprang. Alexander tried to explain to
200

his priests how it was that the three Persons, the three Gods of the Trinity, were but one God. Arius took great pains in trying to understand the arguments of his Bishop. But this was the greatest mistake he could have made. For he did not understand. It seemed to him impossible, if the Father, as the Bishop assured him, had begotten the Son, that He should not have preceded the Son. It also seemed to him impossible that the Son should be of the same substance as the Father, since God was by definition the only one of His kind and indivisible. Whereupon he set to work to organise conferences in which he tried to prove that the Word, that is to say the Son, had been created by the Father. " Then the Son was a created being," objected his opponents.

Bishop Alexander summoned a council of over a hundred Bishops from Egypt and Lybia. The majority were in agreement with him that the Word had existed from all eternity like the Father; the minority shared the opinion of Arius. The latter section gradually found their supporters increasing in numbers, including priests and votaries of all kinds, among whom were " seven hundred virgins." Arius gathered them all together and founded a schism.

Arius seems to have been a charming man, tall and thin and with a pale face which looked as though it were illumined by an inner flame; the expression of his eyes and the tone of his voice were extremely sweet. With his limpid melancholy he possessed the gift of persuasion. He was a poet and a musician. He put his doctrines into various popular refrains, some suitable for fishermen, others for millers, merchants or boatmen, refrains which were suited to the different tones of voice among the people. His numerous disciples used to chant them at table at the end of the meal.

The doctrine of Arius was accepted by some of the Emperors, including Constantine the Great; it obtained the approval of more than one Council, and even of one of the Popes, Liberius, whom martyrology has included in the ranks of the saints. Arian missionaries converted the Visigoths, the Ostrogoths, the Burgundians and the Lombards; but the charming Emperor Julian, disgusted by all the squabbles between the Arians and the Orthodox, deserted Christianity in order to return to the little owls of Minerva, the hounds of Diana and the white doves of Venus.

The history of Arianism is full of absorbing interest, but we cannot enter into it here. Suffice it to say that when the Franks, hairy and bloodthirsty pagans, arrived in Gaul, they found all the Bishops of the country supporting the orthodox doctrine which taught that the Son existed from all eternity and was consubstantial with the Father, whilst the heads of the various principalities which had come into being between the Rhine and the Pyrenees were followers of the Arian heresy.

The end of the fourth century is marked by the dismemberment of the Roman Empire. On the death of Theodosius (395) the government was divided between his **Large Estates** two sons, Honorius and Arcadius. Arcadius, the **and Colonies.** Emperor of the East, took up his residence at Constantinople, whilst Honorius, the Emperor of the West, lived at Rome, or rather at Milan. At Milan his chief interest was farming; in Rome he gave in 403 the last gladiatorial show of which mention is made. In Gaul his authority existed only in name. The Christian Church had drawn to herself all the vital forces of the nation, and the only power that existed beside her was that of the landed aristocracy.

The landed aristocracy had developed after the disaster of 276; for the land still belonged to them. They rebuilt their villas on a new plan. In the devastated country the large estates spread all the more easily on account of the ruined condition of the neighbouring domains. Deprived of all resources, the medium-sized and small properties allowed themselves to become absorbed. The laws laid down in the code of Theodosius tried to inaugurate a reaction, by imposing a fine of forty pounds in gold upon a great landowner for every minor estate he had taken under his *patronage*. But the great landowners had become more powerful than the laws, or rather in their own domains they made their own laws.

Ausonius and Paulinus of Pella have described the domains of the fourth and fifth centuries. To reach the villa or mansion of the overlord it was necessary to pass through hamlets consisting of the huts of the serfs and cultivators. The lord's palace was called the *prætorium*, a characteristic appellation

202

to which the Romans attached the idea of judicial power and military command. The domain, like the feudal fief of later days, contained all that was necessary for the life of the master, the overlord—the baron as he was called in the Middle Ages— and his dependants. The principal dwelling was the villa—or what the Middle Ages called the palace; then there were the buildings for the slaves, and the villages inhabited by the serfs and cultivators, together with barns, granaries, cellars, stables, mills, ovens, presses, forges and workshops and small factories in which the women spun and made clothes. A great villa such as that which Pontius Paulinus Leontius, the Commander of the Prætorians, had built in the reign of Constantine (first half of the fourth century) in the Gironde not far from Bordeaux, was like a small town, surrounded by deep moats and lofty ramparts strengthened by means of tall towers. It included storehouses for provisions which would have sufficed to resist a siege, and provided a place of refuge for the inhabitants of the neighbourhood. What was this but a feudal castle? And indeed, the villa of Leontius actually bore this title; it was called *burgus*, " burg," from the German word; it was also called *castellum*, stronghold, castle.

The master of the villa held the title of " senator," by which the rich landed proprietors came gradually to be designated. The " senator " was the " baron " of the fourth century. He lived in his villa, surrounded by his clients—the " dependants " of the eleventh and twelfth centuries, to whom must be added his freedmen and slaves.

The " senator " occupied himself with the development of his domain, and above all with the development of agriculture; he discussed the tillage and the crops with those who had charge of them, made plans for irrigation and directed the carrying out of them, arranged for the cutting and storing of the hay, superintended the grape harvest and did not even disdain to put a hand to the plough himself. At the time of the invasions of the Visigoths some of these landed " senators " raised bands of cavalry at their own expense and put the aggressors to flight; others equipped regular armies on their domains, the strength of a whole legion; for the military character of these Gallo-Roman " senators " must never be overlooked. In addition to his agricultural activities and all the industrial work necessary for his own subsistence and that of his people, he maintained a permanent troop of armed men. Jacques Flach writes that about his double capacity of landed proprietor and general of an army there could be no doubt. His troop of soldiers was formed from his *familia*—the mesne of the eleventh century—slaves, cultivators and free clients, the latter being the vassals. The free clients, the vassals, served on horseback, the others on foot. The members of the *familia* were bound to the " senator " by oath, just as the vassals were afterwards bound to their overlord. If necessary the " senator " supplemented them by means of mercenaries. In his case might was right, and he usurped and exercised an authority that no one was strong enough to dispute, so that he became, not only a landed proprietor and a military chief, but, if he so desired, a judge and legislator as well.

But this exactly describes the feudal lord of the eleventh and twelfth centuries. One last feature completes the likeness —the extension of the patronate by the ties of vassalage.

" The weak," says Salvienus, " handed themselves over to the powerful, in order to be defended and protected by him." Salvienus waxes indignant at the thought, and gives us the most precise details on the matter.

" In order to obtain this protection," he writes, " the miserable wretch had to hand over almost everything he possessed to the man whose protection he sought. The support given to the father cost the children their heritage. And thus countless numbers of the poor were despoiled of their small possessions." And, what made matters worse, these unfortunate people were still forced to pay taxes on goods they no longer possessed. For they were taxed as before.

And thus the free population gradually dwindled in numbers and whole towns put themselves under the patronage of a suzerain. All this sheds a bright light upon the formation of mediæval feudalism, though the latter was animated by a moral force from whence there sprang a most fertile social life bound together by a reciprocity of rights and duties between the weak and the strong.

To this movement of concentration in the hands of the great

the Emperors would have liked to offer a strenuous opposition; but in order to prevent the *minores*, to use a mediæval term, from seeking the protection of the strong at the expense of their own property and liberty, the Roman State would have had to give them protection itself; and of this it was incapable.

"The peoples of Gaul," writes Zosimus, "detached themselves from the authority of Rome, and tried to be sufficient unto themselves, fighting for their own interests and dismissing the Roman officials in order to govern themselves in their own way."

From these numerous similarities between the great Gallo-Roman domain of the fourth and fifth centuries and the fief of the eleventh and twelfth, it would seem that the latter was the child of the former, its continuation, or at all events its transformation. This is a conclusion which naturally occurs to the mind, and the majority of historians have allowed themselves to be seduced by it. Nevertheless we do not agree with it.

We have already seen how feudalism was established in Gaul in the time of Cæsar similar in every way to the feudalism of the Middle Ages. After Cæsar it was destroyed by several centuries of Roman rule, so that Gallo-Roman feudalism certainly did not spring from it, any more than did the feudalism of the eleventh and twelfth centuries from that of the fourth and fifth. Similar circumstances produce similar results. In a time of insecurity and in the absence of protection afforded by the State, local patronates are formed, public authority is split up between private individuals and under the same conditions; for human nature is very simple and in similar circumstances passes through a similar evolution.

The farmers had become cultivators. The cultivator was not a slave, nor even a serf. He was recognised as a free man, but he was not allowed to leave his land, any more than a soldier was allowed to leave the colours. Moreover, he enjoyed all the rights of citizenship, like a soldier. He was a free man, but chained down—the law speaks of the *nexus colonarius*, the bond of the cultivator.

This state of affairs possessed great disadvantages, which are obvious at a glance; but it also had advantages. The cultivator was not allowed to leave his little property, but it was secured to him. No proprietor could eject him from it. And from what has gone before the value of such a guarantee will be realised. The proprietor who sold his estate sold with it the labour of his cultivator, whom no change of master could alienate from the soil.

The cultivator married whom he pleased provided it was a woman of the same domain. " Exogamy " was not allowed without the consent of the proprietors of the two estates to which the future married couple belonged, a consent which, however, was easily obtained by means of an exchange of persons. The son of a cultivator was obliged to be a cultivator on the same domain as his father.

The master was not allowed to separate the cultivator from the plot of ground he tilled, nor could he force him to do the work of an artisan or render him personal service, or send him to work another part of the domain. The cultivator was not numbered among the troops of slaves or mercenaries who gathered in the corn and vine harvests under the command of the " monitor." He worked as he pleased on the ground to which he was attached, on the sole condition of giving to his master part of the produce he derived from it. Cultivators might be seen going to sell for their own profit in the market of the neighbouring town such produce of their labour as they reserved for themselves.

A man became a " cultivator " after an interval of thirty years. A farmer who had cultivated a given plot of land for thirty years or more thenceforward formed an integral part of it. Amongst these cultivators there were, from the end of the third century onwards, numbers of Germans to whom lands had been conceded individually on condition that they put them under cultivation.

The obligations of the cultivator towards his patron varied considerably; sometimes he made payment in kind, sometimes in money, and sometimes in labour; but once established they were never altered. Constantine expressly forbade proprietors to demand from their cultivators a different form of payment from that to which they had been accustomed. And thus it came about that the lot of cultivators varied considerably according to circumstances; some working large and prosperous farms from which they derived an easy competence, others living in abject misery under conditions which the hardest toil could never make sufficiently remunerative.

After the cultivator class came that of the freedmen, old slaves who had won their liberty under very varying circumstances. The manumitted slaves still bore the brand of their origin. They became very numerous in Gaul in the fourth century, and occupied an appointed position in society which brought them a certain recognition. Their condition seems even to have been better than that of the common people. They had won their freedom by their work, their intelligence, and their skill, and seemed to form a sort of popular aristocracy. The position occupied by the freedmen in Rome is well known. Many of the Roman nobility were very much displeased by it, and it was largely in order to criticise the power of the freedmen that Tacitus wrote his *Germania*.

The bond between the freedman and his old master was not severed. Morally the freedman still formed part of the latter's household. He still came to pray at the altars of his patron's *gens*, and superintended the upkeep of the tomb in which his old master slept with his ancestors. And in various ways he continued to render him homage.

At the bottom of the social scale came the slaves. Nevertheless their lot was not always one of misery. It partook of a patriarchal nature, as they were attached to the same house from generation to generation. They were often bound to their masters by strong ties of affection and devotion. Sometimes the slave was even buried in the family tomb by the side of the master he had served. Funeral inscriptions make mention of this. On more than one altar may be read an invocation to the gods from him who built it, beseeching them " on behalf of his son and his slave."

The rich possessed slaves by the hundred. Families in modest circumstances had a family of slaves attached to the house. The occupations carried on by the latter were of infinite variety ranging from the fine arts, letters, music and dancing to the roughest of toil.

The Church did not forbid this form of servitude. The

207

clerics and the monasteries had their slaves, and the Councils devised the means of securing their possession. But the Church endeavoured to ameliorate their lot. For the mere fact that she preached the equality of all men before God in a society where the new faith was very strong resulted in accomplishing much towards their future emancipation; and by this means rural slavery was transformed into serfdom of the soil. The change did not take place all at once, by virtue of any single law, sovereign decree, or general consent. We have seen that troops of slaves worked on the large domains, and it often happened that one or other of these bands became allotted to the cultivation of a particular piece of land; and thus the slave became a serf. And, by an inverse process, more than one free cultivator, hereditarily attached to the cultivation of a particular spot, saw his holding transformed into serfdom, even if it were only because the ground he worked did not suffice to support him, and he himself desired the change in his position.

Lastly, outside the various social classes we have just described, the people properly so-called, the inhabitants of the towns and the country districts, lived outside the limits we have outlined. We know little about them. The rich alone knew how to write, or rather they were the only people who were written about. They could still take an interest in the cultivators, the freedmen, and even the slaves who formed part of the social hierarchy of which they, the rich, were the highest in the scale; but these vague, floating masses, who had nothing in common with them, failed altogether to rouse their interest.

BIBLIOGRAPHY.—Works of Catullus, Julius Cæsar, Cicero, Dio Cassius, Jordanes, Plutarch's Life of Cæsar, Apollonius Sidonius, Strabo, Suetonius' Life of Cæsar, Tacitus, various editions. Barthélemy, *Alesia, son véritable emplacement*, from *Rev. des questions hist.*, 1867. Ernest Desjardins, *Géographie hist. et Administ. de la Gaule romaine*, 1876–93. Aug. Longnon, *Études sur les pagi de la Gaule*, 1869. Am. Thierry, *La Littérature profane en Gaule au IVe siècle, Revue des Deux Mondes*, 1873. Boissier, *Les Rhéteurs gaulois au IVe siècle, Journal des savants*, 1884; reprinted in *La Fin du paganisme*, 1891. Cam. Jullian, *l'Avènement de Septime Sévère et la bataille de Lyon, Rev. hist.*, 1889. Julien Havet, *Les Origines de Saint-Denis*, from *Bibl. de l'Ec. des Chartes*, 1890. Am. Thierry, *Hist. de la Gaule sous la domination romaine*, 4th ed., 1878. Hirschfeld, *Lyon in der Römerzeit*, 1878. Cam. Jullian, *Ausone et son temps*, 1891. Friedländer,

Gallien und ihre Kultur unter die Römer, Deutsche Rundschau, 1877, Fustel de Coulanges, *La Gaule Romaine,* 1891. Cam. Jullian, *Gallia, tableau sommaire de la Gaule sous la domination romaine,* 1892. Jullian, *Le Fondateur de Lyon, Munatius Plancus,* 1892. Cam. Jullian, *Ausone et Bordeaux,* 1893. Hirschfeld, *Aquitanien in der Römerzeit,* 1896. Mohl, *Introduction à la chronologie du latin vulgaire,* 1899. Mohl, *Les Origines romanes,* 1900. R. Holmes, *Cæsar's conquest of Gaul,* 1899. Guglielmo Ferrero, *Grandeur et décadence de Rome,* 1903, *sq.* 5 vols. C. Bayet, *Le Christianisme,* in *Hist. de France,* edited by E. Lavisse, 1903. Ém. Esperandieu, *Recueil général des bas-reliefs de la Gaule romaine,* 1907–1910, 3 vols. Cam. Jullian, *Hist. de la Gaule,* 1908, *sq.* 6 vols. Bonnard, *La Gaule thermale,* 1908. [Maxime Petit], *Histoire de France illustrée,* 1909. De Pachtere, *Paris à l'époque gallo-romaine,* 1912. J. Morin, *La Verrerie en Gaule sous l'empire romain,* 1913. Fr. Cumont, *Comment la Belgique fut romanisée, Ann. Soc. archéol. de Bruxelles,* 1914. Cam. Jullian, *Vercingetorix,* 6th ed., 1914. Cam. Jullian, *De la Gaule en France,* 1922. Aug. Longnon, *La Formation de l'unité française,* 1922. P. Imbart de la Tour, *Histoire politique des Origines à 1515,* in *Hist. de la Nation française,* edited by Gabr. Hanotaux [1922]. Cam. Jullian, *Le Paris des Romains,* 1925.

209

CHAPTER IV

THE MEROVINGIANS

The great invasions. The Alemanni occupy Alsace. The Franks take Cologne and Treves (418). Clodion. The Burgundians installed as occupants of the valley of the Rhone and the Franks north of the Somme. Attila and his Huns. Aetius. His victory on the Catalaunian Plains (June 4th, 451). Clovis. A royal brigand. History of his reign. How he became a Catholic and conquered part of Gaul. Saint Clotilda. Gregory of Tours. A great prince : Theodoric, King of the Ostrogoths. His letters to Clovis. Intervention of the Emperor of the East. The Gallo-Roman aristocracy is not deprived of its lands. The sons of Clovis. Character of each of them. They divide their father's kingdom between them, but one of them, Clotar, reunites it under his own rule after the death of his brothers. The great man of the group : Theodebert, grandson of Clovis. His expeditions into Italy ; his designs on the throne of the East. Fresh partition between the grandsons of Clovis. A bloodthirsty dilettante : Childeric, King of Neustria. Galswinthe. Fredegonde. Brunehaut. Murder of Galswinthe. War of Chilperic against his brother Sigebert, King of Austrasia. Gontran, King of the Burgundians. Clotar II sole King. Torture of Brunehaut. The good King Dagobert. The decline of the Merovingians. Mayors of the Palace and Sluggard Kings. The Bishops : their authority, their power, their moral, political and social influence. They are the real leaders of the people. The great Merovingian domains and immunity.

WE have seen how the barbarians, in addition to their terrible invasions, succeeded in making a peaceful penetration of Gaul. Established there as cultivators, they lived under the protection of Roman Law, but were regarded as citizens of inferior rank. The law forbade marriage between a Gaul and a German woman, just as it did between a free man and a slave.

The Great Invasions.

The Germans presented themselves in large numbers on the frontiers, demanding admission into the frame-

210

work of the Roman Empire. In 370, the Emperor Valentinian informed the Burgundians that he wished to raise several thousand recruits from among them. Eighty thousand presented themselves but were hurriedly sent back.

The leudes—from the same root as the German *leute*, people —consisted of groups of Germans of low origin, who were attached to the Roman armies and established in compact masses on the lands they were commissioned to defend. Others had come in as agriculturists, but on condition of undertaking military service. Many of them became Roman citizens, and some, abandoning their German names, succeeded in reaching the highest rank. The tribes of leudes were settled chiefly along the frontiers, but some were found as far as Noyon, Rheims, Le Mans, Bayeux and Coutance, Clermont in Auvergne and Rennes.

The bodyguard of the Emperors gradually came to be formed largely of barbarians, and especially of Germans. And thus the barbarians came to exercise great influence, and even had a voice in the election of the head of the State. It was German auxiliaries who in the year 360 proclaimed Julian the Apostate Emperor Augustus in Paris. They raised him on a large shield, clashing their bucklers, as was the custom of their country.

The "great invasion" began in 405. The Suevi, the most important of the German nations, headed by Radagaisius, swooped down on Italy, where the famous Stilico inflicted a bloody defeat upon them in front of Florence. But the movement had been unloosed. There were the Burgundians, the Vandals, the Alans (406–407), the latter a Scythian race from the Caucasus. "Nearly all the Alans are handsome, and somewhat fair. Their greatest glory is to kill a man. They make trophies of the skin taken from the heads of the vanquished. They worship in no temple. Their god is a scimitar planted in the ground (Ammianus)."

The Alemanni occupied Alsace. "Numberless tribes," writes Saint Jerome, "invaded Gaul from the Alps to the Pyrenees, from the Atlantic to the Rhine—Quadi, Vandals, Sarmatians, Alans, Gepidæ, Heruli, Saxons, Burgundians and Alemanni. Mayence was taken and sacked, and thousands of men were massacred in the church. Worms succumbed. Rheims, Amiens,

211

Arras, Thérouanne, Tournai and Strasbourg fell into the hands of the barbarians. Aquitania and the districts of Lyons and Narbonne were ravaged." A devastating flood swept across the fertile fields of Aquitania, crossed the Pyrenees, and spread over Spain.

The Franks founded their power on their bonds with the Empire. They seized Cologne and Treves (418). "I have seen the ground heaped up with dead," writes Salvienus, "bodies of both sexes, naked and torn, exposed to the birds and the dogs. The stench of corpses infected the living." "The ravaging of Gaul lasted a long time" (Stilico).

The seat of government was moved back from Treves to Arles.

And now the Franks were masters on both banks of the Rhine from the mouth to the Hercynnian Forest. The widows of the best Gallo-Roman families entered the service of the invaders' wives. Under the leadership of Clodion, they pushed as far as the Somme; but at Hesdin-le-Vieux, on the banks of the Canche, Aetius met them and inflicted a severe defeat upon them. Sidonius gives us the details. "On the neighbouring banks of the river, the Franks were celebrating a marriage according to Scythian rites. The maiden was fair as was also the bridegroom. On the chariots were all the preparations for the feast, plates, dishes and cauldrons full of food, the whole decorated with garlands of flowers." Everything, including the bride, fell into the hands of the conquerors (436).

The bonds with Rome were renewed by Aetius, who allowed the Franks to keep their new conquests on condition of swearing fealty to the Empire and providing soldiers. And thus the Franks were settled among the natives in the usual circumstances—a partition of lands and houses. The Franks preferred to leave the walled towns to the Gallo-Romans, and established themselves in the country on the large domains. Numberless villas had been destroyed for generations; these the Franks rebuilt in their own way.

The Burgundians were installed in the basin of the Mein. They appeared on the Rhine and took up their abode in the region of Worms, where they founded a kingdom celebrated in literary history through the Lay of the Niebelungen, which hymns their great deeds and their misfortunes. Unfortunately the *Niebelungenlied* has not come down to us in its original shape. In its present form, which seems to date from the thirteenth century, it is no longer even an epic poem, like the *Chanson de Roland* and the *Chanson de Guillaume d'Orange,* but a romance of chivalry.

We now lose sight of the Burgundians until the year 435, when Aetius inflicted upon them a crushing defeat in which their King Gunther met with his death. Aetius, in answer to the supplications of the vanquished, made peace with them; but after the year 437, the Huns, led by Attila, appeared and put to the sword all that remained of the Court of the Burgundian Kings and part of the people. This forms the plot of the *Niebelungenlied.* The Burgundians had already been converted to Arianism.

The Roman Empire welcomed the fugitive nation and allowed it to settle on the banks of the Rhone. They were established there as defenders of the land, as " guests," that is to say, as soldiers.

According to law, the inhabitants were bound to give up to them a third of their houses and slaves, and half their land and woods. The " guests " settled down with their wives and children. Towards the end of the fifth century we find the Burgundians living in this way in Savoy, in Dauphiny, in the basin of the Saône and on the upper reaches of the Loire, at Lyons and in the surrounding district. They seem to have been the least rough of all the German tribes, and the most adaptable to a new form of civilisation. They were workers and liked a sedentary life. Apollonius Sidonius, Bishop and poet, had no complaint to make against these seven-foot giants, except that they greased their hair with rancid butter and exuded an odour of garlic and onions.

The Goths came from the shores of the Baltic and southern Sweden. We know a little more about their feats and achievements, for they had a historian—Jordanes. In the fourth century they spread over the plains of southern Russia and Roumania of the present day, divided into two great nations, the Visigoths or the Goths of the West, and the Ostrogoths or the Goths of the East. Like the Burgundians, they had been converted to the Christian religion in its Arian form.

About 376, the Visigoths and Ostrogoths were invaded by formidable inundations of Huns, and retired upon the Roman Empire. Theodosius stopped them. After his death (396) Alaric and then his brother-in-law Ataülf (412) resumed their victorious progress. Ataülf overran the south of Gaul and Spain. At Narbonne he married Placida, the daughter of Theodosius, and sister of the two Emperors Arcadius and Honorius. As a wedding present the bridegroom gave his wife the booty taken from her own people in Rome. Ataülf had conceived the ambition of defending the Roman Empire, but he perished at the hands of assassins in 415. He was succeeded by his brother Vallia, to whom Honorius ceded the territory between Toulouse and the Atlantic, together with Bordeaux and certain towns in the neighbouring provinces, under the usual conditions, that is to say, as guests and defenders of the Empire (419). Toulouse became the capital of the new kingdom, which gradually extended its borders, acquiring Narbonne and then Nîmes, and finally crossing the Pyrenees and including a part of Spain.

Like the Visigoths, all these barbarians who settled down in Gaul had promised to serve the Empire faithfully and to use their forces in a friendly fashion for the preservation of the majesty of the Roman people—*majestatem populi Romani comiter conservare*. Thus they formed encampments throughout Gaul, just like the Roman encampments.

The Gallo-Romans—and this is an important fact—were not the subjects of the new arrivals who had settled in their midst, but continued to be under the jurisdiction of the Empire.

The Burgundians, Goths and Visigoths seem to have lived on friendly terms with the Gallic people. The energetic administration of Julian had only put a stop to the extortion of the imperial officials for a short time. But the Goths and Visigoths were more considerate. " The subjects of the Empire who came under their rule," writes Salvienus, " desired nothing less than to be forced to return to the rule of Rome." And certain Gauls together with their families and modest belong-

214

ings even left the districts still under the administration of Rome and came to settle among the Burgundians and the Visigoths, who did not weigh them down beneath such a heavy burden of impositions and taxes.

Thus in the first quarter of the fifth century we find three kingdoms established in Gaul—the Franks north of the Somme, the Burgundians in the basins of the Saône and the upper Loire and in the valley of the Rhone, and the Visigoths in the south, between the Rhone and the Atlantic. The Alemanni had spread over Alsace, the Saxons, a seafaring folk, swarmed along the sea-coast from the Scheldt to the Loire, and finally a Celtic people from Great Britain by continually sending small groups of settlers came to occupy the greater part of the Armorican peninsula.

It must be remembered that the Gallo-Romans were Catholics, the Visigoths and Burgundians Arians and the Franks pagans who worshipped Wotan, Thunder, the Sun, the Earth and the Moon.

As for the Huns, who made their appearance in the second half of the fourth century, they were the most barbarous of the barbarians, a terror even to the latter themselves. They were Tartars. They were an extremely vigorous race, with small, tawny, round heads supported on thick necks. They wore turned-down caps, cloth tunics and goatskin breeches. A contemporary writer compares them to caryatides, because they walked with their bodies bent forward " like two-legged animals," due no doubt to their life on horseback.

" This people," writes Ammianus, " are of unbounded ferocity. They cover the cheeks of their children with deep wounds in order to prevent them from growing beards later on."

According to the same historian, the Huns did not know how to cook or to season their food, but lived on roots and raw meat. Their method of cooking consisted in sitting on the meat for a time when they were on horseback. They built no houses, " but shunned them as they would shun a sepulchre." They used their chariots to live in, and these formed the only shelter they had for family life. In the domain of military art they knew nothing beyond impetuous onslaughts, with a terrific din and clatter, and furious shouts; they were also

215

skilled in shooting arrows with points made of sharp bone. They fought with the sword and the lasso.

" If you ask one of them whence he comes," says Ammianus, " he can only answer that he was born far away from the place where he was conceived, and brought up yet further away."

Attila, their chief, was a tall, vigorous man, broad-chested and ferocious-looking, with small, very bright eyes which were never still; his beard was sparse and his nose short and flat, and his complexion dark like the rest of his race. He loved war, which he carried on, not only as a fighter, but as a skilled soldier. Gifted with a rare intelligence, he could be trusted to keep his word, to be faithful in friendship and amenable to supplication.

The historian Priscus, who was sent to Attila by Theodosius the Younger, has described his celebrated camp in Pannonia (Hungary). It was a sort of town enclosed by a fence of shining polished wood, the parts of which were joined with such consummate art that the joins could not be seen by the naked eye. Within the enclosure, instead of houses there were numberless tents arranged in orderly fashion. They were all spacious with entrances resembling porticoes. In the centre was the tent of Attila, larger and vaster than the rest, and made of magnificent materials.

It was in 451 that the barbarian hordes crossed the Rhine between Worms and Bingen under the leadership of Attila. On the 6th April Metz was taken and burnt, and the inhabitants massacred. Paris was threatened, and in an agony of fear the Parisii would have deserted their town and sought refuge in the depths of the woods, had they not been calmed and reassured by the voice of a young girl—Saint Geneviève. Geneviève is said to have been a little shepherdess from Nanterre; she may have come from Nanterre, but she was never, any more than Joan of Arc, a shepherdess. Her parents were well-to-do, just as were the parents of Joan of Arc. In the case of Geneviève the mistake was circulated in the seventeenth century owing to the false interpretation of an allegorical engraving, depicting Geneviève praying on the walls of Paris, the inhabitants being represented by sheep, whilst outside the enclosure the Huns were portrayed as wolves. The menace to Paris ended in smoke. Treves was defended by its Bishop Saint Lupus and Orleans by its Bishop Saint Aignan, just as Metz had been by its Bishop Auctor. The power and prestige of the Bishops became consolidated. Aetius hastened up with all the forces he could collect. Franks, Burgundians, Armoricans and Visigoths flocked to join his standards.

Aetius was one of the great figures of the period. From the age of twenty he was to be seen indefatigably barring the road to the barbarians from one end of the Empire to the other. He was born in Mysia (the present Serbia and Bulgaria). In his youth he had lived for some years among the Goths. Alaric, who had become fond of him, trained him in the profession of arms, after which he spent several years with the Huns. And thus he learnt the manners and customs, and the strong and weak side of the barbarians. His administrative and diplomatic gifts equalled his military genius. He conquered one after the other the Visigoths, the Franks, the Burgundians and the Bretons of Armorica. " In him," says Jordanes, " was vested the whole fate of the Empire."

Attila was besieging Orleans and the defence of the town was being directed by Saint Aignan. On the 4th June, 451, Aetius forced the Hun to raise the siege. The decisive battle, the celebrated Battle of the Catalaunian Plains, was fought between Troyes and Châlons-sur-Marne. It was one of the greatest events in European history, the most important in the history of France since the siege of Alesia.

Attila had under his command not only hordes of Huns, but also Ostrogoths, Gepidæ, Thuringians and Alemanni, who followed him as subjects or tributaries. Aetius, on the other hand, had under him Franks—under the command of Meroveus —Visigoths, Burgundians and Saxons, who rendered him obedience as " Roman soldiers."

Blood flowed in such profuse abundance, writes Jordanes, that the stream which watered the plain was transformed into a torrent by it. The soldiers, brought to its banks by thirst, drank blood.

As his army was flinching, Attila retired into his camp, which he had surrounded by the thousands of chariots which followed in the train of the barbarians. Jordanes gives a picture of him here, among his own people, " like a lion who, hard pressed by the hunters, stands in the mouth of his lair, whence he dare not emerge, but still makes the forest tremble with his roaring." The enemy was afraid to attack him, and Attila beat a retreat, not forgetting as he retired to sack the town of Treves. In the following year he hurled himself upon Italy.

Three years had elapsed since his great victory when Aetius was murdered by the Emperor Valentinian III. Terrified by the enthusiasm he inspired in the army, Valentinian lured him to Court and killed him with his own hands. One of the greatest of the Romans was killed by the head of the Empire out of jealousy of his valour.

With the death of Aetius the history of Rome may be said to close.

In the fifth century the Franks were divided into two groups —the Salians established in the north, in the Netherlands, as far as the Somme, and the Ripuarians, the " river-side folk," settled between the banks of the Rhine and the Meuse—whence their name.

Clovis.

Each of these groups was subdivided into tribes, and each of these tribes had a chief whom writers called " a king,"— kinglets like the kings of Homeric Greece. Ennodius, Bishop of Pavia, writing about this period, remarks in connection with an army commanded by Theodosius the Great, that the barbarian kings of the Germans were so numerous in these parts that they alone required all the resources of a district without counting their men. The German historian Junghans declares that in this way the territory of the Franks under its numerous princes was " cut up into numberless bits."

Over the tribe of the Salians, established in the district of Tournai, there had reigned since 481 a young chief named Clovis—which is the same as Louis—great-grandson of a certain Clodion, who by settling the Salians about 440 in the region of Flanders, Brabant and Tournai, had ended the era of migration for this people.

The Franks were a race of robbers. Historians declared that " war was the ordinary avocation of the Franks." They gave the name of war to what is usually known as brigandage. Speaking of the Alemanni, the first cousins of the Franks,

Abbé Dubos writes, " They made a regular business of over-running Italy and going there to reap their harvests sword in hand. These brigands were living the same kind of life when in 496 they were driven out of their country by Clovis." His was also the same " kind of life " and " business " as that of the Franks, but it was not carried on in Italy. Theodoric the Great assigned territory to the conquered Alemanni on the northern frontier of his Empire. Ennodius writes to him :

" You have established a body of Alemanni in Italy. You allow yourself to be protected by those who plundered you. You have preserved them as a national body, and have given to Italy as her guardian angel a people who used continually to invade her territory."

What Theodoric did for the Alemanni, Aetius, the master of the Roman militia in Gaul, had done for the Franks after he had conquered Clodion. He had settled them in the north of the country, transforming into " guests "—we have already seen the meaning of this word—the former robbers and vagabonds.

They were curious soldiers. A band of brigands encamped in the woods, living in the swamps and marshes, like the brigands of classical times, in those huge forests which covered Belgium, the dark " coal-bearing " forest which is the continuation of the Ardennes. The Franks formed a sparse population here, scattered about in small groups. Gregory of Tours gives Clovis 3000 companions—no doubt an exaggerated figure. The Franks devoted themselves to hunting in their woods and fishing in the rivers that ran through them. They had tame deer to act as decoys to the wild deer. They practised the breeding of cattle, sheep and goats, and above all, of huge black pigs, which were very wild and fierce. We have seen how much the pork produce of this district was appreciated in Italy in the second century. The Franks also kept bees for honey, by which they set great store. Their agriculture in the open spaces enlarged by felling the trees, and on the confines of the woods, was quite primitive, and chiefly in the hands of the women. They practised " war," and when they were not pillaging, they spent their days in getting drunk on coarse beer and in playing games of chance to the accompaniment of swearing and fighting. An embryonic industry was the task of slaves, unfortunate wretches whom they had carried off in the course of their " wars " from more civilised peoples.

The most popular branch of this industry was that of the jeweller. Just as the first Romans had chosen the wolf and the Gauls the boar as their sign, so the Franks had taken the bee. On the tomb of Childeric, in Tournai, there are bees carved in gold. Some historians interpret the *fleur de lis* of the Capets as a development from the wearing down of the Frankish bee. And it is indeed curious that Napoleon I should have replaced the *fleur de lis* by the bee.

The Franks wore a sort of cloak, half linen and half leather, which came down very low over their bodies, covering half their legs, under which a blouse with narrow sleeves and breeches covered the body closely. They were overloaded with amulets, bracelets and rings. The women wore necklaces made of beads of gold, amber or glass. The men shaved their faces, leaving only the moustache. Their hair, generally fair or red, was gathered up in a tuft on the top of the head. Thus they kept their hair long on the top and short at the back. Only members of the royal family kept the whole of their hair long and allowed it to fall right down their backs as far as the waist. The slaves had their heads shaved.

Whether they were fair or red-haired, the Franks generally had green eyes.

Their chief weapon was the double-headed axe, with the iron fastened into a handle of ox or horse bone, the famous battle-axe, which they were skilled in hurling to a distance. They also had a kind of javelin shaped like a hooked harpoon. " They hurl this dart at the first onslaught," says Procopius, " and if it happens to be thrown swiftly and enters the body, the spikes stick out through the skin, whilst the handle pulls in the opposite direction, and the wounded man cannot extricate himself from it. Or else they succeed in hooking their harpoon into the enemy's shield and thus depriving him of it."

The horsemen, who were few in number, were armed with a short strong lance, generally made of iron, the end of which was very pointed and also had a double edge.

Procopius gives us a picture of the Franks in their encampments : " Some were sharpening their battle-axes and their lances, others were setting their darts; one man was mending what he had broken. They have hardly any armour and do not require any skilled artisan to forge it. They merely have a few smiths who know how to resolder it when it snaps or breaks. The Franks do not wear greaves or breastplates. Most of them fight bare-headed. They do not use bows, or slings, or balistas."

Their houses consisted of huts made of mud or wood, covered with branches or straw, similar to those of the primitive Gauls, but even more rudimentary.

Such was the life of the Franks towards the end of the fifth century, between the Meuse and the North Sea. In the whole of that region there were only two towns—walled encampments —Tournai, where Clovis lived, and Cambrai, where Ragnachar, another Frankish chief, was in command.

The organisation of society was rudimentary—based upon the family which had swelled out into a primitive clan. Each of these small homogeneous groups was under the authority of a chief, and over them, in command of all the bands, was a head chief, whom the writers call " king " for want of a better name. Between the individuals, grouped into families, and this chief, there was no intermediary. The chief had absolute authority and power of life and death.

We have but little information about the lives and actions of the Franks at this period; we only know that they were plunderers. Treves, among other places, underwent a terrible ordeal. The town was sacked by the Franks, who made no attempt to keep it, or to settle down in it and administer it. They preferred to leave to the industry of the inhabitants the task of amassing a little wealth again, after which they returned and pillaged it a second and third time. Truly " war " was the daily " business " of the Franks.

Clodion seems to have had a son named Meroveus, whom we have seen at the head of his band, under the command of Aetius, in the Catalaunian Plains, and of whom we know nothing beyond the fact that he gave his name to the dynasty. In order to understand how an almost unknown prince could have named a line of kings, we must realise the influence wielded by poetry. He was said to be the son of a sea-god, whence his name. The wife of Clodion was walking along the shore when she is supposed to have been surprised by a god rising out of the waves. The people composed songs celebrating the great deeds which led to her seduction, little poems some of which have been preserved in Latin verse of barbarous form—songs which the women themselves used to sing, beating time with their hands and feet. In connection with the expedition of Clotar II against the Saxons, Hildegaire, Bishop of Meaux, writes, " From this victory was born a popular song which, on account of its very rusticity, flew from mouth to mouth, and the women sang it in chorus, beating time with their hands." In these songs Meroveus played a great part, and through them loomed large in the minds of men.

Meroveus died young, and was succeeded by his son Childeric (457). Though we have no information about Meroveus, we have plenty, even too much, about Childeric. But it is nearly all legendary. He allied himself with the Romans established in Gaul against the Saxons who were swarming along the coasts, and threatening to take Angers; and also against the Bretons who had made a victorious advance as far as Bourges and had entered that town. In 463 we find Childeric, still in alliance with the Romans, waging war against the Visigoths, who, in their turn, were threatening Angers.

Later on we find him fighting against the Alemanni. In this alliance with the Roman elements in the country Childeric and his Franks had aroused the attention of the Catholic Gallo-Romans who were subjected to Arian princes. The Arians, who were Christians, and held Christ and the Gospels in honour, interfered with the Catholics in their worship and occupied their basilicas. The Catholics thought that the barbarians, being pagans, would prove indifferent to their religion and show more tolerance. Moreover paganism was on the decline and the conversion of an idolatrous prince was much more likely to occur than that of an Arian prince. Thus we find the Lingones, the Catholic Gallo-Romans of the Langres district, and the subjects of a Burgundian king who was an Arian, turning their eyes towards Childeric. This fact is important.

In order to understand what follows, we must take into
222

consideration the political situation of Gaul in the second half of the fifth century. We have seen how various barbarian peoples had been established, but under certain conditions, as guests, or, in other words, as soldiers defending the Roman Empire—the Franks in the north, the Burgundians in the valleys of the Saône and the Rhone and the Visigoths south of the Loire—these were roughly the boundaries. Instead of payment they had been given lands. " Behold the barbarian," observes Eumenes, " he sows and he reaps; if the Empire wants to raise men, he hastens up; he obeys every order, and submits to punishment without a murmur, and under the name of soldier he regards himself lucky to be a slave."

The western cantons along the coast were occupied by leagues of Armoricans and by the Saxons, who had renounced the sovereignty of Rome. There remained one part of the country which was not governed by any barbarian prince, but was subject to a Roman ruler, a lieutenant of the Emperor, who bore the title of " master of the militia," but who had also made himself independent, if not in theory, at all events in practice, just like the barbarian kings, and behaved just as they did. This district, which Gregory of Tours calls " the kingdom of Syagrius," was bounded on the north by the Somme, where it had for neighbours the Salians, on the east by the valley of the Moselle, where its neighbours were the Ripuarians, on the south, as far as the heights of Auxerre, by the kingdom of the Burgundians, and finally on the east by the Armorican league, which had freed itself from the Empire by repudiating the authority of the Roman general which represented it. The " kingdom of Syagrius," as it was called by Gregory of Tours, from the name of the military chief who ruled it in the time of Clovis, had for its capital Soissons. And it was indeed a kingdom untainted by provincialism. The military chiefs who ruled under imperial mandate, acted as sovereign monarchs. The Roman general, with whom Childeric entered into alliance against the Visigoths, the Armoricans and the Alemanni, was called Paulus. He was succeeded by Egidius, the Count Gilles of old French historians. He was a member of an illustrious Gallo-Roman family, the *familia Syagria*, which could boast of a consul in its ranks—Afranius Syagrius (382).

This " Count Gilles " was a man of valour. Contemporaries
are full of praise for his military virtues. His death, at the
beginning of the year 461, was a great grief to the district he
ruled. It is not correct to say that his son Syagrius succeeded
him. Syagrius never had the title of " Master of the Militia,"
a title at that time considered far superior to that of king.
Syagrius only succeeded his father in the much more restricted
functions of governor of the city of Soissons, the word " city "
meaning, not only the town, but also the territory of which it
was the capital.

Syagrius too seems to have been a man of merit, but he lived
in times that became ever more and more troublous. And he
did not exercise the great power his father had enjoyed. He
knew the Germans so well and spoke their language so correctly
that the Franks and Alemanni were on their guard in his presence
in case they committed a solecism in their own tongue.

Childeric died when he was still young—about forty—at
Tournai. His tomb was discovered in the seventeenth century,
and a likeness of him with long hair on a ring. He was buried
with his charger and his weapons. The death of Childeric is
placed in 481. He was succeeded by his son Clovis.

The Roman Empire of the West had just come to an end in
the person of Romulus Augustulus, who was deposed after the
capture of Rome by a barbarian chief, Odovacar, prince of
the Heruli (476). The last nominal Emperor of the West,
Flavienus Julianus Nepos, who took refuge in Dalmatia, was
assassinated in that country on the 9th of May, 480, and Gaul
opened her arms to a fresh destiny.

Several writers of the period, particularly Salvienus, have
depicted the Franks as brave, affable and generous barbarians,
though they were lying and treacherous. Procopius, in speaking of them, says, " This nation breaks its faith more easily
than any other." And Clovis seems to have been a man of
this character, possessed, moreover, of a subtle, crafty and
deceitful barbarian intelligence.

Clovis was sixteen when he came to the throne. He naturally
began his reign in the district of Tournai, his little Empire.
His tender years explain why the first years of his rule passed
by without any important undertaking. It is true that his

224

history is difficult to follow. His sole historian, Gregory of Tours, wrote a hundred years after his death, and, in his simplicity of mind, merely re-echoed the various legends and anecdotes current about the subject of his history. We have already mentioned the poetic traditions of the time, circulated in the form of songs. Many such songs were composed about Clovis and we shall see how the king of the Franks himself contributed to their number. Several historians, Gabriel Monod, W. Junghans, and Godefroy Kurth, believe that Gregory of Tours made use of them and turned them into prose, a theory to which Maurice Prou very rightly objects that " Gregory nowhere makes any reference to these poems." Fustel de Coulanges also observes, " Some modern writers maintain that Gregory must have made use of the Germanic songs in praise of Clovis and the Franks; this is pure hypothesis, without any foundation in fact. Gregory of Tours, who gives his authorities, never mentions them." Nevertheless these songs existed, and in addition there were popular legends and hagiographic tales. Henri Bordier seems to point to the chief source used by Gregory of Tours. When Queen Clotilda became a widow, she retired to Tours, and lived there for thirty-four years close to the sacred basilica. Gregory became Bishop of Tours in 573. He must have collected the tales told by people who had heard them from Saint Clotilda.

Clovis secured the triumph of Catholicism in Gaul, and through Gaul, in the world. The Bishops and the sacred writers who deal with him were filled with immense gratitude to him, and in their sincere enthusiasm they made a travesty of his acts and deeds. The few letters and diplomas which are said to have been written by him are apocryphal as well as the most important texts upon which the history of his reign has been reconstructed. About the civil administration of the Frankish prince we are also in total ignorance.

But this fact has not discouraged his panegyrists, in the front rank of whom must be placed the great historian Godefroy Kurth. " The greater part of the narrative left us by Gregory of Tours," they say, " is legendary or comes from a poetic source." Whereupon they proceed to build up a history of Clovis upon this self-same narrative, discarding as poetical

225

anything that does not suit their purpose and accepting anything which supports their point of view.

Everything that has been written in connection with the marriage of Clovis, the vow of Zülpich, the vase of Soissons, the baptism of the Frankish king and the conversion of his army by Saint Remi—to mention only the most important facts—is merely the embroidery of legend. All that remains are the fundamental outlines, the woof upon which the imagination of the sixth century set to work.

Clovis united under his rule a large part of Gaul; this much is certain. His conquest may be divided into two parts; we are not speaking from the chronological point of view, for the chronology of the history of Clovis is impossible to determine. The first part, which Clovis must have had great difficulty in carrying out, was his struggle against the kinglets of the Franks and Salians in his neighbourhood, for, as we have seen, there was not only a Frankish king at Tournai, but there was also one at Cambrai, another at Thérouanne, and yet another at Dispargum—Dispargum, the mysterious, which seems to have disappeared to-day—and in many other places, not to mention the Ripuarians whose capital was at Cologne. Gregory of Tours makes all these princes relatives of Clovis. All that is certain is that by a series of sudden attacks, murders, ambuscades and perjuries, Clovis succeeded in uniting all these peoples under his own authority. In this little epic, dripping with blood, Clovis, at the head of his three thousand companions, hiding in the woods, armed with their axe with its horse-bone handle and their famous dagger, the skramasax, seems a regular bandit chief, greedy of gold and power, to whom all means are good and the quickest are the best. Gregory of Tours describes Clovis to the grandson of the hero : " When Clovis put to death all the kings who were opposed to him, he had neither gold nor silver."

Gregory exposes this debauchery of crime with quasi-religious emotion, as a work of brigandage in which he could see the hand of God. It would be impossible to find a more typical example of the way the critical faculty of a good man can be utterly destroyed by a fixed idea. The sole matter of importance for Gregory of Tours was to have right ideas about the

Holy Trinity, and to believe that the Son had existed from all eternity like the Father; this point once settled, the rest did not matter.

The following dialogue, which the saint himself repeats, lays bare his state of mind. Gregory had entered into a discussion with an Arian, " a man devoid of all capacity for finding ideas," says the Bishop. Agila, the Arian, was having a theological discussion with his opponent, when the latter began all of a sudden to cover him with abuse. The Arian replied :
" Do not blaspheme against a law you do not observe. We for our part, although our belief may not be the same as yours, do not blaspheme against it, because it cannot be regarded as a crime to believe this or that. There is even a proverb among us that if a man passes between the altars of the Gentiles and the church of God, he does no wrong in honouring them both."

These words laid bare to Gregory the " stupidity " of his interlocutor, and saying that he did not wish " to cast his sacred pearls before filthy swine," he abandoned the discussion and left the place.

It must not be imagined that Clovis had from the beginning conceived the vast plan he ultimately realised. He saw that there were territories to be occupied and treasures to be pillaged ; but he worked by stages, gradually widening his field of action as his means of execution increased. After having extended his power in the regions about him with all the temerity and wanton spirit of youth, among the Salian Franks themselves, he cast his eyes on the territory which still remained Roman in his own neighbourhood.

Clovis seized the situation quite clearly. In the so-called " kingdom " of Syagrius, the authority of the Roman chief no longer possessed any basis since the disappearance of the Western Empire, and the Gallic population were impatient under the yoke of the Romans. Orosius, writing in the fifth century, says that numbers of Gallo-Romans preferred to go and live among the barbarians a life of poverty but of independence, rather than remain among the Romans as tributary serfs. Salvienus says the same.

Syagrius had only inherited a fragment of his father's authority, and was only obeyed in a very restricted area—the

227

city of Soissons. Moreover, his " kingdom " was riddled with Bagaudæ in revolt against the exactions of the Treasury and against the nobles. Hostile groups of them occupied whole cantons and other rebels were continually swelling their ranks. " Subjects of the Empire," says Salvienus, " they became strangers to it without leaving its territory." It was the Bagaudæ who had opened Gaul to Attila, and they became formidable auxiliaries for Clovis.

The expedition against Syagrius, the Roman King of Soissons, which Junghans places in 486, probably did actually take place between the various slaughters carried out by Clovis in order to secure peaceful possession of his throne and increase his power. The power of the Roman chief had lost its foundation, as indeed had also that of the Burgundian and Visigoth monarchs, for they all enjoyed their position as defenders of the Empire in Gaul. But the kings of the Burgundians and the Visigoths continued to rely on their own subjects, whilst the authority of a man like Syagrius, depending as it did upon his soldiers themselves, was weakened by the disappearance of the Emperor.

Thus the field was opened to Clovis, who was young, intelligent, audacious and utterly devoid of scruple.

As for reasons for attacking his neighbour, he brought none forward—which was just as well. It is better in such wars of plunder not to attempt any sort of justification. They are rendered even more odious if, like Cæsar, at the beginning of the Gallic Wars, the aggressor invokes the rights and majesty of the Roman people in order to excuse a wicked attack.

It was quite a small war. Neither side put more than 3000 combatants into the field, and even these figures were doubtless not reached. Syagrius more particularly does not seem to have been able to raise any troops but those belonging to his own domains. One can imagine the young Clovis, leading his band of savage warriors, fair giants, with the backs of their heads shaved, and the hair on the top knotted up into a tufted crest above their foreheads, with their battle-axes and their hooked harpoons. " Such an army," says Augustin Thierry, " could not do without brigandage even in a friendly country."

Syagrius was defeated in the neighbourhood of Soissons (486) and took refuge with Alaric, King of the Visigoths, who ruled at Toulouse. Clovis demanded his surrender, threatening the Visigoths with his victorious army, reinforced by the soldiers of Syagrius who had come over to his side. Alaric was afraid of treachery on the part of the Gallo-Romans, and feared the hostility of the Burgundians. Syagrius was handed over. Clovis had him put to death in the depths of a dungeon " in order to avoid openly provoking his followers," says Godefroy Kurth.

Clovis inherited the whole of the kingdom of the late Roman. The majority of the soldiers who had rendered obedience to Syagrius, thenceforward fought under his command, though keeping their weapons and their ranks. The colours with the device of the bronze wolf mingled with those of the golden bee. " The Roman soldiers and warriors," says Procopius, " who had been left in Gaul for the defence of her frontiers, unable to return to Rome, or surrender themselves to the Burgundians or the Visigoths, who were Arians, ranged themselves on the side of the Franks together with their ensigns, and put into the hands of the Franks the places they were guarding for the Romans, though they kept their own customs, lands, laws and national dress."

Clovis became master of all that constituted the " Treasury," that is to say the coffers and the public lands of the Romans— money and villas. The latter were numerous, and formed the foundation of the wealth which was to be one of the elements of his power.

Clovis transferred his capital from Tournai to Soissons, where he installed himself in what has somewhat pompously been called " the palace of Syagrius." His power extended as far as the Loire. Moreover, nothing was changed in the condition of the Gallo-Romans, who from that time forward had to acknowledge the Frankish king as their chief.

The war against Syagrius was followed by the war which Clovis waged against the Thuringians, or rather against that portion of the Thuringian peoples established at the mouths of the Rhine and the Meuse—Gallic Thuringia. Between the Franks and the Thuringians there existed that ferocious and pitiless rivalry characteristic of hatred between barbarians.

Thierry, the eldest son of Clovis, reminded his brother and his Franks of all this. "You should remember the time when the Thuringians hurled themselves violently upon our fathers, who were suing for peace with them and giving hostages. But the Thuringians killed the hostages, and attacked our fathers, taking away all they possessed, and hanging the children to the trees by the sinews of their thighs. They killed two hundred young girls, whom they bound by their arms and legs to the necks of horses whom they goaded on and forced to tear them in bits; others they stretched out along the roadside bound to stakes, and made heavy chariots drive over them, and after thus breaking their bones, left them still alive a prey to the birds and dogs."

As compared with the Thuringians, Clovis no doubt had a far superior force of men and armaments at his disposal. His hopes of victory were none the less disappointed; his attack failed (491), and the Thuringians preserved their independence.

The marriage of Clovis with Clotilda, the niece of Gondebaud, King of the Burgundians, took place about the year 493. But the exact date is uncertain. Clovis was then twenty-seven or twenty-eight. He was already married and had a son, Thierry, who afterwards succeeded him. We do not know whether he was a widower, or whether he had repudiated his first wife, or whether he still kept her after marrying a second. Clotilda was a Catholic, and had a sister who was a nun. Legend has woven its most brilliant colours about this union which gives the impression of having been a happy one. Clotilda seems to have had a noble nature. Did she impart some of it to her husband? Had she any influence over him? Popular songs and the oldest writers represent her in a somewhat different light from that in which the hagiographers have placed her, and one which brings her closer to her barbarian husband.

It may be asked why the Frankish king consummated this union. Clotilda was a Catholic and Clovis had need of the Bishops. She was the daughter of a Burgundian prince, and Clovis, after making himself master of the Soissons district, had cast his eyes on Burgundy.

It is important to remember the great power of the Catholic Bishops in Gaul in the fifth century, not only from the moral and religious, but also from the social and political point of view. Of all the institutions of the Roman Empire the Church alone remained. The Bishops were the venerated chiefs of the cities, and had far greater power than the municipal magistrates in their decline; they disposed of vast material resources, which were continually swelled by gifts from the faithful; but they were impatient of the suzerainty of the Arian princes in Gaul, the kings of the Burgundians and the Visigoths.

The campaign of Clovis against the Alemanni is generally placed in 496.

The Alemanni were first cousins of the Franks, they had the same marauding customs we have already described, and, at this period, the same beliefs. " They worship certain trees," says Procopius, " and offer them propitiary sacrifices, just as they do in the neighbourhood of the waters of certain rivers, and of certain hills and forests, where with great devotion they immolate horses, oxen and other animals, whose throats they cut." Procopius adds : " I can see nothing pleasing on their little altars, which are covered with the blood of so many animals."

The pretext given seems to have been an attack on the part of the Alemanni against the Ripuarians, whose King, Sigebert, who lived in Cologne, was a relative of Clovis, according to Gregory of Tours. It was in order to avenge this kinsman— whom Clovis later on did not hesitate to assassinate in the most terrible circumstances—that he seems to have gone to war. The army of Clovis consisted of a group of Frankish warriors and Gallo-Roman auxiliaries, that is to say, Roman soldiers engaged to work under his orders. The victory was won by Clovis at some place which it is impossible to identify. It has been located at Tolbiac (the Zülpich of to-day, south-west of Cologne), through the mistake of a sixteenth-century historian, Paul Emile, who confused the battle fought by Clovis against the Alemanni with an earlier battle at Tolbiac fought by Sigebert, King of the Ripuarians of Cologne, against these same Alemanni. It was in consequence of this first battle of Tolbiac that Sigebert, who was wounded in the leg, became lame, which Clovis used as a pretext for having him killed by his son. Some historians, and notably Sybel, have suggested the neighbourhood of Toul as the field of battle. But this is a long way from Tolbiac. As a matter of fact only one thing is certain, and that is that Clovis with his Franks and Romans defeated the Alemanni and subjected their nation to his authority.

This battle, called the battle of Tolbiac, has remained famous on account of the vow of Clovis. Seeing his army wavering, the Frankish King apparently promised the God of Clotilda to worship Him if He gave him the victory. After the eighteenth century, certain French historians, Abbé Legendre and Gaillard, maintained that this " mercenary vow " was not a prayer, but " a bargain that did not deserve to be carried out." We regard the tale as legendary, though it was in keeping with the superstitions of the time.

This was followed by the King's baptism. Here again only one thing is certain, and that is that the young prince was baptised, very probably on Christmas Day, 496, and possibly in the town of Rheims. The certainty of these four facts declines in the order they are mentioned. Some historians are in favour of the town of Tours, and others of Attigny.

A certain number of Franks seem to have been baptised at the same time as their king. " I do not know whether we can place much confidence in their conversion by Saint Remi," says Fustel de Coulanges. At all events it is certain that this conversion was far from including the whole of the Salian Franks, as is proved by the efforts to convert them which were afterwards made by Saint Vaast and other apostles.

Even those of the Franks who were baptised did not bring a very profound faith into their new religion. And in the sixth century we find the northern regions occupied by Franks reverting to paganism. The Bishoprics had disappeared, and fresh missions were required.

Procopius depicts the Franks fighting in Italy under the orders of Theodebert, the grandson of Clovis, still practising their bloody sacrifices, casting horoscopes from the blood of the victims, and obedient to the hints of their sorcerers.

It was in the imagination of the Gauls that the ceremony of baptism made a deep impression.

Saint Avitus, Bishop of Vienne, wrote to Clovis to tell him the

232

joy with which his conversion had filled him. The Catholics, said Saint Avitus, had hitherto been forced to place their faith in eternity, leaving to God the task of deciding whether they or the Arians possessed the true faith. They felt they must leave the decision to the Day of Judgment. But now all was changed. Avitus advised Clovis to spread the doctrines of salvation to the Germanic peoples plunged in the darkness of paganism, and to send them missionaries without delay. For hitherto it was only Arian missionaries who had led the barbarians to the Christian faith.

As for Saint Remi, Archbishop of Rheims, he advised the King to show all deference to the Bishops and to ask their advice on all things.

At this period the throne of Italy was occupied by a magnificent prince, the most brilliant figure of the age—Theodoric the Great, King of the Ostrogoths. He had his capital at Ravenna. We have already seen how he welcomed the fugitive Alemanni and gave them lands to cultivate on his northern frontier, in Rhetia, which, in accordance with the Roman system, he handed over to their care.

The orders he sent to his subjects in the province of Noricum, between the Alps and the Danube, asking them to facilitate the exodus of the fugitive Alemanni, have been preserved. The oxen harnessed to the chariots of the exiles, worn out by the length and difficulty of the road, were to be exchanged for fresh oxen in good condition.

Theodoric wrote Clovis a letter full of the greatest interest, proving the height of power to which, in that disorganised state of society, a band of hardy and unscrupulous ruffians, under the leadership of a young, audacious and intelligent chief, could attain by means of a few cleverly organised attacks. Nothing sheds greater light on the character and attainments of Clovis in the fifth and sixth centuries than the exploits of Robert Guiscard and his brothers in the eleventh century in Italy; frankly brigands, although possessed of a more refined culture than Clovis, they founded splendid kingdoms and acted as protectors of the Papacy.

The letter of Theodoric also contains an astonishing detail to which sufficient attention has not yet been paid, one of the rare facts in the life of Clovis of which we have precise information, thanks to a contemporary document of unimpeachable authenticity. Having conquered the Alemanni after his victory over Syagrius, Clovis asked Theodoric to supply him with a bard to sing his glory on the zither. The bard was sent. This is a fact of the greatest importance, proving that the famous poems in honour of the Frankish warriors not only actually existed, but that they were lays not in a Teutonic tongue—as the Germans naturally maintain—but in the Latin language; for obviously Theodoric did not send a Teuton to Clovis from Italy. Moreover, the fragments of poems which have been preserved are actually in Latin. This fact also confirms the hypothesis of Fustel de Coulanges when he says, " Probably it was not so much popular poetry as a Court literature."

The following is Theodoric's letter in an abbreviated translation:

" We congratulate you," wrote Theodoric to Clovis, " inasmuch as at the head of the Franks you have victoriously defeated the Alemanni; but do not hold them all responsible for the crimes of a few; show clemency to the fallen, and calm your fury against those who in their terror have sought refuge across our frontiers. Let it suffice for you to know that the pride of the conquered king has been humbled together with that of his whole nation; let it suffice for you to have made a people without number fall beneath the edge of your sword, or beneath the yoke of slavery. Learn by my experience. The wars which I have found most profitable have been those which I ended in a spirit of moderation. . . . We also send you the bard who can play on the zither for whom you ask. He is skilled in his art. May he give you pleasure by celebrating your power and glory by striking his fingers on the strings and raising his voice in harmony. We have confidence in his success inasmuch as you have inspired him."

Imagine with what audacity as well as circumspection Clovis must have acted during these first years of his reign (481–496)— the Frankish kinglets about him hewn down with the battle-axe, the " kingdom " of Syagrius conquered with the consent of its own " subjects," the Gallo-Romans, the kingdom of the Alemanni subjected with the help of the Roman army. " Clovis," says Godefroy Kurth, " could now turn his attention without fear towards the south."

If we examine the Burgundians, established in the valleys of the Saône and the Rhone, and the Visigoths south of the Loire, all of whom were much more formidable than Syagrius, we find the situation was even simpler. The Arian missionaries, by means of prolonged and arduous efforts, of which we know nothing, because the Catholics destroyed all record of them, had converted the majority of the barbarian peoples, the Suevi, the Visigoths, the Ostrogoths, the Burgundians, the Vandals, the Gepidæ and the Lombards. This constitutes a long page in the history of modern civilisation, in which no doubt might be found many acts of devotion and self-sacrifice, of faith and enthusiasm on the part of apostles, and the martyrdom of more than one missionary; but it has been torn up. The result, however, remained; the Burgundians and the Visigoths as well as the Ostrogoths and the Vandals were Arians, whilst the Gallo-Roman population, under the guidance of their Bishops, were Catholics. We have already described the position of the barbarians in these cantons, where they had settled down as soldiers of Rome, as well as the great administrative power and authority over the cities which the Bishops had in their hands. Clovis saw the situation at a glance : he became a Catholic.

From that day forward he could hope to dominate Gaul. The whole of the Gallo-Roman population was on his side. Cries of joy arose from the Bishops. At last they had a strong power on their side, with a formidable army at its disposal; and behold they were free from heretical princes. Their life, their power and their influence were transformed. The doctrine of " Consubstantiality " had won the day; the Son was of the same essence and the same origin as the Father; the world was Catholic, the faith was saved.

As for Clovis—if we take him as Gregory depicts him—and we must do so or else discard him altogether, since the Bishop of Tours is his sole historian—it would be ridiculous to suppose that the bandit without faith or law, with his hands stained with the blood of his own people and of all whom he found across the path of his ambition, whose life was nothing but a tissue of knavish crimes, could have brought the smallest modicum of sincerity into the business. The identity of the three Persons of the Trinity was for him a political and military affair. Moreover, had he any idea of what this theological discussion meant? Henry IV thought Paris well worth a Mass; Clovis thought Gaul well worth his assent to the identity of the Father and the Son, and no neophyte ever affirmed his new faith with greater ardour.

After a series of murders of great number and variety had made Clovis the only Frankish prince in Belgium and Holland, as far as the country of the Frisians and the Saxons in the north, the Thuringians in the east and the Alemanni in the south, after the murder of Chararic and his son, of Ragnochar, King of Cambrai, and his two brothers, and several other personages, after he had made himself master of the kingdom of Syagrius and of the territory of the Alemanni who had fled to Italy, the young Frankish chief thought he might extend his enterprises even further. " Having exterminated many more kings," writes Gregory of Tours, " and even his nearest kinsmen, Clovis extended his power over the whole of Gaul. Thus he was able to say : ' Woe is me, for I am left like a traveller among strangers and have neither kith nor kin to help me in adversity ! ' " " He said this out of guile," says Gregory, " in order to find out whether there was anybody left to kill."

In order to understand this passion on the part of Clovis for killing all his relatives, we must remember that the Franks were free to raise on their shields any prince they chose to power, on condition that the man they elected was a member of the royal family, whom they believed was descended from the gods. Thus, according to Gregory of Tours, Clovis imagined that if he killed all the males in his family there would be nobody left to contest his crown.

" Every day," writes our episcopal chronicler, " God made the enemies of Clovis fall in this manner, because the King walked with a pure heart before the Lord and did that which was agreeable unto God."

The Burgundians occupied the basins of the Saône and the Rhone together with Savoy, but did not go down to the

Mediterranean. Avignon was in their hands, but Arles belonged to the Visigoths. On the throne of Vienne (Burgundy) there reigned Gondebaud, the uncle of Clotilda, an interesting figure, a man of letters, speaking Latin and Greek, taking an interest in theology, a wise legislator, carrying on the government by means of Gallo-Roman ministers and in such a way as to be acceptable to their own people. He was a member of the Arian faith, but far from persecuting the Catholics he took counsel with their ministers, and had placed his trust in Saint Avitus, Bishop of Vienne.

Clovis declared war against the Burgundians in the year 500. The Catholic population were favourable towards him as well as a certain party among the Burgundians themselves. Godegisel, Gondebaud's own brother, to whom the Burgundian monarch had confided the administration of part of his kingdom, with Geneva as its capital, betrayed him to the Franks. A battle took place in the neighbourhood of Dijon.

Gregory of Tours gives a charming description of the town of Dijon in the sixth century. It was still nothing more than a " castle with very strong walls," " built in the middle of a fairly smiling plain," says Gregory, " the land of which is so fertile that if the fields are ploughed only once before being sown, they nevertheless produce very rich harvests. The castle is bounded on the south by the River Ouche, which abounds in fish. On the north is another little river, the Suzon, which flows into the castle through one of the gates and out through another, surrounding the ramparts with its calm waters, but before entering the castle it works the mills with astonishing rapidity. Dijon has four gates facing the four points of the compass, and the ramparts are strengthened by thirty-three towers. The wall to a height of twenty feet is built of quarried stone, and its total elevation is thirty feet high by fifteen wide. On the west is a line of fertile hills covered with vines which provide the inhabitants with such a fine Falernian "—it is clear that the good Bishop is a connoisseur—" a wine so good that they despise that which comes from Châlons."

It was in this " fairly smiling " plain that Clovis gave battle to Gondebaud. The struggle continued throughout the day, foot by foot, but towards evening Gondebaud saw the victory slip from his hands owing to the defection of Godegisel, his brother, who went over to the enemy together with all his forces. Gondebaud shut himself up in Avignon, where Clovis set siege to him; but Gondebaud made victorious sallies. Clovis, no doubt, attacked by other Burgundian forces, found his communications menaced, and was forced to raise the siege and beat a retreat. It was a signal defeat.

We must not indeed imagine these Frankish armies in the epic guise of rough and valiant warriors. Fustel de Coulanges describes them as follows : " A wretched rabble who pillaged, burnt and killed an inoffensive population, and often, at the first sight of the enemy, disbanded themselves. It would be difficult to imagine a more repugnant spectacle." That which constituted the backbone of the armies of Clovis after his easy victory over Syagrius was the Roman cohorts attached to them.

Gondebaud governed his domains as an independent sovereign till the day of his death, trying to give them greater unity and to bring about the fusion of the Burgundian and Gallo-Roman elements. His code—the loi Gombette—has justly remained famous. It would have been well if Clovis had had a similar title to glory standing to his credit.

Weakened by the disastrous issue of his campaign against the Burgundians, Clovis thought it better to remain quiet for a time. Moreover, he had to organise his previous conquests. The course of the Loire separated him from the kingdom of the Visigoths, taking the term " kingdom," of course, to mean what we have described above. Clovis cast covetous eyes upon this kingdom on account of its wealth. He laid his plans with some skill, making peace with the Burgundians, and promising them Provence, which together they were to take from the Visigoths. It was the dream of the Burgundians to descend the Rhone as far as the sea. The Burgundian kings were in constant touch with the Court of Constantinople, which had honoured them with the titles of " Masters of the Militia " and " Patricians." They were proud of being its officials. The Eastern Empire regarded Theodoric the Great, King of the Ostrogoths in Italy, as a rival, because he aimed at reviving for the benefit of his own sceptre the Roman Empire of the

West, of which the Byzantine Court considered itself the heir. "Byzantium," says Godefroy Kurth, "put weapons into the hands of the Franks and hurled them against the Visigoths."

Clovis was aware of the alliance of Theodoric with the Visigoths. Theodoric might have crushed him at a blow, but he also knew that the Ostrogoths of Italy would be held in check by the Byzantine fleets.

Finally Clovis was urged on by the Bishops.

The words put in his mouth by Gregory of Tours sum up the situation :

" I am impatient," said Clovis, " at the thought that these Arians should possess part of Gaul; let us march forth with the help of God and, after conquering them, subject the country to our rule."

Without taking sides in theological controversies, we may be allowed to render homage to the Arians, as we have already rendered homage to the Catholics, and shall do again. The doctrine of the Arians was the doctrine of Christ; they acknowledged the Gospels and practised the same morality as the Catholics; in fact they were Christians. They had proved themselves possessed of the greatest virtues, just like the Catholics; like them they had had their martyrs, and, like them, suffered persecution, and in the difficult and dangerous task of converting the barbarians they had preceded them and set them a glorious example. Their doctrine was a noble effort to explain what was inexplicable in the doctrine of the Trinity. Moreover, the difference between them resided not so much in the conclusions to which the Arians had been driven as in the mere fact that they wished for an explanation; the Catholics aimed at imposing dogma without commentary. Both were right from their own point of view. The Catholic doctrine— an act of faith—secured the unity of the Church, her cohesion, her greatness and her permanence. And it was this that the Nicene Fathers understood so well. When once it was admitted that a logical, rational, and comprehensive explanation of the mystery of the Trinity could be found, explanations would result in hair-splitting differences and produce as many different sects. A similar difference to that which divided the Arians and the Catholics afterwards separated Catholics and Protestants. The Arians are the Protestants of the fourth and fifth centuries, and, for the reason we have just adduced, they were destined, like the Protestants of the Reformation, to become divided up into a certain number of sects. At all events the Arian who had a controversy with Gregory of Tours was right when he told him that it ill became him to despise anyone because in all good faith he held such and such a belief, above all when this belief was, like Arianism, closely akin to Catholicism, and full of beauty, idealism and devotion.

Theodoric the Great, aware of the intentions of the Frankish king, and of the alliances he had formed for the realisation of the infamous blow he was preparing, made up his mind to intervene. It is a poignant episode. In the darkness of the reign of Clovis it forms a ray of light shed by contemporary documents; in that rough and sinister fifth century it surrounds with a halo of glory a barbarian prince trying to play a part which in the twentieth century we should like to see filled by the League of Nations.

" Beware of those who derive satisfaction from a conflict in which they take no share, and pray God that such an iniquity shall not influence your decision. I beg you to believe," writes Theodoric to Clovis, " that he who would precipitate another into ways of violence does not give him good counsel."

These letters are admirable. The following is an abbreviated translation.

First of all Theodoric wrote to Clovis as follows :

" Heaven has ordained that kings should be brought into touch with each other by the ties of kinship "—Theodoric was the brother-in-law of Clovis and the father-in-law of Alaric— " so that their tranquil souls may give the peoples the peace they desire. This is a sacred thing and should be upset by no act of violence. In what pledges can we have faith if we repudiate sentiment? Wherefore we are the more surprised that for trivial reasons you are preparing to engage in the direst conflict with King Alaric, so that those who fear you are filled with joy by your disagreement. In the flower of your strength you are both of you rulers of two great peoples. With what a terrible upheaval will you afflict your kingdoms if you allow the two factions (Arians and Catholics) to enter into a

240

clash of arms undisturbed. May your valour not unexpectedly become a cause of calamity for your country!—for the kings a petty quarrel but for the people a terrible misfortune. Freely and affectionately will I say what I think. Such is the impetuosity of man's temper that it drives you to flourish your weapons at the first word. But that which we wish to obtain let us, on the contrary, await as the award of arbitration. Let the conflict die down, cast away your arms. I am an old man, and I speak to you as a father and a friend. And remember this much, that he who rejects our advice will have us and our allies against him. We are sending you two ambassadors, and also to King Alaric. May no malicious hand place snares between you! Keep the peace and silence your differences through the voice of friends who will act as intermediaries. To these friends we are also addressing ourselves, so that the peoples, after having enjoyed a long peace, may not be overcome by a sudden disaster. Lend an ear to the counsels of one whom you have always seen smile upon any good fortune that has befallen you. He who tries to precipitate his neighbour into violent conflicts is certainly no trusty counsellor."

After this Theodoric addressed himself to the King of the Visigoths in no less emphatic terms :

" Although you have a multitude of kinsmen to strengthen your courage, although you have not forgotten that the might of Attila gave way beneath the hand of the Visigoths, remember that the bravest of peoples, like your own, grow soft during long years of peace; wherefore take care not to expose to the hazard of war those who for so long have lost the practice of arms. Do not abandon yourself to blind rage. How much wisdom is there in moderation, the guardian angel of the nations ! It is desirable to rush to arms only when justice cannot find even the smallest crevice in which to lurk on the enemy's side. Wait until our ambassadors have reached the King of the Franks, so that common friends may settle your dispute by arbitration. Does the murder of a kinsman or the invasion of your territory offend you? Your quarrel is still a matter of words. A settlement will be easy if you do not rush to arms. Disregarding all family bonds, we and our allies will oppose with picked troops and justice, the sword of kings, him who

241

first breaks the peace. Do not allow yourself to be influenced by those who take malicious joy in conflicts arising between their neighbours. May Heaven keep you from such iniquity. Any evil that may befall you finds in us an adversary as well as those who wish you harm."

Theodoric had been informed of the offensive alliance which was being made between Clovis and Gondebaud, King of the Burgundians. He wrote in emphatic terms to the latter:

" It would be a great wrong to plan without warning an immediate conflict between two kings who are dear to me. I could not suffer it that princes, who are bound to me by family ties, should fight against one another. You all of you have in your hands the pledges of my good will. . . . It is my part, with words of reason, to curb the passions of two young kings. In the effervescence of their youth they owe respect to age. I am obliged to speak roughly for fear lest my neighbours go to extremes. With this object I am sending my legates to my son [son-in-law] Alaric so that he may see—before I march out against the King of the Franks with my allies—whether the quarrel cannot be reasonably settled through friendly mediation. No man can doubt that the outbreak of war would cause me the greatest displeasure. The bearers of these letters will make other communications to you by word of mouth. I trust that your prudence will order all for the best, as usual, with the help of God."

These missives were completed by a last letter addressed by Theodoric, as a sort of circular, to the Kings of the Thuringians, the Warnians and the Herulians. The Thuringians were neighbours of the Franks between the Elbe and the Saale; the Warnians were a Germanic people of the north, between the Elbe and the Oder as far as the Baltic; the Herulians were Germanic tribes some of whom were established in Italy. Sidonius speaks of them as follows: " The Herulians, whose cheeks are daubed with blue and whose complexions are of the same colour as the sea the most distant shores of which they inhabit."

Theodoric saw quite clearly through the ambition of Clovis: " Arrogance, which is hated of God, should be banned by common accord. He who would bring trouble upon a nation by a

242

premeditated crime will not spare others. The greatest of crimes is the contempt of right and truth. The man who has overcome one great adversary in hateful combat will think he should overcome all. [The war against Alaric and his family are clearly foreseen.] Wherefore I beseech you, who are conscious of your own valour and are doubtless irritated by hateful presumption, to send your ambassadors together with mine to my brother Gondebaud [King of the Burgundians] and to Clovis, King of the Franks, in order that they may abstain from attacking the Visigoths out of respect for justice, and set forth to discover the right of nations, or else let him who despises our offer of arbitration await our combined attack. I will say what I think without circumlocution. He who would act in violation of all equity is preparing to destroy the kingdoms of all of us. Remember the friendship shown you by the aged Euric [King of the Visigoths, and father of Alaric], the help he gave you, the number of wars with which your neighbours threatened you that he warded off. Show your gratitude to his son. If a kingdom like his falls, you will be attacked in your turn. I charge two ambassadors with verbal messages so that, with the help of God, we may act in common accord. Do not hesitate to spread your valour beyond your frontiers, for fear lest you may soon have to fight on your own ground."

In writing this last letter, Theodoric had only the faintest hope that peace would be maintained.

The treasures of Alaric shone with too seductive a brilliance. Clovis knew that the Burgundians would take the Visigoths on the flank, whilst he himself would make a frontal attack; he knew that the menace of the Byzantine fleet would prevent Theodoric from taking action, and he knew that in Aquitania he would be supported by a considerable section of the people headed by their Bishops. And, indeed, several of the latter had to be expelled by Alaric, who convicted them of being in touch with the Frankish King.

Clovis left Paris, where he had taken up residence, and marched on Poitiers (507). Alaric had made a desperate appeal to all his subjects. As Theodoric had reminded them, the Visigoths had lived in peace for a long time, and they naturally found themselves at a disadvantage with the Frankish warriors.

They were attacked in the rear by the Burgundians. The Catholics were making terms with the invader, for on crossing the Loire Clovis published a declaration reassuring members of the Catholic clergy, the attendants in the churches, widows and orphans and all who owed allegiance to the Gallo-Roman clergy.

The decisive battle was fought at Vouillé in the deep valley of the Auxance. Alaric was beaten and fell in the fight, it is said at the hand of Clovis himself, who seized his treasures and his lands, as he had seized the Roman coffers after his victory over Syagrius. Once again massacres took place. The slaughter was terrible and recalled the butcheries of Cæsar.

Countless numbers of Visigoths, reduced to slavery, were taken out of the country in chains. Even the " peace " promised to members of the Church was not respected. Numbers of nuns were reduced to slavery.

Auvergne alone still held out. The admirable people of these parts, who had fought against Cæsar with the energy we have already described, opposed the Frankish hordes with equal loyalty of heart. To bring them to submission a special campaign, under the leadership of Thierry, or Theodoric, the eldest son of Clovis, was necessary.

It is maintained that in 508 no Arians survived in Aquitania; they had been completely annihilated.

The power of Clovis extended thenceforward to the Pyrenees.

On his way home the leader of the troops stopped at Tours to make handsome offerings in the basilica of Saint Martin. The treasures of Alaric provided him with the means. In this connection an anecdote is told, the first repartee attributed in the annals of France to a head of the State. On reaching the tomb of St. Martin to return thanks for his victory, the Frankish warrior, as was customary, gave his horse as a gift to the church, though reserving to himself the right of buying it back again. He offered a hundred gold pieces for it, but the animal reared and refused to come out of the stable. He was obliged to double the sum :

" Assuredly," said Clovis, " Saint Martin is a mighty good help, but he drives a mighty hard bargain."

These were high achievements which were followed by a less

glorious sequence of events for the conqueror. In return for their able help the Burgundians were to have been given Provence. The Greeks, who were allies of Clovis, had just disembarked in Apulia from a fleet of two hundred vessels, and were spreading fire and slaughter everywhere. Theodoric divided his forces, and sent one half against the Greeks and the other to Provence. Arles was being besieged by the armies of both the Franks and the Burgundians. The inhabitants were holding out, and the Franks and Burgundians redoubled their efforts. The towers and the walls of the ramparts were crumbling away; still the people of Arles held out, when the generals of Theodoric arrived upon the scene. One was called Tulum and the other Ibbas. Saint Cæsarius, Bishop of Arles, had won a great reputation in the besieged town on account of his charity towards the infidels, doubtless the Arian Burgundians, whom the Arlesians had taken prisoner on their sorties, and whom they had herded together in their basilica. It must be remembered that Clovis, who had made war on the Visigoths because it really distressed him too much to see this fair kingdom in the hands of Arians and heretics, did not hesitate, in order to secure the success of his enterprise, to enter into alliance with the Burgundians, who were no less Arians and heretics. Saint Cæsarius visited the prisoners and gave them food and clothes, and ransomed as many as he could according to his means—a beautiful and inspiring example of which the Catholic clergy in Gaul provided many an instance.

Theodoric's generals fell upon the Franks and Burgundians who were besieging Arles, like cats fall upon a group of sparrows. Arles was relieved.

Theodoric hastened to write the victorious Arlesians the following charming letter (winter of 508–509) :

" Although the most urgent duty is to come to the help of the inhabitants and to show proof of interest more particularly towards men, we think we ought to divide our gifts between the citizens and the ramparts which should be put back into repair. May the prosperity of the town, combined with that of its citizens, be recovered through the good order of your buildings. We are sending you funds for the repair of the walls of Arles and her ancient towers, and we are preparing victuals which will lighten your expenses. They will arrive as soon as the weather becomes propitious for navigation. Courage ! Have faith in our promises and confidence in the good will of God, for our words are as well stocked with benevolence as the shops are with food."

Thus Theodoric saved for the Visigoths the districts of Narbonne, Carcassonne, Béziers and Nîmes, which became Septimania. He kept Provence, including Orange, Avignon, Arles and Marseilles, thus securing the communication of his own country with Spain. In the organisation of his conquests he displayed all the intelligence that history has associated with his name. In their manner of life the inhabitants found that nothing was changed except the name of their king. Their ancient privileges were preserved. An Arian prince, Theodoric nevertheless had restored to the Catholic church of Narbonne all that she had lost. He took a pride in alleviating suffering, and forestalling the wishes of his subjects even before they were expressed :

" Under a benevolent prince," he writes, " there should be no need to clamour for remedies long delayed; goodness should not wait to be asked. Vows shine with a sweeter brilliance when they are made after the prayer has been fulfilled." And again :

" Justice is only perfect when it discovers the oppressed before being drawn towards them by the hands of suppliants."

But to return to Clovis, from whom we have wandered far. On all these events, on the defeat of the Franks before Arles, Gregory of Tours preserves a pious silence. His hero did not shine here in a brilliant light.

As a reward for having conquered the Visigoths, and having thus ruined the policy of Theodoric in Gaul, Anastasius, the Emperor of the East, honoured Clovis with the title of patrician, thus making him the lieutenant of the imperial crown beyond the Alps, a title of honour to which he soon added that of consul, the greatest privilege which could be conferred at that time by the heir of Cæsar and Augustus. The inaugural ceremony was carried out at Tours, on the 1st of January, 509, with the greatest solemnity. The clergy enhanced the beauty of the proceedings with their most gorgeous ceremonies. Clad in the consular robes, the white toga with the purple border, over which flowed his fair ringlets, the royal ringlets, his feet shod with white slippers, armed with the ivory rod, and surrounded by the incense of episcopal consecration, the barbarian must have turned his thoughts towards his youth, not yet far behind him, in the forests of the Menapii, amid the thatched huts filled with the quarrelsome shouts of the Franks, and the great wild pigs and the bees buzzing round their hives full of golden honey.

From that day forward all the Catholics, and even those of the Gallo-Romans who had remained true to paganism, could recognise no other prince but Clovis.

The capture of the treasure of Alaric was the last memorable act of Clovis. Three years later he died in Paris (511). He was buried in the church of the Holy Apostles, which he had had built, and which in the tenth century became the church of Saint Geneviève. The tower, called the Tower of Clovis, to-day fitted into the Lycée Henri IV, is all that remains of it. His widow, Clotilda, retired into a monastery at Tours, where she survived for many a long year (till 555) devoted to good works.

The personality of the founder of the Frankish monarchy in Gaul arouses but little admiration in our minds. Cæsar filled us with repulsion, but repulsion mingled with admiration. Clovis inspires us only with disgust. In short, his greatest act was, following the example of Julian the Apostate, to have chosen Paris as the capital of his kingdom. His military successes amount to very little—victories won at the edge of the sword against neighbouring Frankish kinglets, and the easy defeat of Syagrius, who no longer possessed the means for offering serious resistance. In his case it was war on the part of the head of a State against a private individual. In Thuringia Clovis failed. He beat the Alemanni, a robber people, with the help of Roman centurions and soldiers. His campaign in Burgundy ended in a retreat which suspiciously resembled flight. He triumphed over Alaric only with the help of the Burgundians and the majority of the inhabitants of the country, the towns opening their gates to him. The lieutenants of Theodoric vanquished his armies with the greatest ease and Clovis, finding himself confronted by a serious adversary, took care not to continue the struggle.

The way in which the founder of the Frankish monarchy in Gaul consolidated his " conquests," however, had important consequences. It has been a matter of surprise that Clovis and his Franks should have left the Gallo-Romans in possession of their lands. But this is easily explained. Clovis owed the greater part of his successes to the inhabitants of the " conquered " districts themselves, who were favourably disposed towards him. After the victory, the Frankish chieftain seized the domains of the Roman Treasury and the treasure of Alaric : that was all he could do. And even so he had more than he needed for rewarding his companions in arms, especially as they were fine fellows who were much better adapted for pillaging villas and estates than administering them.

If he had despoiled them Clovis would have set against him the territorial aristocracy, who would have turned him and all his band out of the country. So naturally the Gallo-Romans were not dispossessed of their property. The Franks did not act from generosity ; respect for landed property was a necessity in their case.

Benjamin Guérard also points out that Clovis and his successors never reigned over the territories of Gaul, nor even over the people who inhabited them, but only over the armed bands that scoured the country and gave themselves over to plunder without distinguishing between friend and foe. Neither Clovis nor his successors ever carried on any sort of administrative system.

The King of the Franks died in his bed, still young, in his forty-fifth year, after a life well filled with murder. He killed with his own hands, or had killed through his intrigues, at least ten kings or sons of kings—Syagrius, put to death in his dungeon ; Alaric and the King of the Alemanni—the two latter at least killed in the din of battle ; then there were Sigebert, King of Cologne, and his son Cloderic, Chararic, King of the Morini, and his son, the King of Cambrai, Ragnachar, and his brother Richa, the King of Le Mans and his brother, all murdered by Clovis or by his orders, the father sometimes being killed by the son.

And the sinister line of kings of which he was the founder will display before our eyes a group of criminals beside whom the

248

creations of Shakespeare will appear as models of moral worth and virtue.

Benjamin Guérard, the historian who knows this period best, writes in his immortal *Prolégomènes* : " Under the first race, there was consistent progress only towards barbarism." Such too was the opinion of Guizot and of Fustel de Coulanges, and we may perhaps be allowed to subscribe to the verdict of the three greatest historians of the nineteenth century.

Clovis had four sons—Thierry, or Theodoric, the offspring of his first marriage, and Clodomir, Childebert and Clotar, born from **Sons and** his union with Clotilda. He also left a daughter **Grandsons** named Clotilda after her mother, who married **of Clovis.** Amalaric, the son of Alaric, King of the Visigoths, the alliance proving most unhappy owing to their religious differences. Clotilda, the daughter of Saint Clotilda, was an ardent Catholic, whilst Amalaric, whose father had been killed by his wife's father, and he himself dispossessed of his lands because he was an Arian, had on that account remained all the more deeply attached to his beliefs.

The four sons divided the kingdom between them. The eldest, Thierry, or Theodoric, received the eastern portion with Rheims as its capital; it included the towns of Cologne, Treves, Strasbourg, Metz, Toul and Verdun. He had, moreover, part of Aquitaine, including Auvergne, Velay, Quercy and the Limousin.

Clodomir had included in his share the districts of Orleans and Chartres, Anjou, La Touraine, Le Berry and Poitou.

Childebert, the third son, had the north-western portion, with Paris as capital. Amiens, Rouen, Beauvais, Coutances and Le Mans were included in his lot. Lastly, the fourth son, Clotar, received the Soissons district, together with Laon, Noyon, Cambrai, Tournai and, towards the north, the whole country as far as the Meuse.

Theodoric, or Thierry, the eldest, was twenty-five at the time of his father's death. The four brothers were associated together in the government, or rather the exploitation, of their States. They placed their capitals on the extreme edge of their territories so as to keep in communication with each other—Rheims, Orleans, Paris and Soissons.

Like their father, Theodoric, Clodomir, Childebert and

Clotar were leaders of armed bands, who, like brigands, divided the booty they took. Rape, pillage and murder followed each other just as before. The following passage from Gregory of Tours describes their exploits. It was in the year 531 :

" The Franks, who owed allegiance to King Theodoric, said to him : ' Your brothers lead their soldiers into Burgundy; if you do not take us there too, we will leave you and go with your brothers.' Theodoric replied : ' I will take you to Auvergne, where you will find gold and silver, cattle, woven materials and slaves to bring home.' Content with this promise, they obeyed his will."

Each of the sons of Clovis showed certain marked characteristics. They were one generation nearer to Gregory, whose information about them consequently carries greater weight.

Theodoric was a fighter, rough and energetic. He undertook a second campaign against the indomitable people of Auvergne, and this expedition gives the whole gamut of the horrible scale— massacre and rape, slavery, pillage, burning and drinking bouts and ruined habitations. Everything was sacked.

The Franks left Auvergne in a state of desolation. After which Theodoric turned his warlike activities towards Germany and the Thuringians. He defeated Hermannfried, King of Thuringia, on the banks of the Unstrutt, a small stream which runs into the Saale, and enticed him to come to him after the battle on pretence of entering into negotiations. The two kings were walking on the walls of Zülpich when Hermannfried fell into the moat and was killed. Theodoric had completed his victory. He also coveted the possessions of his brother Clotar, who had been his ally on this expedition. Gregory relates how Thierry had enticed his brother into his tent, where he had posted assassins. Clotar saw the feet of these fellows sticking out beneath the drapery behind which they were hidden, and kept his escort with him. Theodoric did not know what to say to his brother, whom he had invited only in order to kill him. He pretended that he had asked him to come so that he might present him with a silver platter. When Clotar had departed with the precious gift Thierry regretted having given it to him. He had a very remarkable son named Theodebert. As we shall see presently, this Theodebert was the great man of the Merovingian dynasty. On account of the difference in age between Theodoric and Clotar, Theodebert was almost a companion for his uncle, and one day when he was larking about with him he succeeded in " getting back " the silver platter. " Theodoric," says Gregory of Tours in conclusion, " was very clever at such tricks." The eldest son of Clovis became one of the favourite subjects of ancient German poetry, in which he was regarded as a legendary hero.

About Clodomir, King of Orleans, we have fewer details. He was killed in 524, in the campaign against Burgundy, before his thirtieth year. " In this war," writes Procopius, "having thrust himself too far forward in the *mêlée*, he was pierced through the breast by an arrow and fell down dead. The Burgundians, perceiving his long, dishevelled locks falling over his shoulders and down his back, knew that they had killed the leader of their enemies; for the kings of the Franks do not have their hair cut. They allow it to grow so long that as a rule it hangs down to their waists; they divide it in front and let it hang down behind, and they do not allow it to become dirty and matted like the Turks and other barbarians, but scent it with pomade and sweet smelling oil and arrange it with a comb. This is regarded as a beauty of royalty and is allowed only to kings."

Clodomir left three children, three sons, who were confided to the care of their grandmother, Saint Clotilda, who lived at Tours. Childebert and Clodomir regarded this as a favourable opportunity for enlarging their domains. They asked their mother to entrust the children to them, as they intended to put them in possession of their father's heritage. Clotilda sent the two elder boys. She heard that they had reached their uncles through messengers who presented her with a pair of scissors and a dagger—Childebert and Clotar gave their mother the choice for her grandsons of either the cloister or the tomb. The reply of the proud queen is famous; she preferred to see her grandsons dead rather than subjected to the tonsure. Here again we have a Clotilda very different from the saint of the hagiographers. The scene which followed is no less famous. Clotar seizing the elder of the two boys and sticking a dagger into him before the eyes of his little brother, who begged for mercy on his knees, Childebert intervening on his behalf, Clotar thrusting his brother back and killing the younger as he had done the elder. The last of the sons of Clodomir—Clodoald abbreviated into " Cloud "—was hidden in a small place in the neighbourhood of Paris. He devoted himself to the worship of God, and future generations made him a saint and gave his name to the village which had provided him with shelter— " Saint Cloud." Clotar, infuriated that one of his victims should have escaped him, at least gave himself the pleasure of massacring all the staff which had been attached to the young prince.

Childebert, King of Paris, who had tried to save his nephew from death, was the most civilised of the three brothers, and preferred peace and tranquillity to the bloody game of war. If we may believe Gregory, he loved letters and justice. " He was the first of our kings," writes the Bishop of Tours, " who knew Latin, whilst his father and grandfather (Clovis and Childeric) only spoke ' Sicambrian.' " By Latin must be understood the popular " Roman " language in process of developing into French.

As for Clotar, the last of the sons of Clovis and Clotilda, he was the monster of the family, of that family so fertile in the production of monsters. We have just seen the virtuosity with which he set to work to kill children. His son Chramnus rebelled against him, and then took refuge with Chonober, a Breton King. Clotar followed him, killed Chonober and shut up his son Chramnus together with his wife and children in a cottage to which he set fire. He refused to leave the place until the flames had consumed the building and all it contained. " Chramnus," he said, with the deepest emotion, " is of all my children the one I loved best," and he compared himself to King David chastising his son Absalom for rebellion.

Clotar was married six times. He had several legitimate wives at the same time as well as various additional conjugal helpers. Montesquieu is of opinion that these marriages were less a proof of incontinence than " an attribute of dignity." As Clotar extended his sway over the whole of Gaul, and an Empire far wider than that of Clovis himself, his dignity was very great.

252

On the death of his brother Clodomir, Clotar, as we have already seen, murdered his children, and married his widow. On the death of his nephew Theodebald, Clotar married his widow in the same way—Valrada, daughter of the King of the Lombards. He felt himself bound to marry all the widows in his family. He was very fond of Ingonda, whom he had also married. She sent for her sister Aregonda to Court, and begged Clotar to find a husband for her. Clotar inspected Aregonda and found her charming; " I have seen your sister," he told his wife, " and I have given her for husband the greatest noble in my Court."

Thus Clotar had the two sisters as wives each in turn.

He lived on his estates, on the great farms, going from one to the other, from Braine to Attigny, from Attigny to Compiègne, and from Compiègne to Verberie, he and his suite consuming the produce and the revenues, hunting and fishing with his retainers and from time to time choosing out some pretty girl from the homes of his dependants, the administrators, cultivators, serfs and slaves on his domains.

On the huge farms which somewhat resembled the great agricultural establishments of modern France, the Merovingian kings were far happier than in the more elegant Gallo-Roman villas. These farms were large rustic dwellings of a non-military nature. They were entered by means of porticoes, either in the antique style or in carved wood. About the chief building occupied by the sovereign were the houses of the heads of companies who had attached themselves to him together with their men by bonds of fealty. Then came a whole scattered village in which lived, not only the labourers on the estate and their families, but also the artisans required by the royal Court and its retinue—wheelwrights, carpenters, curriers, ironmongers, weavers, armourers, as well as gold-smiths. There were also women's workrooms for dying cloth, and sewing and embroidering.

In large covered enclosures the synods of the Bishops were convoked, or other assemblies which used to be terminated by banquets worthy of Pantagruel, at which whole boars, roasted on iron spits, were placed on the tables.

When the produce of one of these large farms, which had been turned into giant storehouses, had been exhausted, the Court changed its residence.

Clotar succeeded in uniting the whole of Gaul under his authority, an end which Clovis had never achieved, in the following way. After the death of Clodomir and the murder of his sons he divided the latter's territory with his brother Childebert. Theodoric, who died in 543, had been succeeded by his son Theodebert, and the latter, who died in 548, was succeeded by his son Theodebald. The latter died in 555 without issue. Clotar laid hands on his domains, and Childebert having died in 558, he found himself the sole heir of the Merovingian State, which had grown to extraordinary proportions.

And indeed the sons of Clovis had succeeded in conquering where their father had failed, securing Thuringia, Burgundy and Provence, and even adding the territory which Theodoric had conceded to the Alemanni.

From this terrible family of barbarian princes, Theodebert, the son of Theodoric and grandson of Clovis, stands out conspicuously. He succeeded his father in 534 at the age of thirty. He was rough, brutal and cruel, like the other princes of his family; he was also cunning and sly like his grandfather, but endowed with real military genius. He was everywhere triumphant, against the Thuringians, the Visigoths, the Suabians, the Saxons, the Danes and the Bavarians. He crossed the Alps, leaving death and destruction in his path, sparing neither old men, women or children. The Po washed away the white bodies of strangled maidens. Whereupon the young hero found himself master of northern Italy, of Liguria and Venetia. He coined money at Bologna. He was endowed with a cunning and unscrupulous gift for diplomacy. He was really a second edition of Clovis, but gifted with greater versatility. Some historians have tried to see in him a prototype of Charlemagne. At all events it is certain that as early as the sixth century he conceived and partly realised the vast conceptions of that great Emperor.

Procopius has described his campaign in Italy. Justinian, the Emperor of the East, and Witigis, the King of the Ostrogoths, were fighting for the peninsula. It was a bitter and prolonged conflict, bristling with sieges and battles, in which the illustrious

Belisarius covered himself with glory at the head of the imperial armies.

Theodebert, King of the Austrasian Franks, received from Justinian letters couched in the following terms : " The Goths have forcibly invaded Italy, which from days of old belongs to our domain, and will not give us reparation. They are doing us so great an injury that they have forced us to war. We have desired to inform you of this, resting assured that you would lend us your aid, as much for the sake of the good and true belief in God which we share in common, as for the hatred we bear to the Goths, because of the heresy of the Arians which makes them detestable to all true Christians." To these letters was added a goodly sum of money, with the promise of an even greater amount after the fight. Theodebert concluded an alliance with Justinian and the Romans against the Ostrogoths, after which he entered into a similar alliance with the Ostrogoths against the Romans. Whereupon he set forth at the head of his army.

Both Romans and Ostrogoths were expecting him with his Franks, both equally hopeful that he would prove a powerful ally. Theodebert crossed the Alps (539) and arrived in Liguria. " And the Goths," says Procopius, " having heard that Theodebert, the Frankish chief, was in the neighbourhood with a large army, rejoiced in good hope that, through him, they might make an end of the Romans."

Theodebert reached the banks of the Po, which he crossed by means of a fortified bridge. The Ostrogoths allowed the Franks a free passage, but no sooner was Theodebert master of the bridge and the fortress than he made his soldiers seize the wives and children of the Goths, cut their throats and throw their bodies into the river, " offering to the gods of the river these first fruits of war "; for, though the grandson of Clovis and his men had been baptised, they still continued to worship the gods of the woods and rivers. The Frankish army then reached the camp of the Goths, who were still in ignorance of these " first fruits." They joyfully allowed them to enter; whereupon the Franks set to work with their battle-axes, their skramasaxes and their harpoons. Any of the Gothic army who were not massacred took flight in the direction of Ravenna. The Romans who, from their camp, could see the fugitives, thought that

255

Belisarius had inflicted a defeat upon them. They advanced in all confidence, with demonstrations of friendship, to meet the Franks, their allies, whom they were impatiently awaiting. But the latter set to work incontinently to kill them as they had already killed the Ostrogoths. The Romans in their turn fled in terror, leaving to the Franks their camp full of provisions.

Belisarius wrote to the King of the Franks :—

" I do not believe, Theodebert, that it befits a decent man, though he be a prince and chief of so great a number of soldiers, to make use of lying and deceit. Moreover, it is a villainy, of the vilest and most abject in the world, to break an oath given in writing and to disregard agreements entered into. After having promised to undertake this war against the Goths, you come and attack us. . . ."

Theodebert beat a retreat before Belisarius, just as Clovis had done before Theodoric; but it was only to return to the charge, and to profit by the constant struggle, complicated by religious dissensions, of Catholics against Arians, and Romans against Ostrogoths. Numbers of Franks and Alemanni swept down upon Italy in his train. When he returned to Gaul Theodebert left them under the command of a lieutenant named Buslin or Bultin, who sent to him from Italy quantities of treasure which he won by pillage. Thanks to these fresh resources, Theodebert raised a considerable army which he recruited with Lombards and Gepidæ in addition to Franks and Alemanni. His object was to march through Thrace against Constantinople, and to place the imperial crown upon his own brow. Thus the Roman Empire would have been revived in the sixth century with a grandeur that Charlemagne himself did not succeed in endowing it with. But a premature death put an end to these fair schemes.

Theodebert died at the age of forty-three through an accident in the hunting field (547).

The Franks whom he had let loose in Italy were constantly receiving fresh recruits, who were only too pleased to come to pillage those fertile districts. They continued to fight, plunder and shed blood in their customary fashion until the year 555, when, in the neighbourhood of Casilinum, on the Volturnus, in Campania, they were surrounded and massacred in one of the most terrible battles of history by the Romans under the command of the Persian General Narses.

Theodebert, writes Gregory of Tours, proved himself great and full of goodness. He governed with equity, showed respect for the Bishops and enriched the churches. He spread his benefits with a generous hand, and lived in the odour of gentleness and piety.

Theodebert had been very much in love with a young widow named Deutheria. She was, says Gregory of Tours, a lady of rare merit and great prudence. A signal instance of this prudence is shown in the following tale, also recorded by Gregory of Tours. Deutheria had a daughter who was fairly tall and exceedingly pretty. For fear lest she should please the King, her mother had her put in a chariot harnessed to two wild bulls and hurled from the top of a bridge into the Meuse.

Theodebert's heir was Theodebalt—or rather Thibault, as the old French historians call him—a young man feeble in mind and body. He became King in 538 at the age of fourteen, and died in 555.

Left sole master of Gaul, except Septimania, Clotar, the last son of Clovis, governed it in his own way, as a mediocre monarch, heavy-handed and devoid of any aim or political idea. In that great Empire he looked for nothing but the satisfaction of his primitive and brutal vanity, the possession of resplendent treasures and the satisfaction of gross appetites. In 556 he headed an expedition against the Saxons and suffered a severe defeat.

On his death at Compiègne in 561, he left four sons, Caribert, Gontram, Sigebert and Chilperic. Once more a division of property took place, first in 561, and again in 567, one of the brothers, Caribert, having died without issue.

The figure of Caribert remains a mystery, Fortunatus having nothing but good to say of him and Gregory of Tours nothing but evil. Caribert prided himself on his literary tastes and on being able to speak Latin correctly.

To describe these partitions, with their divisions and sub-divisions, in detail, would be wearisome; one point only in the partition of 567 is interesting, and that is the importance already acquired by the town of Paris, which was so large that the three brothers decided to leave it undivided, none of them having the right to enter it without the consent of the others.

The partition was, moreover, extremely complicated, the principal towns in the same region being frequently divided between the three brothers. Roughly speaking, Sigebert received north-eastern France, which was soon afterwards called Austrasia, the Kingdom of the East—the word from which the " Austria " of to-day is derived—together with Auvergne and the districts of Velay, Vivarais, and Albi; Chilperic received north-western France, Neustria, which meant " the newest Kingdom," *Neuester reich*, the Franks having established themselves in it later than in Austrasia, together with the districts of Limousin, Quercy, Bordeaux, Auch, Bigorre and Comminges; finally Gontram had Champagne, Burgundy, and the districts of Berry, Lyons, Dauphiny and Savoy and, in addition, Saintonge, Angoumois and Périgord. These divisions are only given roughly, each of the three princes having insisted on receiving slices of land in his brothers' domains.

The chief reason for this division was that the northern regions endowed the owner with power, on account of the leudes and dependants, and the southern regions provided red and white wine, which had assumed a vast importance in the eyes of the Franks and other barbarians, who had become insatiable tipplers ever since the divine juice of the grape had made them despise the fermented barley on which their ancestors had become drunk.

After the death of Caribert, Clotar's eldest surviving son was Gontram, who had received Burgundy as his portion. His was **Chilperic.** a singular mentality, a mixture of sweetness and violence, furious outbursts of rage disordering an otherwise almost ecclesiastical tenure. For the sake of a hunting horn he would have several of his men tortured; he would kill one of his leudes for having hunted a buffalo on his lands. He prided himself on being a lover of justice and allowing himself to be guided by the wisdom of the Bishops. A benefactor of the Church and of religious foundations, he imagined he could thus atone for his numberless crimes, and the chroniclers of the day, who all belonged to the Church, laid great stress on this. " He was full of goodness," says Fredegar,

258

"and in an assembly of Bishops seemed to be one of them. Generous in almsgiving, and loved by his leudes, he reigned in wisdom and prosperity." As he passed for a saint he had perforce to work miracles. Gregory of Tours tells how a good woman had her son dangerously ill of a fever. She secretly cut off a piece of fringe from the King's mantle and dipped it in a vessel full of water, and by this infusion her son was immediately cured. Gregory adds, "Ofttimes have I heard devils pronounce his name in terror when they were agitated by fury."

Queen Austrehilda, the wife of King Gontram, died in September 581. Before she yielded up the ghost she asked her husband to have the two doctors, who had attended her but failed to cure her, put to death. And Gontram in pious acquiescence had their heads cut off.

But the most interesting personality among the sons of Clotar was Chilperic, King of Neustria. Gregory of Tours regards him as a monster. Chilperic thought that the churches and the religious establishments were becoming far too rich owing to accumulations of gifts from the faithful who, by overwhelming them with the goods of this world, hoped to open the road to heaven for themselves. But Chilperic argued, " Our Treasury is impoverished by this means and our power handed over to the Bishops." So he annulled numerous wills made in favour of the Church and revoked the gifts his father had left it. It is also certain that Chilperic committed abominable crimes from the beginning of his reign to the end—crimes which had become the regular stock in trade of the Frankish princes.

This barbarian had aspirations towards literature and reform; he had artistic tastes and aimed at establishing the glory of his rule on other bases besides that of assassination. One of his attempts at reform is of considerable interest. Several sounds in the Germanic languages could not be expressed by the letters of the Latin alphabet—the *th* of modern English, the guttural German *ch*, in such words as *auch, rauchen*, and lastly the sound represented in modern English by the letter *w*, as in *we, will, what*. Chilperic decided that the sound *th* should be represented by the Greek ξ, the guttural *ch* by χ, and the *w* in question by the letter ϕ; he also wanted the long o, the French $\hat{o}$, to be represented by ω, reforms which were both good and practical. Those numerous German words, about which modern scholars are always arguing, would thus have been given a correct form adapted to their pronunciation. Chilperic's reforms, moreover, only applied to Latin and the Roman language, that is to say, to the popular idiom in process of becoming French. As the man of letters he prided himself on being, the Frankish prince despised Teutonic dialects.

As a matter of fact the means to which Chilperic had recourse on behalf of his reforms, energetic though they were, do not seem to have been altogether happy. He gave orders not only that all teaching should thenceforward follow the new method, but that all the books then in existence, written, as we know, on parchment, should be erased with pumice stone and rewritten in the new way. Finally, he decided that anybody who refused to follow his system of writing should have his eyes put out—which was perhaps not the best way of teaching them to write.

After having reformed orthography, Chilperic tried to put order into the Church. The interminable discussions between Arians and Catholics about the Trinity had ended in irritating him also. He wrote a little theological treatise to prove that the Trinity was God without distinction of persons, saying that it was unseemly to say that God was composed of three *Persons*, as though it were a question of human beings. The Father, according to Chilperic, was the same as the Son, and the Holy Ghost the same as the Father and the Son, these three so-called Persons merely representing the different activities of the divine Being, Father, Son and Holy Ghost, in its diverse manifestations for the welfare and salvation of men—a scheme which, for a barbarian prince, was not badly conceived.

Chilperic discussed the matter with the neighbouring Bishops —Salvius of Albi and Gregory of Tours, but when they heard what he had to say they only flew into a fury. If the Bishop of Albi, wrote Gregory, had only had the parchment containing the edict in his hands—for Chilperic had formulated his theology in royal edicts—he would have torn it to pieces. The holy prelates had recognised the heresy of Sabellius, condemned by the Synod of Alexandria.

Gregory of Tours said to Chilperic, "Let this matter be, pious King; we must follow the teaching of Hilary and Eusebius." Chilperic, who knew neither Hilary nor Eusebius, thought they were still alive. Inflamed with rage, he replied, "I see clearly that, in this matter, Hilary and Eusebius are my enemies!" And no doubt he had a search made for them in order that he might have their eyes put out.

Chilperic was a poet. He composed Latin verses, religious chants, and hymns modelled on those of the priest Sedulius, famous at that time. Aimoin, a monk of the tenth century, has preserved a fragment in honour of Saint Germain. The poet Fortunatus thought Chilperic's verses admirable; Gregory of Tours thought them execrable. The King did not observe the rules of prosody, he mixed everything up together. At all events these tastes of the barbarian King make of him an interesting personality.

Chilperic also had artistic aspirations. Once when Gregory chanced to be with the King on his farm at Nogent-sur-Marne, the latter showed him a great basin of chased gold encrusted with precious stones. "I made that in order to elevate and polish the Frankish nation," he explained to the Bishop, "and I shall make many others if I have time."

He loved old and rare ornaments, and surrounded himself with Jew dealers who unearthed them for him. On another occasion when Gregory was with him at the royal villa at Nogent, and presented himself before him in order to bid him farewell, he describes how he found him with a young Jew named Priscus, with whom he was very friendly, and whom he employed to buy all kinds of precious things.

And now we come to a scene of modern life and find Chilperic a feminist. He wanted to break the Salic law and allow his wife to inherit some property and have the right of succeeding her husband on his death, thus showing himself to be far in advance of the ideas of his contemporaries in this respect. But we have no desire to return to the atmosphere of that terrible period. When the town of Limoges rebelled, Chilperic increased the number of wooden horses used for torture and had crowds of miserable wretches stretched on them, not sparing the clergy.

Like his father, Chilperic had a large number of wives, perhaps even more than the latter. It would be impossible to enumerate them; they were so numerous that the chroniclers became quite confused over them all. One of the first was called Audovera.

Audovera had in her household a young girl of Frankish descent called Fredegonda, of great beauty and courageous spirit. Chilperic fell in love with her. The King had gone with his brother Sigebert, King of Austrasia, on an expedition across the Rhine, when Audovera gave birth to a daughter. Fredegonda persuaded her mistress to act as the baby's sponsor herself, and a Bishop, either ignorant of the canonical regulations or else acting as an accomplice, celebrated the baptism. Chilperic on his return discovered that his wife had acted as godmother to her own daughter. He sent the guilty Bishop into exile and forced Audovera to take the veil like a widow. The repudiated Queen went and shut herself up in a convent in the Mans district where Fredegonda, fifteen years later, had her put to death.

Sigebert, King of Austrasia, and brother of Chilperic, had married a daughter of Athanagild, King of the Spanish Visigoths—the Princess who was to play so great a part under the name of Brunehaut.

Chilperic, wishing to increase the glory of his crown by an alliance of similar magnificence, sued Athanagild for the hand of another of his daughters named Galswintha, a sweet, fragile creature whom Augustin Thierry describes as follows : " She was a sweet and melancholy figure who moved across the stage of Merovingian barbarism like an apparition from another century."

Athanagild gave his daughter a rich dowry, and Chilperic as a marriage settlement assigned her five towns in Aquitaine, and Galswintha, tearful and terrified, made her way to the awful kingdom of the Franks filled with a vague presentiment of her destiny. She only remained a few months with her husband the King. In 567, the same year in which she became his wife, Chilperic, at the instigation of Fredegonda, had her strangled in her bed, after which he married Fredegonda.

One can imagine the household of these two creatures, the

King, barbarous, cruel, suspicious and jealous; the Queen wicked, vindictive, and full of hatred and low ambition. There were violent scenes, with cries and blows. Chilperic was suspicious of his wife, who gave him only too good cause. Fredegonda had three sons, one after the other—Samson, Clodebert and Dagobert. They all three perished in an epidemic. Whereupon Fredegonda remembered that Chilperic still had a son by Audovera, named Clovis.

The young Clovis was in love with a girl in Fredegonda's suite. Fredegonda was possessed of the idea that the girl's mother was a sorceress, who by her wiles had caused the death of the young Princes. The unfortunate girl was flogged until the blood ran down her back in the presence of Clovis, and the mother was put to torture and made to confess what was wanted of her. Clovis himself was sent in chains to Noisy-sur-Marne, where shortly afterwards he was found stabbed to death and at the same time Audovera, Chilperic's first wife, and the mother of Clovis, was strangled in the convent in Le Mans in which she had sought shelter. There remained one child of the marriage between Chilperic and Audovera—a daughter, the sister of Clovis. She was handed over to the soldiers and shut up in a convent in Poitiers.

In 583 another son, called Theodoric, whom Fredegonda had by Chilperic, also died. He too was supposed to have been the victim of sorcery, and several women in his service and one or two women from Paris, who were reputed to be witches, were burnt alive, drowned or quartered.

Mummolus, the prefect of the palace, was looked upon with displeasure by Fredegonda, who declared that he had been the instigator of the crime. He was hanged from a rafter with his hands tied behind his back in order to wrest a confession from him. But in vain. He was then bound to a wheel and flogged with straps for such a long time, says Gregory, that the executioners were tired out; thorns were stuck under the nails of his hands and feet, but his life was spared. After this he was dragged in a chariot to Bordeaux, where he was born, and died as soon as he arrived.

One daughter of Fredegonda and Chilperic survived named Ridegonda. Gregory of Tours has left a significant picture of the relations between mother and daughter. They were always quarrelling and hitting and kicking each other without mercy. One day, when the mother had succeeded in making her daughter bend over a coffer, on the pretext of getting out some jewels from the bottom of it, she shut down the lid on her head and was engaged in strangling her when servants ran up in answer to the cries of the victim.

And this same Fredegonda, convicted of the most atrocious crimes, yet contrived to burn the tax-gatherers' registers in order to lighten the burdens of the poor in remembrance of her own lowly origin. When a certain family feud, one of those hereditary quarrels which developed on such a large scale in feudal times, was laying bare a whole district, and the unfortunate inhabitants saw their property being pillaged and their lands ravaged by the partisans of both sides, Fredegonda pacified the country by destroying the two families root and branch and thus delivering the people from the scourge.

Gontram, King of the Burgundians, who claimed to be a lover of justice, had forced Chilperic to give back to Brunehaut, the wife of Sigebert, King of Austrasia and sister of Galswintha, the five towns of Aquitaine which he had given Galswintha as her dowry. Chilperic agreed, but lost no time in going to war with Sigebert. The latter retaliated by having himself proclaimed King of Neustria—the kingdom of Chilperic—at Vitry on the Scarpe. He drove back the forces opposed to him and blockaded them in the town of Tournai in which Fredegonda was shut up. Sigebert felt assured of victory when he was murdered by the emissaries of the woman whom he already regarded as his prisoner (575). The King of Neustria now only had one enemy left—a woman, Brunehaut, the widow of Sigebert. And indeed Brunehaut was quite capable of defending herself.

It is very difficult to form an exact estimate of the character of Brunehaut. Gregory of Tours is full of her praises. She was, according to him, of a pleasing disposition, honest and decent in her morals, prudent in her councils, and amiable in conversation. The daughter of Athanagild, King of the Spanish Visigoths, and sister of Galswintha, she had married Sigebert I, King of Austrasia in 566. Brought up in the Arian religion, she was converted to Catholicism on the occasion of her marriage. She was very beautiful; on this point everybody is of one accord. She was energetic and intelligent, and clever in reaching firm and well-considered decisions.

Brunehaut acted as Regent of Austrasia in the name of her little son Childebert II, who was proclaimed King at the age of five, and maintained the royal prerogatives which the Austrasian nobles were already attacking in their efforts to turn their domains into small independent States. She introduced a system of land registration and, in re-arranging the taxes, aimed at freeing the poor and making the rich pay—a policy which, as we know, was long regarded as monstrous. She tried to put great and small on an equal footing of justice and, whilst combating the abuses arising from privileges of rank and birth, she nevertheless endeavoured to safeguard the aristocracy by maintaining the right of primogeniture and preventing the division of hereditary estates by continual partition. The foundation of a large number of abbeys, amongst them some of the most important, was due to her— in fact she was a veritable " statesman."

Meroveus, a son of Chilperic and Audovera, had escaped the fury of Fredegonda. He saw Brunehaut, who happened to be in Rouen, fell passionately in love with her and persuaded the Bishop Praetextatus to join them in marriage, a union which the ideas of the age repudiated, on account of the consanguinity of the parties. The fury of Chilperic, fomented by Fredegonda, who recognised a rival in Brunehaut, knew no bounds. The newly-wedded pair had taken refuge in a monastery. They left it under guarantees of safety given by the King of Neustria, but although he allowed Brunehaut to return to Austrasia, he had her son shut up in the monastery of Saint Calais, near Le Mans. The unfortunate Prince made good his escape, and rejoined Brunehaut in Austrasia, but the nobility, who were chafing under the reforming rule of the Queen, had no intention of having the King foisted upon them as well. Meroveus had to take flight once more, and was wandering about in the neighbourhood of Rheims, when he was overtaken by the emissaries of Fredegonda. In order to escape falling into the hands of this cruel woman, he asked a faithful vassal who had followed him to kill him with a knife. Fredegonda completed her vengeance by having the Bishop Praetextatus, who was an old man, stabbed at the very foot of the altar (577).

A few years after the murder of Praetextatus, Chilperic himself fell beneath the assassin's knife. He happened to be staying at the royal farm of Chelles, indulging in the pleasures of the chase, when one evening, as he was returning from the forest at dusk and was just about to leave the saddle, with his hand resting on the back of a servant, he was struck two blows, one under the armpit and the other in the stomach. A few moments afterwards he died (584).

Some ancient chroniclers, and especially the author of *Les Gestes des Francs*, once again saw in Fredegonda the instigator of the murder. For some time past the Queen's misconduct had been the cause of increasing the violent scenes between her and her husband. Nevertheless, Sunnegisil, the High Constable, who had armed the hand of the murderer, brought no accusation against her, and the Queen pointed to the Grand Chamberlain Ebrult as the author of the crime.

After the death of the King Fredegonda took refuge in Paris, in the cathedral church, under the protection of Bishop Ragnemod. She took with her all she could carry of the royal treasures.

On the orders of Childebert, the son of Sigebert and Brunehaut, King of Austrasia, Sunnegisil was seized, put to torture and then cast into gaol, where he was flogged every day with birch rods and leather thongs. As soon as his wounds healed they were opened up again so as to renew his suffering. He confessed not only that he had participated in the death of Chilperic, but that he had also joined in a plot against Childebert himself.

Chilperic was buried in the basilica of Saint Vincent, to-day called Saint-Germain-des-Prés.

Notwithstanding Chilperic's artistic tastes, his collection of rare treasures of art and his desire to reform literature and theology, civilisation suffered a fresh terrible reverse in his reign. The Frankish warriors, who were masters of the country, knew no form of labour except that of rapine and pillage, and saw wealth only in the brutal possession of gold. They melted down the precious vases stolen from churches or taken from tombs. The roads became battlefields on which the merchant was robbed and killed by lords of high descent, who, it is true, could sometimes be appeased by being plied with drink.

Anything could be got out of them by means of wine, writes Augustin Thierry, " even to a promise of lending their support at Court to such and such a candidate for a vacant bishopric."

What under such conditions was to become of the peaceful pursuits of the mind? The most distinguished Gallo-Romans allowed themselves to be swept along by the barbarian floods. They too became fighters and robbers, nocturnal brigands and highwaymen.

And if we examine the generations that followed, the picture is still obscure. Gregory of Tours, who died in 595, was the contemporary of Chilperic, who was murdered in 584; and if we compare the society he depicts in his chronicle with that of which we have an outline in the so-called chronicle of Fredegar (first half of the seventh century) we find the latter enveloped in still further obscurity. As Guizot has observed, the pictures drawn by Gregory of Tours are enlumined by a certain ray of light; they reveal vague reflections of Virgil and Sallust, and the very theological discussions they contain bear witness to intellectual preoccupations; but the social life presented by Fredegar is nothing but darkness and confusion. The grossest barbarism had invaded even the episcopal thrones—a thick fog which here and there was pierced with difficulty by the shy rays of some quiet candle burning on the rough wooden table of a modest monk bending, in the silence of the monastery, over a manuscript of ivory hue.

Gontram, King of Burgundy, and brother of Sigebert and Chilperic, undertook the education of the little Clotar II, the **Clotar II.** son of Chilperic and Fredegonda, who was six months old, just as he had undertaken the education of Childebert II, King of Austrasia.

Clotar II was proclaimed King of Neustria.

This Merovingian monarch, who was a brutal, violent and

267

pilfering despot, nevertheless exercised a great influence over the country by the very fact of his existence, which kept factions in check, and was a last brake upon internal dissensions. In what light does Chilperic appear to us? Hardly had the news of his death been announced than disorders broke out (584). The people of Orleans and Blois fell upon the inhabitants of Dunois, pillaging, killing, delivering houses and crops over to the flames, and carrying off anything they could lay their hands on. Whereupon the inhabitants of Dunois, joining with the people of Chartres, invaded their assailants to pay them back in like coin. Gontram, King of Burgundy, the protector of his two nephews in Austrasia and Neustria, took up the reins of authority and order was restored.

Fredegonda died in 597, and Brunehaut, rid of her terrible rival, ruled in the name of her grandson Theodebert II, who had become King of Austrasia on the death of his father Childebert II (595), whilst another of her grandsons, Theodoric II, had become King of Burgundy. The two brothers came to blows in 610. " With the help of God," writes Fredegar, " Theodoric conquered Theodebert and the battle was once again fought in the Plain of Zülpich (612). Theodebert was led in chains before his brother, who had him put to death. The King of Austrasia (Theodebert) had with him his little son, Meroveus. At the command of Theodoric a soldier seized the child by the leg and dashed his brains out against a wall. Whereupon Theodoric laid hands upon his brother's treasure." And thus Austrasia was reunited to Burgundy.

Soon afterwards Theodoric died also and Brunehaut once more assumed the reins of government in the name of Sigebert II, the bastard son of Theodoric. She was ruling despotically, though observing the traditions of a regular government, when the nobles of the country, under the leadership of the Mayors of the Palace in Austrasia and Burgundy, in a movement at the head of which were to be found the ancestors of Charlemagne—Saint Arnoul, Bishop of Metz, and Saint Pepin de Landen, rose in rebellion, assassinated Sigebert II, proclaimed Clotar II, who was King of Neustria, King of Austrasia and Burgundy also, and delivered Brunehaut up to him. And thus Clotar was able to wreak on this old woman—Brunehaut being close on seventy—the implacable hatred of his mother Fredegonda.

Clotar began by putting to death two of his great-grandsons, the children of Theodoric II, after which he put into execution the sentence he had passed upon Brunehaut—a terrible scene, a description of which has been preserved in the so-called chronicle of Fredegar.

After the old woman had been tortured for three days, she was put on a camel and promenaded through the ranks of the soldiers, who covered her with insults and mockery. When this moral torture seemed to have lasted long enough, they tied the Queen quite naked by her hair, and one arm and a leg, to the tail of a fiery horse, and her poor body soon became no more than a torn and bleeding mass (613). And Fredegar, after having described this beautiful punishment, goes on to say of the Prince who had ordered it : " Clotar was full of sweetness, learned in letters, fearing God, the protector of churches and priests, and abandoning himself with great zest to the hunt as well as to women." The portrait is a mediocre piece of work.

After this Clotar had a few more prominent personages assassinated, and notably a certain Boson, whom he suspected of being in love with the Queen, at the same time applying himself to the best of his ability to the government of his vast estates. He succeeded in reducing the taxes and in restoring the royal domain, and is regarded as the best of the Merovingian kings. Master of Neustria, Austrasia and Burgundy, Clotar re-united in his own hands the territories of the whole of Gaul, which had been continually divided up ever since the death of Clotar I, but in each of the three districts he was obliged to appoint its own Mayor of the Palace. This, as we know, was the title of the chief of the King's household, who thus found himself placed at the head of the officials and the nobles. Landry was Mayor of the Palace in Neustria, Radon in Austrasia and Warnacaire in Burgundy. And the latter Clotar was obliged to promise to keep in office for life. He tried to depose him after a conspiracy attributed to his son, but was unable to do so owing to the opposition of the nobles. The three kingdoms were reconstituted under one King, but with divisions and political separations far deeper than any that had existed under the sons of Clovis and of Clotar I, each of the Mayors of the Palace becoming a veritable Viceroy; for it was found necessary to make their office permanent, which was the first step towards making it hereditary. But still the Austrasians were not content. They wanted a sovereign of their own and Clotar was obliged to send them his young son, Dagobert, in this capacity (622). "In the thirty-ninth year of his reign," writes Fredegar, "Clotar associated with him in his kingdom his son Dagobert and set him over the Austrasians, keeping for himself the territory stretching towards Neustria and Burgundy, beyond the Ardennes and the Vosges." The young Dagobert, who must have been about seventeen, had as his advisers Saint Arnoul, Bishop of Metz, and Pepin de Landen, who had become Mayor of the Palace.

These facts call for attention. No historian who has deplored the partitions under the Merovingians has failed to ask himself whether they were not a necessity. Austrasia, Neustria, Burgundy and Aquitaine—each of these States had its own traditions, customs and ways, each was imbued with a spirit of independence. The Austrasians obeyed a Neustrian King grudgingly or not at all. They lent him no aid when he was obliged to fight recalcitrant subjects, rebellious tributaries or aggressive neighbours. The monarch imposed upon them reigned over Neustria, and they regarded with indifference the incursions of Saxons or Slavs or of the Normans who had just made their appearance. And if the King had been an Austrasian, the Neustrians would have thought and acted in the same way.

Thus the division of France into Austrasia, Neustria and Burgundy was a necessity. Aquitaine was still exhausted by the terrible massacres under Clovis, but as soon as she recovered her strength, she displayed the same spirit of independence.

Of all errors of thought the most common among historians is to attribute to men of another epoch the ideas of to-day. The conception of a united France, conscious of her destiny, could only be formed in the course of centuries, as the result of the superhuman efforts, sacrifices, suffering and glory of which we know the history.

Clotar II died on the 10th of October, 629, and was buried in the church of Saint Vincent (the Saint-Germain-des-Prés **Dagobert.** of to-day) in a suburb of Paris, writes Fredegar. His epitaph has been found.

His son Dagobert, who was twenty-four, convoked the leudes of the kingdom of Austrasia of which he was the Sovereign. They arrived in arms, and with this imposing force at his disposal he sent deputies to the Burgundians and the Nuestrians demanding them to proclaim him King also. The reply of the leudes and Bishops of Burgundy reached him without delay, and he took their oaths of fealty at Soissons. Dagobert had a brother called Caribert, to whom part of the kingdom should have reverted, but he seems to have been feeble in character. His maternal uncle, Bromulfo, undertook to defend his rights, and to stop his agitation, Dagobert, in true Merovingian fashion, had him assassinated.

But we have already mentioned the desire on the part of the three sections of Gaul, Austrasia, Neustria and Aquitaine, each to have their own separate government—Burgundy had gradually become more and more closely united to Neustria— and so determined were they that Dagobert decided to give the administration of Aquitaine to Caribert. The latter established himself at Toulouse, and about the year 633 even subjected to his power the whole of Gascony, a part of which had declared its independence. Shortly afterwards Caribert died, leaving one son, Chilperic, who was not long in following his father to the tomb. Dagobert was suspected of having put him out of the way. At all events the fact remains that the whole heritage returned to his hands.

Following the example of his father, Clotar II, Dagobert had a very large number of wives. He married them, repudiated them, married others at the same time as he kept the first and took others without any formality. By Nanthilda Dagobert had a son called Clovis, by Ragnetruda another son called Sigebert. The order in which the Queens of France succeeded each other under Dagobert is for that matter impossible to decide. We cannot even tell which of them were officially Queens as distinguished from those who were so in practice. However that may be, Dagobert did for his son Sigebert, the son of

Ragnetruda, what his father had done for him; he handed over to him the kingdom of Austrasia, the leudes of that country insisting upon having a King of their own; after which Dagobert decided that the kingdoms of Neustria and Burgundy should at his death devolve on his son Clovis. He convoked the nobles and Bishops of Austrasia to make them swear on the relics that this partition should be respected; and the Austrasians consented. The only stipulation was that the Duchy of Dentelin, which the Austrasians had seized, should be returned to the Neustrians and subjected to the rule of Clovis. The Duchy of Dentelin, with its curious name, which played so great a part in the history of that period, included the cities of Boulogne, Thérouanne, Arras, Noyon, Cambrai and Tournai.

We might think we were reading of treaties made between different States. Nevertheless it was after the long reign of Clotar II and the twelve first years of the reign of Dagobert, who both united the whole of Gaul under their rule, that these divisions took place.

It was not the territorial partitions between the sons of the Merovingian kings that created the divisions of Gaul. Procopius, on the contrary, emphasises the unity of policy and government under the four sons of Clovis and the four sons of Clotar I, which filled him with admiration. In speaking of these partitions, Fustel de Coulanges points out that sometimes a town was divided into two or three parts, " and thus we find the kings fighting for a half or a third of a city." From which it becomes clear how superficial these divisions were; in the north it was a question of armed forces, for the north provided armed bands; in the south it was a question of *pots de vin*, both literally and figuratively; whilst, on the other hand, we know there were profound divisions under the apparently unified government established by Clotar, and after him by his son Dagobert, in Austrasia, Neustria and Aquitaine. Was it not the victorious Clotar II, the sole master of Gaul, who had to recognise the independence of Austrasia?

The reason for this division was the same as that which was to lead to the rise of the power of the leudes and the destruction of the Merovingian dynasty—the local life which was gradually organised under the guidance of its direct leaders, the leudes and the Bishops, in groups which became ever more and more compact and by joining together increased their powers of resistance; whilst the government of the princes who succeeded each other after Clovis was unable to wield any real power over the country, any centralised power—the very idea raises a smile.

In the vigour of his youth, Dagobert did not fail to shed a certain military glory over his reign.

In the year 578 the Basques had descended from the Pyrenees, and laid bare the vineyards and the fields, carrying off the inhabitants and their cattle; and these incursions were repeated. The Basques or Vascons ended by installing themselves in the district, which was to be called Gascony after them. Their language, Euskarian, represented the ancient Iberian tongue, although the erudite Auguste Longnon disputes this—an " agglutinative " language which cannot be made to fit into the so-called Indo-European group of languages. In 602, Theodebert II and Theodoric II had undertaken an expedition against the Basques which ended in an agreement, leaving them a national Duke under the vague suzerainty of the Franks. But the indomitable little race returned to their pillaging manœuvres. In 637 Dagobert brought them into subjection, for a time at least, for, after him, their Duke Yon renewed the conflict, and became the head of an independent State which was ruled in succession by the Dukes Hunald and Waïfar or Gaifier.

Dagobert forced the Breton chiefs to present themselves before him in his villa at Saint Ouen as obedient subjects. He conducted expeditions as far as the Elbe, against the Wends, who were led by a common Frank called Samo, who seems to have been an extraordinary character. Under the walls of Egra, Samo defeated the army sent by Dagobert. He had abjured Catholicism in order to embrace the religion of the Slavs. He had twelve wives and thirty-seven children.

The young King of the Franks had the Salic law revised. In 628–629 he paid a visit to Burgundy in order to conduct an inquiry into the manner of government and the administration of justice in that country. The chroniclers, Fredegar and the monk of Saint Denis, speak of this with emotion. " His arrival," says Fredegar, "filled the Bishops and leudes with fear, but gave great joy to the poor, for the King rendered them justice." A description which unexpectedly raises before our eyes the image of Saint Louis. "At Langres the King judged great and small with so much equity that every man regarded him as pleasing before God." The chronicler thought it necessary to add : " Neither gifts, rank nor station had any weight with him." Similar scenes were enacted at Chalon-sur-Saône, and afterwards at Auxerre, Autun and Sens. The young Prince neither ate nor slept, for he would not allow anyone to leave his presence without having obtained justice. It was during this journey that Dagobert, "having entered the bath before daybreak," says Fredegar, had Bromulfo put to death; after which, on reaching Romilly, he repudiated his wife Gomatruda in order to marry Nanthilda, a daughter of the people, "but of an admirable beauty," observes the monk of Saint Denis.

The reign of Dagobert is the most brilliant period in the monarchy of the fifth and sixth centuries. He may be regarded as the Louis XIV of the Merovingians. If the Roi Soleil had the good fortune to be served by great ministers, Dagobert had the still better luck of being served and advised by saints; for he was surrounded by saints, from Saint Arnulf, Bishop of Metz, who was his teacher, to Saint Eloysius, Bishop of Noyon, who was his treasurer and goldsmith. His referendary was Saint Ouen, Bishop of Rouen, and as members of his council he had Saint Cunibert, Bishop of Cologne, and Saint Amand, Bishop of Tongres.

Saint Eloysius dazzled the Court by the splendour of his golden girdles. He made a throne of solid gold for the King and for the basilica of Saint Denis a great golden cross incrusted with emeralds, amethysts and rubies. "The blessed Eloysius, who was held to be the most skilful goldsmith in the kingdom," says the monk of Saint Denis, "helped also, no doubt, by his piety, executed with admirable art, not only this cross, but also all the ornaments in the basilica. The goldsmiths of to-day [end of the seventh century] are accustomed to say that there is hardly a man, however skilful he may be in other ways, who can work gold in this way and encrust it with

274

precious stones, owing to the fact that, for many years, the science of melting rare metals has fallen into desuetude."

Dagobert died when he was still young on the 19th of January, 639, in his villa at Epinay-sur-Seine. He was a King who had been very fond of money, and left behind him a reputation for avarice; but he founded the Abbey of Saint Denis. He committed a few murders, so as not to break the traditions of his ancestors, and brought joy to the hearts of countless numbers of fair and honest dames.

His pious biographer, the monk of Saint Denis, sums up his reign in the following precious lines :

" King Dagobert, it is true, committed a few reprehensible actions from the religious point of view, for no man can be perfect. Nevertheless it must be believed that all the alms and the prayers to saints, with which he adorned the monuments and enriched the churches, more than any of the kings who had gone before him had done, in order that he might reclaim his soul, must have obtained for him without difficulty the pardon of all-merciful God."

Such was the psychology of the time, the psychology of the chroniclers, all of them ecclesiastics, to whom we owe our knowledge of the people we are studying and of all these kings, conquerors and captains, rapers and robbers, murderers, traitors, knaves and perjurers who pass before our eyes in an uninterrupted procession. But what can you expect? As the good monk says, nobody can be perfect, and so many magnificent gifts to the churches, monasteries and servants of God, with the help of the prayers of the saints which enriched the altars, could not fail, in the end, to secure their eternal salvation.

Prematurely exhausted by his numerous wives, Dagobert died—of old age—when he was thirty-four (639). His eldest **Mayors of the** son, Sigebert, who was seven or eight at the time, **Palace and** had already been King of Austrasia for six years; **" Rois** whilst his son Clovis, who was four or five, had **Fainéants."** just been recognised King of Neustria and Burgundy. With the death of Dagobert the rule of the Merovingian kings really came to an end, and we enter upon the era of the administration of the Mayors of the Palace and the reign of the " *Rois Fainéants* " or Sluggard Kings. *Fainéant* did not mean a king who did not wish to do anything, like the modern word "*feignant*," feigning, not "*fainéant*"—"*fainéant*" meant one who was unable to do anything.

The picture drawn by Eginhard, the historian and adviser of Charlemagne, is famous :

" Except for the title and the means of existence allowed him by the Mayor of the Palace, the King possessed no property of his own except one domain, which brought but little revenue, and a house and a few servants to provide him with the necessaries of life. When he had to go on a journey he drove in a chariot drawn by a yoke of bullocks and led by a rustic drover. It was in this equipage that he presented himself at the Palace, or the popular assembly, which met once a year for the good of the kingdom, and then returned to his home."

The truth of this picture has been contested, but it cannot be destroyed. A general outline is given in it with strokes that are too vivid for us to allow them to be blotted out.

The Mayoralty of the Palace was an institution peculiar to the Merovingian epoch. We have already described the great Gallo-Roman domains, many of which became the property of the Merovingian kings who, as we have seen, made them their favourite places of residence. Landowners who did not administer their domains themselves, handed them over to the care of a steward, who took the title of *major*, meaning " greater," since he was set in authority over his subjects. The *major domus*, the " mayor " of the household, became in the royal household the " Mayor of the Palace."

At first, in the sixth century, the Mayors of the Palace exercised relatively unimportant functions; but their power continued to grow. At the beginning of the eighth century the authority of the Mayor was greater than that of the King himself. He had the direction and administration of the royal palace and jurisdiction over all the visitors and dependants within its walls. Under the embryonic bellicose government of the early Merovingians the Palace was the State. The towns were ruled by the Bishops, and the country districts by the large landowners. The Dukes and Counts, who represented the royal authority outside the Palace, were themselves nomi-
276

nated by the Mayor, who was the head of the administration. The Mayor of the Palace was supreme in the royal domains and the farms and villas the produce of which constituted the regular resources of the monarchy. In the absence of the King, the Mayor presided over his tribunals and commanded his armies. It is easy to imagine how frequent these " absences " became under dissipated, incapable kings, or minors.

How quick must have been the growth of the power of the Mayors during the minority of little princes like Sigebert II and Clovis II! We have already described the " recommendation " by means of which men who were too weak to defend themselves and their property placed themselves under the protection of important personages. The King had such *protégés*, and amongst them, in a higher social scale, those who had put themselves in *trust* with the King by close bonds of association attaching them to his person. These antrustions formed his bodyguard, and were drawn from the ranks of warriors of high social standing and birth. They were attached to the King by oath. But even over them the Mayors of the Palace extended their authority.

Benjamin Guérard, with his usual clarity of thought, sums up the situation very vividly when he depicts the Merovingian kings as " ruling, or rather dominating, not so much the country and peoples of Gaul, as the armed bands which overran and pillaged it." The King had his " band," which was the largest and strongest; the Mayor of the Palace had his. From the day on which the Mayor's band became stronger than the King's and the Mayor even laid hands on the royal band, the power of the King ceased to exist.

After the death of Dagobert, Neustria, whose King was a child of five, was governed by the Mayor of the Palace, Aega, and Austrasia, whose Sovereign was a child of seven, by the Mayor Pepin de Landen, an ancestor of Charlemagne. They were both men of worth. The monk who acted as the guide of Dagobert in his lifetime has left us a portrait of Aega. " He surpassed all the nobility of Neustria. He was of noble birth, rich, a friend of justice and clever in speech and reply; but a few accused him of avarice." In the fourth year of the reign of the little Clovis in Neustria, that is to say, in 641,

Aega died. The Queen, Nantilda, went with her little son to Orleans, which was in the kingdom of Burgundy, and there convoked the nobility, the Dukes and the Bishops of the country. They arrived in great numbers, and the Queen, says Fredegar, " by the unanimous vote of the Bishops and Dukes raised to the dignity of Mayor of the Palace Floachat, who was a Frank by birth, and gave him her niece Ragnoberta in marriage."

From this time forward the Mayors of the Palace were no longer even in the nomination of the King or his representatives, but were appointed by the nobles. The following comparison is characteristic. If we examine the list of the Mayors of the Palace who succeeded each other up to the death of Dagobert, we shall find that their number is greater than that of the kings who reigned during the same period in Gaul; whilst, after Dagobert, the number of the kings is larger. Up to and during the reign of Dagobert the kings deposed mayors who had ceased to please them, replacing them by others whom they preferred. But after Dagobert it was the mayors who deposed the kings.

Amongst the nobility of the kingdom, the most important were the Bishops. " They formed," says Maurice Prou, " an aristocracy more powerful than the aristocracy."

The Bishops. The Bishops were the princes of those barbarian days, and it might almost be said that from the fall of the Roman Empire to the accession of the Capets, that is to say, for five hundred years, the Bishops were the leaders of society, not only from the religious point of view, but in every possible way. It was they who raised Charlemagne to power. And this period constitutes the great epoch of the Church, when she was strong, fertile and creative.

The Catholic Church was not during the first few centuries of her existence the huge centralised body into which she subsequently developed. The Pope was called the Bishop of Rome; he took precedence over his colleagues, but he did not rule them, and had no voice in their election. The unity of dogma, which was upheld with such severity against the heretics, such as the Arians, the Sabellians and the Pelagians, depended upon episcopal assemblies, Councils and Synods, but not on a
278

single pontifical decision. The Catholic world was composed of a federation of churches each one of which was governed by its own Bishop and held sway over the territory of a city.

Thus the Church borrowed her administrative boundaries from the Roman Empire and animated them with the intense vitality which at that time constituted her active power. The identity of the Gallic Bishoprics with the Roman cities was, with few exceptions, almost complete.

The Bishops were great personages, not only on account of their prestige and secular power, but also frequently owing to their personal valour and their family position. Many of them in the fifth century were of senatorial descent. And, in keeping with the spirit of tradition which had grown up through various careers and trades being kept in one family, all the Bishops of Tours, as Gregory of Tours points out, were, with about five exceptions, relatives of his own. The priest Euphronius had been raised to the bishopric of Tours. King Clotar, who was in favour of another candidate, inquired into the motives underlying the election. The reply was, " Euphronius is the nephew of the Bishop of Langres," and the King gave way.

In those days of lively faith, the authority of the Bishops was very great. See how they spoke to the King. Saint Germain, Bishop of Paris, said to Sigebert, " If you do not depart from your intention of killing your brother [Chilperic] you will return victorious, otherwise you will perish."

The Church held a man in her power through the crimes he had committed, the remorse with which they had inspired him, and the threat of eternal damnation which would be his punishment and from which she alone could absolve him. She held him by fear ; but she also held him by beauty, mildness and joy. Her doctrine founded on hope brought comfort to sorrowing souls. The ceremonies of her worship, in which all could join, with their magnificent services, their hymns and chants, the splendour of the setting, the perfume of the incense and the charm of the heavenly music, provided the utmost beauty those days could offer. On liturgical feast days the sufferings of every wounded heart could not fail to be alleviated.

Moreover, the Bishop, with his high authority, in his vestments glittering with gold and precious stones, surrounded by the magic of the religious ceremonies, seemed to the masses a sacred being. He was called upon in his own lifetime to work divine miracles; and he succeeded, not by reason of his virtues, but from the very fact that he was a Bishop. And if a Bishop did not work the cures expected of him, it was because he did not wish to do so; and he was held responsible. " If I die," said Ulfus to Saint Germain (Bishop from 555 to 576), " you will be responsible, and the King and my family will come and demand a reckoning from you." We do not know whether the threat moved the holy prelate, but the fact remains that Ulfus was cured. It was regarded as great good fortune to possess a few words written by a Bishop on a scrap of parchment; they were boiled, and the infusion thus produced was more efficacious than the prescriptions of the leading lights of medicine.

And of this authority the Bishops made good use. They developed the works of peace; they maintained the right of asylum in the holy places. And this right of asylum was extended not only to the basilica, but to the atrium leading into it and the ecclesiastical buildings surrounding the vestibule. The Councils did all they could to guarantee the right of asylum, which was open even to murderers. It provided a refuge for slaves, whose masters were not allowed to have them back until they had sworn not to inflict any corporal punishment upon them.

The moral authority of the Bishops was doubled by their secular power. The domains in the possession of the episcopacy were very considerable and they constantly increased in size. They were inhabited by serfs and cultivators—and slaves—who were not allowed to leave them. Certain Bishops, like the Bishop of Le Mans and the Bishop of Cahors, who possessed over thirty domains, found themselves rulers over 15,000 or 20,000 subjects—princes of a little kingdom. And these domains continued to grow, partly through their own development and partly through the gifts of the faithful desirous of accomplishing a pious work. The Councils formally forbade any alienation of episcopal property. A Bishop was only allowed to concede the use by usufruct of this or that portion of land, so that the right of possession was not violated. These were the rights of mortmain. By the end of the eighth century the property of the Church included a third of Gaul.

The Bishop was supported by the mass of the people by whom he was elected. The basilica was the place in which the inhabitants of the town—and of the city—met together to discuss their common interests, frequently under the guidance of the Bishop. He was the protector of the weak who sought shelter beneath the pastoral crook; and his power increased accordingly. In every way and from every direction, private individuals of all sorts and conditions tried to release themselves from the chaos of the various conflicting authorities in Gaul, in order to come and " recommend " themselves to the Bishop, whereby the number of his subjects continued to increase. When, towards the end of the sixth century, Chilperic said that public authority had passed from the Crown to the cities, he meant to the Bishops.

The writers of the sixth century congratulated the Bishops, who proved themselves the active defenders of their flocks. The Bishops opposed the exactions and injustices of which the Counts representing the royal power continued to be guilty. They played the part of *defensor civitatis*, defenders of the Gallo-Roman city, though without having directly inherited the position by virtue of an edict or a law. The transmission of authority had been made by force of circumstances.

" The Bishops," says Fustel de Coulanges, " seem to have been regular political chiefs without rivals in their respective cities." The town in which they lived rendered them obeisance, and they arranged for its defence against all aggression. Consider Autun, Rheims, and Sens. They were ruled by their Bishops, who conducted the manœuvres in sieges, and put themselves at the head of the sorties directed against the enemy.

Bishops, and among them saints, might be seen raising troops, marching out to war, and fighting valiantly. When Ebroin, the Mayor of the Palace, was in the midst of a conflict with Saint Leger, Bishop of Autun, who with his men had engaged him in battle and was on the point of surrender, reinforcements under the command of Saint Genès, Archbishop of Lyons, arrived just in time. With the revenues from his church and from the city, to which he frequently added his own personal resources, the Bishop undertook the construction of public works, he built or restored monuments, strengthened the ramparts, constructed aqueducts, made canals, and embankments along watercourses. The poems of Fortunatus, Bishop of Poitiers, give us many examples.

In their councils the Bishops themselves decided the division of their revenues—a quarter for their " household," another for the poor and a third for the clergy of their diocese; the remainder was consecrated to the maintenance of the churches and other monuments.

The Bishops in their cities performed the functions of judges. In this department their authority far exceeded that of the Counts. They dealt in equity rather than in law, aiming at protecting the humble, settling the interminable and murderous feuds between the great families, the bloody vendettas, and were magnificent justices of the peace. And in important affairs, in order to give their authority still further weight, they called in the assistance of the notables of the city.

" Maurillon, Bishop of Cahors, was a man just in the judgments he delivered, a zealous defender of the poor against bad judges. In the words of Job : ' I delivered the poor that cried . . . and him that had none to help him . . . and I caused the widow's heart to sing for joy.' " (Gregory of Tours.)

Their authority extended to military matters. King Gontram sent an expedition into Septimania against the Goths. It ended in disaster. On the return of his vanquished army he arraigned the generals before a tribunal on which four Bishops were seated. They protected their flocks against the officials of the Palace, and against the kings themselves. When the Mayor and the Count of the Palace came to Gregory of Tours to raise taxes, the latter vehemently informed them that they must respect Saint Martin. From fear of arousing the anger of the saint, had not King Clotar had the registers of the land survey burnt ? Had not King Caribert promised to raise no new taxes ? Had not King Sigebert acted in the same way ?— and now, fourteen years after the death of his father, King Childebert was trying to get money out of the people of

282

Touraine ! In the end, out of regard for Saint Martin and in terror of his anger, and at the command of the King himself, the collectors departed without having accomplished their mission. The same thing happened at Bourges. The inhabitants heard that an official of the Palace, named Garnier, was on his way to levy taxes in the town. They appealed to the Bishop, Saint Austregisile. The latter went out to meet the collector and barred his road. Neither rage nor violence could move him and Garnier also had to return empty-handed.

Thus the Bishops came to regard the levy of such taxes as did not directly serve the needs of their flocks as iniquitous and contrary to the will of God. Gregory of Tours tells us how certain tax-collectors and their colleagues were struck through the anger of Saint Martin in the lives of their nearest and dearest. The zealous pastors, as we may well imagine, had no difficulty in making those whose spiritual guidance was confided to them share their views. And this condemnation of taxes which were regarded as unjust impositions was largely responsible for the gradual weakening of the power of the King.

The importance of the episcopal elections was in keeping with the interests at stake. At first, before the arrival of the Franks in Gaul, it took place in a general assembly of the faithful, under the eyes of the Bishops of the province. " Let the Bishop, who is to be above all, be chosen by all," wrote Pope Leo the Great. The election of the most illustrious of all the prelates is described by Sulpicius Severus. The Bishops of the province had gathered together at Tours, the capital. They wished to appoint a new Pontiff, but the people with loud shouts demanded Saint Martin. The prelates, who belonged to senatorial families, found this little to their taste. Martin was of mean descent, he was poor and sordidly clad—*veste sordidum ;*—but the people would not cease from shouting that they wanted Martin. And thus it came about that Saint Martin was placed upon the episcopal throne of Tours.

Venerandus, Bishop of Auvergne, had just died, and his colleagues in the province had arrived to appoint his successor. But the assembled people were unable to come to any agreement as to their choice, when a priest named Rusticus happened to pass through the crowd. He was well loved for his good works.

This incident was regarded as a sign from God, and Rusticus was elected by acclamation.

These customs of the primitive Church still retained their vigour under Clovis, though the King had already arrogated to himself the right of presenting candidates, who on that account alone stood the best chance of carrying the vote. And thus, between the provincial Bishops, under the presidency of the Metropolitan, and the people a new factor was introduced, that of the King. To the right of presenting candidates, the Merovingian dynasty, from the time of Clovis, added that of confirming the election when it had been made.

It is easy to understand that, with the right of presentation and the right of confirmation thus arrogated to themselves by the kings, the episcopal elections soon fell entirely into their hands. In 515, four years after the death of Clovis, the Arverni chose Quintianus to succeed their Bishop Eufrasius who had died. But another personage of the district, a very rich man, presented himself before King Theodoric and by means of gifts persuaded him to designate him as the successor of Eufrasius, and it was he who, in spite of the election which had already taken place, occupied the episcopal throne. And this custom unfortunately became universal, and simony was the rule. Even the kings who professed the greatest devotion to the Church, like King Gontram of Burgundy, disregarded the protestations of the Pope, and sold the bishoprics for ready money.

Furthermore there were quarrels, intrigues and conflicts between the popular electors themselves. When the bishopric of Autun became vacant in 657, the choice of the new Bishop led to such violent struggles that blood was spilt. One of the two candidates was killed in the fray, and the other was driven out of the town. The conflict lasted for two years, when Queen Bathilda, who was acting as Regent during the minority of her son, Clotar III, appointed Saint Leger to the see of Autun (659).

In Paris a Syrian merchant named Eusebius won the crozier and mitre by bribing the electors. And behold him on the episcopal throne proceeding to canonical investitures and administering his diocese as though he were in his counting-house. The Bishop's palace was packed with Syrians conducting all manner of business in their outlandish jargon.

At other places, such as Gap, Embrun and Rheims, the episcopal thrones were occupied by ruffians who won them, not by spending money right and left like the Syrian Eusebius, but in the way that Clovis had won his throne, with the battle-axe and the dagger.

Gontram, King of Burgundy, rewarded one of his officials, who had informed him of the treachery of the patrician Mummolus, by appointing him Bishop of Geneva; but in spite of these facts, it must be confessed that the choice made by the princes generally fell upon men of merit. A prelate like Cautin who, as Bishop of Clermont, committed the most atrocious crimes, was an exception. The princes liked to appoint to sacred offices one or other of their palatines whose moral worth and capacity they had proved; for even the worst of the Merovingian kings—and it is difficult to choose between them— found it in their own interest to give to the people leaders who could maintain order, peace and prosperity. The choice of the princes frequently fell upon members of the laity. A few, like Chilperic, appointed ecclesiastics only as exceptions. His son, Clotar II, who has the reputation of being the best of the Merovingian kings, by an edict of 614, expressly reserved to himself the right of appointing to the bishoprics those of his officials whom he considered deserved a reward for their services. And the people, for their part, found it to their advantage to have a Bishop who, by his close connection with the Court, was able to obtain them numerous favours.

These appointments from the laity must not surprise us, since we find the Bishops themselves, when an episcopal vacancy was placed in their hands to fill, deciding in favour of lay candidates. The town of Bourges was the capital of the province, *Aquitanica Secunda*. It was the custom, when the election of a metropolitan Bishop became necessary, for the prelates of the whole province to meet together to superintend it. Apollonius Sidonius, Bishop of Clermont, went to Bourges for this purpose, and found the people divided into opposing factions. So great was the number of candidates for the see, writes Sidonius, that sitting close up against one another they

285

would not have found room on two benches. Some of them were scattering money right and left. Finally the crowd declared it would abide by the choice of the Bishops, and the latter referred the decision to Sidonius. The Bishop of Clermont asked for a few days for reflection and at last declared his choice. It was in favour of a layman named Simplicius. In enumerating his qualifications for the archbishopric of Bourges Sidonius mentioned as among the most important the fact that he came of a noble family, that he was immensely wealthy and that his administrative gifts had been proved. Simplicius was also a man of virtue and pure faith, which was not to his detriment.

Moreover, Simplicius was married, and according to the Bishop of Clermont, his wife was a lady of no less distinction. Sidonius ended his statement to the people of Bourges by reminding them that they had sworn to abide by his decision. And by virtue of this Simplicius was declared " in the name of the Father, and of the Son and of the Holy Ghost " Archbishop of Bourges, and installed, together with his wife, in the Archbishop's palace. Later on he was canonised.

The intervention of the Bishops in civil administration was, moreover, regarded as legitimate by the King and the Count who represented him in the city ; the Bishops, on the other hand, considered themselves bound to the King by ties of fealty. In 585, at the Council of Macon, the Bishop of Cahors was excommunicated by his colleagues for having supported Gondovald, the supposed son of Clotar, who was trying to dispute possession of the throne with those he called his brothers.

Thus the Bishop came, in a certain sense, to be considered a royal official. " The Church of Gaul," says Maurice Prou, " was a national Church of which the King was the temporal head,"—a logical development of the policy inaugurated by Clovis and the consequences of which became evident under Charlemagne.

In order to make his power respected by the Counts and by the King himself, the Episcopacy, in those profoundly religious days, wielded the redoubtable weapon of excommunication which terrified the princes, even the most villainous among them. They were one and all believers and trembled before the thunders of the Church in proportion to the crimes with which they were charged.

Lastly, the power of the clergy, guided by their leaders, was destined to become even greater in consequence of the immunities—one of the outstanding features of the period. By means of immunity, the domain thus covered became a privileged district into which the royal officials were denied admission, either for the levying of taxes, the administration of justice or the recruiting of men. The territory thus immunised was free from all public authority, and the master of it acted as an independent suzerain.

The first example of such immunity under the Merovingians occurred in the reign of Clovis. The King awarded with the domain of Micy, situated between the Loire and the Loiret, an old priest, named Euspice, and his disciple, Maximinus, with the object of securing for them an inviolable retreat for the practice of the holy life. This property was to be free of all taxation. The King increased it by the concession of a wood of oak trees, and pasture lands, adding the right of having windmills turned by the streams. We are not told whether all this fitted in very well with a life of prayer, but the fact remains that Euspice and Maximinus found themselves endowed with a domain which was free from public authority through the privilege of immunity.

Marculf's definition of these concessions of immunity is comprehensive :

" The favour we bestow," said the Merovingian King, " is such that in the ecclesiastical domains of this Bishop no public official shall be permitted to enter, whether to hear cases or to collect the *freda* [fines for disturbances of the peace], but it shall belong to the Bishop and his successors in full ownership. Wherefore we ordain that neither you [the King was addressing one of his officials] nor your subordinates, nor any person holding public office, shall enter into the domains of that church, in whatsoever part of our kingdom they may be situate. We forbid you to demand the right of sojourn or payment in kind or to have any agents there."

As we have already said, the domains of the Church extended over a third of Gaul.

If we take into account all the details given above we shall realise the growing importance of the Bishops in the kingdom of the Franks and the ever greater part they were to be called upon to play.

Having discussed the Bishops, we must now turn to the masters of the great domains.

As we have already seen, the Frankish conquest had altered the division of the land very little. Clovis seized the domains **The Merovin-** of the Roman Treasury, and the State lands. **gian Domains** There were, with very few exceptions, no other **and the Right** expropriations. **of Immunity.** And thus the large estates continued, after Clovis, to be the chief instruments for the exploitation of the land, just as they had been before his time.

The domain was called *villa*, or *fundus*, whence the French word *fonds*, real estate. The villa had a name, the name of one of its owners, which was handed down under succeeding owners. In the early days an owner was often called Flavius; the domain of such a man became in the north Flavy, in the south Flaviac; Flavinius was responsible for Flavignac, Flavigny and Flavin; Sabinus for Savigny, Sévigny, Savignac, La Savinière, Les Savinières, etc., names which are still to be found in the place names of France, since, for reasons to be given later, the majority of modern French villages—nine out of ten of them—have developed out of the old Merovingian domains. Many of these villas even became towns. The villa Sparnacus, which was sold to Saint Remi, is to-day Epernay. The tenants on the domain, whose various plots covered the countryside, were grouped together in houses close to each other, at a short distance from the *casa dominica*, the mansion of the master. And in every villa, in every domain, there grew up around the life on the estate and the practice of agriculture, a whole system of industry calculated to make the villa self-supporting. There was a monastery served by a priest whose livelihood was assured by the proprietor of the estate. The majority of the rural parishes of France owe their origin to this. The officiating priest found himself endowed with two or three manses, the manse being a collection of lands judged sufficient for the support of a family.

288

The buildings and the lands composing a villa were divided into four groups. The first included the mansion of the master, the *casa dominica*, with its various buildings of all kinds. In front of the mansion there was a court, which played a great part in the life of the community, and was enclosed by walls to which the buildings for the household staff were contiguous; beyond which came a kitchen garden, a small park and an orchard. This first group was surrounded by a wall or a moat enclosed by a palisade. Gregory of Tours describes one of these residences, which he calls a *château*, which was besieged by Theodoric, the son of Clovis. It was the Chastel-Merliac (Cantal, in the arrondissement of Mauriac). "In the middle was a pond with sweet water for drinking; in another part there were fountains so abundant that they formed a stream of fresh water which ran out through the gate of the place; in short, this fortress enclosed such a large space that the inmates cultivated the ground inside it and gathered fruits in abundance."

A second group consisted of the neighbouring lands directly exploited for the profit of the master by a population of slaves or serfs; this constituted the former's manse.

A third group included lands upon which there lived serfs, cultivators or *lites* (enfranchised slaves), as well as free men, cultivating the lots they had been assigned or which they voluntarily held from the master. They cultivated them for their own personal profit and as they pleased in return for the rendering of dues, which might take the form, in varying proportions, of payment in kind, rent in money or in labour, that is to say, work done for the benefit of the proprietor. These were slave manses (occupied by slaves or serfs) or ingennils (*ingénniles*) occupied by free men.

The manse consisted of a farm to which was attached a certain amount of land which belonged to it for ever and in principle could never be taken away. It generally constituted a rural establishment which was more or less self-supporting and capable, as we have just pointed out, of ensuring the livelihood of the family who worked on it.

The master of the domain furthermore exercised rights of marriage, was entitled to the best piece of furniture in a legacy, and when the deceased left no heirs, the possession of the whole heritage. He also had the right of levying fines for certain misdemeanours.

Finally, the fourth part of the domain included lands of some importance which, at the pleasure of the master, were common to all the tenants, serfs, *lites* and cultivators—meadows and pasture-lands, commons and forests, the latter providing wood, acorns and pasturage for pigs. They were the origin of the common lands of a village.

Thus the importance of a Merovingian villa was far greater than that of the seignorial domain which existed under the *Ancien Régime* in France and which were only the remnants of it. " What corresponded with the Merovingian domain were the cattle, the village and all the lands of the community taken together " (Fustel de Coulanges).

Small domains were sometimes wedged into these large estates, and their fate was far from enviable. They were suffocated. Unfortunate owners of a few acres wedged into the lands of a rich lord were to be found who were obliged to submit to servitude and give up their fields and vineyards to him in order to be able to live.

A single property aimed at including land and produce of every imaginable kind—cornfields, meadows, vineyards, flax fields, willow groves, tall forests and copses. The overlord placed at the disposal of his tenants, free men, cultivators, serfs and slaves, for their common use, mills, ovens, presses, forges and a brewery, from which the compulsory feudal services of the Middle Ages were not derived, but which had a similar origin and *raison d'être*. The mills were worked by water or by labour; windmills being still unknown in Europe.

Thus each of these great domains constituted an economic unit which was self-supporting. The produce of the ground was consumed on the spot and needs of all kinds were supplied by the work of the inhabitants. The same system prevailed in the royal villas. From the importance assumed by the domains in Gaul of the seventh century it is easy to see how insignificant the industry of the fortified towns became. The decadence in this respect as compared with the work of the artisans in

Gallo-Roman times, not to mention the Gallic industries in the days of Vercingetorix, was far-reaching.

The villages properly so-called, the *vici*, as they were termed in Latin, tended equally to disappear. The whole of Gaul was organised into domains and villas. Fustel de Coulanges declares that in Gaul of the seventh century he has only been able to discover about fifty villages as compared with twelve hundred villas. And even so these villages do not seem to have been centres of culture or of life, but merely stations along the great highways, placed at cross-roads, places of exchange at given points, regular stopping places with houses for shelter and rest, stabling for horses and what we call inns, together with wheelwrights' sheds for repairing carriages and harness. Or else they were little religious centres, where the remembrance of some venerated saint or some legendary event attracted the faithful and gave birth to a small local industry.

We have enumerated the causes which had led to the concentration of the possession of the land in ever fewer and fewer hands—the exactions of the Treasury, the depredations of the marauders, the scourge of the invasions and internal troubles. It was necessary to form groups around powerful individuals and thus create centres of resistance.

In a state of society which was becoming ever more and more troublous, the weak and isolated man could not protect his land. He accordingly " recommended " himself, that is to say, placed himself under the protection of a powerful personage. It was his only alternative. He might have sold his property perhaps. But what could he have done with the money in a world in which commerce and industry had been destroyed? Personal property had ceased to have any value. He was obliged to keep his land by remaining attached to it and cultivating it under the protecting rule of an overlord.

In a villa each living was worked by the tenant, whether serf, cultivator, or free man, who was attached to it, and the domain of the master was developed by the work of all.

The owner of an estate very rarely looked after it himself, but confided the care of it to a steward, whom the Romans called *villicus* and the Merovingians, as we have already observed, called *major*, mayor.

The ties which constituted the unity of the villa were so strong, so binding and so firmly rooted in the soil, that even the partition of the domain could not break them. We must bear in mind the various hereditary bonds which kept a man on the piece of land he inhabited and which also subjected him to the rule of the villa. It sometimes happened that a villa was divided up between several proprietors without its unity being destroyed as far as the tenants inhabiting it were concerned. In this respect a Merovingian villa might be compared to a modern industrial concern, the administration of which is divided up between several people without its unity being interfered with as regards the shareholders and the working staff.

When the Franks arrived in Gaul these villas were only fortified by palisades and ditches, which formed an obstacle against aggression. They were situated in fertile plains on the banks of rivers and streams which facilitated their cultivation, but the consequences of the growing chaos under the barbarous administration of the Merovingians may well be imagined. All intellectual and artistic life and all culture were gradually stifled and sought a silent refuge in the monasteries. All the amenities of existence were withered at the root, and brutality and violence everywhere carried the day, so that the Gallo-Roman land-owners themselves came to adopt the tone of the royal Court.

Imagine these domains separated from each other by long distances, cut off by wide stretches of forest, marshland and uncultivated or devastated territory. The villas, with all their rustic belongings, followed the example of the monasteries, and left the easily-cultivated plains and the navigable rivers in order to climb the hill-sides, hoist themselves on to the heights and there fortify their position. They surrounded themselves with walls, and many of them became fortresses. And Glasson, in his history of French institutions, was able to write : " The proprietor of a huge villa, surrounded by his cultivators and his slaves, was indeed a veritable *seigneur*." And this was the name by which his tenants knew him.

He became, says Fustel de Coulanges, within the limits of his domain, " the head of a State."

The head of a State whose importance continued to be

great. The population of a domain was sometimes over a thousand souls, acknowledging no other authority than that of the master, who exercised the right of jurisdiction over them, even over the free men. Far from opposing this authority the Kings supported it. It was in the royal interest for a " seigneur " to rule his property well, to maintain peace and order and increase his prosperity, for the King's government was incapable of accomplishing this. For the task of administration the traditions of the ruler and organised units are prerequisites, and the royal authority under Chilperic, Clotar II, and Dagobert had neither the one nor the other. The *de facto* administrators were the Bishops and the heads of domains. The villa of the eighth century had become an institution for public order.

We have just said that the majority of modern French villages are derived from Merovingian villas. In the seventh century the word " villa " still meant a domain, in the eighth it already designated a village with its lands. In addition to the word " village " we also find *villaris*, meaning an " annex," a dependent hamlet of the village. The villa, that is to say the village, formed a rural parish to which the *villaris*, the dependent hamlet, was attached.

The proprietor of a large domain, the " seigneur," found his authority still further increased by the development of the right of immunity. We have already described this right as enjoyed by the Church, but it was no less important in the case of the laity.

The following is a definition of it according to Marculf :

" ' We ordain,' says the King, ' that such and such a person, a man of good repute, shall hold in full possession the villa bearing such and such a name, and that no royal official shall have the right of entering it for the purpose of imposing judicial fines, or for any cause whatsoever.' "

But this did not mean that the King renounced his rights ; he still exercised them through the medium of the seigneur, the Bishop, the Abbot, or the great landed proprietor. Fustel de Coulanges says that, by the right of immunity, the royal authority, far from being weakened, was actually strengthened. And indeed it was under that one of the Merovingians whose power was the most secure, under the monarch, who in those troublous times enjoyed the most firmly-established authority, under Dagobert I, that the right of immunity made the greatest strides in its development.

The man enjoying this privilege, the beneficiary, became in return the " loyal servant " of the King. The favour thus conferred upon him bound him to his sovereign by exceedingly close personal ties. He owed him fealty. The King continued to exercise jurisdiction, to levy taxes, to recruit men-at-arms, and to levy the fines inflicted in his name, but he no longer did so directly, but through the medium of a loyal servant to whom he had delegated his power, a servant who was, so to speak, responsible to him. And it is certain that in principle the right of immunity fortified the royal authority as long as those who enjoyed the privilege were mindful of their duties and faithfully discharged on behalf of their prince the royal prerogatives he had conceded to them. But what happened in the course of time ? The inhabitants of a domain, who had a relationship only with their overlord, soon came to regard him as the only one entitled to exercise authority over them, and gradually the tenant became transformed into a subject. And thus the authority of the overlord grew stronger and stronger and led him to form in his own mind the desire of making it entirely independent. Added to this there were the endless civil wars of the Merovingian kings, their private murders, the disorders produced by the fresh invasions, the Slav, German and Saracen invasions, which together with the long minorities of the reigning princes, during which regents and above all Mayors of the Palace ruled, who pleased one party but not another, made people feel that they were not bound by ties of fealty as they were to a monarch.

And the movement which, following upon the granting of the right of immunity, gradually detached the owner of the privilege from the royal power, was further legalised by the fact that the former having pledged his faith to the King, and become his faithful servant, and the King having in return taken him under his protection, under his tutelage and promised to defend him and his, no longer found himself in a position to fulfil his part.

294

Fustel de Coulanges has shown how the right of immunity, granted over and over again from the sixth to the eighth century, imperceptibly modified the social constitution of Gaul. It profoundly modified the subjection of the nobility to the throne, and it also altered their authority over their subordinates. In his domains, which continued to grow ever larger and larger, the overlord became the sovereign and was no longer bound to his own sovereign except by moral ties and by the sentiment— very strong, it is true, in the case of loyal souls in periods of order, but exceedingly unreliable among the selfishly inclined in times of trouble—the sentiment of loyalty.

*　　*　　*　　*　　*　　*　　*

Let us now sum up the situation in Gaul towards the middle of the seventh century. In Austrasia and Neustria two children occupied the throne and their minority was followed by other minorities. A powerful aristocracy had divided the kingdom between them, great landed proprietors who were sovereigns in their own domains, Bishops all-powerful in their cities, Abbots who ruled over their monasteries, numerous concerns and wide territories; and finally Dukes and Counts, the representatives of the King in the provinces, but who had in fact become hereditary and independent rulers. Between all these " *majores* " —the " greatest " in the land—hierarchies and groups had been created. The system of protection, fealty and recommendation which we have described formed ranks in society through the creation of protectors and protected, a hierarchy maintained by ties which were strong in a different way from the tutelage of the kings, since they were direct. An example drawn from Fredegar will make the picture more vivid.

The patrician Willibad was summoned to Chalon-sur-Saône in the name of Clovis II. The powerful overlord, well aware of the immunity he enjoyed owing to the existence of the Mayor of the Palace, came followed by a strong retinue. " Brave and courageous men," says Fredegar. It was a regular army which would not have hesitated to give battle to the supporters of the King.

And if we turn to the frontiers we find that in Germany the peoples who had been subjugated by the descendants of Clovis had raised their heads again and claimed their independence—

the Thuringians, the Alemanni and the Bavarians had liberated themselves, and were ruled by their own princes. The Armoricans along the coast, and the Basques or Vascons in Gascony, once more appeared as free marauding peoples. The separatist spirit, which we have already noted in the case of the Austrasians, the Neustrians and the Burgundians, continued to grow, and formed ever deeper and deeper divisions throughout the greater part of Gaul. And the invasions started afresh, Slavs and Saxons in the north-east, and later on, in the south of Gaul, the Saracens !

Nevertheless, in spite of this general decline, in spite of the obvious threat, not only of disorganisation, but of annihilation, the idea of royalty still maintained its power, and was preserved, not only by tradition, but also by necessity; for the people who formed the substratum of the nation in the midst of these endless, diverse and unco-ordinated bids for wealth and power still lived and worked, the people of France !—the old Celto-Ligurian stock—a fine, strong race, which kept its unity, though nothing else did—a basic unity and an uncorrupted soul. Eight hundred years had passed over its head since the death of Vercingetorix, bringing in their train heavy trials and burdens—the Roman conquest, the Roman administration, the Roman system of fraud, weakness and shame, followed by the victory of the Franks, their robbery, pillage, barbarism, anarchy and their mad acts of bloodshed and filth—but still the people worked, toiled, loved and suffered, indomitable in their vital strength. If heroism existed, let us not connect it with the name of Cæsar, Clovis or Charlemagne; heroism was there—in the masses ! It made its virtue shine forth by breathing strength into Christianity and endowing it with its sublime impetus; and it preserved the means of salvation through its living faith. Royalty was represented by unworthy princes and became incarnate in children; it was surrounded by conspiracies and rivalries, treacherous and bloodstained, but nevertheless it was royalty with the spirit of Christianity ineradicably rooted in the spirit of the people. Christianity alone was able to maintain social unity and sovereign justice between the conflicting parties, the rival overlords and clashing interests. In Gaul, thus divided, a prey to the worst forms of violence,

296

affording a spectacle of complete chaos and anarchy, there remained but one force for the preservation of union and unity, and one alone. Whether placed in the hands of a feeble child, a sluggard king or a bloodthirsty madman, it remained nevertheless the greatest power of the age, for it was founded upon the immutable energy and faith of a whole people devoted to that which assured its salvation.

BIBLIOGRAPHY.—Salvienus, *Works*, edited by Halm, 1877. Apollonius Sidonius, edited by Baret, 1879. Grégoire de Tours, *Historia Francorum*, edited by Omont et Colon, 1886–1893, 2 vols. Poems of Fortunatus, edited by Leo from *Monum. Germ. hist.*, series in 4to. *So-called Chronicle of Fredeggar and his Continuators*, edited by Gabr. Monod, 1885. Marius d'Avenches, edited by Mommsen, 1893. *Gesta regum Francorum*, edited by Krusch, 1888. Aimoin, *Historia Francorum*, edited by D. Bouquet; *Rec. des Hist. de la Gaule*, Vol. III. Roricon, *De Gestis Francorum*, edited by D. Bouquet, *ibid.* Jordanes (Jornandes), edited by Mommsen, 1882. Cassiodorus, edited by Mommsen, from *Monum. Germ. hist.*, *Auct. antiquiss.*, XII, 1894. Paul Diacre (Warnefried), *Historia Langobardorum*, edited by Waitz, 1878. Zosimus, *Historiæ Romanæ*, edited by Mendelssohn, 1887. Procopius, *De Bello Gothico*, edited by Dom. Comparetti, 1885. *Vie de Saint Rémi*, edited by Krusch, from *Monum. Germ. hist.*, *Auct. antiquiss.*, Vol. IV. Prosper Tiro, edited by Mommsen, from *Chronica Minora*, Vol. I. *Vie de Saint Léger*, from D. Bouquet, *Rec. des Hist. de la Gaule*, Vol. II. *Gesta Dagoberti*, edited by Krusch, 1888. The *Niebelungen*, edited by Bartsch, 1870–1880, 3 vols. *Loi Salique*, edited by Holder, 1879–80. *Loi des Burgondes*, edited by Bluhme, from *Monum. Germ. Hist. Leges*, Vol. II. *Loi Romaine des Wisigoths*, edited by Haenel, 1849. *Formulaire de Marculfe*, edited by Rozière, 1860, 2 vols. Ampère, *Hist. Litt. de la France av. Charlemagne*, 3rd ed., 1870. Bayet, Pfister et Kleinclausz, *Hist. de France*, edited by Ern. Lavisse, Vol. II, 1913. Abbé Dubois, *Hist. crit. de l'établissement de la monarchie franque dans les Gaules*, 1735, 3 vols. Fustel de Coulanges, *La Monarchie Franque*, 1888; *L'Alleu et le domaine rural pendant l'époque mérovingienne*, 1889; *L'Invasion germanique et la Fin de l'Empire*, 2nd ed., 1891; *Les Origines du système féodal, le bénéfice et le patronat*, revised and completed from the MSS. of the author by Cam. Jullian, 1890. Am. Gasquet, *L'Empire byzantin et la monarchie franque*, 1888. G. Goyau, *Hist. religieuse*, from *Hist. de la Nation française*, edited by Gab. Hanotaux, Vol. IV. Guérard (Benjamin), *Prolégomène au Polyptique de l'abbé Irminon*, 1844. Imbart de la Tour, *Histoire politique des Origines à 1515*, from *Hist. de la Nation française*, edited by Gabr. Hanotaux, Vol. III. Junghans, *Hist. de Childéric et de Chlodovech*, translated by Monod, 1879. Kurth (Godef), *Clovis*, 2nd ed., 1901. *Hist. poét. des Mérovingiens*, 1893; *Sainte Clotilde*, 1897. Lenormande, *Restitution d'un poème barbare relatif aux évènements du règne de*

Childebert Ier., from *Bibl. de l'Ec. des Chartes*, 1839–40. Levillain, *Le Baptême de Clovis*, from *Bibl. de l'Ec. de Chartes*, 1906. Littré, *Étude sur les Barbares et le Moyen Âge*, 1867. Longnon (Auguste), *Géographie de la Gaule au IV*ième *siècle*, 1878; *Origine et formation de la nationalité française.* Maury (Alf.), *Les Forêts de la Gaule*, 1867. Meillet, *Introd. à l'étude comparative des langues indo-européennes*, 3rd ed., 1912. Pertz, *Die Geschichte der Merovingischen Hausmeier*, 1819. [Maxime Petit], *Histoire de France illustrée.* Picavet (François), *La Littérature française en langue latine*, from *Hist. de la Nation française*, edited by Gabr. Hanotaux, Vol. XII [1922]. Prou (Maurice), *La Gaule Mérovingienne.* Waitz, *Ueber die Anfänge der Vassalität*, 1856.

CHAPTER V

THE CARLOVINGIANS

The founders of the Carlovingian family, Saint Arnulf and Saint Pepin de Landen. Gallo-Roman ancestors. Charles Martel. His military valour. Victory of Poitiers (October 17, 732). Causes of the final retreat of the Arabs. The policy of Charles Martel towards the clergy. Childebrand. The benefices. Pepin the Short and Carloman. Retreat of Carloman to Monte Cassino. Alliance between the Papacy and the French Monarchy. Pepin has himself proclaimed King (751). Stephen II places himself and the Church of Rome under the rule of the King of France. Pepin's campaign in Italy. The Exarchate of Ravenna. Wars in Aquitaine. Duke Waifar. Early wars of Charlemagne. Partition of the kingdom of the Franks between the two sons of Pepin the Short, Charlemagne and Carloman. Charlemagne. Death of Carloman. Charlemagne seizes his heritage. The policy of Big-footed Bertha. Charlemagne breaks off relations with the King of the Lombards. Campaign in Italy. The General Assemblies under the Carlovingians. The Saxon Wars, Wittekind. Ecclesiastical nature of the government of Charlemagne. Dukes, Counts and Marquises. Capitularies and *missi*. Louis the Pious King of Aquitaine. Spanish campaigns. The disaster of Ronceveaux (August 15, 788). Rolando, Duke of the Breton Marches. Campaign against the Huns. Appearance of the Normans. Charlemagne, Emperor of the West (December 25, 800). The Empress Irene. The Imperial Palace at Aix-la-Chapelle. The Court. Portrait of Charlemagne. End of his reign. Charlemagne loses his eldest sons. His lassitude. Death of the Emperor (January 28, 814). Reign of Louis the Pious. His struggles with his sons. Judith of Bavaria. Partition of the Empire. The higher clergy against the Emperor. Pitiful end of Louis the Pious. Charles the Bald. His alliance with his brother Louis II, the German Emperor. Battle of Fontanet. The oaths of Strasbourg (841). Partition of Verdun (843). The Normans arrive in Paris (845). Edict of Quierzy-sur-Oise (877). Charles the Bald, Emperor of the West. His death (877). Last days of the Carlovingian dynasty. Norman, Hungarian and Saracen invasions. Charles the Fat, King of France. Anarchy.

France organised by her local forces. Robert the Strong. Rivalry between the last of the Carlovingians and the Robertians. Abbot Hugh. A national dynasty. Conclusion.

CHARLEMAGNE, who was King of the French from 768 to 814, was the son of Pepin the Short.

Pepin the Short, so-called on account of his small stature, was the son of Charles Martel, who was the son of Pepin d'Heristal. The latter derived his name from the locality of Heristal, on the Meuse, between Liège and Maestricht, where he had built a palace for himself in which he frequently resided.

The Carlovingian Family.

The father of Pepin d'Heristal was called Ansegis and his mother Begga. The latter was canonised. Ansegis was the son of Saint Arnulf, Mayor of the Palace in Austrasia and afterwards Bishop of Metz, who was married and the father of a family before his entry into the Church. Begga was the daughter of the first Pepin, called Pepin de Landen or Old Pepin, who was also numbered among the saints, and a young woman of Aquitaine, of senatorial rank, who brought her husband large domains as her dowry. Saint Arnulf and Saint Pepin de Landen had been appointed by Clotar II tutors of his son Dagobert. They formed the trunk of the Carlovingian family to which Charlemagne gave its name. Saint Pepin de Landen succeeded Saint Arnulf as Mayor of the Palace in Austrasia.

According to a tradition accepted at the Court of Charlemagne, Saint Arnulf, who had been appointed Bishop of Metz by royal favour, was descended from the family of Ferreolus, one of the great houses of the most Romanised province of Gaul—the Narbonnaise. His father, Ansbert, who was of senatorial rank, had married Blithilda, one of the daughters of Clotar I. We have already observed that Saint Begga, the mother of Pepin d'Heristal, was the daughter of a Gallo-Roman. Thus the family into which Charlemagne was to be born had as much Roman and Gallo-Roman as German blood in its veins; but since the immediate ancestors of the restorer of the Western Empire were Mayors of the Palace in Austrasia, and Austrasia, through its ever-increasing hostility to Neustria, had emphasised its German character, Charlemagne had come to use the German

300

language in private life. His education, moreover, had been very much neglected; he did not even know how to write.

At the end of the seventh century the Carlovingian family possessed vast domains and was distinguished on account of the important offices, and particularly that of Mayor of the Palace, held by several of its members, and the number of faithful retainers it has thus succeeded in attaching to it.

Finally, the Carlovingian family shone out among the rest on account of the number of saints it had produced—nine Bishops, seven saints, of whom the first was Pepin de Landen, and three female saints, of whom one, Tarsilia, had raised a man from the dead. " Your family is holy "—*sancta gens*— wrote Pope Stephen III to Charlemagne and Carloman in the year 769.

In addition to this the heads of the family were successively men of the greatest valour—Pepin de Landen, Pepin d'Heristal, Charles Martel and Pepin the Short. Resounding victories, one of which saved Christendom, served to heighten its glory.

After the death of Dagobert II, King of Austrasia, Pepin d'Heristal, with the help of his brother Duke Martin, seized the government of that kingdom (680). Thierry III, King of Neustria, and Ebroin, his rough and violent Mayor of the Palace, marched out against them and defeated them; but the war was renewed a few years later. The Austrasian leudes wanted a government of their own. Thierry III and his Mayor, Berthar, suffered a decisive defeat at Tertry, between Péronne and Saint Quentin (687). Pepin d'Heristal had Berthar put to death, after which, says the continuator of Fredegar, " he seized the person of the King, the royal Treasury and the office of Mayor of the Palace."

In all these struggles, the interests of the King were not at issue. Thierry was the reputed King of Austrasia, as well as of Neustria and Aquitaine. And he continued to be so regarded. The Austrasian leudes, however, fought for a Mayor of their own against the Neustrians who wished to impose theirs upon them, and at this time the latter were in power.

Pepin d'Heristal, say the chroniclers, governed the kingdom of France for twenty-seven years, and his rule seems to have been both firm and skilful. The designation of Mayor of the

Palace was no longer sufficient for him, and he conferred upon himself that of Duke of the Franks. Foreign sovereigns sought his alliance and exchanged ambassadors with him. The office of Mayor of the Palace had attained such a high degree of power that royalty seemed to be completely overshadowed by it.

Pepin d'Heristal carried on his government with three aims in view, all of which had but one object—the increase of his power.

He tried to abolish the division between the kingdoms of Neustria and Austrasia by giving them a common King, Clovis III, the son of Thierry, in 691, Childebert III, the second son of Thierry, in 695, and lastly, Dagobert III, the son of Childebert, in 711.

Secondly, whilst allowing these princes to remain titular monarchs, he did not permit them to take the smallest share in the government, even for the sake of appearances; and, lastly, at the beginning of each new reign, he saw to it that the dead King should be succeeded by the prince whose rights to the throne were the most obvious, so that no loophole could be left for discussion, thus reducing the influence of the Great Ones who used to meet together when a new King had to be appointed. The proposal made by Pepin d'Heristal was such that it could not fail to be carried by acclamation.

It was Pepin d'Heristal who had all the posts, offices and honours, including the appointment of Bishops and Abbots, in his gift, and disposed at his pleasure of whatever remained over from the taxes, as well as from the produce of the royal villas. On his death, in 714, his heirs were his grandsons, children who were actually appointed to the government under the tutelage of their grandmother Plectruda; but the Neustrians were quick to revolt and appoint Ragenfred their Mayor, whilst the Austrasians also rebelled and chose a natural son of Pepin d'Heristal, an energetic soldier whom history has glorified by the name of Charles Martel, so roughly did he hammer his enemies in battle. His mother was called Alpaïde. Charles Martel, Mayor of Austrasia, in his turn imposed his authority upon the Neustrians and became, in fact, King of France. Thus the Carlovingian family grew slowly but surely ever greater, strengthening its power and authority from one generation to the next, by the extension of its domains, which had become the largest in Gaul, by increasing its riches, by holding the highest offices and multiplying its " faithful retainers," by the holiness of a large number of its members and the miracles they worked, and lastly by the personal valour of the leaders who guided its destinies.

Thus the family descended from Pepin de Landen and Saint Arnulf found themselves at the head of the Austrasian aristocracy and, by this fact alone, at the head of the State. The King no longer exercised any authority over his own lands, but only over persons. Thanks to the system of recommendation and patronage, this power over individuals had become clearly defined, but the King's faithful retainers, the leudes, and the antrustions had in their turn, by means of recommendation and patronage, secured retainers who were personally attached to them and had thus also increased their power. Society was becoming co-ordinated. Every large landed proprietor, outside the State, reorganised it on his own lands, from which the right of immunity had ousted the agents of the King. On their vast domains several hundreds of Bishops, Abbots and overlords, rich in lands and men, exercised sovereign rights and raised taxes. At the apex of this aristocracy arranged in groups and orders of rank there shone resplendent the Carlovingian family. The crowned King was King, but without power of any sort.

On the death of Pepin d'Heristal, Charles Martel was in the fortress of Cologne where Plectruda, his father's widow, had **Charles** had him incarcerated. He was rescued by the **Martel.** Austrasian leudes, and at their head he defeated the Frisians, who had invaded Austrasia, and afterwards the Neustrians, under the leadership of their Mayor, Ragenfred, at Vincy-les-Cambrai (717). He renewed his campaigns against the Frisians, whom he defeated on the coast; against the Saxons, whom he challenged five times; against the Bavarians; against the Alemanni, whom he defeated twice, and against the Neustrians and the Aquitanians. He displayed an unbridled activity, swift to discover and destroy any plots formed against him. In Aquitaine, Duke Eudo still kept his power, but the advance of the conquering Saracens obliged him also to appeal to the Duke of Austrasia.

Ever since the beginning of the eighth century Christian Europe had been exposed to a terrible menace. In 711 the African Arabs had invaded Spain and made themselves masters there. In 720 they crossed the Pyrenees, penetrated into Septimania and took Narbonne. In 721 Toulouse was threatened. Eudo, Duke of Aquitaine, succeeded in holding them in check for a time, but after the fall of Nîmes and Carcassonne and the sack of Autun (725) the danger became deadly.

Eudo implored the help of Charles Martel.

The great victory which the valiant Mayor of Austrasia won near Poitiers over the Mussulman troops under the command of Abd-er-Rhaman, a hundred years after the death of Mahomet, saved Christian Europe (October 17, 732). By an extraordinary coincidence this defeat suffered by the Arabs took place at the very moment when the Berbers of north Africa in Maghreb rose in a general rebellion which threatened their rule in countries which were essential to them for their invasions into Europe; and the Saracens, obliged to use their forces on the African continent, were forced to abandon their grandiose dreams of conquest. For the struggle in Maghreb, fed by religious dissensions in the bosom of peoples who had been converted by force, raged for many a long year. The Saracens appeared again as marauders, but their great conquering onslaught had been ended at least in western Europe.

Campaigns followed in Burgundy (733), in Aquitaine (735), in Provence (739), by means of which Charles Martel secured his rule over Gaul. Thierry IV, surnamed Thierry de Chelles, died in 737, and Charles Martel dispensed with convoking the assembly qualified to acclaim the new King, contenting himself with leaving the throne empty. The remainder of his rule was regarded by the royal notaries as a sort of interregnum. They dated their acts in such and such a year after the death of Thierry IV and thus established their chronology.

Again when Eudo, Duke of Aquitaine, had been re-established in his States by the conqueror of Poitiers, the latter left him his independence, and when, subsequently, he, in conjunction with

Hunald, the son of Duke Eudo (who died in 735), passed an edict declaring him, Charles Martel, suzerain of Aquitaine, he did not act as King of France, but Hunald declared that he held his States in fealty and homage to Charles personally and his two sons Carloman and Pepin. The latter was destined to become the real founder of the dynasty.

The Arabs, after their retreat in 732, had remained masters of Septimania, whence they continued to molest Aquitaine. But several of the more powerful overlords in that country, and even counts, impatient of the Frankish domination, supported their manœuvres. In 735, the Saracens seized Arles and Avignon, whence they made incursions as far as Burgundy (736). " The Duke Charles," writes the continuator of Fredegar, " having raised an army, marched towards Burgundy, subjected to his power the town of Lyons, together with the lords and prefects of that province, appointed judges as far as Marseilles and Arles, and returned laden with booty to the capital of his Empire."

There was a fresh campaign in 737. The Saracens had returned and captured Avignon. Charles Martel advanced as far as Narbonne. The Emir of Cordova sent help for the besieged town from Spain. But Charles Martel, once again victorious, had a great massacre of Saracens and completely destroyed Nîmes, Agde and Béziers, and ruined a number of castles and strongholds, after which he returned to his northern provinces.

In 741, the year of his death, Charles received ambassadors from Gregory III, who sent him the keys of St. Peter's tomb and begged him to come to his help against the Lombards of Italy. Charles hesitated. The strength of the Lombards was not known to him, and he was afraid of another offensive on the part of the Arabs.

Moreover, the present sent him by the Holy Father did not represent sovereignty over the city of Rome, as some historians have maintained. The keys were reproductions of the original, only valuable because they had been made by melting down part of the chains worn by Saint Peter. They formed a kind of decoration like the order of the Golden Fleece, which the King of Spain bestows to this day. These keys were also worn hung round the neck. Over twenty persons, including several women, had been honoured in the same way.

Charles Martel thanked the Sovereign Pontiff for his good grace in sending to his Court the Abbot of Corbie and a monk from Saint Denis named Sigebert, laden with rich presents, but refused to commit himself.

We can already see the outlines of the policy the pontifical Court was afterwards to adopt.

Against the Emperor of Constantinople who, as the heir of the Roman Emperors, claimed the suzerainty over Italy, on the one hand, and on the other, against the Lombards established in the north of the peninsula and along the coasts, the Pope solicited the help of the Frankish princes. " The Sovereign Pontiff," writes the continuator of Fredegar, " and Duke Charles agreed by treaty that the Roman people should abandon the cause of the Emperor and that the Pope should appoint Prince Charles consul of Rome."

Charles Martel, whose strong right arm had routed the Saracens, was a rough and magnificent warrior. Rome came to him as a suppliant, and he himself supported with his armies the missionaries he sent to Germany; but the main object he had in view was his own power and the glory of his sword, and his chief concern was to secure the means of triumph. In order to bind to him the leudes who formed the main strength of his armies, he gorged them with booty, and this booty he took where he found it, in the vast domains of the clergy. Bishoprics and abbeys were plundered by him. The Bishop of Vienne, in order to avoid witnessing the rifling of his church, took refuge in the shelter of a monastery. Under Pepin the Short, the son of Charles Martel, forty-one places were restored to the Abbey of Saint Denis which Charles Martel had taken from it, and their restitution seems to have been far from complete. But it is only fair to add that the Holy See itself, in order to allow Charles to carry on his campaigns against the Saracens, had placed the goods of the clergy at his disposal.

Charles, it is true, went even further. Not satisfied with dividing between his " faithful retainers " a large proportion of the treasures of the Church, he also appointed them to the bishoprics and abbeys. He made his nephew Hugh Bishop of

306

Paris, Bayeux and Rouen at the same time, as well as Abbot of Saint Wandrille, Fleury-sur-Loire and Jumièges. Milon, his companion in arms, was promoted to both the archbishoprics of Treves and Rheims at the same time. As may easily be imagined, many of these prelates had been very badly trained in the functions they were called upon to fulfil. Some of them did not know how to read. They were, moreover, indefatigable hunters and good soldiers, always ready to arms. Gerold, Bishop of Worms, died sword in hand against the Saxons, and his son inherited the episcopal throne as though it were an heirloom. These noble prelates, who made armed attacks upon the convents in their own or neighbouring provinces, took them by assault and plundered them as though they were conquered places, took but little interest in their flocks or their clergy, who were obliged to go in for trading in order to make a living. To win a bishopric it was deemed unnecessary to enter the Church, which was a mere waste of time; a Bishop had other things to do than to say Mass and wear the tonsure.

Thus Charles Martel, although he had saved them, was as much hated by members of the Church as he was loved by his own men-at-arms. Saint Boniface, Archbishop of Mayence, the apostle of Germany, declared to Carloman and Pepin that their father was most certainly damned. Pepin the Short was convinced of it. A few years after the death of Charles Martel, when his tomb was opened at Saint Denis, it was found that his body was not there. In its place was discovered a great serpent —others say a black dragon—which could only have been the devil. The monks of Saint Denis told this tale to all comers. In 858, more than a hundred years after the hero of Poitiers had left this world, the clergy used to assure Louis II of Germany, the grandson of the great soldier, that his great-grandfather was in hell because he had given the goods of the Church to the laity.

Charles Martel died on the 22nd of October, 741, at Quierzy-sur-Oise, after a reign of twenty-six years. He was always and everywhere a magnificent victor, and rendered possible the work of his successors, Pepin the Short and Charlemagne. With great sweeps of his sword he had opened up the way for their policy, though doubtless he knew not what he did. But through him the policy of the Carlovingians was outlined in all its grandeur and in part realised.

Beyond this we know almost nothing about his personality and character, except that he was very handsome, very tall and very strong. Of all that line of men of valour who succeeded each other as rulers of Austrasia, from Pepin de Landen to Charlemagne, he was perhaps the most remarkable; but the ecclesiastical chroniclers, who only mention him with mistrust, have been sparing in details about his character and actions except in connection with his military exploits.

Before his death, Charles Martel had disposed of his power in favour of two sons he had by Rotruda. To Carloman the elder he had assigned Austrasia, Alemannia and Thuringia; to Pepin the younger, Neustria, Burgundy and Provence. He disinherited almost entirely Griffon or Grippon, the son he had by Swanahilda. Of these two women, Rotruda and Swanahilda, we do not know which was his legitimate wife, possibly both at once, possibly neither.

The Merovingian King still remained King in name. Grippon did not fail to claim his rights. He was conquered, taken prisoner and shut up in Neufchâteau in the Ardennes, whilst his mother Swanahilda was forced to take the veil in the convent of Chelles. As soon as he regained his liberty, Grippon renewed hostilities against Pepin the Short, and died in 751 at the hands of Theodouin, Count of Vienne, and Frederick, Count of Transjurane Burgundy.

Pepin d'Heristal, the father of Charles Martel, had had another son by Alpaïde of whom most of what we know is to be found in two lines by Boileau :

> Oh ! le plaisant projet d'un poète ignorant
> Qui de tant de héros va choisir Childebrand ! [1]

The poet in question was Carel de Sainte-Garde, the King's almoner, and his poem is entitled *Childebrand, or the Saracens driven from France.* According to the third continuator of Fredegar, Childebrand was the valiant ally of Charles Martel, particularly in the campaign of 737. But there was a far more

---

[1] Oh ! the delightful plan of an ignorant poet who from so many heroes goes and chooses Childebrand !

cogent reason for the " scheme " of Carel de Sainte-Garde—in the seventeenth century the descent of Robert the Strong was still traced from Childebert, in order to legitimise the accession to the throne of the Capets, the ancestors of Louis XIV.

The lands and goods of which Charles Martel despoiled the clergy in Gaul were given by him to his men at arms as benefices.

The Benefices. The benefice, together with the right of immunity and recommendation, formed one of the three elements constituting society under the Carlovingians. The benefice was a concession of land, money, offices or dignities, made by princes, overlords and even private individuals, with the object of obtaining from the recipients, help, succour and services of all kinds. Benefices were also called " honours."

The benefice, which existed in the Merovingian epoch, derived all its importance and development under the Carlovingians. The origin of the benefice has been traced by some to ancient Germany, as was also the origin of feudalism. But the benefice from the sixth to the eight centuries was the product of the circumstances in which it was developed; and similarly feudalism owed its origin to the accession of the Capets.

Similar circumstances produce similar institutions without its being necessary to trace their successive appearances as due to cause and effect. The eighteenth century knew the meaning of municipal stocks and the nineteenth Parisian loans, but the latter were not the outcome of the former.

Some historians have regarded lands thus given as benefices as a distinct category of lands called " *allodia*," that is to say, freeholds, the possessor of which had no burdens imposed upon him. But nothing of the kind can be read from the texts in which all lands are described as " *allodia* "—*allodia* upon a number of which the benefices were superimposed, whilst others remained free.

The benefice was conceded as a life interest, and ended, not only with the life of the recipient, but also with that of the giver. Presented as a personal honour, it had to be renewed when either of the contracting parties ceased to exist.

The bonds formed by the benefice were very precise in character. They imposed the duties of protection upon the

309

giver in regard to the person, who by the very deed of gift became his vassal, and the duties of fealty, help and succour on the latter towards him who had become his overlord. The chief obligation of the beneficiary consisted of military service, and it was above all with the object of increasing their forces, by multiplying the number of their men at arms, that the Carlovingian princes distributed benefices. The policy of Charles Martel sheds a very clear light upon this point of view. Moreover, the concession of benefices was closely allied to recommendation; it was the complement of the latter. The bond between the overlord and the vassal could be established in two ways—the humbler person might come and place himself under the ægis of the more powerful by means of recommendation, as we have already described, or the more powerful could attach the humbler to him by means of a beneficiary concession which involved all the consequences of recommendation.

All this obviously bore a very close resemblance to the feudalism of the ninth century; nevertheless the difference between the two institutions is very great. The feudal tie involved of necessity military service, whilst the benefice only imposed it in certain cases, which were, it is true, exceedingly numerous. But in other instances it was conceded in return for the payment of rent in money, or in work of various kinds. It might even be conceded as an act of grace with no tie except a moral obligation.

Should the beneficiary fail in his duties, the benefice was forfeited. The beneficiary had to look after the benefice conferred upon him, keep the lands in good order, and maintain the buildings in good repair. We find the princes forcing the holders of royal or ecclesiastical benefices to superintend the tenants of the domain, whether cultivators or serfs, and feed them in times of scarcity. One of the capitularies of Charlemagne stated that the possessor of a burnished coat of arms who did not carry it with him to war would be deprived both of it and of his benefice.

Although the benefice was essentially a life-interest, it more and more frequently became hereditary owing to the general conditions of the epoch. In the first place it seemed only natural to keep the son in his father's benefice, and later the transmission took place as a matter of course. The ideas of the
310

age as well as the force of circumstances gradually led to the hereditary principle being regarded more and more as a right. The beneficiary came to consider the title he held as his own property, which, under certain conditions, he was allowed to cede to a third party. The holder of an important domain would give away a portion of it to another beneficiary, who would hold it from him under similar conditions to those which bound the original beneficiary to his overlord. Others aimed at converting their benefices into their own private property, into independent *allodia*. The princes had a hard task to combat this tendency. " Let him who holds a benefice from the Emperor or the Church," said Charlemagne, " take nothing therefrom into his own patrimony." An ingenious process consisted in transferring to others a benefice held from the sovereign, only to buy it back again for ready money and hold the domain as an *allodium*, that is to say under an independent title.

Benjamin Guérard points out in a capitulary of 757, not only the word *beneficium*, but the words *seigneur* and *vassal*, bearing their historical signification. As for the word " fief," *feodum*, that was not found until the eleventh century to designate an institution very similar to the benefice, but having no direct connection with it.

A benefice given to a man at his own request and for a definitely limited period was called precarious. It applied to little except Church property and did not involve military service.

On the death of Charles Martel, his two sons, Carloman and Pepin, divided Gaul between them, Carloman taking Austrasia and Pepin Neustria and Burgundy. They both assumed the title of Mayor of the Palace.

Pepin the Short.

We have already seen how Charles Martel had seized the sovereignty of Burgundy, Neustria and Austrasia, at the expense of his nephews, the sons of Pepin d'Heristal. And now we find Theudoald, one of the latter, claiming his share, which consisted of nothing less than Neustria and Burgundy. His pretensions were settled by having him assassinated.

In the following year, on the 2nd of April, 742, in a place in Neustria which has remained unknown, historians are generally agreed that the child who was destined to become Charlemagne was born. His father was Pepin the Short and his mother Big-footed Bertha, the daughter of Caribert, Count of Laon.

Nevertheless it was necessary to have a King. The presence of an undisputed chief, of a keystone to the social arch, was a necessity. And this supreme head required to be invested with a moral character which placed him above all rival competitors, aspirants and factions. The proclamation of either Carloman or Pepin as King would immediately have given rise to divisions and conflicting claims; one great lord or another would have risen up in arms, supported by his partisans, and an era of violent struggles would have been inaugurated of which no one would have been able to foresee the development or the end.

Carloman and Pepin, therefore, set to work to find a prince to wear the crown, and finally succeeded in unearthing from the depths of a quiet abbey a Merovingian of doubtful lineage whom they set upon the throne with the title of Childeric III (743). Like his immediate predecessors, Childeric was King only in name. The interregnum since the death of Thierry de Chelles had lasted six years.

The two brothers, Carloman and Pepin, got on extraordinarily well together. Between them they conducted a campaign against the Aquitanians who had rebelled under the leadership of their Duke Hunald, the son of Duke Eudo. It was the usual warfare of the period, consisting of pillage and devastation. Bourges was sacked and the two brothers returned laden with much booty and followed by a number of prisoners.

In 744 Carloman conducted a campaign against the Saxons, who, in the course of repeated incursions, had pillaged Austrasia. He and his brother Pepin, moreover, carried on the policy of their father, endeavouring to render the barbarian people innocuous, not only by inspiring them with terror of the Frankish armies, but by drawing them to the faith and practice of the Christian Church by means of missions. The two princes drew ever closer and closer to the Church. The great problem of the secularisations practised by Charles Martel for the benefit of his warriors, and which Carloman and Pepin had also indulged in during the first years of their reign, remained in abeyance. Several Councils, and especially the Council of Soissons (744), offered the following solution—ecclesiastical property and domains, which had been alienated for the benefit of the laity, were to remain the property of the latter, but only in usufruct; and the clergy thus despoiled were to remain the possessors of the property, at the expense of the armed forces on behalf of the " beneficiaries " and in receipt of rent calculated to a fraction. It was the clergy who had the best of the bargain. At the same time the organisation of the bishoprics was reformed under the direction of the two princes. In each episcopal see a Chapter of Canons was established with rules framed on the pattern of those in monastic institutions.

The accord between Pepin and Carloman afforded a spectacle rare indeed for hundreds of years in the relationship of two brothers; when suddenly Carloman declared that he wished to renounce the pomps of the world and retired into a monastery.

" Inflamed by a holy love of piety," we read in the continuator of Fredegar, " Carloman placed his kingdom, together with his children and his son Drogo, in the hands of his brother Pepin, and went to Rome, where he entered the Church of the Holy Apostles and took his place in the ranks of the monks. By means of this succession the power of Pepin was more firmly established."

This " succession " was also settled after the manner of Clovis. The worthy French historians of the eighteenth century pointed out, in connection with this entrusting of the children of Carloman to the hands of Pepin the Short, " It was like giving sheep to the wolf to guard." What happened to the unfortunate little things? Let us hope that they were not murdered, like Theudoald, who took the extraordinary step of laying claim to his share of his grandfather's heritage. However that may be, nothing more is heard of them.

There has been much discussion as to the motives leading Carloman to assume the monk's cowl. Was it because, like Charles V later on, he was disgusted with the pomps and vanities of the world?

Gaillard, in the eighteenth century, speaks as follows :

" Carloman, persuaded on the faith of the clergy that his father, Charles Martel, was damned, tormented by the idea and disgusted with his age, went and buried himself in a cloister, either because this allowed him still to hope that his repentance might make up for his father's failure in that respect, or because the terrible picture of a father devoured by eternal torture made him fear the dangers of earthly glory for himself."

Kleinclausz cites the remorse with which Carloman was devoured for a terrible massacre of Alemanni he had ordered in 745 to account for it; or thought that perhaps it was due to the great need for a life of peaceful contemplation felt in that rude age by so many souls who had been drawn into the whirlpool of the world. Perhaps too the sacrifice of Theudoald, in which Pepin had made him share, filled Carloman with horror for the demands made upon a sovereign. At all events, from the day on which Pope Zacharias imposed the tonsure upon him, the noble prince became an edifying example to all with whom he came in contact. He first of all went to a monastery (to-day the Cloister of Saint Sylvester) which he had built on Monte Soracte, in Etruria, fifty miles from Rome (748), but since his personality attracted too many visitors to it he fled to the wilds of Monte Cassino, where he confined himself to the commonest of tasks, which he carried out in all simplicity and a humility he tried not to make too apparent.

There remained to carry on the government Pepin the Short and his puppet King.

Pepin was short of stature but extraordinarily robust, and the chroniclers have handed us down epic tales about him. His was a nature full of fire and audacity, and the energy of his resolutions and the rapidity with which he carried them out were reminiscent of his father, Charles Martel.

He was thirty-seven years old. Divested of all family ties he breathed freely. In diplomas he had himself described as "he to whom the Saviour has confided the cares of government," and he thought the moment had at last come when, by means suggested to him by his devilry, he might approach the great task before which his father and grandfather had recoiled.

In 751 Pepin sent to Pope Zacharias the famous embassy consisting of Fulrad, Abbot of Saint Denis, and Burchard, Bishop of Wurzbourg, in order to consult the Sovereign Pontiff on the subject of the King who ruled France without authority.

Zacharias apparently replied, "It is better to call him King who wields the power than him who is deprived of it."

This reply on the part of the Sovereign Pontiff has been universally applauded. But perhaps we may be allowed to express our opinion regarding it. If it is authentic, it was an outrage, more especially on the lips of the Head of the Church, the heir of the doctrine of Christ and charged with the duty of carrying it out in peace, mildness and loving kindness.

What was to become of the great maxim: "Render unto Cæsar . . ." if the astounding theory ascribed to Zacharias was to prevail? What was to become of justice?

Might is right, said old La Fontaine sadly, whilst the Sovereign Pontiff proclaimed it as a principle of equity.

That Pepin, by an act of authority, and supported by the nobility of the kingdom, in one of their assemblies of March or May, should have had himself proclaimed King would have been an act of usurpation, but an act before which history would have been forced to bow; but against an act of spoliation cunningly carried out in complicity with the Holy See it is the duty of every honest man to rise up in indignant protest.

To the credit of Pope Zacharias and of the Holy See, which has played so great and glorious a part in history, the authenticity of the famous reply to Pepin is very far from having been established. Modern historians accept it, but it is not to be found in the most ancient annals of France. There is no trace of it in the life of Zacharias by the librarian Anastasius, nor in that of Saint Boniface, who consecrated Pepin King of France, a life written by his disciple Willibad of Eichstädt. The Pope does not mention it in his correspondence with Pepin and with Saint Boniface; and finally, as the historian Gaillard so justly observes, it would be astonishing if, in a matter of such great importance, only a verbal reply was given and was regarded as sufficient.

It is more likely that it was a rumour cleverly circulated by Pepin himself to make his usurpation more acceptable, and repeated by Eginhard. The matter was not carried through without an effort. When the designs of the Mayor of the Palace became evident, protestations were raised and troubles broke out. The alleged declaration of Pope Zacharias served to allay them, and Pepin gained thereby all he lacked to enable him to lay hands on the crown—moral support of a singularly strong nature in those days when men's minds were dominated by a faith so lively that we can only with the greatest difficulty form the vaguest idea of it.

The poor little Merovingian King had in his favour his long hair, which was still venerated by the Franks, but which was soon to be shorn; he had the lays celebrating his heroism and his ancestors, but which were soon to be replaced by lays infinitely more beautiful in favour of the Carlovingians; on the other hand, Pepin had power and the alleged approval of the representative of God on earth.

In 751 Pepin convoked a General Assembly of the Great Ones at Soissons and succeeded in having himself proclaimed King and his wife Bertha saluted as Queen. Childeric III received the tonsure and was returned to the monastic life from which he had been so cruelly torn. The place of residence chosen for him was the monastery of Saint Bertin. His son, Thierry, was imprisoned at Saint Wandrille.

The election at Soissons was confirmed by a religious consecration—anointing at the hands of the Roman Pontiff or his representative.

The anointing of a King was a novelty, at least in France, for it was practised in Spain and among the Anglo-Saxons and Bretons. Under the Merovingians the coronation had been an exclusively military ceremony; Pepin added that religious element which had the result of placing him in the minds of his contemporaries far above the princes whose place he was taking. He himself declared that he was the elect of God and that he ruled by right divine; but in despoiling the Merovingians he took care not to mention the holy unction brought from heaven by a dove at the baptism of Clovis.

Pepin was crowned King of France in the town of Soissons by Saint Boniface, the Legate of the Holy See, apostle of Germany and Archbishop of Cologne. The royal prerogative of being crowned in the archiepiscopal see of Rheims dates only from the twelfth century. Pepin had himself anointed together with his wife, Big-footed Bertha, which was in itself an innovation and

316

also a clever device. For the sons born of their union were forthwith designated heirs to the throne.

The coronation of the King by Saint Boniface (752) was repeated two years later—the 28th of July, 754—in the basilica of Saint Denis by Pope Stephen II, who had come to France. Not only did the Sovereign Pontiff confirm the consecration made in his name by the Archbishop of Cologne, but he went much further by hurling an edict of excommunication against any who, in the course of time, might dare to elect a King from any other race than that upon whose usurpation he was bestowing his blessing: *Ut numquam de alterius lumbis regem in œvo presumant eligere;* let no man in the future, said the Pope, dare to chose a King from outside this family " which has been raised by divine piety and consecrated by the intercession of the Holy Apostles."

When Hugh Capet, with the concurrence of the higher clergy of France, took away the crown from the Carlovingian Charles of Lorraine, did he regard himself as excommunicated together with the distinguished prelates who crowned him on his election ?

After having consecrated him King of France, Stephen II further proclaimed Pepin a " Patrician of the Romans." This was a title to which, even in the time of Clovis, great importance was attached and which was regarded as superior to that of King. The patrician was the delegate of the Emperor in the countries in which he was established. Since then the patriciate had become an honorary dignity. And thus it came about that all the exarchates who administered Italy as lieutenants of the Emperor were patricians. It is only right to add that the Sovereign Pontiff had not the smallest authority for conferring any such dignity. He had the power of appointing Cardinals, Legates, Bishops and Abbots; in all that concerned the patriciate, the Byzantine Empire alone might have had a right to intervene; but after all, what did one usurpation more or less matter !

Stephen II made not only Pepin but also his two sons " patricians."

It must be confessed that these numerous favours and generosity were very far from being disinterested. If we may use a colloquial expression, it was not for love that Stephen II proclaimed Pepin the Short King of the Franks and a Roman patrician. He wanted his help against the Lombards, who were aiming at seizing Rome. As a matter of fact—and it is only fair to him to mention it—the Pope had at first sought help from the Byzantine Court, which should have been his natural protector. But having received only the cold shoulder on the shores of the Bosphorus, he had tried to come to an understanding with the Lombards. At last in despair, he addressed himself to the Franks. " Saint Peter himself," said the Pontiff, " has consecrated Pepin by appointing him the saviour and defender of the Church."

The agreement between Pepin the Short and Stephen II was clearly enunciated. " We have commended our Church into your hands," wrote Stephen to the King of the Franks, " and you have promised to undertake her defence." This is the " commendation " we have already mentioned, binding the protector and the protected by definite bonds; it is the system of clientage whereby, in return for a promise of submission and fealty, a powerful man undertook to protect the weaker brother whose patron he was. And indeed, as Fustel de Coulanges points out, the Sovereign Pontiff acknowledged himself a subject of the King of France. And it was this fact that Charlemagne took care not to forget; and, as a matter of fact, Leo III wrote to him in 796 renewing his oath of fealty.

For the time being it was a matter of keeping the contract and going to war against the Lombards. In order to lead an army of Franks into Italy it was necessary to obtain the consent of the Great Ones of the kingdom at a General Assembly. Pepin convoked them at Crécy-sur-Oise, and presided over the meeting with Pope Stephen seated beside him. The King of the Franks was feeling confident of obtaining the unanimous vote of his Bishops and leudes, when suddenly, to his complete amazement and unbounded displeasure, there appeared upon the scene a personage whom he was very far indeed from expecting—his elder brother Carloman. The noble monk had left Monte Cassino, in order to come and defend the man he regarded as his suzerain, and to uphold the cause and the rights of Astolpho, King of the Lombards. He came to defend with wholehearted loyalty the cause of a King, his overlord, whom they were preparing, in order to satisfy the exigencies of the political situation, to despoil of his States.

What an apparition! Carloman, with his imposing figure, was revered for more than one reason by the great assembly before which he had presented himself, respected on account of the family to which he belonged, the supreme dignity from which he had voluntarily retired, and the sacred character he had assumed.

Carloman spoke with force and authority. What, he demanded, had Astolpho and his Lombards done to the Franks and to Pepin? If Austrasia, Neustria and Burgundy had any complaint against their neighbours, surely their differences could be amicably settled. And thus the gracious intervention of Theodoric the Great between Clovis and the Visigoths was repeated once more, though its spokesman was not a powerful prince, but a high-spirited monk, bearing the white tonsure and the black frock of Monte Cassino.

After so many centuries of bloodshed the voice of Carloman rang forth with poignant emotion. The monk, the son of Charles Martel, and brother of King Pepin, spoke with simplicity and all the force of conviction; he won the day. So deep was the impression he made that the nobility of the kingdom refused to vote in favour of war. Carried away by the words they had just heard, they demanded negotiations, and 12,000 gold pieces were offered the King of the Lombards to induce him to come to an agreement with the Pope.

Overcome with confusion and vexation, Pepin saw that his fine enterprise had failed. He flew into a terrible passion and arranged with Pope Stephen that " so zealous a subject as Carloman, and one so eager to defend the interests of his prince, should be subject only to his own brother." And Carloman was refused leave to return to his cell on Monte Cassino, under the suzerainty of Astolpho. He was shut up in a monastery at Vienne (Isère), where he died, in what historians have been allowed to term his prison, shortly after his arrival. His body was taken to Monte Cassino, where they engraved the following curious epitaph on the tomb of the great penitent, who had left his retreat in order to interrupt the intrigues of the world with a few words of equity, goodness and peace :

" Here lies Saint Carloman, King and monk of Monte Cassino,
—the cell surrounded him with a halo more brilliant than did
the throne, the cowl than the purple, the daily service than the
sceptre, submission than power. . . ."

Several historians have accused Pepin the Short of having rid
himself of his brother in the same way as he had of his nephew
Theudoald, and his conduct affords only too great a justification
of their suspicions.

However that may be, when once he was free from his incon-
venient relative, King Pepin was able to carry out his plan with
a free hand. He did not succeed in overcoming the hostility of
the nobles towards the Italian war; the impression made by
Carloman remained indelible; but he was clever at managing
men, at seducing them by benefits conferred and by promises,
at conjuring up dazzling visions before their eyes, and, if
necessary, at moving them by threats. After further hesitation,
protestation and disorders, he at last succeeded in going to war.
He crossed the Alps at the head of a powerful army, defeated
the Lombards and received the famous exarchate of Ravenna
together with the Pentapolis on the coast of the Adriatic, which
included the towns of Ravenna, Rimini, Pesaro, Faro, Cesane,
Sinigaglia, Ancona, Jesi, Forli, Urbino, Cagli, Gubbio and Narni,
which the King of the Franks presented to the Sovereign Pontiff,
thus creating the temporal power of the Papacy (754).

As a matter of fact, the exarchate was not actually wrested
from the Lombards, but from the Byzantine Emperor, who
was its suzerain. But Byzantium was a long way off; she
did not enforce her rights and the matter was not closely
investigated.

The expedition into Italy was repeated in 756, after fresh
efforts on the part of Pepin to overcome the hostility of his
leudes. The gift of the exarchate was solemnly confirmed.

Paul III, the brother and successor of Stephen II, continued
the policy of union with the King of the Franks. He sent
Pepin choristers to teach the choir of the royal chapel; he sent
him rare books and beautiful manuscripts; for Pepin, who
had been educated at Saint Denis, had a taste for literature; he
made him a present of a clock, which the old chroniclers called
a " night clock," because it told the time by night and not only

320

during the day, like the sundials which were the only timepieces then known in France.

In the reign of Pepin the government took a decided step in the direction of the ecclesiastical monarchy finally realised by Charlemagne. The capitularies had formulated the canons of the Church and had given them the force of law. If called upon to do so, the Counts and other representatives of royal authority were bound to give armed support to the ecclesiastical judges. A private individual, whose crimes had become notorious, was tracked down and punished by the secular arm of the law, which also had the right of inflicting capital punishment.

The advent of the vigorous Carlovingian dynasty changed the very character of royalty. To all appearances the political constitution remained the same as it had been under the last of the Merovingians, with the exception that the hereditary principle was applied to the benefices as well as to offices and served as a weapon of power in the hands of the great princes who guided the country's destiny—Pepin d'Heristal, Charles Martel, Pepin the Short and Charlemagne. The Kings were no longer children held in tutelage or unfortunate wretches under indictment, but intelligent, active and energetic chieftains, endowed with a valour that made them popular, and the prestige of whose victories, together with the sacred halo bestowed upon their family by the pontifical unction, raised them above the heads of other men. They conceived great designs and knew how to carry them into action. Benjamin Guérard sums up the situation in one brief sentence pregnant with truth—" The Merovingians had taken Gaul away from the Romans, it was now a question of taking it away from the leaders of factions."

These leaders had been glutted by Charles Martel with the property of the clergy, after which he had subjected them to a certain discipline; Pepin the Short drowned them in floods of pontifical unction and diplomacy; Charlemagne encased them in ecclesiastical cement out of which they were unable to stir, though this task of clerical administration carried out by the clumsy hands of great warriors, beginning with Charles Martel, met with vigorous resistance. It is impossible to describe the whole process, but we can at least cast a glance on the epic campaigns of Pepin in Aquitaine.

Here he found a magnificent adversary in the person of Duke Waifar, the son and successor (745) of Duke Hunald, with whom Charles Martel had concluded a treaty of fealty and homage. In 751 Waifar granted asylum to Grippon, Pepin's brother, whom the latter had despoiled. War broke out and lasted for seventeen years. Terrific struggles took place of which we are given a picture in an admirable poem entitled *Garin le Loherain*. It is an epic of the twelfth century, but in its brutal savagery reproduces the spirit of a much older work.

It was in these campaigns that Charlemagne had his first lessons in the art of war under the guidance of his father (761). We can form some idea of these expeditions from the description given of the year 763 by the continuator of Fredegar :

" In 763, having convoked all the Frankish warriors, Pepin went to Nevers, where he held a council of war with all his nobles. Whereupon he crossed the Loire and laid waste Aquitaine as far as Limoges and above all set fire to Waifar's domains. In many monasteries he drove out all the inmates. After this he immediately marched upon Issoudun and took the town, and afterwards ravaged the vine-bearing cantons of Aquitaine from which the monasteries, the churches and the poor, as well as the rich, procured their wine. Waifar raised a large army composed chiefly of Gascons and Basques; but the Gascons took flight and were massacred." The Franks went home laden with booty. In the following year the same process was repeated.

Waifar waged this war for the independence of his country as Vercingetorix had done before him, and himself laid bare whole territories in order to deprive the enemy of the means of subsistence. He retired into the mountainous parts of Dordogne, and afterwards into the strongholds of Auvergne, where the spirit of the great Gaul still hovered and where it was impossible to reach him. At last Pepin brought the war to an end by having his indomitable adversary assassinated by hired ruffians in the forest of Ver in Perigord (June 2, 768).

And Pepin, says his chronicler, " returned in great triumph to Saintes, where his Queen Bertha had remained."

Thus Pepin brought Aquitaine under his rule, with the exception of the Duchy of Gascony, which he was obliged to leave in the hands of Waifar's son. The latter nursed in his heart a ferocious hatred for the Franks of which he subsequently gave striking proofs.

Pepin did not long survive his enemy. He was already ill when he left Aquitaine to return northwards. On his arrival at Saint Denis he convoked an assembly of the chief personages in the Palace and in their presence divided his kingdom between his two sons. The elder, Charles, the future Charlemagne, was given Austrasia and the portion of Neustria situated north of the Oise and Aquitaine with the exception of the ecclesiastical province of Bourges; the younger, Carloman, had Thuringia, Hesse, Alemmania, Alsace, Septimania and that part of Aquitaine which had not been given to his brother. Pepin also left a daughter, Giselle, who received the Abbey of Chelles.

Pepin the Short gave up the ghost on the 24th of September, 768, at the age of fifty-seven, after a long reign, which decided the fate of his dynasty together with that of France and of the Papacy.

" Pepin wished to be buried at the door of the church of Saint Denis, with his face to the ground, the position of penitents, to expiate—what ? " asks the historian Gaillard. Doubtless the death of Theudoald, of Carloman and his sons, of Grippon, of Remistain, and Waifar?—" Not at all," says Abbé Suger, " but to expiate the usurpations by Charles Martel, his father, of the property of the Church. This was the infamous crime which filled men with terror even five hundred years later, and then more than ever. . . ."

The two sons of Pepin the Short were placed on their thrones a fortnight after the death of their father—Charles, whom we **Charlemagne** shall now call by his historic name of Charle- **the King of** magne, at Noyon, and Carloman at Soissons. **the Lombards** Each of the two princes took possession of that **and the** part of their father's kingdom which had been **Exarchate of** allotted to him. Charlemagne was twenty-six **Ravenna.** and Carloman seventeen.

The government of the two brothers was carried on far from smoothly, and was constantly interrupted by struggles, quarrels and disagreements. They got on as badly together as Carloman and Pepin, the sons of Charles Martel, had

323

agreed well. Their father had hoped to bind them together by giving them joint control in Aquitaine; but the result was exactly the opposite. And if we turn to what we to-day call foreign policy, the discord was no less virulent, Charlemagne supporting the aspirations of the Court of Rome and Carloman those of the King of Lombardy.

Big-footed Bertha, the mother of the two young men, did her best to keep them friendly. She was a woman of great force of character and moral worth. In that barbarous eighth century she reminds us of Blanche of Castille, the mother of Saint Louis. It is a pity that contemporary writers have not left us more details about her. But at least we know the magnificent project she conceived and that she at first succeeded in realising in spite of the obstacles placed in her path. It was a question of nothing less than securing the peace of Europe by the union of the principal crowns—those of the Franks, the Lombards and the Bavarians, and of placing them all on terms of friendship with the Court of Rome.

Tassilo, Duke of Bavaria, was the son-in-law of Desiderius, the King of the Lombards. The former, a man of great energy and activity, was threatening the rule of the Franks across the Rhine. Bertha conceived the plan of marrying her son Charles to the other daughter of Desiderius, and, in order to make the alliance still stronger, to complete it by the union of her daughter, Giselle, with the latter's son, Adalgis. By this means concord would be established between the Franks and the Holy See, on the one hand, and the Lombards and the Bavarians on the other, and the peace of Europe secured. This was the policy outlined by Theodoric the Ostrogoth in the sixth century—peace, and the idea of securing peace by means of family bonds between the rulers was revived by a woman.

As soon as Pope Stephen III heard of the plans of the French Court, he was mad with rage. An alliance between the Franks and the Lombards! His terror may well be imagined. He wrote a vehement letter to Charlemagne. Any such union, he declared, would be " diabolical." Charlemagne had in his own kingdom the most beautiful and amiable girls in the world. " Love them, it is your duty ! " He had before him the example of his father, his grandfather, and his great-grandfather, which

324

forbade him to take a wife outside his own country. Unlike the women of France, who were so charming, the Lombards were repulsive and smelt bad. Moreover, how could the Lombards, a people who had brought leprosy into Italy, be allowed a place in the human race? Furthermore, was not Charlemagne already married to Himiltruda, by whom he had a son? The bonds of matrimony were indissoluble. "Do not forget," wrote Stephen III to Charlemagne, "that my predecessor prevented King Pepin from repudiating your own mother!" The Pope concluded by hurling the thunders of the Church against whomsoever dared to mention such a project again, condemning him to everlasting fire stoked by the devil, whereas, if he showed himself obedient to the voice of the Pontiff, Charlemagne would be rewarded with eternal joy in the presence of the saints and all the elect of Paradise.

Neither Charlemagne nor Big-footed Bertha allowed themselves to be convinced by the pontifical arguments. Charlemagne repudiated his young wife, Himiltruda, and the son she had borne him—the latter we shall hear of again as Pepin the Hunchback—and married Desideria, the daughter of the King of the Lombards.

The year 770 is notable for the Aquitainian campaign. On hearing of the death of Pepin, Duke Hunald thought a favourable opportunity had arrived for renewing the war of independence. He left the cloister, and the whole of Aquitaine rose up in arms. It was in Aquitaine that Charlemagne had served his apprenticeship in arms, and he reappeared at the head of an imposing army. From the first day he proved himself to be the intelligent and resolute soldier, with a marvellous gift for organisation, who was destined to fill the world with wonder. He did not possess much originality in his military designs, nor were they conspicuous for any very great hardihood or ingenuity. His campaigns were monotonous and wearisome, but were remarkable for their rapidity of movement—in this respect Charlemagne was superior to Charles Martel—and above all for their wonderful organisation—mobilisation, commissariat and supplies—which were astonishing for that epoch. Moreover, Charlemagne was everywhere triumphant, and as in the art of war the aim is victory, he must take his place among the great soldiers of the world.

325

Hunald found himself face to face with the young King of France at the head of his army when he thought he was still a long way off, and sought refuge with Lupus I, Duke of Gascony. Charlemagne demanded that the fugitive should be delivered up to him. Lupus yielded, but Hunald managed to escape and found shelter at Pavia, at the Court of the King of the Lombards.

On the 4th of December, 771, the event took place which was destined completely to transform the fate of Charlemagne; Carloman died, leaving his elder brother, at the age of twenty-nine, sole ruler of the Empire.

As a matter of fact Carloman had two young sons, Pepin and Siagrus, who should have inherited their father's domains, but their mother Giberga, remembering the tragedy that had overtaken the children of Carloman, the son of Charles Martel, at the hands of Pepin the Short, and fearing a similar fate for her own sons if they were left to the tender mercies of Charlemagne, took flight with them and also sought refuge at the Court of the King of the Lombards.

The death of Carloman completely altered the outlook of Charlemagne. He was now the sole master of the French kingdom. Wide horizons had been opened up to him and he was full of plans for a patriarchal policy. By supplementing the power of his arms through the high prestige of the Papacy no ambition seemed beyond his reach. It was necessary, he thought, to have the support of the Pope, whose own authority would be further increased by the fresh power the Holy See would derive from an alliance with the warriors of France. Bertha had made her son promise never to repudiate the daughter of King Desiderius, but Charlemagne, casting to the winds every consideration that appeared hostile to his ambition, after the death of his brother sent Desideria away, and married Hildegarda, a Swabian. He was thirty at the time, and she was his third wife, all three being alive. Adalard, the King's first cousin and one of the most remarkable men of the day, outraged by this act of treachery, ostentatiously quitted the Court and retired to his abbey at Corbie. As for his sister Giselle, who was betrothed to the son of King Desiderius, Charlemagne forced her to return to the Abbey of Chelles. The indignation of the King of the Lombards may well be imagined;

it was impossible for him to pardon this cynical, twofold insult.

The wars of Charlemagne against the Saxons began in 772; it was a struggle which was perpetually renewed and constituted the greatest feat of his reign—a contest lasting thirty-three years (772–804).

The territory of the Saxons was situated in the plains of Germany from the valley of the Rhine to the Elbe. Saxony of the eighth century did not include modern Saxony, but only Westphalia and Hanover. The Saxons had adhered to their ancient customs which were so much belauded by Tacitus. They still practised human sacrifice.

The thrust of the peoples who constituted part of the Scandanavia, which the Gothic historian Jordanes had already called the Factory of the Nations, was still continuing towards the south-west. From Scandinavia it made itself felt in Germany, and from Germany in Gaul.

War against the Saxons was therefore declared, says Eginhard, in 772 : "It was prosecuted in every direction with equal vigour. It is difficult to say how often the Saxons presented themselves before the King as conquered suppliants, how often they promised to do as they were demanded, delivering up hostages, receiving ambassadors, and sometimes so weakened as to declare themselves ready to embrace the Christian faith, without, however, being able to overcome the desire to break their engagements."

In 773 the war against the Lombards broke out. Charlemagne had repudiated the daughter of King Desiderius under the influence of Pope Adrian. Desiderius retaliated by invading the exarchate given by Pepin to the Holy See. The supremacy of Lombardy had succeeded that of the Ostrogoths in Italy; and it was the ambition of Desiderius to found in the peninsula a great Empire similar to that which the Merovingians and Carlovingians had established in Gaul.

In answer to the Pope's appeal, Charlemagne twice asked Desiderius to return the exarchate to the Sovereign Pontiff. Receiving no satisfaction, he opened the campaign in the month of August 773. We have already mentioned the opposition on the part of the nobility of the kingdom to the Italian war under

Pepin the Short. This was renewed under Charlemagne. They regarded the repudiation of Desideria as perjury. Many of them, and among their number some of the highest in the land, had given themselves as security to the King of the Lombards when the marriage was celebrated, plighting their faith as a guarantee for their sovereign. But Desiderius met Charlemagne's efforts at reaching an agreement with such hostility that their scruples were silenced.

At the approach of the French in arms the Lombard army took to flight. Desiderius shut himself up in Pavia, and Charlemagne appeared before the walls of the town.

In this connection we have the account of the monk of Saint-Gall which has become justly celebrated. The author wrote at the end of the ninth century, at the request of the Emperor Charles the Great, to whom his work was dedicated, a hundred years after the events he describes. And just as Gregory of Tours wrote about Clovis, so did the monk of Saint-Gall treat the subject of Charlemagne. According to the chronicler, his tale of the exploits of Charlemagne was derived from the accounts given him by a certain Adalbert, the father of one of his fellow monks in the monastery.

L. Halphen believes he has identified this monk with Notker the Stammerer. He followed historical sources—more especially, as L. Halphen has pointed out, the chronicles of Eginhard—and poetical sources, epic lays in process of formation. As for the episode which follows, Gaston Paris says :

" The episode of Desiderius and Otkar is overburdened with ornament very far removed from primitive simplicity, and although the basis of this beautiful tale was without doubt some popular version, we can find no trace of that form; the lay provided the chronicler only with his subject, his presentation of it is entirely his own."

Here is an abbreviated version of this " beautiful tale."

Desiderius had shut himself in Pavia with Hunald, Duke of Aquitaine, whilst his son Adalgis had gone to Verona with the widow and children of Carloman.

Count Otkar, one of the great nobles of France, who had rebelled against his suzerain, was with Desiderius. One day they were standing on the top of a high tower from whence they

328

could see the plain spread out below. In the distance Charlemagne's army was visible. First of all came the machines of war " such as might have been used in the armies of Darius or Cæsar."

Desiderius asked Otkar :

" Is not Charles with this great army? "

" No."

Endless chains of common soldiers then appeared.

" Surely Charles is advancing with all that crowd? "

" No," replied Otkar, " not yet."

Thereupon followed the bodyguard who rested not night or day.

At the sight of them the Lombard King, filled with terror, exclaimed :

" Of a certainty that is Charlemagne."

" No," replied Otkar, " not yet."

Next came the Bishops, the Abbots, the chapel priests and the Counts in all their splendour.

In tears Desiderius cried, " Let us go down and hide ourselves in the bowels of the earth."

Then Otkar said, " When you see the cornfields tremble, and the Po and the Ticino lashing the walls of the town with their waters blackened by steel, then will it be time enough for you to believe in the arrival of King Charles."

Hardly were the words out of his mouth than they saw rising out of the west a black cloud, which obscured the light of day, and as Charlemagne continued his advance the flash of the steel arms cast over the town a veil darker than night. Charlemagne came forward clad from head to foot in a coat of mail, his head encased in a steel helmet, his left hand clasping a steel lance which he held perpendicular, as his right hand remained immovable on the hilt of his invincible sword; his shield was of steel, his horse was an iron grey; those who surrounded him, and those who followed, the whole army seemed made of steel. Steel covered the whole countryside. Steel that is so hard was borne by men who were harder still. Otkar and Desiderius were struck dumb, and at last Otkar murmured in a whisper :

" There is Charlemagne."

Notwithstanding all this array of steel the siege of Pavia

329

dragged on interminably. It was still in progress when Charlemagne left for Rome, where he was given a triumphant reception by the Pope. He confirmed the gift made by his father to the Holy See, and added to its importance, whereupon he returned to Pavia.

The capital of King Desiderius only opened its gates in June 774, after having held out for eight months. Desiderius was taken to France with his wife and daughter and shut up in a monastery, doubtless at Corbie. His son Adalgis was still holding out in Verona. He succeeded in making good his escape and found refuge at Constantinople at the Court of Constantine Copronymus. Charlemagne seized the widow and children of his brother Carloman, and the fate of these miserable wretches is also shrouded in mystery.

Pope Stephen II had hurled the threat of excommunication against any who in the future should dare to place upon the throne a prince who did not belong to the Carlovingian family; he had forgotten to hurl the thunders of the Church against members of this family who might despoil the children of their father's heritage.

Charlemagne naturally seized the treasures of Desiderius. He had himself proclaimed King of the Lombards and his brow was encircled by the iron crown at the hands of the Archbishop of Milan. The golden crown of the Kings of Lombardy was known by this name because inside it was fastened an iron ring which was supposed to have been fashioned by nails from the Cross. This crown may be seen to-day at Monza in Italy, the place where Charlemagne was probably crowned.

The situation in Italy remained none the less disturbed. The Byzantines were still in possession in the south of the peninsula of Apulia, Calabria and Sicily. The Papal State had not yet been consolidated. Venice was still wavering and Charlemagne turned a deaf ear to the exhortations of the Sovereign Pontiff, who urged him to take more drastic measures. The incursions of the Saxons, revolutionary movements in Aquitaine, and the Saracen menace, which was still hovering in the balance, called his attention in other directions.

We have already seen how Charlemagne used his qualities as a military organiser; in Italy he proved that he possessed gifts

330

for political organisation. The kingdom of Lombardy, which was destroyed by the fall of Pavia, had lasted for two hundred years. The French King respected the form of government already established, and the conquered people hardly realised they were under his yoke. He only put garrisons in the capital and in a few frontier and sea-coast towns, as a protection against danger. He respected the property and customs of the inhabitants, leaving every man free to follow as he pleased either the laws of Lombardy or those of France. Paul Diacre, who was a Lombard, said that the conqueror " tempered his victory with wise clemency and moderation." And, in 781, Charlemagne went so far as to give the Lombards a King of their own in the person of his son Pepin, who was then fourteen years of age, with an autonomous Ministry.

It has already been mentioned that Adalard had left the Court of Charlemagne as a protest against the repudiation of Desideria, thus giving the Lombards a signal proof of sympathy, and it was he whom Charlemagne chose for the position of Prime Minister to the infant King. Finally he made up his mind to justify his Italian policy before a General Assembly of the French nobility.

These General Assemblies—*conventus generalis*—form one of the chief institutions of the Carlovingian epoch. They were **The General Assemblies.** frequently summoned twice a year, once in the spring and once in the autumn. The autumn Assembly consisted only of the most important of the nobility and the principal counsellors of the King. It discussed questions of government, of peace and of war. Unless action were urgent its decisions remained in abeyance until the more popular Assembly met in the month of May, when they were submitted to the ratification of the people; but, as Hincmar is careful to point out, " in such a way as to lead to the belief that nothing had been decided or even discussed previously."

These sessions coincided with the convocation of the army, and thus it came about that they took place in enemy countries or on the frontiers—the assemblies, for instance, which were held during the course of the Saxon wars, at Paderborn, Worms and Ratisbonne. Under Louis the Pious, the son of Charlemagne, the Assembly was generally convoked at Aix-la-Chapelle; under Charles the Bald in Neustria, in the west of France.

The General Assemblies were developments on an enlarged scale of the Merovingian *champs de Mars,* thus called, according to Hincmar, after the God of War, or, as is more probable, after the month of March in which they were held. Under the Carlovingians they were called *champs de mai,* the date of their convocation having been put later in the year by Pepin the Short, in order to allow the Bishops and Abbots to celebrate the festival of Easter in their own dioceses and monasteries.

The General Assembly was also called "*plaid*" *placitum* or "synod." Although it was originally convoked, not only in Austrasia, but also in Neustria and Burgundy, it fell into desuetude in the two latter kingdoms.

As the army which composed it consisted of the bulk of free citizens, it was also called "the Popular Assembly," *populi conventus*; but it was popular only in name, as Fustel de Coulanges has pointed out. Even in the beginning, when it included all the free citizens, it constituted, as a matter of fact, a reunion of the nobles, each of whom was accompanied by his followers. The chief alone counted.

Under Clotar II and Dagobert the military character of the meeting declined, and the Assembly came to occupy itself more and more with civil and ecclesiastical questions. With Charlemagne the military side once more took the ascendancy, but gradually faded into insignificance under Louis the Pious and Charles the Bald.

Even the Bishops, who attended the Assembly, came with their followers, supporters and vassals. Thus thousands of men found themselves gathered together in one vast convention, though they were divided into groups of very different characters, each chief, Bishop, Abbot, Count or Captain of a band, being followed by his own men, in some cases the number being only eight or ten, and in others several hundreds surrounding their "patron."

If the weather was fine, says Hincmar, the Assembly was held in the open air. It must have presented a picturesque spectacle. Tents dotted the plain, and the rallying cries, the divers ensigns and the great variety of costumes presented a lively medley.

Only the nobles took part in the debates; they were the only ones to express an opinion, though they had ascertained beforehand the views of the supporters and vassals who had accompanied them. Thus the General Assembly really consisted of hundreds of private assemblies each of which was represented before the King by its chief.

The procedure in case of bad weather is the proof of this. In such circumstances the Assembly met for debate under cover, away from the multitude. It had various places at its disposal, one of which was specially reserved for the Bishops and clerics of the highest rank, so that they might meet, says Hincmar, without mingling with the laity.

The laity also had their debating hall. " The Counts and other lay dignitaries," says Hincmar, " according to their rank, separated from the rest of the crowd early in the morning, until the deliberations in the presence or absence of the King began. Then these nobles, the clergy on their side and the laity on theirs, presented themselves at the hall appointed for them, where seats had been prepared in their honour. Away from the crowd, they sat all together or separately according to the nature of the business to be discussed, spiritual, secular or a mixture of the two." The Assembly had food brought to it from outside as it required it and convoked those whom it felt it ought to consult or listen to.

Ernold the Black depicts Louis the Pious presiding over one of these reunions and addressing his vassals from his throne above them.

The high officials and the Great Ones of the kingdom, gathered together in the Assembly, had received details of the administrative or other arrangements which the King himself, says Hincmar, had made under divine inspiration. The King was not present at the debate. By means of messengers chosen from amongst the Palatine officials, the Assembly in the course of its deliberations addressed questions to the King on points on which it was doubtful and received his replies. No stranger was allowed to approach the hall so long as the result of the discussion had not been communicated to the King.

Meanwhile the King mixed with the crowd, questioning one and another in a friendly way, cracking jokes with the young men, listening to complaints and giving encouragement. It was here that Charlemagne increased his popularity. His simple, affable manners, combined with the prestige connected with his family and great deeds, easily won men's hearts. His majestic gait, his natural ease and cordiality shone forth with brilliance and charm. The King learnt what was taking place in the provinces, the wishes of the people and their moral and material condition. Those who came from the frontier districts were able to give him information about the neighbouring nations, whether they were well disposed or hostile.

The result of the debate once communicated to the King, the final decision rested with him. Nevertheless it would be wrong to suppose that these discussions were purely formal. A huge army was gathered together in battle array, surrounding its leaders; it constituted the whole power of the King. It often happened that the sovereign consulted the Assembly of the Great Ones on points about which he himself was puzzled and was willing to be guided by their opinion. The capitularies were only published after they had been approved by the leaders of the people. They often bore traces of the advice they had given.

A number of Carlovingian capitularies are merely the result of suggestions formulated in these Assemblies in the name of the nation by the nobles who represented it. It sometimes happened that the two sections of the congress, the clerics and the laity, did not find themselves in agreement. In 846, for instance, the lay Assembly only approved a part of the chapters due to the collaboration of the King and the Bishops.

The final decision made by the King was communicated by the monarch himself to the assembled people, in order to be ratified by them; but this was merely a formality. Whereupon the Counts and Bishops were presented with copies of the common decisions with instructions to make them known throughout the kingdom.

The Carlovingian Assemblies possessed judicial powers which even included the right of inflicting capital punishment, and they seem to have been singularly prodigal in their exercise of the latter right. Charlemagne appears to have referred cases of high treason to them in order that he might not seem to use,

334

or rather abuse, his power in dealing with matters in which he had a personal interest. In 786 the Assembly of Worms condemned certain Austrasian nobles who had rebelled to have their eyes put out. In 788 Tassilo, Duke of Bavaria, who had broken his pledges to the King, was condemned to death by the Assembly, a sentence which Charlemagne commuted to one of imprisonment for life in a monastery. It was also a General Assembly—*universus christianus populus*—which condemned Pepin the Hunchback, the Emperor's own son, to pay the last penalty of the law. Other instances occurred in the ninth century.

At spring and autumn Assemblies the later Merovingians received the annual gifts which their subjects felt they ought to make them for the good of the State and in order to secure the royal favour, a custom which survived under the Carlovingians.

As the frontier of the French kingdom extended it became more difficult to gather together all the subjects of the King at the plaids which were gradually deprived of their military character, and from the time of Louis the Pious the plaids were confined almost entirely to questions of administration and legislation. The records still said that the people were convoked, but the Assemblies consisted only of the high officials, the prelates and some of the nobles.

Thus a number of capitularies were submitted for the ratification of the Carlovingian plaids. The capitularies were not laws, but regulations for the administration of the kingdom, sometimes not even that, but merely instructions drawn up by the King for his agents, or confidential notes for their use.

They must therefore be distinguished from what might be termed laws, if the meaning of this word were not too strict and general for what was meant at this period. On the framing of the laws, that is to say, the decisions whose effects were to be permanent and which were not concerned with individual cases, the influence of the General Assemblies was even greater. They were drawn up by men of acknowledged capacity under the direction of the King and submitted for the approval of all. The law, said the Edict of Pitres (864), is made by consent of the people and the decision of the King, *lex consensu populi et constitutione regis*. Even the conquered Saxons were called upon to approve the capitulary which decided the modalities of their government.

These celebrated institutions—the General Assemblies or Carlovingian plaids—give the impression of having been on the whole extremely liberal, leaving the people, or at all events the governing class, great influence in the ruling of the State; but, as Fustel de Coulanges points out, their power was greater in appearance than in reality. The nobles consulted their men before they took part in the discussion at the May plaid, but these men were entirely subservient to them and the overlord said whatever he pleased; the King consulted the Bishops, the lords and the high officials, but here again they were all his dependents, and their part consisted chiefly in lending support to the royal decisions by their presence. Their activities, as has been pointed out, were above all moral and due to the mere reunion of such an imposing multitude in arms; without reversing the royal decision they could hold it in abeyance or modify its practical application, as we have seen it do in connection with the Italian policy after the intervention of Carloman.

We must now return to the Saxon wars.

The kingdom of the Carlovingians was surrounded by a double rampart of enemies or rivals. On the north-east were **The Saxon Wars.** the Saxons and other German peoples, whom Eginhard terms ferocious, on the south-east the Lombards, on the south the Aquitanians and the Gascons, on the west the Bretons; these constituted the first rampart. The second consisted of more distant nations, at least two of whom were a formidable menace, the north men, the Normans from the Scandinavian countries, and the Saracens from Africa; finally, in the east there were Byzantium and her Emperors.

The Lombards had been conquered.

In 774 the Saxons, profiting by the absence of Charlemagne, who was detained in Italy, renewed their incursions. They did not make a general invasion under the guidance of one supreme chief, but various tribes in succession hurled themselves upon Austrasia, massacring, pillaging and burning wherever chance led them. With his usual extraordinary rapidity of movement,

336

Charlemagne appeared before them with his army when they thought he was still on the other side of the Alps. He divided his forces into four columns; three of these flung themselves upon the Saxons and overcame them, the fourth had only to contemplate the backs of a multitude in flight.

Thus, says Eginhard, the war with Saxony was renewed (774). " Never was a war longer or more atrocious; for the Saxons, like nearly all the nations of Germany, were endowed with natural ferocity; they worshipped devils, showed themselves hostile to our religion, and saw nothing dishonourable in violating all laws, human and divine. Moreover, the nature of the frontiers between their own country and France meant that an incident might at any moment break the peace; consisting almost everywhere of level plains, except at a few points where large woods and mountains formed a line of demarcation, these frontier regions were constantly the scenes of murders, rapine and incendiarism. In the end the Franks became so exasperated that regarding it as insufficient in the future to give blow for blow, they made up their minds to break out into open warfare."

The Saxons had found, if not a leader, at least a marvellous inspirer, in the person of Witikind, who made himself the soul of the national defence against the foreigner. Scholars have recently called him Widuking. Why could they not leave names celebrated in history the form hallowed by time?

Witikind was the Vercingetorix of the Germans. He was a far greater and finer figure than Arminius, a blameless hero whom we respectfully salute. He came from that part of Saxony corresponding with modern Westphalia. Like Vercingetorix he was of noble family and had great possessions. He was an organiser of uprisings against the stranger rather than a leader in battle. After the successive defeats of his fellow countrymen, he sought refuge in Denmark, with the object of seeking help there in order to march at the head of his own people against the Franks; but he never succeeded in bringing about a general insurrection.

The year 775 was marked for the Saxon patriots by a signal success, the victory of Lidbach, a defeat which Charlemagne sought to blot out in the following year, when his armies seemed to have achieved the conquest of Saxony. The soldiers marched forward followed by missionaries; for the King of France regarded the conquest of an enemy people only in the light of their conversion to Christianity.

Saxons were baptised in large numbers, so that in 777 Charlemagne thought he might convoke the vanquished, who appeared to be entirely subjected, to the May Assembly, held at Paderborn, in their own country. And indeed, various tribes arrived in arms under the leadership of their chiefs, just as the Austrasians and Neustrians did. But Witikind was not amongst them, having sought refuge together with his companions in Denmark.

A rude awakening followed. Neither defeat, baptism, soldiers nor missionaries could succeed in breaking the indomitable nation. Charlemagne remained in Saxony throughout 779 and a part of 780.

The year 782 was marked for the Franks by a defeat even more cruel than that of 775 at Lidbach. Charlemagne had left two armies in Saxony, one of which was under the command of Count Theodoric, the best of his lieutenants. The other had three leaders, the Chamberlain Adalgis, the Constable Geilon and the Count of the Palace Worad. The latter army was surprised by bands led by Witikind and massacred to a man on the right bank of the Weser, at a place which historians call Sünthal or Süntelgebirg, according to whether they name it after the valley or the mountain.

Charlemagne knew how to be merciful to conquered rebels, but he could not pardon success. He entered Saxony with a powerful army, laying waste everything in his path, and forcing to be delivered up to him 4500 Saxons who were regarded as the chief helpers of Witikind, who had again sought refuge in Denmark. These 4500 patriots were all beheaded at Werden on the same day. The atrocity of this act of vengeance has remained famous in the annals of Germany.

These rivers of blood were completed by the terrible capitulary of the Saxons in which Charlemagne, as a Bishop in arms, informed the conquered how he expected to see them practising religion :

" Whosoever shall not respect the fast days or shall eat meat in Lent shall be put to death; whosoever, at the instigation of the devil, shall burn one of his fellow-creatures, man or woman, or shall give their flesh to be eaten, or shall eat thereof himself, shall be punished with death " [in this case at least capital punishment is justified and the clause sheds a sombre light upon German civilisation at the end of the eighth century]. According to article VII the burning of a corpse " according to pagan rites " was also to be punished with death. Article VIII condemned to punishment by death any Saxon who, in order to escape baptism, " should hide himself among his fellow countrymen."

Article IX.—" Whosoever shall sacrifice a man to the devil according to pagan rites shall be put to death." Here again is something which sheds light upon German civilisation in the time of " *Karl der Grosse.*" By devil Charlemagne meant the ancient gods of the Saxons, Wotan and his fellow divinities, to whom numbers of Germans in our own day would fain return.

According to Article XI, whosoever should be guilty of disloyalty to the King of the Franks would be punished with death.

There is not a single article in his bloodthirsty edict which is not concluded with a threat of capital punishment.

"The pagan," says M. Halphen in conclusion, "is tracked down like a wild beast, and there is perhaps not another example in history of such a ferocious way of imposing the outward semblance of civilisation."

Finally Charlemagne had recourse, when all else failed, to the last expedient—that of wholesale deportation.

Towards the end of 785 Witikind abandoned the struggle in answer to the appeal of the French King and his promise that the past should be forgotten. Charlemagne stood godfather to him in person and covered him with gifts. But nothing is known of what became of him. Some historians regard him as a saint and others believe him to have been the ancestor of the Capets, of Saint Louis and Louis XIV. Let us turn our thoughts reverently to the death of Vercingetorix. At least Charlemagne here gave proof of the vast superiority of his character as compared with Julius Cæsar, and also bore witness to the fine moral progress achieved by Christianity in the Roman world.

In prosecuting the conquest of Saxony, and the assimilation

of the Saxons by means of religion, Charlemagne acted in conformity with the nature of the royal authority—we had almost said of the priesthood—vested in him.

As early as the time of the Merovingians the Kings had occupied the position of the temporal chiefs of the clergy, and **An** now the ceremony of consecration, an innovation **Ecclesiastical** introduced by the Carlovingians, reinforced this **Monarchy.** authority. " The act of consecration," says Fustel de Coulanges, " was a sign of loyalty and submission on the part of the Bishops; the King became the Head of the Church." Having received the blessing of God, he had power to bless men, and in this respect the *Chanson de Roland* gives a true picture of Charlemagne.

The Carlovingian kings sat in the episcopal synods and presided over the councils. They gave their opinion on questions of ecclesiastical ruling and even took part in the discussions raised in connection with articles of dogma, discussions in which their opinion was final.

Carloman and Pepin were present at the meetings of the councils together with their councillors and certain leudes appointed by them. For the sake of convenience they arranged for these religious sessions to coincide with the assemblies of the soldiers, for no council was allowed to meet without authorisation from the King. The leudes, like the King, took part in the debates.

Naturally under Charlemagne this system was still more rigidly enforced.

Like the spring and autumn Assemblies, the councils had only the right of proposing a motion, even in the case of ecclesiastical matters and questions of faith. The decision communicated to the public depended on the royal pleasure.

The opinion expressed by Charlemagne at the synods and councils was frequently opposed to that of the Bishops, and even of the Sovereign Pontiff. He was stricter in the application of Church principles than the clergy themselves, and his opinion always prevailed. When the vote on the decisions of the council had been taken they were submitted to the King for ratification, and he was at liberty to accept, reject or amend them as he pleased. At the end of the eighth century it was not the Pope who was infallible, but the King. " Herewith the articles that

340

we have drawn up, we, the Bishops and their supporters," we find at the end of the acts passed by the councils held at Arles, Tours and Mayence in 813. "These articles will be submitted to our imperial master that his wisdom may add what is lacking, and correct aught that is contrary to reason." The decisions of the council could only be acted upon with the King's consent. As many as four hundred and seventy such decisions, introduced by Charlemagne in his capitularies, have been recorded. "Whosoever," says the tenth canon of the Council of Soissons, "shall transgress this decree, which three and twenty Bishops and other priests have established, with the consent of the King and his noble Franks, shall be tried by the King or by the Bishops or by the Counts."

Indeed the ecclesiastical side of his prerogatives attained such great importance that half the legislative acts of Charlemagne, the ruler of this vast Empire, were concerned with matters of Church discipline and doctrine and the acts and behaviour of the clergy. He continued the reform of the episcopal churches outlined in 760 by his cousin, Chrodegang, Bishop of Metz, which resulted in the institution of canonic rule. The system was completed in 826 by his son, Louis the Pious. In his capitularies he dealt with the reform of the monasteries suggested by Benedict of Aniane, which were finally adopted by Louis the Pious. He entered into the minutest details—rules of ritual, the liturgy and chants of the Church. It was not only in Germany that he persecuted the pagan practices of which his father, in his capitulary dealing with the Saxons, had made a list (744), but in Gaul too he showed himself implacable against them, even in remote country districts where they still survived in hidden crevices of the popular mind—magic formulæ against the scourge of bad weather, against hail, drought and thunderbolts, incantations against disease, love charms, enchanted talismans, funeral feasts at the tombs of the dead, thank offerings at fountains, springs and the great forest trees.

Charlemagne also took a high hand with the Bishops, his subordinates, keeping them in his tutelage the while. He called himself "the defender of the churches," a definite title which imposed duties and bestowed rights. These churches were under the " protection " of the King, in the ordinary meaning of the word. Bishops and Abbots found themselves placed under his "tutelage" and swore oaths of fealty to him. The prelate placed his hands in the hands of the King and said, "I will be faithful and obedient to you as a man should be to his lord." Charlemagne had episcopal sees in his gift as well as monasteries. Like Charles Martel, he bestowed them as benefices, on the same conditions as the counties and the treasury domains. "With this church or this abbey," he argued, "I can make for myself a loyal supporter." But, unlike Charles Martel, he only gave them to the clergy, the bishoprics at least, though he did not excuse recipients from military service. A petition presented in 803 by a group of leudes in favour of the Bishops opened with the following words :

"We bend the knee before Your Majesty and make this prayer, that the Bishops may not be crushed by the burden of having to go to war, but that when we go forth in arms with Your Majesty they may remain in their parishes."

Neither bishoprics nor abbeys could be assigned without the King's consent. Charlemagne even dispensed with the pretence of election. He nominated directly to ecclesiastical offices the candidates who suited his convenience, and the best way of attaining them was through influence at the Palace. From the time of the Merovingians, as we have already seen, the higher clergy were largely recruited from the ranks of the palatine officials. Among the clergy about him Charlemagne picked out men of sound morality, firm in their faith and gifted with administrative ability, and placed them at the head of the bishoprics.

Moreover, without the authority of the King the prelates would have found themselves helpless. "Without the patronage of the King of the Franks," writes Saint Boniface, "I can neither govern the people among the faithful, nor correct the clergy, the monks and the nuns; without his instructions, I cannot succeed in stamping out pagan rites in Germany, nor the sacrilegious worship of idols."

Charlemagne combated heresy in whatever form it made its appearance. He prosecuted the heresiarch who destroyed the souls of men as he would the robber who killed travellers on the high road. He presided over the council convoked in 794 to pass sentence on the heresiarch Felix, Bishop of Urgel, and over another council in 809, in which was debated the question which ever since Arius was continually being reopened, of the procession of the Holy Ghost. Charlemagne went even further; he would not allow his subjects to commit any sin. Willy nilly, he insisted on leading them to paradise, by force if necessary.

His capitularies sometimes resembled sermons : " Love thy neighbour as thyself.—Blessed are the peacemakers for they shall be called the children of God.—Shun sin that thy faith may be strengthened. . . ." These are specimens of Charlemagne's legislative style. He not only recommends charity, he makes it obligatory. His capitularies prescribe worship, fasting, the observance of the sabbath, and regular attendance at the sermon. Everyone had to know the Lord's Prayer and to repeat it every day, and in the task he undertook of securing the practice of the Christian religion, he chose as his helpers, not only the higher clergy, the heads of monasteries, whose duty it was to circulate throughout the country a knowledge of the capitularies and to secure their observation, and for whom the task would naturally have been too great, but even in the meanest rural parish, the humblest country priest, the lowliest officiating minister.

" In the most distant villages," writes Georges Goyau, " the unity of civil and religious life was maintained. Whether built of wood or loam, at the mercy of fire, or made of stone, like the church which is still standing at Germigny-les-Prés (Loiret), these Carlovingian sanctuaries acted as mayoralties, courts of justice and notaries' offices; in case of invasion they became depositories, granaries and places of refuge. They resembled moral fortresses in which the peasant could place his person, his family and his goods in safety under the protection of the saint who, by his intercession in heaven, might perchance arm the hand of God, and by his prestige on earth might disarm the violence of the foe." The " rector," an ecclesiastical functionary who ruled a regular community of priests, deacons and clerics, had the royal mandate to seek out all malefactors and have them excommunicated.

The churches preserved the character given them by the

Merovingians; civil as well as religious life found shelter within their gates. People met together in them, not only to pray, but also in order to talk—they were meeting-places for gossip. At certain hours the basilica became a forum, in which the merchants had their stalls—a regular exchange.

Let us examine the picture as a whole; far from being separated, as in our own day, Church and State were closely united, and formed one whole, from the top of the huge hierarchy, at the pinnacle of which was the King, soon to be Emperor, the sovereign chief of his leudes, his men at arms, and, through them, of the whole people, who was also the head of the Church, controlling the higher clergy, forcing the sap of his ordinances to circulate to the smallest branches of the huge tree, administering and governing the whole nation through the agency of the clergy much more than by means of the Counts, who acted chiefly as judges, or his famous *Missi Dominici*, who were merely inspectors.

As a matter of fact, even the *Missi* were charged by Charlemagne with religious duties. In 802 the Emperor, in Article XIV of the capitulary concerning them, said : " We are desirous that they should win eternal life for us." The capitulary of 806 contained the following words : " Let each man, in the carrying out of his mission, take care to arrange everything according to the will of God."

The Gallic clergy did not find a lenient master in Charlemagne. The monk of Saint-Gall calls him " the pious overseer of the Bishops," a pious overseer indeed, who kept his subordinates well in hand. He used to summon the Bishops to his presence in order to question them and dictate their line of conduct, and when we behold the humility of an archbishop in the presence of a Count of the Palace or of a mere priest who occupied a low rank in the ecclesiastical hierarchy, but who had access to the King either as nuncio or chaplain royal, it is easy to imagine the attitude of the highest dignitaries at the foot of the throne, and their complete abasement. The King observed the most respectful attitude towards them, but this merely served to cloak his position of absolute authority and his vigilance against the smallest deviation from duty. The King gave his commands and charged the Bishops with the

344

execution of his behests. They were merely officials. The Royal Commissioners, the *Missi Dominici*, acted as zealous inspectors of the monasteries, visited the bishoprics and sent their reports to the King. They summoned the prelates before them and questioned them about the management of their dioceses. None of the clergy were allowed to leave the country, even to go to Rome, without the royal permission.

Charlemagne superintended the doctrines of the Bishops and the teaching they spread abroad, and he was never tired of reminding them to remain strictly faithful to the dogmas. " Visit your dioceses, see to it that everything is in conformity with the rules of the Church, and that your clergy are instructed in their profession." He forbade the Bishops to hunt, to ride on horseback through the forests surrounded by howling packs of dogs or to hunt with the falcon or hawk. He would not allow them to wear golden belts holding knives with handles studded with precious stones, or to put on spurs or baldricks, nor could they entertain pretty women.

Leo III, the successor of Adrian, sent Charlemagne the keys of Saint Peter's tomb, as Zacharias had done in the case of Pepin. Charlemagne responded by sending his son-in-law Angilbert, Abbot of Saint-Riquier, on a mission to Rome. Angilbert went loaded with gifts, but also with instructions. The King of the Franks laid down the law to Leo. He recommended him to observe the canons in terms which would have filled a Gregory VII, an Innocent III or a Boniface VIII with the greatest amazement.

When he crossed the frontier his conduct was still the same. His chief care was to spread the faith. He sent missionaries as far as Sweden, and the advice he gave to foreign princes was almost always directed towards the strengthening of Catholicism.

It has been maintained that the preference shown by Charlemagne for his wars against the Saxons rather than for conflicts which would have been simpler and more fruitful was due to his desire to draw pagan peoples to the doctrines of Christ. The oldest German historians regarded him as a defender of the faith rather than as a conqueror, and called him " the apostle of Saxony and Westphalia." It was the same with regard to his wars against the Huns, whilst he spared the Greeks, ruled over by the fair Irene, who had her son's eyes put out in order that she might keep the throne herself, but who was a Catholic.

Charlemagne established in his vast Empire the most fundamentally ecclesiastical government the world has ever seen. It is important to remember this. The eighth century was an epoch of the profoundest faith. Let us try to picture the state of mind of a great people, like the people of Gaul, at a time when no one doubted the doctrines taught by Christ, but when everyone believed in them with his whole heart and soul. Not only was this belief deep-rooted and absolute, it was also concrete, which made it ten times stronger. Men knew and felt that God and the saints were close beside them, beneath the blue vault of heaven which was not very far above their heads, since in days not long past people climbing on a high tower had almost succeeded in reaching it. And nearer still on the earth itself, God and the saints were active every day in their sanctuaries, where they were friendly with men, hearing their prayers, and playing a direct part in their affairs. Charlemagne was convinced that the triumph of Christian doctrines with their sublime morality and divine inspiration could not fail to secure happiness, peace, concord and prosperity on earth. All this is quite alien to modern thought, but was immovably rooted in the soul of a great and powerful statesman of the eighth century. In addition, Charlemagne found this religion endowed with a strongly organised hierarchy, which spread its roots into the furthest recesses of the country, into the humblest parish. He seized upon this organisation as a means of administration. The idea was simple enough but magnificent in its practical justice, and it constituted the greatness of the restorer of the Western Empire. Charlemagne, as King of the Franks, also found himself at the head of another organisation very different in character, a warlike system which would have been called feudal, had feudalism existed in those days or had it developed out of it. This was the social system consisting of benefices, recommendation, oaths of fealty and the great domains, rising from the serf to the free man, from the free man to the leud, the lord of the domain, the Count, who was a royal official, the palatine officer who was in the King's immediate circle, and finally the King himself, and which placed in

346

the latter's hands a vast conglomeration of active forces. Charlemagne united this to the conglomeration of moral forces provided by the religious organisation.

In addition to these two elements, consisting on the one hand of organisation by means of the clerical hierarchy and on the other by means of the feudal hierarchy, both under the sway of the royal master, there was yet a third, a negative element, if you will, but nevertheless one of great importance—the extreme simplicity of the public administration.

The State of this period is miles removed from a modern State. If we compare the city of Paris with a territory of similar extent consisting of cultivated fields and a few villages, we can draw a picture of the administrative maze presented by modern France as compared with the elementary simplicity of the Carlovingian government. The State—wonder of wonders ! —was not concerned with public services. The only expenses which it had to face were confined to the maintenance of the Palace, a domestic problem, to which were added the gifts the King made to the churches, the nobles and foreign princes. Moreover, the finances were managed by the Chamberlain directed by the Queen, who acted as the imperial housekeeper, as a sort of Chancellor of the Exchequer who was generally exceedingly gracious, often very amiable and sometimes very hard. The Crown revenues consisted of the produce from the royal villas, and from the capitularies we know the care with which Charlemagne superintended their cultivation.

The territory of the villa included several farms with court-yards (*curtis*), each enclosed by a hedge of hawthorn. Each farm had various buildings required for working the estate—cattle-sheds, stables, cowhouses, pigsties, sheepfolds and goat-pens. From the courtyard came the cackling of poultry, cocks and hens, ducks and geese, peacocks, pigeons and doves. Pheasants and partridges were bred. In the copses enclosed by walls wild beasts wandered. Fresh-water fish played an important part in the diet of the Middle Ages. Charlemagne insisted on his fish-ponds being well kept and regularly cleaned, so that the stock of fish might increase. There was a vast variety of vegetables, fruit and flowers. As in the Gallo-Roman villas, a body of artisans was attached to the work of

347

agriculture to provide all that was required in the way of manufactured articles—there were blacksmiths and carpenters, cordwainers and saddlers, brewers and millers, and representatives of more uncommon trades, such as workers in iron, goldsmiths, silversmiths, turners and rope-makers. An interesting section of the Carlovingian villa was the women's quarter, in which the women worked. Charlemagne in his capitulary *De Villis* devoted special attention to them. The rooms had to be warmed with stoves, the gates were to be solidly built, and the surrounding hedges well trimmed; there was to be a large hall for the winter evenings. The variety of articles made by the women is surprising—pottery, vases and utensils of all kinds, linen, wool, woad and madder for dyeing, carding combs and boards, and soap. They wove wool and linen and made cloth and serge for the use of the Palace.

Moreover, we may well imagine all that the King received from his country villas—wool and linen materials and plates and dishes; in the way of food, pork of all kinds, pickled pork and bacon, ham, various meats, either smoked or preserved in brine, especially goat's meat, and fish in large quantities. Fish was so plentiful that Charlemagne used to sell it. His farmers sent him cheeses, butter, mustard, vinegar, flour, vegetables and fruit. He was supplied with butcher's meat, including even cow beef from animals that had to be killed because they were lame and horses killed not necessarily because they had anything wrong with them. He received large quantities of honey which took the place of sugar and produced a fermented liquor known as mead. Charlemagne insisted on the wine being made cleanly without being pressed by the feet. His villas supplied his Court with ale, blackberry wine and liqueur. He sold the horns and skins of his goats. He and his people clothed themselves in wolf skins, with which the tenants of his domains could supply him in good condition.

In addition to the produce and resources of the Royal domain, there were the gracious—and obligatory—gifts made by the nobles and the leudes at the annual assemblies, as well as the tribute paid by the vassal nations and lucrative spoils from enemy country—the treasure of the King of the Lombards and of the Avars, more especially, provided a sumptuous booty.

348

Such, in its great simplicity, are the outlines of Charlemagne's government—the religious hierarchy, the lay hierarchy, each acting by means of their own forces and their internal energy, in touch with the King only through their leaders and directed by an administration which was still very simple and had nothing to do with public services. Such was the Carlovingian Empire.

Imagine a King endowed with a gift for organisation as great as that of Napoleon I, for example—though lacking the latter's amplitude, versatility, suppleness and brilliance, for the earlier task was infinitely less complicated—and itis easy to see how a man of intelligence, good sense and energy, enjoying good health but not endowed with any exceptional gifts, Louis XIV if you wish, and certainly Charlemagne, was able, surrounded by the glamour of the greatest epic poetry the world has ever known, to cut such a magnificent figure in the annals of history.

Powerful as was the religious organisation in the Empire of Charlemagne, it was not the only one; side by side with **Dukes,** it were the wheels of the civil system, which, **Counts and** however, were closely united with it. The funda-**Marquises.** mental divisions of the Empire were the counties, which were as a rule a development from the cities which the Christians had found in Gaul and on the foundations of which they had established their dioceses. There were a hundred and ten or a hundred and twenty counties in the territory of what is now France, each one under the rule of a Count. But it was not the district that appointed the official, as the department to-day appoints its *préfet*. A county was the territory ruled by a Count and could be changed at the pleasure of the King. There were very large counties, like the County of Auvergne, and very small ones, like the County of Senlis.

Several Counts might be subject to the authority of a Duke, but this was not necessarily the case. It must not be imagined that the Duchies were subdivided into counties, as a department is to-day subdivided into *sous-préfectures*. The authority of a Duke consisted in his right of command over several Counts, which was conferred upon him to meet a passing emergency, but which might nevertheless last a long time.

The Marquises were Counts charged with some special military mission on the frontiers—the *marches* of the country; the Spanish March, the marches of Septimania, Friuli, Benevento and Brittany. The *marca*, the march, was the frontier. The word comes from a German root meaning boundary, limit. The word margin—the margin of a book, or of an engraving, surrounding the text or the picture—comes from the same root. " The Counts of the marches," writes the Astronomer, " are charged with the protection of the frontiers of the kingdom and with securing them against enemy incursions."

The Count, *comes*, companion, was indeed, as the word itself indicates, a companion of the King. All the Counts, with but few exceptions, had held offices in the Palace, where they had been trained in the conduct of affairs, shaped in the policy of the King, and won his appreciation. The Count could be entrusted with the most diverse missions, diplomatic, military or judicial. In the eighth century diplomatists, generals and *préfets* were unknown; there were only Counts, the companions of the King, whom the latter charged at his pleasure with such functions as he thought would be well fulfilled by them.

Consequently the title of Count had nothing to do with the birth or the family of the recipient. Some of the Counts belonged to the noblest families, others to the humblest. Charlemagne even chose some of them from the slave class. Adrevald is a typical example of this. After the conquest of Aquitaine and Lombardy, it was necessary to apply to the Palace for a large number of these " companions " of the King, who had been educated under his eyes to hold public office. It was necessary to provide the new provinces with the requisite political machinery, and, like a reservoir which has been drained in a time of drought, the Palace was emptied. It was then that Charlemagne turned for recruits to the serfs of his domain. One of them called Rahon became Count of Orleans, and a certain Stirminius Count of Bourges. A serf, named Bertmund, was placed in command of Auvergne, the most important county of France.

The chief functions of the Count consisted in dispensing justice, assisted by a council of the chief men of the city, free men, whose presence at his council board was obligatory. These latter were the successors of the Merovingian rachimburgs, but
350

they played a more important part. For in practice their opinion was law, and the Count only acted as president at their head. Charlemagne gradually substituted for these free men, whom the Count used to choose to sit on his tribunal, regular assessors, who soon came to act as magistrates. They were called sheriffs, *scabini*, and made their appearance in 780. They met once a month. The assembly of free men was only convoked once or twice a year to deal with particular business. The mallus, or tribunal, no longer met in the open air, in the picturesque fashion of the old days, but in a hall arranged purposely for it.

The Counts were not given a regular salary like modern officials; they provided their own remuneration from the proceeds of their office, keeping for themselves a third of the fines imposed by the court. In some of the domains the Count enjoyed the disposal of a third of the revenue. They also had the right of hospitality. It is easy to realise the consequences of such an organisation in the long run. The Count no longer received reward for his services from the Court, but, on the contrary, sent money to the King several times a year. And when State offices tended to become, not only inalienable, but also hereditary, this financial independence helped to accentuate the movement.

The Counts were expected to go to Court at least once a year, to give a report of their administration and to receive the King's instructions. They were subject to inspection by the *Missi*, which must frequently have been very necessary, particularly when it was a question of disputes between the Counts and the Bishops. There were bad judges and bad inspectors. Some presided over their tribunals in a state of intoxication, others had men hanged without any further trial. Some of them " had their palms greased "—to use an expression of the period—and the worst among them had no shame in appropriating the property of the poor. Such abuses, however, were rare, and the stern hand of Charlemagne soon put a stop to them.

Finally the Counts were entrusted with the mission of bringing contingents from their districts for the army. Charlemagne demanded personal service from the owner of three or more manses. Those who could not afford more were obliged to join together to defray the expense of equipping one man.

As the King's lieutenant, the Count was an absolute sovereign in his own district. He was supported by the viscount, who was really a substitute performing the functions of the Count when the latter was at the Palace or with the army. The Count also left him to judge matters of minor importance.

The vicars, centurions and tithing-men were subordinates of inferior rank, and, like their chief, moreover, they wielded the most divers powers. They were at once administrators, judges, chiefs of police and captains. They were appointed by the Count.

It is easy to see what would happen when once the sovereign no longer exercised the necessary authority to summon the Counts to appear before him once a year, when the institution known as the *Missi Dominici* had become corrupted, and when the tendency of functions to become permanent and hereditary increased. These changes had indeed come into being at the end of the ninth century, and the result was that the Count became the lord and master of his county.

When, moreover, we remember that the Bishops also had their vicars, vidames, centurions and other agents, who were their retainers—in this case in a private capacity—and when we imagine them, frequently pugnacious and truculent as they were, forming part of the social organisation described above, it is not difficult to understand that they too ultimately became masters in their dioceses. However energetic, determined, active and intelligent a sovereign might be, it became no longer possible for him to assert his power effectively in the circumstances, and it has been very rightly observed of Charlemagne that, at the end of the ninth century, he would not have cut a better figure than his successors.

But, for the time being, the monarch was still master in his own kingdom. In one of the statutes we read : " Let no one dispute the prince's ban, question his deeds or oppose his will." The royal pleasure was, in fact, law.

Charlemagne has been regarded as a great legislator. But his statutes are for the most part regulations of a wholly temporary kind, called into being by circumstances which, fre-

352

quently, were purely local in their effect. He has been praised for the fact that " he never attempted to establish uniformity in the laws governing his Empire." He certainly had the ability to bow before the most diverse customs, and endeavoured to turn them to account in furthering his policy. Under his rule every man was judged according to the law, or rather according to the customs of his nation. And Charlemagne made it his business to find out what these customs were. He had them recorded in writing so that they might be more efficiently applied, and this is one of his titles to glory. And when he wished to modify or amend these customs, he was obliged more than once to abandon his scheme owing to the opposition it provoked. When it was a matter of modifying local customs, he took care to consult the competent authorities. Hincmar describes the procedure in this case as follows :

" When the Great of the land were assembled, they were shown the statutes which the mind of the prince had conceived under divine inspiration, or which had been called for by some need that had arisen in the interval between the sessions. And when they had taken due note of their import, they would discuss them clause by clause. Then their conclusions were placed before the prince, who, with the wisdom that God gave him, adopted a form of law which all had to obey."

Charlemagne himself divided his statutes into three categories. The first included the statutes which he termed " written for themselves," and it consisted of those laws concerned with administration which were valid only for one reign.

The second category included the " additions to the laws." It consisted of those statutes which most resembled laws properly so-called, but with this difference—that they were only the additions or modifications made in regard to the customs of a particular people. That which was valid for the Saxons was not valid for the Aquitanians, and that which was valid for the Aquitanians was not valid for the Lombards. They were, however, permanent in character. In 803, for instance, Stephen, Count of Paris, made known to the people of the city the statute added to the Salic law.

" The statutes were delivered to Count Stephen in order that he might make them known to the city of the Parisians assembled in the public ' mallus,' and have them read before the sheriffs. This he did. And the whole assembly agreed that they should continue valid for all time, and everyone—Bishops, Abbots and Counts—ratified them with their own hand."

As regards the statutes for the *Missi Dominici*, these were laws of a particular kind, and consisted of instructions of the prince to those whom he entrusted with some kind of mission.

This consent given to the laws was not an empty formality. It was preceded by the ratification of the Great of the land, assembled in arms—an assembly of great importance and authority. Again in 813 we behold the Bishops, Abbots, Counts and notables converging on Aix-la-Chapelle from every corner of the Empire in answer to a summons to frame Imperial legislation. These Assemblies constitute the most important part of Charlemagne's institutions, and in them the powerful Emperor displayed his magnanimity, his liberal spirit, and his understanding of the needs of those whom he governed or had conquered. Thus he left to the nations gathered under his sway—the Aquitanians, Saxons or Lombards—their own particular customs, and allowed his agents to interfere with them only in order to make them observe their own traditions more exactly.

The organisation which we have just described did not allow any scope for administrative government. This was impossible. **Aquitaine.** And thus Charlemagne was obliged to grant to the various peoples of his Empire a large measure of autonomy. Except for certain pagan practices, which Charlemagne could not tolerate, even the Saxons retained their own customs, and in the person of his son Louis—later known as Louis the Pious and surnamed the Debonair—he gave to the Aquitanians a sovereign of their own. The partition of the kingdom among the Merovingian princes had been a necessity, and even a ruler like Charlemagne found himself compelled to adopt the same expedient. Thus he gave to the Aquitanians his son Louis, and insisted on that section of the kingdom being governed in accordance with its own customs and traditions and, in a great measure, by men of Aquitanian or Gascon birth. One fact recorded by the historian of Louis the Pious, the chronicler who is known as the Astronomer, is characteristic. In accord-

354

ance with his father's instructions, the young king of Aquitaine wore the Gascon costume—the circular cape, the long shirt that reached down to the knees with its flowing sleeves, and the spurs strapped to the boots. With his javelin in his hand, he thus looked as if he were one of the warriors of the country.

Charlemagne never called upon the Aquitanians to participate in the wars he waged against the Germanic peoples, the Slavs or the Huns; but reserved them for his struggles with the Saracens in Septimania and Spain. Always stimulated by his religious zeal and his desire to guarantee his southern frontiers, Charlemagne continued his struggle against the Crescent. Since the days of Charles Martel a revolution had brought changes into the Arab world. The dynasty of the Omaides had been overthrown by the Abbassides at Bagdad, and the Emirs of Spain, who were hostile to their new masters, had at last appealed for help to the Frankish monarch. In 778, at the head of a large body of troops, he passed through the defiles of the Pyrenees, while another of his armies crossed into Spain over the Roussillon mountains.

In accordance with his usual custom the Frankish king invaded the country which he intended to conquer at several different points at the same time with the view of surprising the enemy, baffling him and terrifying him by exaggerating the gravity of his peril. He took possession of several important places—Pampeluna, Gerona and Huesca—and came in sight of Saragossa. What happened outside this fortress? The Frankish and Arab chroniclers do not agree. Did Charles suffer a check, or did he withdraw after extracting a sum of money from the Mussulmans? The first version, which is the Arabs', is the more probable. At all events Charlemagne beat a retreat. And it was while returning to Gaul that the French rearguard, commanded by Rolando, Duke of the Marches of Brittany, allowed himself to be surprised by a party of Basque mountaineers. Under the cover of their rocky gorges, they suddenly pounced on the Frankish host and destroyed it to a man.

This was the famous Battle of Roncevalles, of which we know the precise date—the 15th of August, 788—thanks to the epitaph of the Seneschal Eggihard, who was killed at Rolando's side.

Eginhard has given a fairly accurate account of the action in the following passage :

" On his return across the Pyrenees, he (Charlemagne] had to suffer from the perfidy of the Basques. As his army was marching along single file owing to the narrowness of the path, some Basques hidden in ambush—for the thick woods abounding in that district are very favourable for ambuscades—swooped down from the top of the mountains and hurled into the ravine the rearguard together with the troops protecting the army on its march, and then, engaging in battle, massacred them to a man, plundered the baggage and finally dispersed with extraordinary rapidity under cover of the gathering darkness. The Basques had in their favour their light equipment and the configuration of the land, whilst the Franks were hampered by the weight of their arms and their position below the enemy."

This is a most valuable description, of astonishing conciseness, from the pen of one of Charlemagne's most important collaborators. Eginhard gives the names of the chief Frankish warriors who perished in the fight, the Seneschal Eggihard, Anselm, Count of the Palace, and Rolando, Duke of the Breton Marches. He adds that Charlemagne never had his revenge for the defeat he suffered.

As late as the eighteenth century Spain was still proud of the day when she defeated Charlemagne at Roncevalles.

Modern historians, following in the footsteps of Eginhard, generally agree in making light of the affair, regarding it as merely a rearguard skirmish. They allow themselves to be misled by the contrast between an episode of slight importance and the incomparable splendour of the poem in which the conquered were glorified. Nevertheless we must bear in mind that this " rearguard " was commanded by the Seneschal, by the Count of the Palace and by the Duke of Brittany, three great personages, the Seneschal and the Count of the Palace being the two chief officials of the royal Court. Is it conceivable that an insignificant body of troops should have been placed under the command of such high authorities ? The epic poem, work of imagination though it is, seems nearer to the truth than the statements of chroniclers anxious to minimise the gravity of the defeat.

356

We must remember that the epic poems, like the *Chanson de Roland*, served as history for the people. A valuable confirmation of this fact is to be found in the chronicle of the Astronomer, who was a contemporary and a friend of Louis the Pious, the son of Charlemagne: " I shall not waste my time," he says, " in giving the names of those who fell on that grievous day; their names are on all men's lips." These lines are extremely interesting. They prove that the old "*geste*," which is the subject of the *Chanson* as it has been handed down to us, dated from the first half of the ninth century, and was no doubt edited by a poet attached to the ducal family of Brittany. It reminds us of the bard and his zither whom Clovis had sent to him to inspire him and celebrate his exploits.

These lines, moreover, prove the historical basis of the poem, since a writer like the Astronomer, attached to the person of Louis the Pious, King of Aquitaine, and in a position to know all about these events, makes mention of the account.

Not only were Charlemagne's conquests in Spain lost, but the Saracens once more took the offensive and made their appearance in Septimania.

In 793 Abd-el-Melec set fire to the suburbs of Narbonne. The Count of Toulouse, Crooked-Nosed William, so called because his nose had been broken by a Saracen scimitar, endeavoured to arrest the march of the Arabs on Carcassonne. A small river, the Orbieu, runs into the Aude, and it was on the banks of this stream that the battle was fought in which Crooked-Nosed William was also defeated (793). This was the epic battle on the plain of Larchamp—the name of a place which it has been impossible to identify—which is celebrated in that admirable poem, a worthy fellow of the *Chanson de Roland*, the *Chanson de Guillaume d'Orange*. The victors returned to Spain, carrying off quantities of booty and prisoners.

Another event of this period may also have served as a basis for several of the old French epics, and particularly of the Lay of Gerard, Count of Vienne, the noble baron who rebelled against Charlemagne on account of an insult he was supposed to have received from the Queen of France. In 785, Hartrad, Count of Thuringia, placed himself at the head of a conspiracy against Charles, which was a source of continual anxiety to him.

The Count maintained that he had cause for complaint against Fastrada, Charlemagne's fourth, but not his last, wife. The conspiracy was discovered. Charlemagne treated the conspirators with leniency and repaired the harm the Queen had done; but Hartrad had his eyes put out. Queen Fastrada died in 794, having presented the King only with daughters.

It was on his return from the siege of Saragossa that Charlemagne found himself the father of his third son, Louis the Pious, the child of Queen Hildegarda. In 781, when the boy was three, he was consecrated King of Aquitaine by the Sovereign Pontiff, whilst Charlemagne made his son Pepin King of the Lombards. An event of the year 787, recorded by the Astronomer, shows how full of life local institutions, with their separatist tendencies, still remained, and helps to explain the rapid dislocation of the Carlovingian Empire after the death of its founder. Adalric, son of Lupus II, Duke of Gascony, who has been held responsible for the attack at Roncevalles, seized Corso, whom Charlemagne had appointed Duke of Toulouse, and forced him to swear oaths of fealty to him. Charlemagne in a rage convoked a General Assembly in Septimania, at a place which the Astronomer calls "*La Morte des Goths.*" Adalric was summoned to attend, but he only came after an exchange of hostages with the powerful King of the Franks. And behold the young Gascon noble making his appearance in the Assembly holding his head up and speaking with proud disdain. " On account of the danger to the hostages," says the Astronomer, " they did not dare to do anything to him." Adalric even received presents, returned the hostages, received back his own and retired in freedom. This episode throws a clear light on Charlemagne's rule in Gaul.

Louis, King of Aquitaine, first served his apprenticeship in arms in 791, when he was in his fourteenth year. Charlemagne performed the ceremony of girding him with his sword, and this the old French historians maintained was " the institution of chivalry and the fashion of arming knights." From that time forward the King of the Franks himself took in hand the education of his son, had him to live with him for long periods and endeavoured to teach him his profession of King. Louis stood in great need of this paternal guidance, as he displayed a weak-

358

ness of character which proved the bane of his reign. In 795 his father expressed surprise at his parsimony and his mediocre manner of life. He discovered that the Great Ones of Aquitaine had little by little despoiled the domains attached to the Crown. It was the old game of the benefices. And the King was forced to send Gilbert, afterwards Archbishop of Rouen, and Richard, the steward of his own domains, as *Missi* to Aquitaine to have the lands restored.

The internal dissensions between the Mussulmans continued to serve the cause of the Franks. The various Emirs had made themselves independent of the new dynasty established at Bagdad and the stronger made themselves masters of the weak. One of them, Abdullah, came to Charlemagne to beg for his intervention, and returned to Spain, with Louis, King of Aquitaine, in command of contingents of armed leudes. Several places in Catalonia, Gerona, Vich, Caserras, were occupied by the Franks. In 800 and 801 Lerida and Barcelona were added, and thus the Spanish March was formed. Crooked-Nosed William, who had been beaten on the Plain of Larchamp, routed the troops the Calif of Cordova had sent for the relief of Barcelona, and thus, after the defeat of Larchamp, a victory was celebrated for William also by the author of the " *geste Guillaume.*" And thus the Spanish March was formed consisting of northern Catalonia and Navarre.

The greater became the extent of Charlemagne's Empire the more numerous were his enemies, so that the King of the Franks now found himself face to face with the infidel,
Huns and Danes. which made him wax ever more enthusiastic in his task of conversion. Across the Pyrenees his Empire reached the frontiers of Spain, where he came into contact with the Saracens; on the Saxon frontier there were the Huns in Pannonia (Hungary), the Danes (Normans) in Scandinavia, and in the shadowy East the Slavonic peoples.

This meant war without ceasing. But the King, thanks to his gifts of organisation and his rapidity of movement, which we have already discussed, was quite capable of dealing with the situation.

The year 790 is a red-letter year in the annals of his tumultuous reign, for it was a year of peace.

In 791 a great expedition took place against the Huns, a regular crusade, for its object was the conversion of the infidel. The priests went about preaching a holy war, as they did later on during the crusades under Philip I. The King's camp was like a busy Abbey where fasts were *de rigueur*, where snatches of canticles were wafted on the breeze and public intercession unfolded an endless chain of prayer, whilst processions marched along flaunting all the brilliance of their sacerdotal vestments.

Charlemagne, as was his custom, invaded Pannonia from three different directions, through Bohemia, Bavaria and Istria. The great Count Theodoric, his best lieutenant, was in command of the columns consisting of Saxons and Thuringians; for Charlemagne, like the Romans before him, knew how to transform conquered peoples into champions of his cause. Theodoric advanced along the left bank of the Danube, whilst the King took the right bank. The Bavarians supplied the commissariat by a service of boats on the river; and, lastly, the Dukes of Friuli and Istria brought troops from Italy. The latter alone engaged in conflict and put the Huns to flight; Charlemagne and Theodoric arrived in time to divide the spoils.

In 792 the conspiracy of Pepin the Hunchback, Charlemagne's eldest son, by his first wife Himiltruda, broke out. Charlemagne had excluded him from the partition of his Empire on account of his deformity. The conspiracy seems to have been very serious, for the King acted with extreme severity, and punishments of all kinds were inflicted. Pepin the Hunchback alone had his life spared. His father had his head shaved and shut him up in the convent of Prüm. It was impossible to enter the portals of any monastery of the vast Empire without coming across a son, grandson, brother, uncle, nephew or cousin of the King, bearing the tonsure and consecrated to the Lord in order to make him keep the peace. The conspiracy of Pepin the Hunchback had been divulged by a Lombard priest whom Charlemagne rewarded by the gift of the Abbey of Saint Denis.

And now a fresh insurrection broke out in Saxony. It burst out in the form of a great national movement. Priests had their throats cut, churches were burnt, and idols set up once more—a rude awakening for the conqueror.

360

Charlemagne had made Count Theodoric Governor of Saxony, and we have seen how the latter had led the Saxons to war against the Avars. But it was precisely a rising of the Saxon troops in his command that unloosed the rebellion. At the passage of the Weser the Saxon contingents mutinied and cut to pieces the detachment serving as their escort. Charlemagne's work was entirely destroyed, and he learnt that the Saxons had even gone so far as to make an alliance with the Huns.

It was at this juncture that the policy of transportation came to be practised on a large scale. In whole districts a third of the population were taken away and settled in France, their place being taken by Slavs, the declared enemies of the Saxons.

The policy of devastation was also renewed with increased fury, and Charlemagne spent the years 795, 796 and 797 in ravaging, burning and pillaging this unhappy country. Towards the end of 797 he at last felt he had realised his object, and on the 25th of October he published his second Saxon capitulary in terms which were more moderate, better considered and more politic than the first. This capitulary sums up the conclusions reached by the Assembly of Aix-la-Chapelle (October 798), to which not only Frankish officials, but delegates from the districts concerned had been summoned to deliberate on the affairs of Saxony. The capitulary of 785 was like an iron law imposed on the vanquished by a victor who considered only his own pleasure; the capitulary of 797 was more like an agreement which took into account the aspirations and needs of the people upon whom it was imposed. Nevertheless the worship of idols was strictly forbidden.

The years 795–797, in which the Saxon war was Charlemagne's chief preoccupation, also saw him prosecuting his campaigns against the Huns (Avars). In 795 their famous ring—formed by means of a series of fortifications in concentric circles—was captured together with all its legendary treasures. The ring, it was said, contained the vast booty collected by Attila on his fabulous expeditions, and, if we may believe Eginhard, Charlemagne's warriors must have enriched themselves beyond the dreams of avarice on these wonderful spoils. The campaign was not conducted by Charlemagne in person, but by Pepin, his second son, under the direction of Herric, Duke of Friuli.

In 796 the Huns acknowledged themselves beaten and asked to be baptised, a request which was becoming the customary form of submission, though the sincerity of these conversions is somewhat dubious.

The war in Pannonia was followed by the war in Bohemia, which developed out of the war against the Huns, just as the latter was a result of the war against the Saxons. It was a real stone of Sisyphus. The Slav peoples of Bohemia had been invading the regions subject to Frankish rule. Charlemagne's second son had been placed at the head of the war against the Huns, and the war against Bohemia was entrusted to his eldest son Charles. The same plan of campaign was again adopted. Three separate armies invaded the country from different directions and combined their movements in concentric manœuvres. Only one expedition was required to bring the country into subjection.

Lastly there were the Danes—the terrible Normans. In their long light boats, black and elongated, without any decks, they made their appearance as elusive pirates. In a legendary but extraordinarily vivid account, the monk of St. Gall depicts Charlemagne following the evolutions of these sinister ships with sad eyes and weeping at the sight of them for the fate of his people :

" What," he cried, " will become of my kingdom and my people ? "

Charlemagne is supposed to have contemplated the distressing spectacle on the blue sea waves from the top of the walls of Narbonne. If the picture is a true one it must have been Saracen ships he was watching. In manning them with Normans the chronicler has depicted what was in the minds of his contemporaries.

The King of France took in hand the defence of her coasts. He had ships built to fight the pirates, and placed them broadside at the mouths of rivers. It was impossible for him to go and strike at the heart of the enemy as he had done in the case of the Saxons and the Avars.

362

As the defender of Christianity, Charlemagne had to show his zeal, not only against infidels and heretics, but even in Rome itself, in order to secure the Sovereign Pontiff the independent and honourable position due to the head of Christendom.

The Emperor of the West.

The position of the Pope was an extraordinary one. Officially he was dependent on the Byzantine Emperor, the heir of the Roman Emperors, who exercised suzerainty over the Eternal City. On the other hand, he also depended upon the Kings of France whom the Papacy itself had invested with the title of patricians, that is to say, lieutenants and sovereign rulers in Rome, in the name of the Emperor of the East. As Roman patricians, the Frankish kings enjoyed the same power over the Eternal City as the Byzantine Dukes, their predecessors.

But this was not all. We have seen how the Pope " recommended " himself to Pepin the Short, and placed himself under the authority of the Frankish King by ties of vassaldom of which distance alone weakened the strength. Lastly, although they were no longer menaced by the Kings of Lombardy, the Sovereign Pontiffs were still harassed in Rome itself by factions which found armed partisans even in the Sacred College and incited the people of the city and the rustics of the Campagna.

The Byzantine Empire, the Roman Empire, in fact, was at this time represented in a most extraordinary manner by a woman who occupied the throne of Constantinople, Irene, a beautiful, proud and cruel Athenian, who had married the eldest son of Constantine Copronymus, and in order to keep her power had had the eyes of her own son put out (797). A woman Emperor, the heir of Cæsar and Augustus, who had ascended the throne on the body of her own son !

The Western peoples had not protested against the transference of the Imperial throne to the East after the fall of Romulus Augustulus (477). An opposition movement had begun to grow in Italy about 730, when the heresy of the iconoclasts, the breakers of religious images, found a supporter in Constantinople in the person of the Emperor. In 731, when an edict of Leo the Isaurian had ordered the destruction of the images in Rome, the imperial officials were driven out. From that moment the Sovereign Pontiff, the Bishop of Rome, became the real governor of the city, like the Bishops in Gaul, though the bonds with Byzantium were not severed.

In the midst of this extraordinary and complicated state of affairs the risings of the month of April 799 broke out against Leo III, a timid and retiring Pontiff, of downcast mien, who bore upon his person the stamp of his humble origin, so different from his predecessor Adrian I, with his princely bearing and proud, haughty and independent character.

On the 25th of April, 799, Leo III, in the midst of a solemn procession, was making his way towards the church of San Lorenzo in Lucina, when he was attacked by an armed band under the command of Paschal and Campulus, high officials in the pontifical palace and nephews of Adrian. The Sovereign Pontiff was riddled with wounds, after which, if we may believe Eginhard, he had his tongue torn out and his eyes put out. He was hurled, covered with blood, into the depths of the monastery of Saint Erasmus, from which he was rescued on the intervention of two *Missi* sent by Charlemagne. On regaining his liberty, the Holy Father hastened to throw himself at the feet of the Frankish King, who was presiding over one of his General Assemblies at Paderborn in Saxony.

After the fashion of the inhabitants of Rome in the Middle Ages, the assailants excused their conduct by bringing the worst accusations against the Pontiff—simony, adultery, perjury, idolatry and murder. The recital became monotonous in its violence, for it was repeated again and again. The scenes which ended in the " attempt " at Anagni, at the beginning of the fourteenth century, were far from being isolated occurrences in the annals of the Papacy.

And thus, as L. Halphen says, " the Pope was not only a victim, he was also accused of crime."

Charlemagne sent Leo back to Rome with a guard to protect him. He had no doubt promised to go there himself soon after, and indeed we find him appearing in Rome on the 24th of November of the year 800. Leo III welcomed him at the door of St. Peter's with all the traditional magnificence of papal functions. Charlemagne was the arbitrator in the case.

On the 1st of December the King of France presided in the basilica of St. Peter over an Assembly similar to that which he was accustomed to convoke in Gaul, in which the ecclesiastical dignitaries mingled with the laity, the officials and the nobility. He summoned the Pope to appear before him, just as in Gaul he summoned conspirators and plotters, or those who had been accused of treason or any other capital crime.

Leo III presented himself on the 23rd of December for examination. Can we rely on the account given by Eginhard? Seeing the important part the biographer of Charlemagne played at Court, I think we may. What a terrible spectacle was afforded by this Prince of the Church at bay, with his hollow eye-sockets, two black holes, his open mouth, another black hole, reduced to defending himself by means of an interpreter in the basilica of St. Peter, before a barbarian King surrounded by his leudes in coat of mail ! Leo III was pronounced innocent, and his aggressors, Paschal and Campulus, were condemned.

The Sovereign Pontiff succeeded in raising himself from this humiliation by means of an act of inspiration which has the appearance of a flash of genius—raising himself with his own hands in such a way as to place himself above his judge, while seeming the while to cover him with the highest honours.

It was the 25th of December, Christmas Day.

The account of what happened appears in the *Annales Royales* :

" Everything being ready on the holy day of Christmas, at the moment when, after having prayed on his knees during Mass before the confessional of St. Peter, the King was about to stand up, Pope Leo placed a crown on his head and the people acclaimed him :

" ' Hail Charles Augustus, crowned by God, great and pacific Emperor of the Romans, long life and victory to thee ! ' "

As we know the imperial power had been divided between two heads, one of which was honoured with the title of Emperor Augustus, and the other with that of Emperor Cæsar, the former of the two titles being superior to the latter.

The *Annales Royales* continue in the following terms :

" After these acclamations the Emperor was adored by the Pontiff—according to the custom of princes in former times, in the pagan fashion—and instead of the title of Patrician he was henceforward known by that of Emperor Augustus."

A similar account is given by the pen of Eginhard.

It is important to remember that there was here no question of a Germanic Empire, as the Germans, in their attempt to glorify themselves, have continually maintained; it was not even a question of a Frankish Empire, but purely of a Roman Empire. So much so that when he acted as Roman Emperor Charlemagne always appeared dressed in the Roman fashion.

In his distress the unfortunate Pope exaggerated his attitude of humility. The coronation was followed by the ceremony of consecration, after which the Pope and the Emperor went to place offerings on the altar of St. Peter.

Eginhard commented on these proceedings in the following much discussed lines :

" King Charles received the title of Emperor Augustus, which at first so much displeased him that he asserted that in spite of the importance of the festival of Christmas, he would not have entered the church had he been able to foresee the intention of the Pope."

What can have been the reasons for the King's displeasure? The following are obvious. The Byzantines regarded the event as an insult to their Crown. There was already a Roman Emperor enthroned at Byzantium. Charlemagne was only an usurper. Conflicts and military expeditions, the anxiety of which would overwhelm the new Augustus, would be distressingly prolonged in the future, through the complications which would probably arise with the Greek Empire.

Charlemagne was all the less desirous of this, seeing that the Empress Irene was a Catholic. It is even known that plans of marriage had been discussed between Charles and Irene and that the initiative had come from the King of the Franks. She would have been his sixth or seventh wife. As husband of Irene, Charlemagne would have found himself undisputed master of the whole of Christendom. It is easy to understand the attractions of such a project upon a mind greedy of universal dominion.

After the coronation there were immediate rumours of war. But Irene having been overthrown by Nicephorus, the Imperial Chancellor, the Franks did their best to settle matters amicably.

366

The version of the Emperor's coronation which they made a point of circulating is given in the *Annales Royales,* which L. Halphen regards as official :

" Inasmuch as in the country of the Greeks there was no longer an Emperor but that they were under the rule of a woman, it seemed good to Pope Leo and to all the Fathers assembled in council, as also to all Christian peoples, to appoint as Emperor King Charles, who occupied Rome, which had always been the seat of the Emperors, and the other places of Italy, Gaul and Germany. Almighty God having consented to put all these places under his authority, it seemed just to them that, in conformity with the demand of every Christian people, he should also bear the title of Emperor. This demand King Charles was unwilling to reject, and submitting himself in all humility to God, and to the desire expressed by the priest and by all the people of Christendom, he received this title together with consecration by the Pope." This was certainly the version that was circulated. In the chronicle of Moissac we read : " Since King Charles was in Rome, deputies arrived to say that among the Greeks the title of Emperor was no longer borne by any man, and consequently the Pope and the Bishops determined to make King Charles Emperor." Other writers of the period could also be quoted.

This seems to have been one of the reasons for the displeasure created in the mind of King Charles by the initiative taken by the Pope; but there is another which is perhaps more important. We have seen that the Pope had " recommended " himself to the King of France, and avowed himself his vassal; we have also seen how Charlemagne ruled his Bishops, appointing them as he would ordinary officials. At this time the Pope was merely the first of the Bishops, he was elected like the rest by the clergy and the people, and, to be valid, his election had to be confirmed by the Emperor. " The Emperor," writes Fustel de Coulanges, " could command the Pope to come to Constantinople, either to take his seat at the Council, or to render account of his conduct and even of his faith." We have just seen how Charlemagne sat in judgment on the Pope. By suddenly seizing the imperial crown in order to put it on the King's head and consecrate him Emperor, the Pope recovered his position, and placed himself above the Emperor who owed his rank and title to him. The details of the coronation of Louis the Pious at Aix-la-Chapelle, which will be given later, provide a singular confirmation of this hypothesis. It makes us think of Napoleon in Notre Dame at his coronation in 1804. Just as Pious VII was about to place the imperial crown on his head Napoleon took it from him and crowned himself with his own hands.

Moreover, the French later on would never admit the theory of Papal supremacy based upon the consecration of the year 800 upheld by Gregory VII, Innocent III and Boniface VIII. On the contrary, it was the doctrine of the royal supremacy that was maintained by them as late as the eighteenth century. They declared that inasmuch as the Pope was subject to the King of France the latter had authority not only to nominate him, but to keep watch over him as he did over his Bishops. Charles IX was reminded of this in a conversation with the illustrious Chancellor de l'Hôpital. The latter dared to tell him that his predecessors would never be forgiven for having allowed one of the most precious attributes of the Crown to lapse—that of nominating the Popes, a right won by Pepin and Charlemagne. On the 2nd of August, 1594, Henry IV declared to the deputies from the town of Beauvais : " I accuse my predecessors of dastardly cowardice for having lost the fair title of being the pillar of the head of the Church, and the right they enjoyed of nominating the Holy Father in Rome." And in the seventeenth century Mézeray, one of the most illustrious of French historians, wrote that Pope Adrian had accorded to Charlemagne the right of appointing the Bishops " and of nominating the Pope, in order to avoid the intrigues and disorders that attended elections."

In conclusion, we may say that the coronation of Charlemagne in Rome on the 25th of December, 800, by re-establishing the Empire of the West, which had ceased to exist in 476, made a vivid impression upon the minds of his contemporaries and helped still further to increase his moral power, but that it had very little effect, in fact none at all, upon the condition of the people and upon the working of the institutions at that time in existence.

In the year that Charlemagne was crowned his fifth wife, Liutgardis, died. She was a gracious, sweet and pretty woman. **The Palace,** She was followed by Madelgardis, Gersuinda, **the Court,** Regina and Adelaide, making a total of nine **the Emperor.** wives; and even so the list is not complete. We know that Charlemagne had twenty children, but he certainly had many more. He regarded as legitimate only the children by his third wife, Hildegarda, who was his favourite. She came from a noble Suabian family, and, according to Thegan, was descended from Godefried, Duke of the Alemanni.

By Hildegarda he had three sons, Charles, Pepin and Louis, between whom he divided his kingdom. The name Louis, which is the same as Clovis, now appears for the first time in the history of France.

To Charles, the eldest of his three sons, Charlemagne gave the territory of Maine as his portion, whilst also reserving for him the title of Emperor, together with the three ancient kingdoms of Austrasia, Neustria and Burgundy. Austrasia had come to include the whole of Germany. Pepin received the kingdom of Lombardy and Louis the kingdom of Aquitaine. The latter alone survived his father. By his first wife, Imiltrude, Charlemagne had had a son, Pepin, who was a hunchback; and we have already seen how he treated him. His second wife, Desideria, daughter of the King of the Lombards, was repudiated without having borne him any children. She was followed by Hildegarda, the mother of the three kings. After his third wife, according to St. Basil and St. Gregory of Nazianzus, his spouses were regarded merely as proofs of incontinence and their children were not accepted as legitimate, although they were not considered bastards either. The fourth wife was the proud Fastrada. She was a daughter of the Duke of Franconia.

If we may believe the chroniclers, she must have been haughty and exceedingly wicked, and as she ruled her husband, Charlemagne must have been cruel and wicked also during her reign. She presented him only with daughters.

Like Louis XIV in later days, Charlemagne took his wives with him on his campaigns, which led them further afield than Maria-Theresa and Madame de Montespan. They spent much more time in camps than in their palace.

Charlemagne took the education of his daughters, Rotruda, Bertha, Gisla, Theoderada and Hiltruda, the two latter the daughters of Fastrada, seriously in hand. He kept them with him and tried to make them good housekeepers. He had them taught to spin linen and wool, which did not prevent them from being great coquettes, fond of fine surroundings, silk dresses and brilliant jewels. Their coffers were full of such things. Their royal father took a delight in granting their wishes, but he would not allow them to marry. Eginhard is of opinion that as they were very beautiful and agreeable companions, the Emperor wanted to keep them with him. And, indeed, he was hardly ever away from them, never eating his supper without them, and taking them with him on his journeys and expeditions. "His sons," says Eginhard, "rode on horseback at his side, whilst his daughters followed with the last squadron of the bodyguard specially entrusted with the task of looking after them." A more powerful motive no doubt was Charlemagne's fear of making any Frankish or Gallic noble whom he admitted into his family too important a personage. We know the constant rebellions that broke out in his reign and how terrified he was of them.

The majority of his daughters took the veil, the rest married without the consent of their father, and even without the help of the Church, which, combined with the conjugal morality of the great King himself, must have made a fine home of the Palace. Thus one of his daughters had as husband the poet who called himself the fair Homer. His genius flourished in the palatine school founded by Alcuin. He became a monk and was made Abbot of Saint Riquier. His name was Angilbert, and he was afterwards canonised. Charlemagne had a very high opinion of him and entrusted him with confidential missions. By his union with Bertha he had a son, the historian Nithard, a man of worth, a clever and valiant soldier, and the best writer of annals of the first half of the ninth century.

By Count Roric, Rotruda had a son named Louis, who became Abbot of St. Denis; whilst Hiltruda with her fantastic amours made a great scandal at Court. "Charlemagne," says

370

Eginhard, "shut his eyes as if nothing had happened, not even the slightest dishonour." And to wipe out any such dishonour the Emperor made Hiltruda Abbess of Faremoutier.

Like Louis XIV, Charlemagne had little to complain of from the fair sex, with the exception of the beautiful Amalberga. It is said that the King pursued her with declarations of passionate devotion, but that the lady refused to listen to him. One day Charles seized her round the waist, she struggled and fell, and apparently broke her arm.

We have seen how badly Charles's education had been neglected. He did not know how to write. In later years he endeavoured to make good his deficiencies by studying grammar, rhetoric, dialectic and especially astronomy. Such curiosity was certainly laudable, but his studies led only to very imperfect results. According to Eginhard, his principal teacher was the famous Alcuin, an Anglo-Saxon, and the most learned man of the age. Charlemagne could, however, understand Latin, which probably means that he knew the Romance language spoken by his Gallic subjects. He appears to have learnt a little Greek.

Eginhard has given us a detailed description of the Emperor as an old man. He was strong and broad-shouldered, above the average height, tall, stout and heavy. He had a protuberant belly and a long neck. His eyes were large and vivacious, his nose was long. In old age he had beautiful white hair. With regard to his beard, it is curious that all the artists of our own day, both painters and sculptors, depict him with a magnificent beard, whilst historians are of opinion that he wore only a moustache, basing their view on the mosaic in St. John Lateran, which represents him with Pope Leo III kneeling at the foot of St. Peter's throne. But this mosaic in its present state was restored at the beginning of the seventeenth century, and before this Charlemagne was represented with a full beard.

Charlemagne had pleasing features, open and full of gaiety; in his conversation he was jovial, cordial and hail-fellow-well-met, but nevertheless gave the impression of great strength and majesty. It is curious to note that this imperious and commanding man had a shrill voice, the voice of a woman. He enjoyed admirable health till the last years of his life, when his doctors wanted to put him on a diet of boiled meat. But he grew angry with them and continued to swallow huge slices cut from joints of game roast on the spit which his officers served at his table. Without being a glutton the Emperor was a hearty eater, and used to complain of the annoyance he felt on fast days, which he, nevertheless, faithfully observed. He was a moderate drinker and evinced a lively horror of drunkenness.

There is a description of the Emperor at table, seated on a throne above the rest of the guests. A golden circlet adorned his brow. Beside him was seated Queen Liutgardis, charming and gracious. Her beautiful long bright hair escaped from beneath a golden diadem, and she wore a necklace of precious stones. The King's sons and daughters sat at table with him, the daughters unlike each other in their different types of beauty. The Nuncio, after having said grace, took his place at table with the rest. The Seneschal, surrounded by a host of cooks and bakers, began by presenting the dishes to the Emperor. There was a buzz of conversation, laughter and jokes all round. Charlemagne was full of conviviality, but at dessert the conversation became serious and theology was discussed; after which one of the Palace poets recited verses.

Or else during a meal the Emperor would listen to music or the reading of some historical narrative generally dealing with ancient times. He loved to listen to the works of St. Augustine, above all the *Civitas Dei*.

The monk of St. Gall has given us some curious details about the arrangement of the meals :

" When Charles was at table he was served by the Dukes and leaders of the various nations. As soon as he had finished his meal, the latter had theirs, and were served by the Counts, the Prefects and the high officials. When these had left the table, the civil and military officials of the Palace sat down; they were followed by the heads of the various domestic offices and last of all came the servants. And thus the people of inferior rank never had their meal before midnight."

Charlemagne was very fond of physical exercise, riding and hunting, but above all of swimming, in which he excelled. In his palace at Aix-la-Chapelle he had a large bath built in which as many as a hundred bathers could easily disport themselves with the Emperor.

The Emperor dressed very simply, and the same was said about him as was afterwards said about Louis XIV, that among his courtiers he looked the most simply dressed. He wore, says Eginhard, the national dress of the Franks, " next his skin a shirt and breeches of linen, over this a tunic bordered with silk, and breeches; leather bands round his legs and feet and, lastly, a jacket of otter or rat skin in the winter." A *sagum*, which means a mantle, of blue covered his shoulders. His gold-hilted sword always hung at his side, suspended from a belt embroidered with gold and silver.

On great feast days, or when he received ambassadors, he wore a sword with a hilt encrusted with precious stones, and refused to wear the dress of the other nations subjected to his rule. He made an exception only in the case of Rome, which was in keeping with his title of Roman Emperor, and wore the tunic and the chlamys.

" On feast days," says Eginhard in conclusion, " the Emperor wore a dress of woven gold, shoes studded with precious stones, a golden fibula to fasten his cloak and a golden diadem adorned with precious stones. But on other days his clothes differed but little from those of ordinary men or the common people."

Charlemagne with his extraordinary activity was busy night and day with public affairs, giving audience during his toilet, and while he put on his clothes and boots listening to lawyers and advocates who brought their cases to him and passing sentence as if he were seated at the tribunal; he also received the household officials and arranged domestic details.

With all the majesty of his princely bearing Charlemagne was full of affability and condescension. Everybody had easy access to him and all doors were open. He chatted amicably with the humblest of his subjects, took an interest in their affairs, taking care to find out how their families were placed and asking news of their wives and children. In all these respects there is an extraordinary likeness between him and Louis XIV.

It is very difficult to judge the exact value of his government. It certainly accomplished a great work. Just imagine the mixture, the hotch-potch of races, leaders of bands, Bishops ruling their cities, great landowners governing their domains, a whole multitude of men attached to different institutions, traditions and customs! What a medley of tongues too! And from this formidable mixture Charlemagne made a unified whole! The idea of patriotism and nationality did not exist. When the *Chanson de Roland* sang of sweet France, it was the Île de France that was meant. Charlemagne's achievement can, it is true, be explained on the score of his energy, his resolute will and his untiring activity, but also by the fact that his work remained entirely superficial. Beneath the cloak of apparent submission each social power preserved its own autonomy in the canton in which it was established. It ruled independently of the Emperor, the Bishop being the sovereign in his city, the landed proprietor in his domain and even the Count in his county.

And thus the extent and brilliance of the Carlovingian Empire, as well as its fragile nature, can be explained. Never has a great Empire, apparently so firmly built, been known to fall to pieces with such rapidity. The renaissance of art and letters which the Emperor tried to conjure into life among his people was also entirely superficial, factitious and vain. It gave birth to nothing and produced nothing; it could not produce anything. It was from the lowest strata of the nation that, after the death of Charlemagne, incomparable masterpieces were to be produced. Poets afterwards sang his glory in songs of epic grandeur, but they did so without his ever having known them or inspired them except by providing them all unwittingly with the weft of their embroidery.

The Germans, very proud of Charlemagne, " *Karl der Grosse*," have tried to annex him. But their contention is foolish. Let us consider it for a moment. It is not even true to say that Charlemagne was German born. As we have already seen there was as much Gallo-Roman as Teutonic blood in his veins. And even if he had been a Teuton he still would not have been a German. Modern France is the outcome chiefly of three races, the Ligurians, the Celts and the Teutons. The numerical importance of the Teutons is hardly less than that of the Celts. Germany too is made up of three races, the Teutons, the Celts and the Slavs. A pure Teuton might be a Frenchman and a pure Celt might be a German. One of Charlemagne's poets puts the following words in his mouth: "France witnessed my birth." And indeed he was born in Neustria, crowned at Soissons and took up his residence at Aix-la-Chapelle, which formed a point of military observation precisely against the Germans. For Aix-la-Chapelle on the west bank of the Rhine was at that time regarded as being on Gallic territory. We know the contempt with which Eginhard, the confidant, collaborator and historian of Charlemagne, speaks of the Teutons across the Rhine, and also the terrible way in which Charlemagne himself fought the Germanic peoples, ravaging without mercy with his Gallic troops the Teutonic territories which were richest in German blood—Westphalia, Hanover and Saxony. And writers of the period also made no mistake about it. Historians of the tenth, eleventh and twelfth centuries without exception identify France, together with her inhabitants, her customs and even her language, says Ferdinand Lot, with the Carlovingian race. They called the French Carlovingians, *Carolingi*. The German chroniclers called Henry I of France "the King of the Carlovingians "— *rex Carolingorum* (*Annales Altahenses*, ad. ann. 1056), to distinguish him from their own German prince.

Finally, to quote Imbart de la Tour, whilst Germany was to find "her national epic in her mythology, her native deities and her Valhalla, France was the first to make of her old Emperor the prototype of her warlike virtues and of her faith." And it was owing to the circulation of the French epics by means of the French bards who sang of Charlemagne, of Rolando and the twelve peers, that the glory of the monarch with the bushy beard finally shone forth across the Rhine.

The renown of the great Emperor of the West not only filled Europe but even crossed the frontiers of the Greek

The Dusk. Empire into Asia. Haroun-al-Raschid, Calif of Bagdad, conceived a lively admiration for him. He was the Charlemagne of the East. Under his leadership eight great battles had been fought, huge territories had been conquered, and the boundaries of his Empire extended into

Europe and Africa, from Spain to India. He had reduced the Greek Empire to the position of a tributary. Haroun, it is said, preferred the friendship of the King of the Franks to that of all the Kings of the earth, and Charlemagne, profiting by this spirit, succeeded in obtaining from him the right of protecting the Christians in the Holy Land, a privilege which France enjoys to this day. Charlemagne extended his patronage to the churches, the hospitals and the religious establishments of Syria, Egypt and Carthage in Africa.

When the King of the Franks expressed a wish for an elephant, Haroun-al-Raschid sent him the only one in his possession. It was called Abulabaz, and arrived in 801 in France, where it lived for twelve years, treated with the greatest deference. Haroun sent Charlemagne many other gifts—a tent of many colours woven of the finest linen and a clock which became even more famous than the night clock of Pepin the Short. A description of it has come down to us. The twelve hours of the day were represented by twelve doors, each of which opened at a given moment, whilst metal balls struck a sonorous basin with the number of strokes corresponding to the hour to be marked. It was a chiming clock. At twelve o'clock a miniature rider on horseback appeared at each of the twelve doors, which then closed and the whole process began again.

At the beginning of the ninth century most of Charlemagne's conquests beyond the Pyrenees had fallen again into the hands of the Saracens, and the Emperor entrusted his son Louis, King of Aquitaine with a new campaign. Louis the Pious took Lerida, but was defeated under the walls of Oliva. From this time forward the heir of the great Emperor displayed that listlessness of character which on the battlefield was far better adapted to pious devotions than to military matters. No longer did Charlemagne's lightning marches take the enemy by surprise and put them to flight before an engagement took place, or three army corps in combined manœuvres invade the land of the foe from different points of the compass, seizing whole towns and castles in their grip. After having ravaged the country in vain, Louis recrossed the Alps.

The year 812 saw a fresh rebellion in Aquitaine, which was

temporarily smothered, as the preceding one had been, in torrents of blood. "The King [Louis the Pious]," says the Astronomer, " advanced as far as Dax and ordered the instigators of the revolt to be delivered up to him. As his command was not obeyed he invaded their lands and allowed his soldiers to pillage everything."

The downfall of Charlemagne's Empire was not far off.

In Saxony the Emperor had apparently obtained results more in keeping with his desires, but by what means ! In 804 the resistance of the country died down owing to fresh transportations and deportations among the people. In this year 10,000 fresh families were uprooted from their native soil and transported to the forests of Flanders and Brabant, which they were given the task of clearing.

Then there were the Normans. Charlemagne had boats built which were grouped together in flotillas at the mouths of the rivers and his son Louis was told to take the same precautions in Aquitaine.

In this second half of his reign, after his coronation as Emperor of the West, a great lassitude seems to have overtaken Charlemagne, who in his undertakings against the Greek Empire, the Normans from the north and the Saracens of Spain was far from displaying the same zeal as he had shown even against the Aquitanians, the Lombards and the Saxons. Age had overtaken him and the look of melancholy which the monk of St. Gall says filled his eyes was perhaps the expression of a disillusioned soul. It is true that the deaths of his two eldest sons, Charles and Pepin, which from the point of view of energy of character and military talent were of much greater account than that of their brother Louis would have been, must have been a cruel blow to him.

The partition of 806 between the three brothers had to be undertaken once more. The old Emperor made another will in 811, appointing his son Louis the sole heir of the whole Empire, with the exception of Lombardy, which he kept for his grandson Bernard, the son of Pepin.

Charlemagne's eldest son, named Charles after him, had died at the age of thirty-five without issue. Pepin, King of Italy, who died when he was thirty-three, had left, in addition

377

to his son Bernard, five little girls whom Charlemagne took to his own Court. Their grace and roguishness were the joy of his old age. We have already mentioned his domestic tastes. The greater part of his property and furniture he left to the episcopal churches of his Empire.

In 813, writes the Astronomer, "the Emperor, feeling that his life was drawing to a close, and fearing that when he was taken from the things of this world the kingdom in which he had established such a fair order would fall into confusion and be assailed by tempests, sent to his son to come to him from Aquitaine."

Charlemagne was at Aix-la-Chapelle. He had summoned the Great Ones of the kingdom. He heard their counsels and begged them to serve his son faithfully and authorised him to assume the imperial title. "They all replied," says Thegan, "that it was the will of God."

"On the following Sunday," continues Thegan, "the Emperor at Aix-la-Chapelle dressed himself in all the imperial insignia, and putting a crown upon his head, walked, surrounded by the greatest pomp and magnificence, to the church he had founded. When he reached the foot of an altar raised aloft in a position dominating all the other altars, he had a golden crown placed upon it, though not the one he himself was wearing. After having prayed for a long time with his son, he addressed him in the presence of the assembled multitude of Bishops and Great Ones. He exhorted him to fear God, to govern the Church wisely and to give her his protection. He adjured him to be just. After his son had promised to do so, Charlemagne told him to pick up the crown that was on the altar and to place it on his head. Louis obeyed him, after which they heard a solemn Mass together, and then returned to the palace. Louis supported his father both on his way and on his return and all the while he was with him."

Thegan also gives us a beautiful picture of the passing of the Emperor :

"After his separation from his son Louis [who had returned to Aquitaine], Charlemagne occupied himself exclusively with prayer and almsgiving and the correction of books. In collaboration with certain Greeks and Syrians he made a careful

378

revision of the four Gospels, but in the following year he was seized with a fever on leaving the bath. On the seventh day he sent for his Arch-Chaplain Hildebold to give him the Sacraments. After receiving them he was overtaken with extreme weakness. The next day, at dawn, he made the sign of the Cross. He then joined his two feet one against the other, extended his hands on his body and, shutting his eyes, sang in a low voice this verse from Psalm xxxix : ' Lord, into Thy hands I commend my spirit.' "

Such was the end of his life, enveloped in peaceful melancholy and sweet serenity, affording a great contrast to the rough years of the eighth century. It was the brilliant sadness of the setting sun. He felt the vanity of the glories of this world, even the greatest of them. He bent over the childish heads of his grand-daughters, passing his pale hands through their long hair, and more assiduously than ever, though with great humility, like a monk in a silent monastery, applied his mind to the sacred books which in his eyes contained the truth.

The great Emperor died on the 28th of January, 814. His body was embalmed and then buried in an antique sarcophagus upon which the rape of Proserpina by Pluto was carved in bas-relief. At the entrance of the vault the following epitaph was engraved : " Here rests the body of Charlemagne, great and orthodox Emperor, who nobly extended the Kingdom of France and reigned happily for forty-six years. He died having passed three score years and ten in the year of Our Saviour 814, the 28th of January."

It is not an easy task to estimate the work accomplished by Charlemagne. It is regarded as a terrible thing that it ended only in hideous disaster.

The following is the opinion of the great historian, Camille Jullian :

" Charged with the protection of Europe against the barbarians, Charlemagne, like the Roman Empire at the height of her power, should have organised a frontier force and a flotilla of boats to keep guard; and since centralisation and unity were lacking, at least have secured and fortified the framework of his Empire. But his army was never anything more than a roaming horde and his flotilla scattered without leaving a trace behind it at the first breeze that brought the men from the north. Never was human dream so quickly dissipated as the Empire of Charlemagne. Never was the subsequent history of an Empire more lamentable than that of the years following the end of his reign. All the catastrophes that had overtaken the world on the fall of Rome were repeated— barbarian invasions, piracy on the high seas, civil wars and the dismemberment of the State."

This conclusion is very true. The question is whether it would have been possible to do any better. The Roman Empire, held up as an example by Jullian, possessed a formidable scaffolding which centuries had built up and traditions of energetic administration. Charlemagne received a kingdom in a state of chaos, given over to brigandage, as Benjamin Guérard says, "a hotch-potch of races, leaders of bands and people attached to different institutions, customs and overlords."

All that human labour, energy and good will could do, Charlemagne no doubt accomplished. In order to found a government he possessed but two supports—religious sentiment and the feeling of loyalty. But the leaders of religion, the Bishops, were the first to disorganise everything; and as for loyalty, we all know how fragile a thing this is when it is not maintained by fear of a powerful hand and hopes of fresh benefits to come.

The common traditions of national life had not yet been formulated. How could they possibly have flourished during the exploitation of Rome? How could they ever have come into being under the infant, bloodstained and clammy despotism of the Merovingians?

The prince who at the age of thirty-six was forced to take upon his shoulders the huge burden of his paternal heritage had given proof of solid qualities in the government of the kingdom of Aquitaine, though it is true that the greater part of the credit must be attributed to his father's guidance. The sweetness and at the same time the weakness of his character had, moreover, already been displayed. He possessed four important villas in Aquitaine, great Crown domains which are mentioned in the capitularies. He moved from one to the other to Doué-la-

Louis the Pious.

Fontaine (on the borders of Anjou and Poitou) from Doué à Chasseneuil (Agenois) from Chasseneuil to Audiac (Saintonge) then to Ebreuil (Auvergne) and back again to Doué. In each villa there was sufficient for the needs of his household without oppressing the people by the exercise of the right of hospitality, and he was even able to feed his army himself. " And although his men," writes the Astronomer, " did not like this method, the Prince, having regard for the poverty of those who paid this tax, and the cruelty of those who exacted it, preferred to provide for the needs of his men by means of his domains than to cause suffering to his subjects."

On taking up residence in the palace of Aix-la-Chapelle on the 27th of February, 814, Louis busied himself with the task of setting it in order. According to the Astronomer, he turned out " the crowd of women who filled it, with the exception of those required for the royal service." He begged his sisters to go and take up their posts at the head of their Abbeys and tried to drive out their lovers. The latter resisted his efforts and one of them was killed whilst the other had his eyes put out. The Imperial Court was to be conducted like a monastery.

" The Emperor Louis," says Thegan, " was of average height; he had large bright eyes, an open countenance, a long straight nose, a broad chest and wide shoulders and strong arms, and was skilled above all in shooting with the bow and the javelin." With his vigorous body, he was agile and indefatigable, though in this body made for battle there dwelt a timid and disconsolate soul, given over to devotion. His contemporaries called him Louis the Pious and historians Louis the Debonair. He remained for hours prostrate on the stones of the churches muttering prayers and weeping. It had been his desire to become a monk like his great-uncle Carloman, but Charlemagne had prevented him. Nevertheless Carloman always remained his ideal. And he was not mistaken with regard to his true vocation. For he was made for the peaceful life of an obedient monk rather than for the government of a tumultuous State.

Like his father Louis dressed very simply, though he also followed his example in displaying great magnificence on solemn occasions. In such cases he showed himself to his loyal subjects, to ambassadors and foreign princes, in a doublet and hose embroidered and fringed with gold, and wearing a golden baldrick, a gold-hilted sword, and boots and cloak studded with gold, and on his head a golden crown gleaming with precious stones.

"He never laughed," writes Thegan; "nobody ever saw his white teeth, even when on feast days for the amusement of the people, mountebanks, mimes and buffoons passed along the table, accompanied by singers and players of instruments; and the people, feeling the gravity of the King, only laughed restrainedly themselves. Everywhere he went he distributed alms and welcomed the sick whom he immediately had nursed." He was learned and knew Latin and Greek, but he was above all versed in a knowledge of the Scriptures. St. Benedict of Aniane had been his master and remained his friend.

His chief pleasure was hunting, above all in the month of August, "when the deer are fattest and up to the boar hunting season" (Thegan). The chroniclers also depict him enjoying the pleasures of fishing.

Like all soft natures who suffer from weakness of will, Louis the Pious allowed his intimates to dominate him—his councillors, his old teachers, sometimes exceedingly mediocre personages, and afterwards his second wife, Judith of Bavaria.

"He gave himself over too much into the hands of his councillors," writes Thegan, "owing to his extreme devotion to psalm-singing and reading." But if he had been endowed with a strong will and an energetic character all the psalms in the world would not have made him flinch.

His first councillors were his father's illustrious ministers, Adalard, Abbot of Corbie, and Wala. Eginhard retired into a monastery. Nithard, Charlemagne's grandson, says that Adalard was the predominating influence in his circle. "The Emperor loved him so much," he writes, "that he did all that Adalard desired. The latter, little mindful of the public weal, tried to please everybody. He persuaded the King to distribute honours and public lands solely with a view to his own private advantage, and thus ruined the Empire."

Was this spoliation of the royal domain the work of the Abbot of Corbie, against whom Nithard seems to have nursed a bitter hatred? We have already seen how Louis, as King

382

of Aquitaine, had stripped bare his domains for the sake of his leudes, partly from weakness of character and partly in order to attach them to him by the bestowal of benefices. As Emperor he continued the same policy.

After remaining at Court for some years, the Abbot of Corbie returned to his monastery and the influence of Benedict of Aniane became predominant, and inaugurated a sharp reaction against the government of the late Emperor.

" The only crime of which those who were jealous of him could accuse him," writes the Astronomer, " was his excess of clemency."

And indeed this was a grave mistake in that bitter atmosphere. Everywhere local forces and private individuals were organising. Depending on the support of those whom they grouped more and more closely about them, of whom they were the leaders, and of whom they became from day to day ever more the true monarchs, the great landed proprietors, whether beneficiaries or immunists, Counts, Abbots or Bishops, no longer recognised any other country than that small country consisting of the more or less extensive lands forming the County, the Abbey, domain or seignorial villa over which they exercised their authority. "Each individual pursued his own course," says Nithard. Benjamin Guérard holds the weakness of Louis the Pious responsible for the general disorganisation. Fustel de Coulanges comes nearer the truth in maintaining that Charlemagne himself would have done no better. The discord, war and fear of danger experienced by the country at the advent of a few bands of adventurers—the Normans— were not the work of the Emperor Louis; the state of society was primarily responsible. The trees that grow in a forest and make a tumultuous rustling are not the work of the owner, but the result of the beech and oak seeds that have shot up out of the ground, the product of the soil and of the rain that has fallen from the clouds, the light shed by the sun and the air breathed in by the leaves, that is to say, the terrible disorganisation produced by the chaotic thrust of all the local forces could not have been occasioned by a single man, whatever his policy may have been, it could only arise from the social conditions forming the life of the nation.

Let us consider the Bishops who provided Charlemagne with his chief instrument of government. One of them, Jonas, Bishop of Orleans, a contemporary of Louis the Pious, writes in connection with the publication of the capitularies : " As soon as the King has published an edict, there is not a man who does not attend open-mouthed or thinks of aught else than obeying the behests of the Prince." Well and good; but the Bishops were to be the first not to obey. They became more and more like the Bishops whom Charles Martel had fought, " tyrants greedy of power," power which they did not hesitate to extend by force of arms. They convoked Assemblies like the King, administered justice in public under the elm in the square. " The clergy of Aquitaine," writes the Astronomer, " applied themselves more to the management of horses, to military evolutions and the exercise of arms than to divine worship."

Like the Counts, the Bishops had been invested with their authority in the cities as delegates of the King, and now, like them, they exercised it as their own personal right. They even usurped the title of Count, when they did not claim it from the King, together with the rights appertaining thereto, the administration of justice from the highest to the lowest jurisdiction, the imposition of taxes, Customs dues, tolls and market charges, and the right of minting money. They maintained small armies at the head of which they paraded with helmets on their heads and built strongholds. The Abbots of the great monasteries, who sometimes ruled over a population of 20,000 to 30,000 souls, did likewise. And the extraordinary fact is that Louis the Pious, who was more religious than nine-tenths of the high dignitaries of his Church, tried to make these higher clergy return to the dress, the practices and the way of life suitable to their estate. As a matter of fact the prelates consented, at a General Assembly held at Aix-la-Chapelle in 817 at the instigation of the King, to publish a magnificent volume in which rules for the use of their monks and country clergy were carefully formulated; but when Louis suggested that they should reform themselves, they found it more expedient to attack him in the exercise of his authority, and finally to subject him to the most terrible humiliation to which a King has ever been exposed.

" The King must be outside the Church, not in his capacity as a man but as a sovereign ! " became the general cry. That same Jonas, Bishop of Orleans, who had waxed so eloquent on the subject of the obedience due to the capitularies, began to speak even more convincingly about the royal abuse of power which had to be stopped. The King was no longer to have the right of appointing Bishops and Abbots as Pepin and Charlemagne had done; the patrimony of the Church, that is to say, the huge domains of the Bishops and Abbots, could no longer be invaded and placed in profane hands, as had been the case under Charles Martel; all ecclesiastical property that had been secularised was to be returned; tithes were to be duly levied and the produce from the fines and confiscations imposed for misdemeanours on the part of the clergy were to be returned to them, whilst fresh donations and immunities were demanded. The shade of Charlemagne must have turned in his gold-encircled vault. Louis the Pious thought he could head the attack made upon him by these helmeted prelates; but the result was disastrous.

In 817, writes Thegan, " the Emperor Louis appointed his son Lothar to succeed him after his death in all the kingdoms which he held from his father and to bear the title of Emperor. On account of this all the other brothers were very angry." These sons were Pepin and Louis, the sons of Louis' marriage with Ermengarde, daughter of Count Ingoramnus. It was necessary to appease them, and Louis accordingly gave to Pepin Aquitaine and a part of Burgundy and to Louis Bavaria.

Fustel de Coulanges has described the nature of this partition. Lothar, the eldest, was to be the sole political head, sole Emperor. His juniors were to render him obeisance and to play no part in foreign affairs without his consent. They could not even marry without his authority; but in the territories assigned to each of them, they were allowed full exercise of suzerain rights, they could dispose of benefices, appoint royal officials, and choose Bishops and Abbots.

" And thus," writes Fustel de Coulanges, " all the loyal subjects of the Empire were divided between them, recommending themselves and binding themselves to one or the other by oaths of fealty. Each of the three brothers thus became, not a sovereign in the modern sense of the word, but the chief of loyal vassals."

Meanwhile, Bernard, King of Italy, and nephew of the Emperor Louis, had rebelled against the authority of his uncle, and invaded Gaul with his supporters. Louis marched out against the rebels as far as Chalons-sur-Saône, where he captured their leader (December 817). Condemned to death by an Assembly of the Great Ones held at Aix-la-Chapelle, Bernard, together with Reginar, who had been a Count of the Palace, had his eyes burnt out. The Bishops who had taken part in the conspiracy were deposed. Bernard and Reginar died a few days afterwards. Nithard holds Bertmund, a serf of the royal domain, whom Charlemagne had made Count of Lyons, responsible for these cruelties.

But Louis had been frightened, and his timid and retiring nature led him to think it necessary to safeguard himself against any similar outbreaks. He had three brothers, born to Charlemagne by three different wives; they were called Drogo, Hugh and Theodoric. "He was afraid," says Nithard, "that they might imitate Bernard and rebel against him." He therefore made them take the tonsure and shut them up in monasteries, where, nevertheless, he concerned himself about their education and their future. Drogo became Archbishop of Metz, and Hugh, who became Abbot of Saint-Quentin, died in 844 sword in hand, in battle against the Saracens, as did also Archbishop Turpin.

In 818 Louis the Pious lost his wife Ermengarde and wasted no time in marrying again, this time taking to wife Judith, daughter of Count Welf of Bavaria, for whom he had conceived a passionate attachment (819). The beauty of this young woman, her grace and intelligence, are mentioned by all writers of the time.

The soul of Louis the Pious was like a trembling leaf in his body. The rough exterior of a Frankish warrior concealed the temperament of a neurasthenic. His piety savoured of a mysticism which led to extremes of passionless exaltation. He used to hear strange noises at night and natural phenomena filled him with fright. Thunder, lightning and hail were all things of terror for him. "These prodigies," says the Astronomer, "used to terrify the Emperor, and he would order

386

prayer and fasting, and distribute much alms in order to appease the divinity," and to complete his sense of security he took to drink.

After the tragic death of Bernard, King of Italy, Louis was haunted with remorse, which was a source of fresh libations, more frequent and more abundant than the occasional bumpers due to the agency of hail and thunder. Recent researches have attributed to drunkenness the intellectual and moral lack of balance of the Emperor Louis.

In 822 he summoned a General Assembly at Attigny; Bishops, Abbots and clerics of every rank assembled there in great numbers, as well as the Counts and the Great Ones. Louis went from one to the other, as his father had been accustomed to do, but, unlike his father, he described to everyone the torments of his soul and the remorse which racked him, telling them about the death of Bernard, King of Italy, and the history of his brothers Drogo, Hugh and Theodoric, and other sins that lay heavy on his conscience, as well as reverting to his father and the sins of Charlemagne and those of his grandfather and great-grandfather, Charles Martel, whose place in the tomb had been taken by the devil. The clergy, who had just published their ideas regarding the power of the King in *L'Institution Royale* by Bishop Jonas of Orleans and *La Liberté des Élections* by Deacon Florus of Lyons, eagerly seized the opportunity of carrying them into practice and bringing to book this Emperor who wanted to reform them and reduce them to the practice of religious duties.

It did not take long to persuade the unfortunate man that there was only one way of unburdening his soul of the load of crime with which it was bowed down, and that was by public confession, confession as public as the crimes themselves had been. Louis began by releasing from their Abbeys his three brothers Drogo, Hugh and Theodoric and reconciling himself with them. And, in the presence not only of the Bishops and the Great Ones, but before a vast concourse of people, the Emperor made a solemn confession of his " crimes." " His shame was such," writes the Astronomer, " that it seemed as if all the pains and penalties which had been lawfully inflicted upon the guilty were solely the result of his cruelty."

The unfortunate monarch took off his crown with his own hands. In the following year, on the 13th of June, 823, Queen Judith gave birth in Frankfort to a son, who afterwards became Charles the Bald.

Whilst in Gaul the Bishops were concerned with destroying the imperial power, Rome still held it in respect. Eugenius II died in 827. His successor, Valentinus, survived him only a month. Gregory IV was elected in his place, but his consecration was postponed. Rome awaited the approval of the Emperor. "This monarch," says the Astronomer, "having given his consent to the choice of the clergy and the people, Gregory was consecrated Pope."

Louis the Pious took his royal duties seriously to heart. During the lifetime of his father, when he was King of Aquitaine, he already used to set aside three days in the week for hearing cases brought by his subjects, listening to their grievances and pronouncing patriarchal judgment. When he became Emperor his other duties did not leave him so much leisure, and he announced that he would hold audience once a week. "We would have you know," he said in one of his capitularies, "that every week we shall set aside one day to hear cases brought before us in our palace."

But the clergy would not allow him to recover himself. At the Council of Paris, in 829, the Bishops discussed the very nature of the royal power. They even dared to attack the principle of heredity, and to decide that Kings did not hold their titles from their ancestors, but from God alone. They also had the audacity to congratulate Lothar and Louis, the Emperor's two eldest sons, for having rebelled against their father and for having appealed to the episcopal body, after which they congratulated them on having understood that "priests shall judge Kings."

This was the beginning of the great struggle which was destined to last a thousand years, until the end of the *ancien régime* in France, concerning the origin of the royal power, and which Philip the Fair tried to decide with the rude energy we know.

And indeed in this year 829 Louis the Pious decided upon the action which was destined to unloose such terrible storms.

888

At Worms, in the presence of his two sons, Louis and Lothar, he handed over to his youngest son Charles, son of the Empress Judith, the whole of Alemannia, Alsace and Rhoetia, together with part of Burgundy, with the title of Duke. In their fury Lothar and Louis left their father and together with their brother Pepin openly rebelled against him. This was one of the great dramas of history pregnant with vast issues which it is very difficult for us to judge, so different were the circumstances from anything we can imagine to-day.

According to the ideas of the age nobody could deny the Emperor's fourth son his rights to the paternal succession, but the partition was destined to bring the most terrible troubles in its train.

The authority of the monarch was not exercised over territories with fixed boundaries, but over men bound by ties of recommendation and fealty. When Louis the Pious declared his son Charles Duke of Burgundy, he did not mean that he was to reign over the Burgundian territory, but that by means of ties of fealty he was to be suzerain over all the Great Ones, all the Bishops, Abbots, Counts and nobility of the country. These ties were cemented by personal oaths. And this was the reason why the Carlovingian kings had the sons who were to succeed them proclaimed King during their own lifetime, binding their subjects to them by the oath of fealty. We must bear in mind that benefices conferred were temporary, and that they came to an end with the death alike of the giver and the receiver; and the same arrangement applied to the bonds of patronage and fealty. In order to avoid the risk of a terrific upheaval it was necessary for the King to secure the continuation of these bonds in the hands of his heirs, and this as much for the security of his subjects as for the King himself. But what happened when, like Louis the Pious at Worms in 829, anyone modified a partition that had already been made and ratified by thousands of oaths? It meant infinite trouble for the Empire. The Emperor not only modified the territorial arrangement in connection with Pepin, Lothar and Louis to the advantage of the newly-born prince, but he brought confusion into the long chain of faithful subjects which had formed behind each of the former, and thus led to numberless and incalculable complica-

tions. One of Lothar's subjects placed by the new partition in
Charles the Bald's share, might be his enemy, and yet he was
called upon to swear him the oath of fealty and allegiance. It
was impossible for a man to swear fealty to two suzerains at
once ; or again one man might hold two or three benefices from
a prince one of which the new partition, by reducing or modifying
the latter's share, might place in the hands of another suzerain.
And this is precisely the reproach brought by one of the Bishops
against Louis the Pious. " You have upset everything, and
have made the people murmur against the various oaths you
demand of them." And Louis himself, in another public confession which the Bishops extorted from him, accused himself
" of having disturbed the peace by demanding contradictory
oaths from the people."

But the struggle had been unloosed and reverberated in the
furthest corners of the kingdom ; and it was destined to be
never ending. Once more Fustel de Coulanges gives us an
admirable description. As oaths of fealty were sworn to a
certain overlord personally, war broke out everywhere.
Historians describe the quarrels of Louis' sons with their father,
and of the brothers between themselves ; but it must be remembered that each of these men had behind him long chains
of faithful subjects who encouraged them to fight and whose
appetites and desires they were bound to satisfy. This terrible
conflict between the members of the imperial family was only
the prototype of a countless number of local struggles repeated
at various points throughout the kingdom.

The sons who were preparing to march in arms against their
father began by attacking the Empress Judith, the mother of
the newly-born prince, whose advent had brought so much
trouble upon the Empire. Louis had chosen as Chamberlain
Bernard, Count of the Spanish March. The Chamberlain, as
we have already said, arranged the public finances under the
superintendence of the Queen, and his functions brought him into
touch with her. This was made a pretext for circulating the sort
of rumour it is easy to guess. Pepin, the son of Louis the Pious,
gathered together a large army and marched as far as Verberie.
He had with him the Arch-Chaplain, Hilduin, and Jesse, Bishop
of Amiens, together with other great lords. He forced Count

Bernard to retire at once and sent the Empress Judith into the convent of Sainte Marie de Laon. The rebels went to fetch her from there in order to extract from her the promise that she would persuade the Emperor to adopt the tonsure and put on the robes of a monk, whilst she herself was to take the veil. Judith, on reaching the Emperor, faithfully kept her word; but the latter was very far from allowing himself to be persuaded. He was quite content that his wife should become a nun, but he himself resolutely refused to give up his sceptre and crown. And Judith was obliged to return, as she had promised, to the conspirators, who shut her up in the convent of Sainte Radegund.

Lothar, the Emperor's eldest son, on his arrival from Italy, approved of all that Pepin had done. And Louis the Pious, says the Astronomer in conclusion, had nothing but the title of Emperor left.

Lothar and Pepin held their father in strict surveillance. "They forced him to live with some monks," writes Nithard, "in order to accustom him to the monastic life." Bernard, the High Chamberlain, had sought refuge in Septimania, but Lothar and Louis succeeded in seizing his brother Heribert, and had his eyes put out.

The higher clergy had made common cause with the rebels "who had understood that priests may judge kings." Hilduin henceforward always appeared surrounded by men at arms.

In April 833 Louis the Pious was driven to the cruel necessity of raising an army and marching out against his sons. A meeting took place in the neighbourhood of Colmar, at a spot called the Red Field, "Rothefeld." Pope Gregory had come from Italy to act as mediator. The two armies were facing each other, when the majority of the Emperor's soldiers left him and went over to the camp of his sons. Lothar took his father to Compiègne, after having sent the Empress to Italy.

"Lothar conducted his father to the palace of Compiègne," writes Thegan, "and there in the presence of the Bishops and several other lords he subjected him to a cruel persecution (October 833). The Bishops ordered him to go to a monastery for the rest of his days. He refused. They then chose an impudent man, Ebbon, Archbishop of Rheims (this Ebbon was a man of low birth who owed his advancement to Louis) to torment the unfortunate Emperor." Louis was dragged to the monastery of Saint Medard at Soissons, where before a crowd of people " the Bishops took away the sword from his side, and by order of those who were his servants, clad him in a hair shirt." The unfortunate Emperor was condemned to give a recital of the crimes with which he was charged and of which the prelates had drawn up a formidable list, and then to divest himself of his arms before the assembled people, after which he was shut up in the monastery of Prüm. The field near Colmar, where Louis the Pious had been abandoned and betrayed by his followers, the Red Field, was from that day called the Field of Lies, " *Lügenfeld.*"

Having made himself master of the Empire, it was not long before Lothar by his arrogance aroused the displeasure of his brother Louis, whom he had reduced to the possession of Germany and Alsace. Louis left Bavaria where he chanced to be and was joined by Pepin, and a reaction took place in favour of the father who had been despoiled, maltreated and outraged by his children. Summoned to set his father at liberty, Lothar refused, saying that he could not be held responsible for the imprisonment of the Emperor, " seeing that it was the result of judgment by the Bishops " (the Astronomer), and seeing, moreover, that his brothers Pepin and Louis, who now posed as his champions, had been the first to deliver him up. But Louis the Younger had superior forces at his disposal. Blockaded at Saint Denis, Lothar was obliged to set his father free (February 834). So strong was the reaction in favour of the spurned Emperor that Lothar was obliged in his turn to retire to Italy, after having declared that he would submit himself to his father's commands and in future bow before him. Louis the Pious insisted that the Bishops who had pronounced his fall should reinstate him with their own hands, and at Saint Denis, amid the acclamations of the people, the prelates replaced the purple mantle upon the shoulders of their imperial victim and girt him once more with his sword. Everybody seemed to be overjoyed, but what filled the Emperor with the greatest satisfaction, greater even than his solemn reinstatement, were the celestial phenomena which accompanied it—violent storms had raged unceasingly and the rain had swollen the rivers to such an extent as to make them unnavigable, but the moment the Emperor was reconciled with the Church the elements calmed down in benign concert and the wind fell, it seemed as if all nature were appeased in serene beatitude, as though in harmony with the joy of the people and the happiness of the King.

On the 2nd of February, at the Assembly of Thionville, the Bishops who had been responsible for the downfall of the Emperor were condemned—Ebbon, Archbishop of Rheims, had to resign his episcopacy; Agobard, Archbishop of Lyons, was deposed, and the rest had fled to Italy with Lothar. The re-enthronement took place on the 28th of February, 835, in the Church of St. Stephen at Metz, after which the seven Archbishops delivered seven sermons. Unfortunately intrigues immediately broke out afresh. It was a question as to who should be second in the Empire, that is to say, first, seeing how feeble was the Emperor and how ruined his prestige. Bernard, the Grand Chamberlain, returned to favour and wanted to rule everything. A simple monk, named Gondebaud, who had worked cleverly for the restoration of the Emperor, had similar pretensions; and the two sons who had become loyal, Louis the Younger and Pepin, expected to govern in the name of their father after having obtained, by a fresh partition, an increase in the portion which at the previous division of the kingdom had been allotted to each.

Violence, pillage and depredations of all kinds raged in various parts of the Empire. The Normans made their appearance along the coasts, from whence they penetrated into the heart of the country, burning, murdering and devastating the land, after which they returned laden with booty. The Saracens, on their side, landed on the coasts of the Mediterranean. Louis sent commissioners to various parts of the Empire " to suppress brigandage, authorising them," says the Astronomer, " in order to drive out the robbers, to demand help from the Counts and the Bishops," who, however, paid no heed. And then the cursed question of the partitions cropped up again.

Judith considered that the portion allotted to her son Charles was not sufficiently important. And Louis, unable to refuse his wife anything, in 837 assigned to the boy who was to be

Charles the Bald all the territory situated between the Atlantic, the Seine and the Rhine; and in September 838 he had him proclaimed King and crowned at Quierzy-sur-Oise, again increasing his territory as far as the Loire. He deprived Louis the Younger, who, of all his sons, had shown him the most affection, of Thuringia, Saxony and all that he still held of Austrasia. Pepin died on the 13th of December 838, and the Emperor asked Lothar, who was still in Italy, to be the guardian of his son Charles. Lothar accepted, and arrived at Worms on the 30th of May, 839, when a fresh partition took place, once more at the expense of Louis the Younger, who was far away on his Bavarian estates, unable to defend his rights before his father, whose weakness of character made him the plaything of those about him.

And thus the Empire was divided by Louis into two sections, the eastern portion, Austrasia, being assigned to Lothar, together with the title of Emperor, but without the right of supremacy over his brother Charles, who obtained the western portion, Neustria and Aquitaine. But the Emperor was chiefly concerned with the appearance of a comet in the heavens: " Let us walk in a better path," he exclaimed all trembling at the sight, and thereupon set to work to drink a vast quantity of wine to drown his fear. He passed his nights in prayer, had innumerable Masses sung and distributed alms in abundance.

Louis was at Poitiers engaged in suppressing a revolt in Aquitaine. The Aquitanians had refused to accept the partition of Worms which placed them under the authority of Charles the Bald, and had proclaimed as their King Pepin II, son of their own King Pepin, who had just died. Another terrible war broke out. " We may judge of its fury," writes the Astronomer, "by the traces of it which still remain." At Poitiers the Emperor learnt that his son Louis, angry at having been despoiled of his States, had invaded the territory that had been taken from him at the head of a band of Thuringians and Saxons. In spite of his age and the infirmities which bowed him down— dropsy and an affection of the lungs—and the rigours of winter, the old Emperor set out at the head of his army. He forced Louis to retire again to Bavaria and to that part of his domains that had been left to him.

394

As his malady had grown worse, Louis the Pious embarked on the Main, and halted on an island in the neighbourhood of Ingelheim. He felt, says his faithful biographer, that his courage was forsaking him. His poor body was falling to pieces and he died of an ulcer on the 20th of June, 840. His brother Drogo, Archbishop of Metz, whom he had forced to go into Holy Orders, affectionately attended him in his last moments. Before delivering up his soul he pointed to the window with trembling hands, calling out in agony, " Houss ! Houss ! " a popular Teutonic expression meaning, " Avaunt ! Avaunt ! " " Whence it seems," says the Astronomer, " that he had seen the devil." He was sixty-four years of age and was buried at Metz by the side of his sainted ancestor Arnulf.

Benjamin Guérard passes a very harsh verdict on Louis the Debonair, " He may have been a good fellow, if you will, even after he had had the eyes of his nephew Bernard put out; but let us not be afraid to say that he was a most hateful monarch, without faith, without firmness and without heart, who thoroughly deserved all the humiliations to which he was subjected and who was capable of destroying an Empire older and better consolidated than that of Charlemagne."

But the great mediævalist goes too far. The work of Charlemagne was fragile on account of its very magnitude. It was impossible to preserve it. Certainly Louis the Pious was an unfortunate character. But he had a right feeling about the part he was called upon to play, though it crushed him. He had been rightly inspired when, in his youth, he had wished to become a monk, owing to the admiration he felt for his great-uncle Carloman—a really great man, who, with Charles Martel, was the most illustrious member of his family. He was ruled by his wife Judith for whom he had an old man's love. He allowed himself to be mastered by the higher clergy, who strangely abused the ascendancy they had over him. And the death of Bernard ! He allowed those about him to do as they pleased, owing to his weakness of character and the feeling of fear with which the rebellion had filled him, after which he was tortured with remorse for the rest of his days. It is perhaps true, as Dr. Janselm maintains, that he was a drunkard. In the latter part of his life, that tortured, torn and humiliated life, like so

895

many others who cannot find in themselves the strength to recover, Louis sought in semi-intoxication an alleviation of a burden too heavy to bear.

But, in many cases, Louis the Pious displayed a majesty of gait and bearing that was quite Shakespearean, reminding us of King Lear, whose old age was also made desolate by his children. And at the end what an impressive nobility he displayed when, with a sudden outburst of energy, he left Aquitaine whose rebellion he had quelled at the head of his faithful supporters, and with his men-at-arms set out for Germany, afflicted with dropsy and a painful asthma which caught his breath, through the snow and the cold, to go and fight one of his own sons and to die in a distant land, on an island in the Main, in the arms of the brother to whom he had once dealt a heavy blow, and at the last moment with his haggard eyes, dilated in the agony of death, filled with the hideous, horrible and terrifying vision of a devil coming in by the window to carry him off.

Louis the Pious, on his deathbed, had sent the golden crown to Lothar, the Emperor designate, and exhorted him not to forget the protection he had promised Judith, who would be left a widow, and her son Charles. But Lothar on the death of his father set covetous eyes upon the whole Empire, since Louis had been reduced to the kingdom of Bavaria and Charles to that of Aquitaine. Louis, surnamed the German, after the States which had been assigned to him, joined forces with his brother Charles and the struggle began.

Charles the Bald.

Each of the two parties tried to win over the greatest possible number of adherents, among them the most powerful; for it was not a question of nationalities. Louis the German, at the head of a strong army, set out to join Charles, who had gone to Aix-la-Chapelle to celebrate the festival of Easter (17th of April, 841). A detail given us by Nithard bears witness to the state of disorganisation into which the whole of France had fallen. " As King Charles was coming out of his bath and was about to dress, messengers arrived from Aquitaine bearing the royal crown and the ornaments for divine worship. It was indeed astonishing that such a small band of men were able to traverse such a wide stretch of country infested by brigands given over to pillage."

Nithard, the grandson of Charlemagne, was concerned in the events which followed. He was one of the negotiators of the agreement of Verdun and his account is invaluable.

The two brothers met in Burgundy together with their armies. Louis' forces were exhausted by their long march and weakened by lack of horses. " Nevertheless," writes Nithard, " they were afraid that if Louis abandoned his brother Charles they would hand down a dishonoured name to posterity."

At the beginning of June 841 Louis and Charles with their men were in the district of Chalon-sur-Saône, whilst Lothar was in Auxerre. Louis and Charles once more tried to come to an agreement, but Lothar prolonged the negotiations—he was awaiting contingents from Aquitaine sent by Pepin II.

In Lothar's army there were many Neustrians—the Abbot of Saint Denis and the Count of Paris, " loyal subjects " from the district of Chartres who were bound to the Emperor by oath. The reinforcements from Pepin II had arrived, but a large number of Aquitanians had attached themselves to the fortunes of Charles the Bald. But Lothar and Louis also shared the forces from Germany. Lothar in addition had contingents from Italy.

Each of these faithful subjects had come to defend his own lands, his offices and his tenures and desired their increase at the expense of the conquered. Victory would secure the conqueror a vast quantity of land, and a number of counties and bishoprics for distribution. Nithard says quite clearly, when mentioning the chiefs who were facing each other : " To yield would have meant betraying those who had placed their trust in them." Apart from any idea of race or nationality each man had attached himself to the party to which his interests or his sympathies called him. The more acute among them waited, before taking sides, to ascertain which was the stronger. A battle was fought on the 25th of June, 841, at a place called Fontanet in the neighbourhood of Auxerre, which has not been identified with certainty. The carnage was terrible. Four thousand men were killed. Each side claimed the victory. None the less the battle was a defeat for Lothar, whose pretensions

897

to supremacy were destroyed; but the campaign was continued, and the two brothers, Louis and Charles, resolved to bind themselves to each other and to their supporters by a solemn oath; whence that famous document, the oaths of Strasbourg, the most ancient writing in the French tongue that has come down to us. We reproduce it below. It shows what the French language was towards the middle of the eleventh century. Louis the German gave his oath in the French language, out of regard for Charles' army, and conversely, Charles swore his oath in German in order to be understood by the army of Louis the German, which consisted chiefly of Germans.

Louis, the elder, spoke first :

"*Pro Deo amur et pro christian poblo et nostro commun salvament, d'ist di en avant, in quant Deus savir et podir me dunat, si salvarai eo cist meon fradre Karlo, et in adhiudha et cadhuna cosa, si cum om per dreit son fratra salvar dift, in o quid il mi altrezi fazet ; et ab Ludher nul plaid numquam prindrai qui, meon vol, cist meon fradre Karle in damno sit.*"

Which meant : " For the love of God and the salvation of the people of Christendom and of ourselves, from this day forward, so long as God shall give me knowledge and power, yea indeed, I will support this my brother Charles with my help in all things, as one should by right support one's brother, and that he may do the same by me, and from Lothar I shall accept no plea which, by my connivance, shall be to the disadvantage of this my brother Charles."

Charles repeated the same oath in German, after which each of the two camps in their turn made the following promise, this time each in their own language :

" *Si Lodhuwigs* "—said the partisans of Charles—" *sagrament, que son fradre Karlo jurat, conservat, et Karlus, meos sendra, de suo part lo suon fraint, si io returnar non l'int pois, ne io ne neuls cui eo returnar int pois, in nulla aiudha contra Lodhuwig nun li ier.*"

Which means : " If Louis keeps the oath he has sworn to his brother Charles but if Charles, my master, for his part, breaks his, and I cannot deter him from so doing, neither to him nor to any whom I cannot deter shall I be of any help against Louis."

With the transposition of the words " Louis " and " Charles," the same oath was sworn in German by the followers of Louis the German.

The two armies were close to each other. Whilst negotiations were being carried on with Lothar, they spent their time in playing various games, for the sake of exercise. The two Kings were present as well as Nithard, who gives us the following description :

" The crowd stood all round to watch the sport, and first an equal number of Saxons, Gascons, Austrasians and Bretons, from either side, charged rapidly against each other as if they were going to fight. Then one side took to flight, protecting themselves with their bucklers, and pretending to want to make good their escape, but suddenly they turned on those who were pursuing them, until at last the two Kings, followed by their young men, shouting aloud on their galloping chargers and brandishing their lances, gave pursuit first to one side and then to the other." This, says Nithard, " was a spectacle worth looking at, on account of the high birth of those who took part in it and the moderation displayed."

The three brothers finally decided upon the partition of Verdun (June 843). This Verdun was not Verdun on the Meuse, whose name has been immortalised by the late war, but Verdun sur-Doubs in Saône-et-Loire. Nithard expressly says : " Verdun, not far from Mâcon."

"Louis the German and Charles the Bald," says Nithard, " each chose twelve of their own men, *and I was one of them*, in order to divide the kingdom among them as they thought fit. Less account was made in this partition of the fertility or equality of the portions than of their proximity [which means no doubt the frontiers] and their suitability [meaning possibly the suitability to each other of the various districts]." This was very far removed from preceding partitions in which the recipients had been guided by very different motives. There were two partitions, of which the second alone is of interest, and took place in the month of August 843. The text of the original treaty has been lost. Lothar, the eldest, kept the title of Emperor, but without the right of exercising supremacy over his two brothers, who became his equals. It was, as a matter of fact, precisely the same as the arrangement made by Louis the Pious. His domain included Carlovingian Italy and a strip of about a hundred and fifty miles in breadth stretching from the North Sea to the Alps and the Mediterranean. Louis the German received the countries situated east of the Rhine together with the districts of Spiers, Worms and Mayence on the left bank " by reason of the wine they produced," a curious echo of the old Merovingian partitions which gave to each of the claimants, who were heavy drinkers, in addition to their share in the northern districts, which were good recruiting areas, territories in the southern cantons with their beautiful vineyards.

This partition, so simple in appearance, became so complicated in detail, that even in the middle of territories assigned to one or other of the brothers isolated patches of land were under the rule of one of the others.

Lothar bemoaned the loss of the imperial suzerainty and the small size of the portion assigned to him, and maintained that it would not provide him with the wherewithal to indemnify those who had attached themselves to his cause. He also deprived of their charges and benefices all those who, once his dependants, had been forced to abandon his side after his defeat at Fontanet.

Charles the Bald, the grandson of Charlemagne, whose birth had brought such great afflictions upon the State, was an interesting figure. He was intelligent, brave, active and unscrupulous, never hesitating to enter into the most solemn alliances, only to break them as soon as his policy demanded it. He was cultured and a good theologian, of which he was very proud. Eric, Bishop of Auxerre, regarded him as a philosopher. And indeed, the intellectual revival which he patronised was far more important than any which appeared under Charlemagne. The theories of Jean Scot on free will are still held in honour and quoted. There were already signs that speculative thought was in process of cultivation and endeavouring to comply with scientific rules.

On the 19th of December, 843, Charles married Hermentruda, daughter of Eudo, Count of Orleans, and grand-daughter of Adalard, who had played such a significant part at the Court of Charlemagne and afterwards in the reign of Louis the

400

Debonair. Charles the Bald, says Nithard, made this marriage in the hope of attracting the greater part of the nation to himself. A curious assertion, for, in that case, what had become of the royal power, seeing that the King was reduced to marrying one of his subjects in order to strengthen by means of his wife's family clients the supreme power invested in himself? Nithard's observation also helps us to understand the importance which a family of " loyal dependants " could acquire in the country by means of the growth of their clientage, and foreshadows the part the Capets were to play.

The partition of Verdun had placed Aquitaine in the portion of Charles the Bald, but the Aquitanians were determined to have a King of their own.

Pepin II, the son of Pepin I, who had been deprived of the kingdom of Aquitaine, collected ever more and more numerous partisans about him. In 844 Charles was obliged to march in arms against him, and set siege to Toulouse. Hugh, Abbot of Saint-Quentin, having brought an army to reinforce him, he thought he could deliver battle in the neighbourhood of Angoulême; but he was defeated. His lieutenants—Ebroin, Bishop of Poitiers, Renier, Bishop of Auxerre, and Lupus, Abbot of Ferrières—were taken prisoner. A curious trio of soldiers! The old military episcopate of the days of Charles Martel, which the unfortunate Louis the Pious had tried so hard to reform, had been resuscitated. At all events the poets of the *Chanson de Roland* who were already writing the *trouvères* at this period, had their models under their own eyes. By the Treaty of Saint-Benoit-sur-Loire, Charles gave up to Pepin the greater part of the province on his swearing an oath of fealty (June 845).

But anarchy continued to grow. In 845 the Normans reached Paris, entered the town, killing and ravaging, and only retired on payment of a sum of money. In Aquitaine they penetrated as far as Toulouse, and pillaged Saintes and Bordeaux. Aquitaine and Brittany were thenceforward continually at the mercy of their depredations. Charles begged for help from his brother Lothar. In 856 the monks of Saint-Martin of Tours were massacred, Orleans was taken and Paris fell for the second time. In addition to the brigandage of the Normans, the great lords, the proprietors of the large domains, who were entrusted with the duty of defending the country, also indulged in rapine and set to work to pillage the land.

The situation became so grave that the Abbot of Saint-Bertin and Count Eudo of Chartres were sent as delegates to Louis the German. If he did not come to their help, said the loyal subjects of King Charles, they would seek from the pagans, to the peril of Christendom, the protection no longer afforded them by their own rulers (856).

The Capitulary of Quierzy (14th of February, 857), which must not be confused with the Edict of Quierzy (877), was promulgated against these brigands housed in palaces. The Counts themselves were threatened with severe chastisement. Whereupon the Great Ones of the kingdom redoubled their supplications at the Court of Louis the German; but it was no longer only against the Normans and the brigands that they asked for help, but against the sovereign who actually aspired to rule them. The German Emperor, busy with a war against the Swabians, had not answered their first appeal.

Amongst the Great Ones who had rebelled against the authority of their King, there is one name worthy of remembrance—that of Robert the Strong.

On the excuse of bringing help, Louis the German led his men at arms forward in 858, sacking everything on his way, and allowing his reiters to commit the worst excesses. He penetrated as far as Orleans, where he received a delegation of lords from Brittany and Aquitaine, but was obliged to return owing to trouble in his own States.

The Edict of Pitres (864, department of the Eure) sheds a curious light upon this society in process of dissolution. The long years of peace which had preceded and which had been favourable to the government of Pepin the Short and Charlemagne had gradually effaced the enclosures, the fortified shelters and entrenchments inside the frontiers. Charlemagne, all of whose efforts, in his lust for territory, were directed against the foreigner, had rather encouraged this gradual dismantling, and had thus destroyed the facilities for local insurrections and capacity for resistance. This was one of the items in his government which, owing to the egoism of its aims, lacked foresight.

402

But what is surprising is that the Edict of Pitres, far from ordering the reparation and reinforcement of the surviving fortresses against the Normans, the Saracens and the other greedy bandits, on the contrary prescribed their complete demolition.

" We desire," said Charles, " that every fortress that has been raised in our kingdom without our permission shall be destroyed." So much more formidable even than the Normans and the Saracens had the native brigands, sometimes very high personages, come to be regarded.

And other clauses in the Edict shed an even more sinister light on the age, more especially Article VI and Article XXXIV.

According to Frankish law, if a free man had to be brought to justice, the summons had to be delivered to him in his own domicile. Now many of those leudes, whose houses had been destroyed by the Normans, took to the highways and practised open brigandage, which they found it all the easier to do seeing that, as their houses had been destroyed, they could not be brought to justice. " Having regard to this evil," said King Charles, " we decree that, in such cases, the Count shall send his agent to the spot where the guilty man's house once stood, and that at this spot he shall give him the summons to appear."

Article XXXIV sheds a particularly terrible light upon the society of the day :

" Several of our Counts," said the King, " have consulted us regarding the free men who, under stress of hunger, have sold themselves as slaves. We have asked ourselves, as also our Bishops and other faithful subjects, what it behoves us to do in the matter."

Charles consulted the records of the Salic law and the Capitularies, but could find nothing in connection with such cases. He then had recourse to Holy Writ, where he found that " a man who has delivered himself up into servitude shall be a slave for six years but shall be declared free in the seventh year." And in the laws of the Roman Emperors, " my predecessors," said Charles the Bald, it was stipulated that if free men, under stress of hunger, had sold their children, the latter could regain their liberty on repayment of the purchase money increased by one-fifth. Charles adopted this latter arrangement due to his " celebrated predecessors," and made it applicable to the parents also.

Such was the state of affairs under the government of the grandson of Charlemagne, which makes us endorse the opinion expressed by the worthy French historians of the eighteenth century, who declared that instead of setting forth for the conquest of the world, as did good King Dagobert in the charming ballad, or going to Rome to receive an imperial title that had become meaningless, Charlemagne would have done better to devote his energies and his organising genius to the arrangement of the dominions he had inherited from his father and which were already sufficiently extensive, in a more stable and co-ordinated fashion.

Charles the Bald, notwithstanding all his difficulties, was, however, still haunted by the same thirst for aggrandisement. It is true that his pretensions to Lotharingia coincided with the aspirations of the country itself.

Before his death, Lothar, the eldest son of Louis the Debonair had, in the usual way, divided his States between his three sons, Louis II, Lothar and Charles (855). Lotharingia (contracted into Lorraine) formed the portion of Lothar II from whom it derived its name.

Lorraine, in which both politically and traditionally Alsace was always included, was separated from western France by the Scheldt and the Meuse, from eastern France by the Rhine and from the south, from Burgundy, by the plateau of Langres, in which the Meuse has its source. Lothar II died on the 8th of August, 869, leaving no heir. Charles the Bald thereupon laid claim to Lorraine, citing the partition of Worms (839) which had assigned a large portion of it to him. But Louis the German on his side also laid claim to Lorraine, whilst the Emperor Louis II, the brother of Lothar II, supported by Pope Adrian II, also maintained he had a right to it. Charles the Bald thereupon replied that the people had the right of deciding for themselves. There is no new thing under the sun. The Austrasians, and above all the Bishops, pronounced largely in his favour. The Bishops of Lorraine maintained that Charles was " the elect of God and the people," " elected by popular acclamation," in short, all that it was convenient to maintain

404

in such circumstances, and Charles was crowned by them King of Lorraine, with great pomp and ceremony, on the 9th of September, 869, in the cathedral of Metz; after which he went to Alsace, where he was also acclaimed.

From Frankfort the Emperor Louis sent King Charles a threatening ultimatum (February 870). But Charles was more cunning than Louis. Charles replied in such a way as to bring about negotiations, which resulted in the Treaty of Meersen (twenty miles north-west of Aix-la-Chapelle). By this treaty Charles' kingdom was substantially increased by territories filched from the old domain of his brother Lothar; he received an important part of the Low Countries, half Lorraine, part of Burgundy and the districts of Lyons and Vienne. This was a good day's work which had far-reaching results and left Charles the Bald an honourable name among the French.

It is true that in 873 he had his son Carloman's eyes put out because he had put himself at the head of a conspiracy of the " faithful," who were dissatisfied with their overlord. Doubtless it would have been a grievous mistake to allow this manner of procedure to die out among the Frankish princes when it had been so brilliantly inaugurated by Clovis and faithfully observed ever since his day.

In the same year the expeditions against the Normans were renewed. The latter had installed themselves as victors in the town of Angers, whence they organised their pillaging operations into the surrounding districts. Charles invested the place, and Salomon, Duke of Brittany, sent him reinforcements. The Normans capitulated. After having hostages delivered up to him, the King of France allowed them to settle on an island in the Loire in order to carry on trade on condition that they were baptised and that those among them who refused should leave the country promising never to return. This was the first attempt at settling Normans in Gaul, similar to that which was so brilliantly successful under their Duke Rollo.

Salomon, Count, or Duke or King of Brittany, was assassinated on the 25th of June, 875, an event which gave rise to terrible anarchy which spread through the country. Each local chieftain laid claim to the title of King and conducted himself accordingly, invading the lands of his neighbours. The situation may well be imagined, further complicated as it was by the incursions of the Normans; for the pirates had returned and installed themselves on the Loire. In the Annals of St. Bertin we read : " The Bishops and other lords who live across the Seine showed great diligence in raising from every side the tribute they were called upon to pay to the Normans who remained on the Seine and its neighbourhood." Perhaps this was what the Normans, in their treaty with Charles the Bald, meant by " carrying on trade " (877).

The famous Edict of Quierzy-sur-Oise (877) was one of the last acts of Charles the Bald. It has been regarded as the constitutional charter of feudalism. It recognised the heredity of offices. The King undertook, " in case one of his Counts should come to die leaving a son of tender years," to put the child in possession of the " honours," that is to say, the offices, of his father. This constituted a fresh and serious weakening of the royal authority and deprived it of its chief weapon of power. But, as Mons. Pfister has justly observed, this same principle of heredity was also to be regarded by the kings as a factor for order and stability. " Every vacancy in an office or a benefice gave birth to jealousy and quarrels; when once the principle of heredity was admitted, the transmission took place without any upheaval."

It has been very rightly observed that the Edict of Quierzy did not inaugurate a new *régime*. The social order of a State cannot be changed by a stroke of the pen in edicts or capitularies. The decision of Charles the Bald merely confirmed a condition of things which already existed and which had arisen from force of circumstances.

After sixty-five years of life, the magnificent Western Empire, founded with so much pomp and ceremony by Charlemagne, was the most derelict object in the general state of ruin. On the death of the Emperor Louis II on the 12th of August, 875, it really seemed that the Empire had ceased to exist; but the Papacy clung to it desperately as though it were a plank which might still bring it to port out of the storm.

Pope Adrian II, the predecessor of John VIII, had once meditated crowning Charles the Bald Emperor of the West. On the death of Louis II, John VIII revived the idea, in the hope that the King of France, as heir of Charlemagne, would protect him against the Saracens, who were becoming ever more and more audacious along the coasts of Italy, just as Charlemagne had protected his predecessors against the Lombards. Charles the Bald, at the head of the most trusty of his subjects, crossed the Alps and made a brilliant entry into the Papal city, where he was crowned Emperor of the West on the 25th of December, 875, Christmas Day, like his grandfather Charlemagne. Whereupon, to complete the similarity, he went to Pavia, the old capital of Lombardy, where from the hands of the Archbishop of Milan he received the Crown of Italy (31st of January, 876). He then returned to France.

But these were but empty glories. The dazzling memory of Charlemagne was a dangerous mirage. The Battle of Andernach (8th of October, 876) in which the forces of Charles the Bald were defeated by the Thuringians and the Saxons under Louis the Younger, the son of Louis the German, sounded a rude awakening. Nevertheless the Pope continued to address desperate appeals to the Emperor Charles the Bald. Charles, the heir of Charlemagne, Emperor of the West and King of Italy, could not turn a deaf ear to them. And it was at this juncture that he drew up the Edict of Quierzy in order to ensure the fidelity, or at least the tranquillity, of the Great Ones during his absence. Charles met the Sovereign Pontiff at Vercelli. A number of Italian lords declared themselves in favour of Carloman, the eldest son of Louis the German. Here were already the Guelphs against the Ghibelins. In France, many great personages, Hugh the Abbot, Boso, Count of Auvergne, openly rebelled, and Charles was forced to return. He died on his way back, at Avrieux, at the foot of Mount Cenis, on the 6th of October, 877.

Mons. Pfister very justly concludes that the task imposed upon Charles the Bald was too much for any human being. " It is impossible for any man to arrest the dissolution of society." It would have been interesting to see how Charlemagne would have dealt with it. Charles the Bald himself most truly remarked : " The invasions of the infidels (the Normans) and the evil designs of those who are Christian only in name have destroyed the power of the capitularies drawn up for the maintenance of order."

Charles the Bald was succeeded by his only surviving son, Louis the Stammerer, who was crowned at Compiègne on the **The Wreck** 8th of December, 877. He was a man of thirty. **and the** He had considerable difficulty in securing the **Rescue.** succession, for the Great Ones of the kingdom had insisted upon an election, which was no longer the simple formality it had been in previous reigns. The "faithful" insisted upon the uttermost farthing for their adhesion, the laity receiving fresh lands and the Bishops the confirmation of their offices and immunities. The Crown became more and more impoverished. Witikind, one of the chroniclers of the day, wrote the following characteristic description of the state of society, "After Louis the Pious the affairs of the Franks fell into disorder, whilst those of the Saxons became more flourishing from day to day."

But this disorder of the Franks, who can now be called the French, was the benign disorder which gives birth to active energies and brings freedom from the fetters of the past. The sap was mounting upwards. In the midst of the tumult the country was co-ordinating its forces and preparing the elements of a civilisation rooted in its own soil. It was the disorder which was burgeoning so magnificently in Gaul at the time when Cæsar appeared and by which he profited in order to spread a stifling and barren culture in a country heroically engaged in a glorious destiny. The temporary prosperity of the Saxons, who can now be called the Germans, was founded on the unity of life and social co-ordination under the hand of one chief, whether King or Emperor, which for the time being endowed them with the power of attacking and dominating their neigh- bours across the Rhine. But the generous and vigorous tumult, in the midst of which so much creative energy was effervescing among the French, was not long before it resolved itself into the most marvellous harvest of social, economic, artistic and literary masterpieces that the world has ever known and the fruits of which were to be spread among those same Saxons, those same Germans, to take root among them and germinate into fresh harvests. "After the reign of Charles the Bald,"

408

writes Fustel de Coulanges, " the Kings no longer took any part in the administration. They no longer drew up capitularies or legislative acts; justice was no more in their hands. Their reign was spent in receiving oaths of fealty . . ." sworn by lords and prelates with the intention of keeping them according to their own pleasure. The King no longer levied taxes.

The lands composing the kingdom of Charles the Bald constituted, as a matter of fact, those parts of the Carlovingian Empire in which the social elements pregnant with a new order of society displayed the greatest activity. More especially in the districts watered by the upper reaches of the Seine, by the Marne and the Oise, there was being forged, in the general disorder and turbulence of the age, around the generating cell of all civilisation, the family, that formidable organisation which was to be known as mediæval feudalism, from which the modern world is derived.

Under the ægis of an impotent monarchy, notwithstanding the efforts of an intelligent King like Charles the Bald, the movement made its appearance through its very resistance to the royal authority, in the midst of the state of brigandage which was everywhere increasing. This state of brigandage was due not only to the Normans, the Vikings, who were spreading throughout central France, but also to the Saracens, who were landing on the coasts of the Mediterranean and travelling up the valley of the Rhone, and lastly to the Hungarians, who had come from Asia and invaded Lorraine and Champagne, and reappeared more than once to carry out their depredations; whilst bands of marauders, noble lords, and landed proprietors whose estates had been ravaged and their houses pillaged—the " vagrants " of the historical documents—lived on rapine and highway robbery. " Robbery and burglary became the custom," writes Hincmar, " and everybody was a brigand. Brigandage was no longer regarded as a crime."

The greatest lords, Counts charged with the maintenance of order, prelates, Abbots and even Kings—like Pepin II, the dethroned King of Aquitaine—joined forces with the bandits from the north, attacking domains, castles and villas, and making trophies of their booty. One may imagine the massacre of the poor, peasants with their throats cut, bodies heaped up along the roadside, unfortunate wretches killed by hundreds or dead from misery and hunger.

But lo ! the first gleam of light shone out through the blood-stained night. We have already noticed a certain Robert the Strong among the rebels of 857–858. His origin was obscure. Richer, a monk of Saint Remi, makes him the descendant of Witikind. Others regard Neustria or Austrasia as the cradle of his race. He exercised his activity in the region of central France, Maine, Anjou and Touraine. In 852 we find him administering the Abbey of Marmoutier, a year later he was charged by the King with missions in Touraine, Maine and Anjou. Charles the Bald conferred upon him the title of Duke, and made him governor of the country between the Seine and the Loire. He fought against the Bretons and carried off a series of successes against the Normans. Charles the Bald, filled with admiration of his courage and energy, entrusted to him the counties of Nevers and Auxerre, which he took away from his own relatives, his uncle Adalard, and his cousins Hugh and Berenger, who had been unable to resist the pirates. And thus the renown of Robert the Strong grew by leaps and bounds commensurate with his power. His Dukedom was only a military lieutenancy, but with the movement which placed everything on an hereditary basis it became not only a sort of State, but the most important in Gaul. In September 866 a strong band of Norman and Breton pirates, from the mouths of the Loire, was surprised by Robert the Strong and his men-at-arms, among whom was Ramnulfo, Count of Poitiers. The pirates took refuge in the fortified church of Brissarthe (Maine-et-Loire), to which Robert and Ramnulfo laid siege. The Normans shot their arrows from the battlements. Ramnulfo fell mortally wounded, as did also Robert, who with warlike valour had in the heat of the action divested himself of his breastplate and morion.

This glorious end sheds an even stronger light on his exploits, his courageous attempts and his successes. His name and that of his family derived ever increasing glory from it. The French required help, authority and protection; they had as much need of security as of the air they breathed. Robert the Strong endowed them with good hope. Father of the two

Kings Eudo and Robert I, and great-grandfather of Hugh Capet, Robert the Strong was the ancestor of the native Kings of France—the Capets whom some historians still call the Robertinians after the heroic founder of their line.

The kingdom was now in a state of complete anarchy and discord. Like the last of the Merovingians, the last Carlovingians no longer ruled over a people, but merely over their own partisans whose number diminished day by day, whilst the more important of their faithful subjects had " faithful subjects " of their own who brought them power and independence of the King. Nevertheless there was a difference, inasmuch as the partisans of the Merovingian Kings were " partisans " in the strictest sense of the word, leaders of bands of brigands who were powerful on account of the terror inspired by their battle-axes and scramasaxes, whilst the partisans of the Carlovingians were first and foremost landed nobility whose power was derived from the importance of their domains and the men attached to them by ties of fealty.

Louis the Stammerer regarded the situation in the same light as his father Charles the Bald had done. He surrounded himself with the best advisers and followed the counsels of Hincmar, Archbishop of Rheims. But what could good counsels avail in such turbulent times ? The whirlwind had been unloosed and the ship of State was being tossed to and fro on wild and stormy seas. What could a pilot do who no longer had the steering gear in his hands, however great his skill and that of the officers about him ?

For it must not be imagined that the kings of this period were inactive or incapable, or that they lacked men of valour to support them. The reign of Louis the Stammerer produced a mind of the first order in the person of Abbot Hugh, son of Conrad, Count of Auxerre and a cousin of the King's. On the death of Robert the Strong (866) Hugh was given his counties of Tours and Angers, together with the glorious Abbey of Saint Martin, as well as other monasteries, whence he derived his title. The hagiographer who wrote the life of Saint Benedict calls Hugh " the most noble Abbot who ruled the State at the head of the armies and of the Councils." Réginon depicts him as a man of bravery and deliberation, modest and simple, humble in his own esteem, a friend of justice and of peace and impressive in his dignity of manner. In the company of Robert the Strong he and the Great Ones had opposed the royal authority, after which he had rallied to the cause of Louis the Stammerer and became his chief supporter.

Louis the Stammerer died on the 11th of April, 879, after a reign of barely two years, leaving the throne to his two sons, Louis III and Carloman. Louis III took Neustria, Carloman Burgundy and Aquitaine. But the legitimacy of the two princes was immediately disputed, the late King having repudiated their mother Ansgarda. And the whole of one faction in the State, at the head of which was Goslin, Abbot of Saint-Germain-des-Prés, offered the Crown to Louis the Younger, the son of Louis the German. Louis advanced as far as Lorraine, where the Great Ones, the majority of whom were faithful to the cause of Louis III and Carloman, found themselves obliged to return to the King of Germany, in order to put an end to his pretensions, that part of Lorraine which Charles the Bald had recovered. And thus various groups of feudalists who, in order to protect themselves against destruction and anarchy, had formed hierarchies of "faithful subjects," began to raise their heads threateningly against the royal power. In the lower basin of the Rhone, Boso, son of Theodoric I, Count of Autun, had made himself a veritable kingdom, including the districts of Lyons, Vienne and Provence. An assembly of Bishops, held at Montaille in Vienne, proclaimed him King. Carloman marched out and laid siege to Vienne, in which Ermengarde, the wife of Boso, was shut up. But the Great Ones recalled Carloman, begging him to come to their help against the Normans. Carloman left a body of troops before Vienne, which only capitulated after a siege of two years.

This prolonged siege of Vienne by Carloman seems also to have inspired the bards, who named the hero Charlemagne instead of Carloman, in whom nobody would have felt any interest; for in the epic cycles all the feats from which they drew their inspiration used to be attributed to one hero. In this same year, 882, the Normans set fire to the towns of Cologne and Treves, Saint Lambert of Liège, the Abbey of Prüm, the palace of Aix-la-Chapelle, all the monasteries of

Tongres, Arras and Cambrai and some of those in the diocese of Rheims. The Bishop of Metz, who had advanced against them, had been killed in battle and his men put to flight.

The Normans had reached Laon, an impregnable town on a fortified hill, and, ravaging the neighbourhood, proceeded to lay siege to Rheims. Archbishop Hincmar took flight with the relics of Saint Remi. Carloman surprised a strong band of pirates who were returning from Rheims laden with booty, and hurled some into the Aisne, the others making good their escape (882).

On the 22nd of February Carloman held an Assembly at Compiègne. In the capitulary he then published there is a clause of the greatest importance : " If a man is caught acting the brigand, he of whom he is the vassal shall conduct him into our presence in order that we may punish the guilty man; otherwise the lord shall pay the penalty for the crime in his stead."

It was not only the pirates who practised brigandage— Normans, Saracens, Hungarians and the landed nobility; the vassals of the latter made a regular habit of it. The King renounced the exercise of his judicial rights, placing the burden of them upon his " faithful subjects." The lord was obliged to seize the guilty vassal and bring him before the royal tribunal, on pain of being punished in his stead if he did not. In short, the lord having been made responsible for the behaviour of his men, the bonds between them were still further strengthened.

In March 884 there was another Assembly of the Great Ones, this time at Vernon. Carloman took further measures to suppress brigandage, pronouncing severe penalties against any who were found guilty of it; he also tried to restore order in his palace by following the instructions of Hincmar. But his efforts were all in vain. He was reduced to paying 12,000 pounds in gold to the Norman marauders in return for a promise that they would leave the country and remain away for twelve years. This was the last act of the young prince who, in such a short reign, gave many proofs of decision and far-sightedness. Carloman died through a hunting accident on the 12th of December, 884. His brother Louis III had preceded him to the tomb two years previously.

There remained to be placed at the head of the kingdom only a child of five, the third son of Louis the Stammerer by his second wife Adelaide. He afterwards came to the throne with the surname of Charles the Simple. For the time being he could not even act as the lay figure of a King.

When the Normans heard of the death of Carloman, they hastened to return to their work of pillage with greater zest than ever. Abbot Hugh sent them an embassy to remind them of their undertakings, to which the Normans replied that their agreement had been made with Carloman, and that if his successor wanted a similar understanding he had only to pay them a similar sum, a type of reasoning in keeping with the ideas of the age. Oaths of fealty and the bestowal of honours and benefices continued to be made on a temporary basis unless the contrary were stipulated.

The reply of the Normans nevertheless filled the Frankish nobles with such terror, we read in the Annals of Saint Bertin, " that they sent to implore the Emperor [Charles the Fat] to come and take possession of the kingdom and went to meet him as far as Gondreville, where they swore him an oath of fealty."

And thus the King of the Germans became King of France. Charles the Fat, the youngest son of Louis the German, was master, not only of the German portions of the heritage of Louis the Pious, but also of Italy. The Empire of Charlemagne was being restored for the last time, but by what hands !

Rouen was taken by the Normans for the third or fourth time on the 25th of July, 885. On the 24th of November the pirates were before Paris, where they were soon joined by a detachment sent by their fellow pirates in the region of Angers. And the siege began which was so memorable on account of the tenacity of the attack and the heroism of the defence. The latter was directed by the Count of Paris, Eudo, son of Robert the Strong, by Bishop Goslin, and by Elbe, Abbot of Saint Germain, who was famed as a bowman.

The King of France, Charles the Fat, was in Italy at the time. He sent an army to the rescue. When the Normans saw it approaching they prepared a strategem of war which was re-
414

peated several centuries later, on the 11th of July, 1302, by the Flemish on the plain of Courtrai against the cavalry of Philip the Fair.

" When the Normans knew that Duke Henry, who was in command of the German army, was coming to the help of Paris, they dug round about their camp several ditches a foot wide and three feet deep and covered them with branches and straw, leaving spaces at certain points which they could use for crossing [exactly like the ditches at Courtrai, except for the fact that the latter were wider]. Skirmishers lured Henry into the trap. . . . He fell into one of the ditches. His enemies, quickly running up, riddled him with blows before he had time to get up, took his arms and some of his clothes. His own men bore his body as far as Soissons, where they buried it in the church of Saint Médard."

Paris was still built on the *Île de la Cité* and spread on to the left bank where buildings covered the sides of the Mont Sainte-Geneviève. The defence of the Petit Pont, which joined the island to the left bank, and of the wooden tower which protected its entrance, has remained famous to this day. The twelve citizens of Paris who were shut up in the tower were massacred in spite of the promise made them by the Normans that their lives would be spared.

Abbot Hugh had been detained at Orleans, where he was suffering from a wound in the foot. Count Eudo succeeded in making good his escape from the besieged town, and, crossing the Norman lines, rejoined the Emperor Charles in Germany and begged his help on behalf of the people of Paris. The Emperor promised to do as he wished and indeed appeared before the town in September 886, at the head of a powerful army; but he did not dare to give battle to Siegfried, the pirate chief, but made a treaty with him which allowed the Normans the right of pillaging " the districts beyond the Seine," out of hatred, according to the annals of Saint Bertin, of the inhabitants of these parts who had refused to submit to his rule. After which he returned to Germany.

The Normans, who were thus spreading in a continuous flood all over France and England, were chiefly Danes, and the French chroniclers of the period call them indiscriminately

" Normans " and " Danes." Their chiefs were called " Vikings " ;
they were the nobles of the country, somewhat resembling the
Frankish monarchs of the time of Clovis. The word contains
the German root meaning " king." They travelled great distances with their men, like the Frankish kings before them,
pillaging and making their fortunes. We have already described
their struggles in France. Alfred the Great several times
defeated those of them who landed in England. The Vikings
also came from Sweden and Norway as well as from Denmark,
but whilst the Danes preferred to come and pillage France, the
Norwegians chose Scotland and Ireland as the scene of their
adventures. They founded lasting institutions in Ireland,
a principality of which Dublin was the capital. Iceland was
also visited by them. As for the Swedes, they preferred to
spread over Russia, where, about 863, they founded the first
Russian States.

At Christiania two of their large barks are still preserved,
having been discovered in tumuli which had served as tombs for
the Vikings. They were long boats, without decks, propelled
by means of sails and oars, each of which was capable of bearing
seventy or eighty men. The Normans were barbarians disciplined
by the orders of their chiefs, skilled in war and particularly in
the art of defensive earthworks. In the tombs of the Vikings
jewels of silver or of graven gold have been found similar to
those of the Frankish kings.

The action of Charles the Fat in refusing to fight on his
arrival before Paris and allowing the Normans to pillage a
part of France has been severely criticised. He has been
accused of cowardice. But the unfortunate prince is to be
pitied rather than blamed. He was ill, and had lost his head;
he was falling to pieces, both physically and intellectually,
in the most lamentable way; possibly also under the corrosive
action of that weakness for strong drink which wrought such
terrible ravages upon the dying race of French Kings.

" The Emperor," says the trustworthy author of the Annals
of Saint Bertin, " lost not only his health, but also his wits.
He convoked a General Assembly at Tribur at the beginning
of November (887) at which the Great Ones of the Kingdom,
realising that his mind was forsaking him as well as his bodily

strength, forsook him and raised Arnulf (of Carinthia) to the throne."

The unfortunate prince, who only a moment previously had been at the head of a vast Empire—the Empire of Charlemagne—was abandoned by all. Out of charity the Archbishop of Mayence tended his more urgent needs. Charles accepted his fall without complaint. All he asked was to drag out his declining days in peace, and even so he became a burden on those entrusted with the mission of caring for him. On the 12th of January, 888, in the monastery of Richemont, his domestic staff, tired of having to look after the invalid, smothered him in his bed beneath some cushions. Such was the end of him who, of all the Kings of France, had extended his authority over the widest extent of territory.

The Empire of Charles the Fat had to be divided, for clearly it was impossible any longer to unite French, Italians and Germans under one Crown.

The chronicler Réginon wrote some memorable words at this juncture : " The kingdoms which had been subject to the authority of Charles the Fat, divided up and separated from each other according to their frontiers, each of them arranging to elect a King, sprung from their own loins."

At last !

With what agonising impatience through the long years of her history have we been awaiting this moment, awaiting it for centuries, the moment when the French, at last, would once again elect a king " sprung from their own loins," and find themselves once more under a government which belonged to them and was worthy of them. We have been awaiting this moment since the day when that hero fell, who was the glory of their race, and who exercised his power over them in all the beauty of single-minded disinterestedness, but whom not all were able to understand, from the day when, with such a magnificent gesture, Vercingetorix came to surrender himself into the hands of Cæsar.

The Annals of Saint Bertin describe the struggles which took place in the competition for the throne of France : " It was not that the French lacked princes who by virtue of their birth, their valour and their wisdom were worthy of command ; but

417

that the equality of their claims and of their power increased the divisions between them and that there was no one candidate who so far surpassed the others that they were willing to submit themselves to his rule."

The Great Ones of the kingdom, Bishops, Counts and lords, elected Count Eudo, the son of Robert the Strong. The Annals of Saint Bertin pass the following verdict upon him :

" He surpassed all the others in his tallness of stature, his handsome countenance, and by his strength of mind and body. Moreover, he governed the kingdom with all the application that could be desired and defended it with indefatigable vigour against the perpetual incursions of the Normans."

And thus we find ourselves once again in France ! And just consider that beautiful and altogether French way of winning the throne, the epic struggles of the father to defend his native soil, struggles in which, after twenty victories, he found a glorious death, with his face ever towards the foe; and the son, equally brave and strong, equally valiant, becomes in mind and body worthy of his father's memory during that fine siege of Paris. Immediately after his coronation, on the 29th of February, 888, we find him fighting against the Normans at Montfaucon in Argonne. He rallied his soldiers together to the sound of the horn, like Rolando at Ronceveaux, " with so powerful a blast that only the mouth of a king could produce its like." We were right in comparing him with Rolando at Ronceveaux.

Good God, we are indeed far from the hideous brigandage of Clovis, far also from the crimes and the underhand policy of Pepin the Short, far even from the methods whereby Charlemagne succeeded in maintaining himself as the sole power in the land and extending his dominions.

The Empire of Charles the Fat broke up into six States— France, Lorraine, Germany, Burgundy, Provence and Italy. The eastern frontiers of France became once more what they had been under the partition of Verdun. Between the Rhine, the Scheldt and the Meuse was formed the kingdom of Lotharingia (Lorraine) separating France from the German Empire.

The task of government was unfortunately exceedingly difficult for Eudo. The incursions of the Vikings were repeated

418

at various points in the country. Eudo exhausted himself in combating them and found himself in his turn reduced to treating with them. And at this juncture, a party among the nobles, tired of a strong government, at the instigation of Fulk, Archbishop of Rheims, acclaimed and had consecrated King of France, in the basilica of Saint Remi, Charles the Simple, the son of Louis the Stammerer. And thus the kingdom in the midst of all its troubles was again divided into factions which unloosed all the horrors of civil war, the faction of Charles the Simple, the Carlovingian, guided by the Archbishop of Rheims, and that of King Eudo, directed by the Archbishop of Sens. Finally Eudo, being an intelligent man and placing the interests of his country above his own—a new departure in the royal annals—came to an understanding with his adversaries, and gave up to Charles the Simple part of his States together with Laon (the Mont Loon of the ballads) as capital. This was the period in which the epics were born, which provides a further reason for the great part played by the town of Laon in the lays which glorified Charlemagne and his " *geste*," meaning his family.

As King Eudo had no children, he himself recommended his officers and the Great Ones of the kingdom to crown Charles the Simple by common accord after his death. He died on the 1st of January, 898. Robert, his brother, was the first to support the election of the Carlovingian, and in return King Charles left him in possession of all the " honours " which he had held from his brother, the counties and the abbeys. And thus Robert became the richest and most influential of all the Great Ones and bore the title of Duke of France.

The reign of Charles the Simple is marked by one important act which had far-reaching results—the Treaty of Saint-Clair-sur-Epte, concluded with the Viking Rollo. Rollo had made himself master of a large part of the province which was afterwards known as Normandy, and had seized Rouen. Richard Le Justicier, Duke of Burgundy, having inflicted a complete defeat upon him in the neighbourhood of Chartres, Charles the Simple thought it was a favourable moment for coming to terms with the vanquished Viking. By the Treaty of Saint-Clair-sur-Epte (911) Rollo was assigned that region of Gaul situated on the right bank of the Seine from Epte as far as the sea. The only condition that Charles made was that Rollo should be baptised together with all his men.

But this was no novelty. We have already seen how one of the predecessors of Charles the Simple acted in the same way and on the same conditions towards the Normans whom he established in the region of Angers.

We know the results of this settlement. The country of the Normans was organised by Rollo, and after him by William Longsword, and soon acquired a prosperity worthy of admiration. The Normans of Normandy preserved their love of navigation and their skill at it and became the glorious sailors who have played such an illustrious part in the annals of France. Rollo and his companions married the women of the country. They abandoned their own language and spoke " Latin," as the chroniclers of the eleventh century call it, but which meant French. It was through the Normans that the great French civilisation of the Middle Ages was spread throughout England, where it shone with its most original splendour. It was in Norman French that the *Chanson de Roland* was preserved ; not that it was composed in Normandy—it first saw the light in the *Île de France*—but because the Normans adopted it as a sort of national song. It was to the measures of *Roland à Ronceveaux* that, under the command of Duke William, they conquered England.

This establishment of the Normans in the part of France assigned to them also determined the particular character of the social and political state of Normandy in the future—in the first place, her pacification and her more rapid settlement, which must not be attributed to the genius of Rollo or of William Longsword his successor, but to the circumstances in which they were placed. They arrived in the country as recognised victors, as rulers of the land which they could set to work to organise with a high hand. Astonishment has been expressed at the rapidity with which they completed their task. The unfortunate province of Normandy had been so terribly ravaged in every sense of the word that it was like virgin soil which it was easy to mark out and build upon. Whilst the rest of France was organised through thousands and thousands of small local

420

groups, and local authorities, isolated in the midst of the upheavals and the anarchy, and unable to avoid entering into
struggles one against the other, in a process of slow, tumultuous
and agitated, but extraordinarily vital and fertile formation
—Normandy was organised by means of one sovereign mind
with disciplined helpers at his disposal. It might be compared
to a park designed and planted by an expert hand—this was
Normandy; whilst on the other hand there was the magnificent
tumult, the disordered burgeoning of the woods, in a struggle
for existence in which the strongest alone could survive or
those who, like the plants beneath the protecting ramification
of the great oaks, had placed themselves under the protection
of the strongest—these were the various provinces of France.

And this peculiar constitution of Normandy, due to her
early history, had numerous and far-reaching consequences.
Viollet-le-Duc has made a curious but exceedingly profound
observation—as is his wont—on the subject of the arrangement of the strongholds of Normandy, and of the rest of
France. In Normandy, he writes, each of the points of
defence, each of these strongholds formed part of a co-ordinated
whole, each had its place assigned to it in the general defence
of the country—the result of the organisation imposed by a
conquering and guiding hand; whilst in the rest of France
each dungeon was built for itself and for the seignorial domain
surrounding it, without any connection with the neighbouring
strongholds, in hostility to which it seems, on the contrary, to
have been constructed.

In the famous provincial charters which were to be granted
to the provinces of France at the beginning of the fourteenth
century by the son of Philip the Fair, these same differences
may be observed. The Norman charter had a different
character from the others, and alone of them all was able to be
put into practice.

Whilst the Duchy of Normandy, with the character of a free
monarchy, was in process of formation, other independent
States came into being in various parts of France, but by means
of a totally different movement, a movement from below; they
were formed by the co-ordination of the living forces of the
nation which had taken root in the soil. William the Pious,

Marquis of Auvergne, created a powerful State for himself in the centre of Gaul. He was master of Auvergne, of the counties of Velay and Bourges. The same process took place in Gascony. Some idea can be formed of this local co-ordination of States, from which mediæval France was to emerge, by the creation of the Duchy of Burgundy in the hands of Richard le Justicier. Traditions had remained particularly strong in Burgundy. We have already drawn attention to them in Celtic days, before Cæsar, and they had not changed. The Burgundians formed a kingdom apart even when they were united with other provinces under the authority of a common King. Richard won his supremacy, like the Robertinians, through his valour against the pirates; and it must be admitted that the Norman invasions, by throwing the State into a general condition of disorganisation, had strengthened the small local groups, which in the midst of anarchy had centred about the genial core of the family, and obliged them to organise and work together in order to resist the common foe. And thus the creation of the national existence was accelerated in the Île de France and in Burgundy and other parts of the country.

The victories of Richard le Justicier over the Normans were numerous and ended in their defeat in 911 under Viking Rollo near Chartres. The deliverance of Chartres, which resulted in the Treaty of Saint-Clair-sur-Epte, had extremely important results, just as the energy and heroism of King Eudo at the siege of Paris had had before it. Duke of the Burgundians, Richard now received the honourable title of Justicier. And here once more we find one of the essential conditions of the work of co-ordinating the primitive cells existing in the organisation of the family. It was impossible to continue for ever fighting one against the other. It was necessary to live, to work, to cultivate the land, to reap the harvest and to carry on some trade. For this at least a comparative condition of peace was necessary and the existence of some authority capable of settling the differences between individuals by means of some pronouncement of equity and able to curb the violence of local wars. Richard was a soldier, like Rollo the Norman; but he was also, like him, a peacemaker : hence the title of honour conferred upon him. " The importance of the grouping by families," writes Jacques Flach, " was proved in Burgundy by the constructive work of the Duchy. Richard of Burgundy also belonged to one of those great dynasties who were offering their services to the people in place of the Frankish King, when the unity of the Empire was shattered and they became the rulers of local nationalities. Through the prestige of his *geste* (family) Richard was able to found a royal dynasty, which is the essential basis for national cohesion and co-ordination."

A similar process took place in all the provinces, though everywhere the work of social co-ordination started from below and worked upwards, except in the case of Normandy, where it began from the top.

Outside and in addition to the provincial dynasties, the person of the King, at the head of the State, was no less of a necessity. Just as each of these individual States, which we may call provinces, would have fallen to pieces without the personality of the Duke, Count or Marquis, who was the keystone of the arch, so the kingdom itself could not have maintained its unity without the kingly office. We have seen how the power of the King gradually declined. Under the last of the Carlovingians it seemed deprived of all means of activity, but nevertheless it still had some strength because it was a necessity. Maurice Prou has very rightly observed that, in the course of the ninth century the personality of the King in France assumed an ever more and more religious character, it became " theocratic " and its sacerdotal side was an essential feature of it. The King, who no longer exercised any power in war, was endowed by the people with supernatural prestige; whereby, to quote Maurice Prou once more, he preserved his supremacy. The King might be a child or a weak man, without energy or strength of character; he might have no domains, or even offices and benefices to be distributed whereby to entice faithful subjects to his cause or keep those he already had; but he was, nevertheless, the King, a sacred person placed high above the heads of all in order to maintain the requisite unity of the country.

The struggle for the possession of Lorraine still continued between the two parts of the old Carlovingian Empire, for Charles the Simple would not allow the rights he had acquired

423

to lapse. In 912, he was elected King of the country, and in the following year we find him master of Strasbourg. The episcopal coins bear his name. " In Lorraine no less than in Alsace," remarks Jacques Flach, " the rights of the Kings of France were never forgotten or abandoned in the tenth and eleventh centuries, any more than they were in later times," although it may be true that the German sovereigns, profiting by the disputes between the last of the Carlovingians and the Robertinians, thought that they might with impunity usurp the territories naturally and historically attached to the kingdom of their neighbours.

In the kingdom of France, the Great Ones, Dukes, Counts, Bishops and Abbots and landed proprietors, on whom the power of the King depended, gave their support sometimes to the Carlovingians, sometimes to the Robertinians, according as their interests, the consolidation or extension of their power, their " honours " and their property directed them. They were moved by no other motives. The idea of race or of nationality never occurred to any of them. Charles the Simple was ruling with a certain intelligence, energy and activity, when, in 920, those who had placed him on the throne came and informed him " that they would no longer obey him if he did not change his ways," meaning if he did not allow them more liberty. And indeed, in 922, his " faithful subjects presented themselves before him, and throwing whisps of straw on the ground, announced that they would no longer acknowledge him as their overlord. Cutting themselves off from him, they left him isolated." And returning to the Robertinians they elected King, on the 29th of June, 922, the second son of Robert the Strong, with the title of Robert I.

Charles the Simple, raising an army among his faithful in Lorraine, marched against his adversaries. A battle took place near Soissons on the 14th of June, 923. Robert I was killed in action, but the arrival of his son Hugh, assisted by Herbert Count of Vermandois, gave the final victory into the hands of the Robertinians. It might have been expected that the son of the late monarch would be proclaimed King, but the choice of the Great Ones fell upon Raoul, Duke of Burgundy. We have already pointed out the importance the Duchy had assumed from

424

the time of Richard le Justicier, and Duke Raoul found himself in addition at the head of the most important abbeys of the district—Saint-Germain d'Auxerre and Saint-Colombe de Sens.

But it must not be imagined that these great local sovereigns, like the rulers of Burgundy, Flanders, Vermandois, Auvergne, Poitou, Aquitaine, Gascony and Brittany, were free from disturbances and quarrels. On the contrary, they were the victims of internal dissensions, just like the Kingdom of France and the Île de France round which the nation was supposed to rally. The same fights and struggles were repeated a hundred-fold on a lower scale, each of the social, religious or secular authorities, overlords or landed proprietors, founders of dynasties or families, defending or developing his place in the sun with the object of maintaining his existence or increasing his prosperity. Just as the Kings lost their power over the Great Ones, so the latter found their authority over their subordinates weakened. An unexpected but very characteristic proof of this may be found in the independence which the country clergy acquired with regard to their ecclesiastical superiors. The Bishop lost his authority over the parishes, which passed into the hands of the proprietor of the domain upon which was built the church administered by the priest and in which the latter's parishioners lived—a proof, among many others, of the increase in the power of the inferior nobility and of the rupture in the relations between the Bishops and the country clergy. Nevertheless the maintenance of divine service had to be secured. The simplest way seemed to be for the priest to marry and transmit his cure to his son, just as the rural tenant transmitted the land he cultivated, a solution which did not mean any weakening in religious tradition, but was the natural outcome of circumstances which it was impossible to control. From the organisation and co-ordination of the social cells within the framework of the landed estates, the life and salvation of the people and of the Church herself in France was destined to emerge.

"France," as Mons. Pfister very rightly observes, "was organising herself for local life."

For we must not confound dissolution with anarchy. A body decomposing by the wayside, melting away and soon to be nothing but a handful of dust, is in a state of decomposition; the wild vegetation, full of life and power, of virgin forests is an example of creative anarchy.

A magnificent testimony suggesting what took place during that marvellous period consisting of the last half of the ninth century to the middle of the tenth is provided by the following observation from the pen of Camille Jullian : " The end of the invasions is marked by the destruction, in 942, of the Saracen settlements known as the settlements of *Fraxinetum* in Provence."

So the invasions had been stopped. Why ? Because, during that period of anarchy in the ninth and tenth centuries, under impotent kings, who, notwithstanding the qualities displayed by some of them, seemed to act like mere puppets in their palaces, the people of France, through suffering and bloodshed, in the midst of struggles, disorders and depredations, accomplished that which, after Cæsar and Augustus, the vast and able Empire of Rome had never succeeded in doing, which Charlemagne in his all-powerful position, with everything that man, one might almost say that God, could desire at his disposal, failed to realise—the People of France succeeded in organising themselves. At last they appeared in their true shape. The free sky was above their heads ; no more Roman bureaucracy, no more heavy, vain and sterile German domination for them ! The day on which they encountered the living forces of the nation which had co-ordinated themselves, the invasions became impotent, beating like waves of froth against an impregnable wall ; for the people of France had built it with a cement made of a mixture which is the strongest and most unbreakable in the world—their own heart's blood and the sweat of their brow.

King Raoul reigned from 923 to 936, during which time he again victoriously fought the Hungarians and the Normans.

Hugh the Great, son of King Robert, who could have mounted the throne on the death of his father but had preferred to have his brother-in-law proclaimed King, left the Crown to the son of Charles the Simple, Louis IV d'Outre-Mer, so called because, in order to make him King of France, he had to be brought back from England. In spite of his gifts of energy and intelligence

426

and his attempts to win back Lorraine from the German princes who had seized it from his ancestors he was unable to stem the rise of the Robertinian dynasty. On the death of Louis, Hugh the Great again allowed the son of the late King to be crowned, on condition of being given the Duchies of Burgundy and Aquitaine.

Lothar enjoyed a fairly brilliant reign from 954 to 986, a period of thirty-two years. He renewed the attempts of his predecessors in Lorraine, appeared at Aix-la-Chapelle and directed against Germany the threatening eagle that surmounted the imperial canopy. The Emperor, Otho III, who had invaded France, was defeated at the passage of the Aisne. The son of Lothar, Louis V, surnamed the Sluggard, like the last of the Merovingians, succeeded him. He was given this surname, not because he did not wish to do anything, but because during his short reign he actually did nothing. He died in the flower of his youth from a hunting accident on the 22nd of May, 987.

Benjamin Guérard, the greatest of writers on mediæval times, in his immortal *Prolégomènes* makes the following observation :

Conclusion. "The institutions of Charlemagne were destroyed by anarchy; nothing remained of Roman Gaul, and France entered upon a new order of things."

This new order is described in the volume following the present one—The Middle Ages, in which we see France rebuilding herself by means of the organisation of local life, and gradually extending her action from the family to the King. This task of formation, which resulted in the creation of feudal France with the monarchy as its crown, which had been begun over a hundred years previously, from the middle of the ninth century, is to be found in the next volume because in the present one it would be impossible to include in all her essential features the France of the Middle Ages.

And, in conclusion, let us glance back, and consider once more the distant beginnings we have already discussed. To what race did those inhabitants of French soil belong who, twenty or thirty thousand years before our era, gave birth to far the most ancient civilisation that the world has ever known ? It is impossible to say. The amazing relics of their activity are

427

preserved in the grottoes of Périgord, incomparable proofs of a nobility of which France may indeed be proud.

After this we saw the formation of the fine civilisation of Gaul, the foster-mother of Roman civilisation, with its exploitation of the mines, its ironworks, its enrichment of the soil by means of manure drawn from the land, its agricultural implements, wagons, furniture, clothes, enamels and even soap for that cleanliness of the body which makes the dignity of man. What does France not owe to her ancestors, the Gauls of the first century before our era? What did the Romans themselves not owe to her?

During the fertile period of their independence the Gauls had kings of epic glory, Ambigatus, King of the Bituriges, who made his arms resound as far as the East and founded kingdoms there. They had Homeric bards who celebrated the glories of the royal lines and that of the gods. Their clergy taught the immortality of the soul and tried to probe the secrets of nature.

What fair destinies were opening up for Gaul when there appeared a man of prey, a spirit of evil who, unfortunately, was also a man of genius, and by a series of terrible crimes Julius Cæsar extended his sway over Gaul, and Rome imprisoned the vanquished in the meshes of her administrative net.

But Rome was about to enter the period of her decline, and Gaul, from whom she drew renewed strength and vitality, became the pitiful victim of this decadence. Rome prevented Gaul from remoulding her national life on lines similar to those which France was to lay down for herself in the ninth and tenth centuries. It is true that under the rule of Rome an end was made to the struggles which gave birth to new social forces, conducted under the leadership of chieftains similar to those who, in the war for independence, displayed all their energies and greatness of soul. But how did Rome replace them? She gave to Gaul only a brittle and fragile peace, which was succeeded by centuries of ruination and barbarism.

In the midst of this tame mediocrity, with its mournful cameos, through the shadows dyed crimson with the blood of the arenas, there shone forth all at once a great light—Christianity. Behold the glorious life-giving force, of which the people of Gaul, in the face of their conquerors, laid hold in order to animate

428

it with their own spirit and endow it with their own generous splendour ! But the frontiers were crossed by bands of savages, the Germans, who returned again and again from the third to the sixth century, repeating their acts of pillage, devastation and the murder of women and children in the most brutal way, spreading the most lamentable havoc and desolation everywhere —annals of blood and ruin for which Rome alone was responsible. Rome had arrested the development of Gaul, she had put a stop to her national organisation, and prevented her from securing her own self-defence. Rome had shouldered these charges only to end in miserable failure, incapable as she was of performing the duty she had undertaken, which proved a burden too heavy for her to bear ; and it was the nation she had conquered in order to " civilise " it by means of exploitation that had to pay the price.

Towards the end of the fifth century one of these marauding bands, as repulsive as the rest of them, the Franks, forming an alliance with a section of the clergy who were threatening the progress of a rival sect, extended their sway over the country by means of bloodshed. The Roman administration was replaced by the Merovingian monarchy. Fustel de Coulanges has remarked, in connection with the rule of these " regenerators," that the history of the world has no more repugnant spectacle to offer than the series of crimes, treasons, acts of cowardice and knavery which the Merovingians heaped up from one reign to the next and of which Gregory of Tours has drawn a vivid picture.

Nevertheless France continued to live on, to work, to suffer and to love, falling back upon her own resources, and suffering these perennial robber bands, commanded by kings, in the way a strong and healthy body suffers the presence of destructive parasites.

The Carlovingians succeeded the Merovingians. They were better people, no doubt, and had in their ranks men of high intelligence and strong will who swiftly built up an Empire of formidable appearance. They understood the resources with which the element of religion could provide them and with its help completed the mechanism essential for their organisation. Nevertheless the latter remained entirely superficial and had no

429

influence upon the lowest masses of the nation, who continued to remain strangers to the Carlovingians, as they had been to the Merovingians. From the death of the great Charlemagne—great above all because France in after generations endowed him, through the genius of her poets, with her own greatness of soul and the charm of her own enthusiastic nature—from the death of Charlemagne the weakness of a hollow edifice was proved by the most lamentable decay, and to the accompaniment of invasions by bands of marauders, we fall back into a hotch-potch of disorder and brigandage.

But these new bands of robbers—the Normans—were fortunately nothing more. They came to lay hands on all they could and went away laden with booty, whilst rendering those whom they despoiled the service of not only destroying their edifices, but also their institutions. They made a general clearance. In their repeated incursions, seconded by the Saracens in the south and the Hungarians in the east, they delivered France from all the ties by which she had been bound to the Romans and the Germans, and which, as the work of strange hands, were entirely unsuited to her. They returned to France her freedom of action and way of life which was to fill the world with amazement.

And thus we are almost tempted to salute these Normans, these liberating bandits ! And glory too to you, dear and beautiful people of France ! How moving is the tale of your formation ! With what suffering, after what a prolonged period of gestation did you not give birth to your glorious civilisation ! Perhaps it was all the more generous and fruitful on that account. Why is it that the greatest masterpieces must always be the creation of suffering ?

BIBLIOGRAPHY.—Eginhard, *Vie de Charlemagne*, edited by Halphen, 1923. The Astronomer, *Vie de Louis le Pieux*, edited by Pertz, from *Monum. Germ. hist.*, SS. Vol. II. Continuators of Fredegar, edited by Krusch, 1889. *Annales Laurissenses majores*, called *Annales royales*, *Monum. Germ. hist.*, SS. Vol. I. *Annales Laureshamenses (Annales de Lorsch)*, edited by Pertz, *Monum. Germ. hist.*, SS. Vol. I. Nithard, edited by Pertz, *ibid.*, Vol. II. Thegan, edited by Pertz, *ibid.*, Vol. II. Paul Diacre, *Hist. gentis Langobardorum*, edited by Bethman and Waitz, 1878. Hincmar, *De Ordine Palatii*, edited by Maur. Prou, 1885. Le moine de Saint-Gall, *De Gestis Caroli Magni*, edited by Pertz, *Monum.*

Germ. hist., SS. Vol. II. Radbert, *Vie d'Adalard, ibid.*, Vol. II. *Annales de Saint Bertin (Annales Bertiniani*, from 862 to 882) (the work of Hincmar), edited by Waitz, 1883. Hariulf, *Chronicon Centuleuse*, edited by Ferd. Lot, 1894. *Polyptique de l'abbé Irminon*, edited by Benj. Guérard, 1844, 2 vols. *Les capitulaires*, edited by Pertz, *Monum. Germ. historica, Leges*, Vols. I and II. Bretius, *Capitularia regum Francorum*, 1883 *sq.* S., *Agobardi, archiepiscopi Lugdunensis opera*, 2 vols., 1665–1666. Abel (S.), *Jahrbücher des fränkischen Reiches unter Karl dem Grossen*, 2nd ed., 1888. Bladé, *Eude, duc d'Aquitaine*, 1892. Émile Bourgeois, *Le Capitulaire de Kiersy-sur-Oise*, 1885. Dahn, *Kaiser Karl und seine Paladine*, 1877. Diekamp, *Widukind, der Sachsenführer . . .*, 1877. Dopsch (Alf.), *Die Wirtschaftsentwicklung der Karolingerzeit*, 1912–1913, 2 vols. Fagniez (Gust.), *Documents relatifs à l'histoire de l'industrie et du commerce en France*, Vol. I, 1898. Favre (E.), *Eude, comte de Paris et roi de France*, 1893. Fustel de Coulanges, *Le Gouvernement de Charlemagne*, from *Revue des Deux Mondes*, January, 1876. Fustel de Coulanges, *Les Transformations de la royauté pend. l'époque carolingienne*, revised and completed from MS. by Cam. Jullian, 1892. Gaillard, *Hist. de Charlemagne*, 1782, 4 vols. Gasquet, *L'Empire Byzantin et la monarchie franque*, 1883. Guérard (Benj.), *Polyptique de l'abbé Irminon, ou dénombrement des manses, des serfs et des revenus de l'abbaye Saint Germain des Prés sous le règne de Charlemagne*, Vol. I. *Prolégomènes*, 1844. Benj. Guérard, *Explication du capitulaire de villis*, 1853. Halphen (L.), *Études critiques sur le règne de Charlemagne*, 1921. Hauréau (B.), *Charlemagne et sa Cour*, 1898. Himly, *Wala et Louis le Débonnaire*, 1849. Kurze, *Einhard*, 1899. Lauer, *Louis IV d'Outremer*, 1899. Lot (Ferd.), *Les Derniers Carolingiens*, 1878. Mercier, *La Bataille de Poitiers et les véritables causes du recul de l'Islamisme*, 1878. Monod (Gabr.), *Hist. poétique de Charlemagne*, 1865. Pfister, *l'Archevêque de Metz Drogon*, in the *Mélanges Fabre*, 1902. Pfister and Kleinclausz, *Mérovingiens et Carlovingiens*, from *Hist. de France*, edited by Lavisse, Vol. II, 1903. Schmidt, *Die Sachsenkriege unter Karl dem Grossen*, 1882. Vétault, *Hist. de Charlemagne*, 1876. Zotemberg, *Les Invasions des Arabes en France*, followed by a study on the invasions of the Saracens into Languedoc from Mussulman MSS., 1872.

INDEX

ACHEULEAN epoch, the, 7
Adalric, independent attitude of, 358
Aedui, the, hegemony of, 56
Aetius, his defeat of the Franks, 212; of the Burgundians, 213; of the Huns, 217; murder of, 218
Alans, the, description of, 211
Alaric, threatened by Clovis, 241; defeated by Clovis, 247
Alemanni, the, appearance of, 179
Alesia, siege of, 117
Alexander Severus, murder of, 138
Allobroges, the, description of, 58
Alphabet, the Greek, used by the Gauls, 52
Ambigatus, his conquests, 48; his kingdom, 55
Ambiorix, his defeat of Sabinus, 98; his struggle against Cæsar, 99, 100; reappearance of, 112, 118
Arianism, rise of, 200
Arians, the, compared with the Catholics, 239
Ariovistus, his empire, 85; defeated by Cæsar, 87
Arius, description of, 201
Arles, siege of, 245
Arminius, defeated by Germanicus, 177
Arnulf, teacher of Dagobert, 274; ancestor of Charlemagne, 300
Art, in prehistoric times, 10, 11
Arverni, the, their premature unification of Gaul, 45; hegemony of, 56
Attila, description of, 216
Augustus, his division of Gaul, 125; worship of, 128; festival of, 138, 139
Aurignacian epoch, the, 9
Ausonius, his lack of originality, 159; tutor of Gratian, 192; made consul, 193; artificiality of, 193
Austrasia, origin of, 258
Austrehilda, has her doctors killed, 259

Bagaudæ, the, rustic rebels, 123; revolt of, 184; in the kingdom of Syagrius, 228
Bards, the, 38

Basilica, description of Gallo-Roman, 145; description of Christian, 173
Belisarius remonstrates with Theodoric, 256
Benefices, the, description of, 309–311
Bernard, rebellion of, against Louis the Pious, 386
Bertha, Big-footed, mother of Charlemagne, 324; her marriage plans for her sons, 324
Bibracte, description of, 55
Bishops, the, governed the cities, 195; their power, 198; hostility of the monks to, 199; most powerful of the aristocracy, 278; rule of, 278–288; corruption in election of, 284
Blandine, martyrdom of, 169
Bordeaux, schools of, 158, 192; walls of, 186
Bourges, description of, 54; siege of, 109
Brunehaut, description of, 264; her regencies, 265, 268; execution of, 269
Burgundians, the, appearance of, 179; settled in Gaul, 213

Cæsar, Julius, his horse, 3; his description of the Ardennes, 16; his invasion of Gaul, 86; excellence of his armies, 90; his campaign against the Belgæ, 92; against the Veneti, 93; against the Rhineland peoples, 94; against Britain, 95; his struggles against Ambiorix, 99, 100; his discipline, 102; his tactics against Vercingetorix, 109; defeat of, at Gergovia, 110, 111
Cæsarius, succours Arian prisoners, 245
Camulogenus, death of, 112
Capitularies, definition of, 335
Caracalla, his extension of the right of Roman citizenship, 137
Carloman, rule of, 312; his abdication, 313; his life as a monk, 314; reappearance of, 318; his death, 319
Carloman, brother of Charlemagne, his

accession, 323; his enmity to Charlemagne, 324; death of, 326

Carloman, son of Louis the Stammerer, accession of, 412; death of, 413

Catalaunian Plains, battle of the, 217

Catullus, his opinion of Cæsar, 97

Celtic language, the, importance of, 131

Celts, the, 25; conquests of Gaul by, 29; their language, 29; their religion, 30; their practice of human sacrifice, 32; their gods, 32, 34; their conquests, 46; their empire, 47

Cerialis, his speech to the Treviri, 135

Charlemagne, genealogy of, 300; birth of, 312; his apprenticeship in war, 322; accession of, 323; his enmity to Carloman, 324; his controversy with Stephen III, 325; his marriage to Desideria, 325; a great soldier, 325; war against Hunald, 326; repudiates Desideria and marries Hildegarda, 326; his wars against the Saxons, 327, 336–340; his war against the Lombards, 327–330; proclaimed King of the Lombards, 330; his mild rule of Lombardy, 331; popularity of, 334; his defeat at Lidbach, 337; his massacre of Saxons, 338; an ecclesiastical monarch, 341; his treatment of the Bishops, 341, 342; combated heresy, 342; his capitularies, 343; his discipline of the clergy, 344; presented with the keys of St. Peter, 345; simplicity of his government, 347; as legislator, 353; invades Spain, 355; defeated at Roncesvalles, 356; his campaign against the Huns, 360; renewed campaign against the Saxons, 361; his victory over the Huns, 361; succours Leo III, 364; visits Rome, 364; presides over trial of Leo III, 365; proclaimed Emperor, 365; his plans to marry Irene, 366; his wives and sons, 369; his daughters, 370; his studies, 371; description of, 371; at table, 372; his dress, 373; analysis of his rule, 374; protector of Christians in the East, 376; death of his sons, 377; death of, 378

Charles Martel, elected by the Austrasians, 302; his victories, 303; defeats the Saracens, 304, 305; honoured by Gregory III, 305; despoiled the Church, 306; death of, 307

Charles the Bald, birth of, 388; made Duke of Burgundy, 389; his territories increased, 394; his struggle for power, 397; defeats Lothar, 397; his covenant with Louis the German, 398; description of, 400; his marriage, 400; his defeat near Angoulême, 401; orders destruction of fortresses, 403; his legislation, 403; crowned King of Lorraine, 405; crowned Emperor, 407; death of, 407

Charles the Fat, accession of, 414; accused of cowardice in dealing with Normans, 416; death of, 417

Charles the Simple, accession of, 414; consecrated King, 419; elected King of Lorraine, 424; defeats the Robertinians, 424

Chellean epoch, the, 6

Childeric, his alliance with the Romans, 222; death of, 224

Chilperic, his crimes, 259; his literary tastes, 259, 261; his reforms, 260; a feminist, 261; his wives, 262

Christianity, preached in popular Latin, 131, 132; persecution of, under Marcus Aurelius, 136, 168; advent of, 166; its socialistic teaching, 169; a revolutionary movement, 197

City, definition of, 126

Civilis, revolt of, 135

Claudius, granted Roman citizenship lavishly, 133

Clotar, murders his nephews and son, 252; his wives, 255; unites Gaul, 254

Clotar II, murders Fredegonda, 269

Cloth trade in Gaul, 153

Clothilda, retires to Tours as a widow, 225, 247; her marriage to Clovis, 230; her choice for her grandsons, 251

Clovis, accession of, 224; his conquest of Gaul, 226; his attack on Syagrius, 228; his war against the Thuringians, 229; his marriage, 230; his campaign against the Alemanni, 231; his vow and baptism, 232; becomes a Catholic, 235; his war against the Burgundians, 237; defeats Alaric, 244; his conquest of Aquitania, 244; his thanksgiving to St. Martin, 244;

honoured with title of patrician and consul, 246; death of, 247; his murders, 248; his sons and grandsons, 249

Commius, revolt of, 112, 113

Commodus, disasters to Roman Empire under, 136; growth of Gallic Church under, 171

Concilium, the, 139

Counts, the, duties of, 349, 352; their remuneration, 351

Cultivators, the, description of, 205

Curiæ, the Gallic, 143

Dagobert, made King of Austrasia, 270; his wives, 271; his conquests, 273; his administration of justice, 274; death of, 275

Decurion, office of, 141; made compulsory, 142

Denis, martyrdom of, 172

Desiderius, marries his daughter to Charlemagne, 324; his war against Charlemagne, 327–330

Deutheria, her treatment of her daughter, 257

Dijon, description of, 237

Diviciacus, his intrigues with Rome, 85

Dolmens, 18

Domains, the, description of, 202

Druids, the, their cult of the mistletoe, 31; their punishments, 34; their practice of human sacrifice, 35; their oral tradition, 36; ignorant of writing, 37; as judges, 37, 38; their power of excommunication, 38; disappeared with rise of Christianity, 130

Drusus, Governor of Gaul, 128

Dumnorix, revolt of, 97, 98

Duumvirs, the, 143, 144

Eloysius, adviser of Dagobert, 274; his skill as a goldsmith, 274

Enamelling, among the Celts, 56

Eudo, King of France, 418; his struggles against the Normans, 418; death of, 419

Franks, the, appearance of, 178; installed in Gaul, 212; description of, 219

Fredegonda, marries Chilperic, 262; death of her sons, 263; her crimes, 263; her hatred of her daughter,

264; her benevolence to the poor, 264; her murder of Praetextatus, 266; death of 268

Freedmen, the, position of, in Gaul, 207

French language, the, origin of, 131-133

French nation, the, composition of, 28

Galba, proclaimed Emperor, 134

Gaul, States of, 54

Gauls, the, description of, 28, 40, 41; their contempt of death, 36; tribal organisation of, 42—45; character of, 49, 50; their houses, 60; their food, 61; their towns, 61, 62; invented soap, 62; their glasswork, 63; their agricultural implements, 63; their roads, 64; their coins, 65; their bread and ale, 65; their clothes, 66; their love of adornment, 67; tenure of property under, 68; feudalism under, 69—72; their primitive method of warfare, 88—90

General Assemblies, the, description of, 331-336

Gergovia, siege of, 110

Germans, the, description of, 174; invasions of, 173; defeated by Marius, 176; and Germanicus, 176; repulsed by Marcus Aurelius, 177; great invasions by, in 175-276, 180; defeated by Probus, 181; entrusted with defence of the Empire, 182; settled in Gaul, 184; great invasions of, 210

Gilles, Count, death of, 224

Gondebaud, defeats Clovis, 238

Gontran, description of, 258

Goths, the, settled in Gaul, 214

Greek, played important part in education, 159

Greeks, the, their admiration of the Celts, 28

Gregory of Tours, compared with Ausonius, 193

Gutratus, death of, 117; meaning of his name, 118

Hadrian, his admiration of the Gauls, 136

Hiatus, the, 12, 13

Hugh, Abbot, adviser of Louis the Stammerer, 411

Huns, the, description of, 215; defeated by Aetius, 217; finally subdued, 362

Iberians, the, 24
Immunity, the right of, 287; strengthened royal authority, 293, 294
Irenæus, Bishop of Lyons, 170; martyrdom of, 171
Irene, the Empress, Charlemagne's deference for, 346; her cruelty, 363; Charlemagne's plan to marry, 366

Judith, wife of Louis the Pious, 386; gives birth to Charles the Bald, 388; attacked by her stepsons, 390; imprisoned in a convent, 391
Julian, his residence in Paris, 155; defeat of Alemanni by, 182; Governor of Gaul, 191; defeat of Germans by, 191; proclaimed Emperor by the Germans, 211
Justinian, his letter to Theodebert, 255

Lake-dwellers, the, 14
Leo III, a suppliant before Charlemagne, 364; tried by Charlemagne, 365; proclaims Charlemagne Emperor, 365
Leudes, the, description of, 211
Ligurians, the, 16; as lake-dwellers, 17; description of, 19; their religion, 20; practised human sacrifice, 21; predominant in the French nation, 28
Limes, the, 186
Lombards, Charlemagne's war against the, 327–330
Lorraine, description of, 404
Louis the German, joins Charles the Bald, 396
Louis the Pious, made King of Aquitaine, 354; birth of, 358; educated by Charlemagne, 358; his campaign against the Saracens, 376; weakness of, 380; his reforms 381; description of, 381; his councillors, 382; his struggle with the Bishops, 384; his struggle with the clergy, 385; divides his Empire between his sons, 385; rebellion of Bernard against, 386; marries Judith, 385; was a neurasthenic, 386; his abasement, 387; rebellion of his sons against, 389; disastrous results of his partitions, 389; makes war on his sons, 391; disarmed and shut up in a monastery, 392; his reinstatement,

392; his re-enthronement, 393; barbarian invasions under, 393; death of, 395
Louis the Sluggard, son of Lothar, 427
Louis the Stammerer, accession of, 408; his death, 412
Lucterus, the lieutenant of Vercingetorix, 106
Luernus, King of the Arverni, 57
Lyons, foundation of, 127; battle of, 137; the martyrs of, 169

Magdalenian epoch, the, 9–12; artistic achievements of, 9–12
Magi, the, 39
Marcus Aurelius, his reign a period of decadence, 136; persecutes the Christians, 136, 168; defeats the Germans, 176
Marquises, the, duties of, 350
Marseilles, foundation of, 51; her trade, 53; her fleet, 53; university of, 159
Martin, elected Bishop of Tours, 194, 283
Mayors of the Palace, the, origin of the office, 269, 276; rise of, 275; appointed by the nobles, 278
Megalithic age, the, 18
Megalithic monuments, 18–21
Meroveus, gave his name to a dynasty, 221
Migrations, the, 22
Missi Dominici, the, their duties, 344, 345
Montmartre, origin of, 173
Mousterian epoch, the, 7

Napoleon, crowns himself, 368
Narses, massacres the Franks, 257
Neolithic age, the, 13
Neustria, origin of, 258
Nîmes, arenas of, 146
Normans, the, appearance of, 362; enter Paris, 401; first attempt at settlement in Gaul, 405; their depredations, 412; bribed by Carloman, 413; their return, 414; besiege Paris, 415; description of, 416; established in Normandy, 420

Papacy, the, anomalous position of, 363

Paris, arenas of, 148; potters of, 150; town of, 153; the Emperor Julian in, 155; martyrs of, 172; made the capital by Julian, 191; importance of, 257; siege of, by the Normans, 414

Parisii, the, description of, 58

Pavia, siege of, 328–330

Pepin de Landen, Mayor of the Palace, 277

Pepin d'Heristal, Mayor of the Palace, 301; his power, 302

Pepin the Hunchback, 325; conspiracy of, 360

Pepin the Short, rule of, 312; proclaimed King, 316; consecrated by Stephen II, 317; defeats the Lombards, 320; his wars against Waifar, 322; death of, 337

Pitres, Edict of, 402, 403

Procurator, the, his office, 140

Quierzy, Edict of, 406

Raoul, elected King of France, 424

Remi, the, description of, 58

Rhetoric, schools of, 158

Richard le Justicier, defeats Rollo, 419, 422; creates Duchy of Burgundy, 422

Robert I, elected King of France, 424

Robert the Strong, his rebellion, 402; his exploits, 410; the ancestor of the Kings of France, 411

Rollo, defeated by Richard le Justicier, 419; baptism of, 420

Roman citizenship, granted to Gauls, 133

Romans, the, short stature of, 28; invade Gaul, 76, 77; exploitation of Gaul by, 78–80

Rome, captured by the Gauls, 47

Roncesvalles, battle of, 355

Saint Cloud, origin of, 252

Saint John, Festival of, 35

Saracens, their invasions, 304; defeat Crooked-Nosed William, 357

Saxons, the, wars of Charlemagne against, 327, 336–240; Charlemagne's savage edict against, 339; rebellion of, 361

Seigneur, the, as head of a small State, 292; enjoyed right of immunity, 293

Senator, the, of the fourth century, 203

Septimus Severus, his policy of decentralisation, 137

Sequani, the, the Empire of, 57

Sheriffs, institution of, 351

Sluggard Kings, the, 276

Solutrian epoch, the, 9

Soul, the immortality of, 36

Stephen II, consecrates Pepin the Short, 310; and turns to him for help against the Lombards, 318

Stephen III, opposes plans of Bigfooted Bertha, 324

Strasbourg, the oaths of, 398

Syagrius, the kingdom of, 223; his restricted authority, 227; defeated by Clovis, 228; death of, 229

Theatres, description of, 147

Theodebert, 250, 251; description of, 254; his treachery, 255; his death, 256

Theodoric or Thierry, son of Clovis, description of, 250

Theodoric the Great, his letter to Clovis, 233, 234; pleads with Clovis, 240; his letter to Gondebaud, 242; his letter to the Arlesians, 245; his benevolent rule, 246

Thermæ, the, description of, 146

Tourassian epoch, the, 12

Towns, description of the Gallic, 143–152

Trees, sacred, 31, 32

Troglodytes, the, 7–9

Universities, the Gallic, 156

Veneti, the, description of, 59

Vercingetorix, description of, 101; his difficulties, 102, 103; outbreak of his rebellion, 103; his allies, 104; his failure in poliorcetics, 108; surrender of, 117

Verdun, partition of, 399

Vergobret, the, 451

Vespasian, Gauls peaceful under, 134

Villa, the Gallo-Roman, 161–164; the Merovingian, 288–293; the Carlovingian, 347

Villages, the Gallic, 160; decay of, in the seventh century, 291

Vindex, insurrection of, 134

437

Waifar, his struggle against Pepin, 322

William, Crooked-Nosed, defeated by the Saracens, 357; his victory in Spain, 359

Wittikind, the Saxon patriot, 327; his victory at Sünthal, 338; reconciled to Charlemagne, 339

Women, in Gaul, 49

Zacharias, his reply to Pepin the Short, 315